You Never Forget Your First: A Collection of New York Rangers Firsts

MARK ROSENMAN AND HOWIE KARPIN

Copyright © 2020 Rosenman-Karpin

"Topps® trading cards used

courtesy of The Topps Company, Inc."

All rights reserved.

ISBN 978-0-578-65599-4

Press Box Publishing

DEDICATION

To Bob Nevin, Walt Tkaczuk, and Brad Park, who made my first Rangers game one I'll never forget as the trio scored goals within 38 seconds of each other in a 9–0 rout of the Boston Bruins on February 23,1969. It was also Park's first NHL goal.

Mark Rosenman

CONTENTS

Acknowledgments   ii

Foreword by Ryan Callahan   v

1	Mike Allison	1
2	Hardy Astrom	14
3	Sean Avery	16
4	Steve Baker	28
5	Barry Beck	33
6	Rick Bennett	38
7	Martin Biron	45
8	Bob Brooke	50
9	Ryan Callahan	57

10	Daniel Carcillo	65
11	Cam Connor	70
12	Tony DeAngelo	75
13	Lucien DeBlois	78
14	Brandon Dubinsky	82
15	Bill Fairbairn	97
16	Theo Fleury	101
17	Adam Fox	108
18	Bob Froese	111
19	Mike Gartner	124
20	Rod Gilbert	135

You Never Forget Your First: A Collection of New York Rangers Firsts

21	Dan Girardi	146
22	Tony Granato	153
23	Gilles Gratton	158
24	Mike Hartman	163
25	Pat Hickey	169
26	Darius Kasparaitis	185
27	Mike Keenan	192
28	Tom Laidlaw	196
29	Brian Leetch	204
30	Mikko Leinonen	216
31	Don Luce	222
32	Henrik Lundqvist	226

33	Troy Mallette	232
34	Dave Maloney	237
35	Stephane Matteau	247
36	Sandy McCarthy	260
37	Rob McClanahan	263
38	George McPhee	268
39	Rick Middleton	280
40	Eddie Mio	286
41	Dominic Moore	291
42	John Muckler	300
43	Don Murdoch	306
44	Rick Nash	313

You Never Forget Your First: A Collection of New York Rangers Firsts

45	Bernie Nicholls	317
46	Chris Nilan	322
47	Mark Osborne	328
48	Brad Park	336
49	James Patrick	339
50	Mark Pavelich	355
51	Dale Purinton	361
52	Mike Richter	366
53	Eddie Shack	385
54	David Shaw	390
55	Martin St. Louis	398
56	Marc Staal	405
57	Pete Stemkowski	410

58	Kevin Stevens	414
59	Jason Strudwick	417
60	Steve Valiquette	421
61	John Vanbiesbrouck	424
62	Aaron Voros	430

ACKNOWLEDGMENTS

Over my lifetime as well as the last 15 years as host of *SportstalkNy*, I have read thousands of books. Like many others, I do not always take the time to read the acknowledgments. Having now gone through the process of writing six books, I have a greater appreciation as to how important these pages are to the pages that follow it, for without the names I am about to list, there would not have been a book to read.

First and foremost, as always, is my amazing wife, Beth, who is always there as an endless source of encouragement, love, and support. My son, Josh, his wife Stefania, and my daughter, Liana, who by the joy and passion in the way they approach everything they do inspire me to do the same.

My late father, Morris, who took me to all my sports firsts and fostered my love of the New York Rangers. My late mother, Estelle, who allowed me to buy every sports book whenever there was a book fair at school and always encouraged me to pursue my passions no matter the obstacles or challenges.

My late sisters, Cheryl and Suzie, who always set great examples for their little brother.

I would like to thank the following members of the press who welcomed me into their workspace with open arms and showed me the ropes including but not limited to Ken Albert, Christian Arnold, Matthew Blittner, Larry Brooks, Matt Calamia, Rick

"Carpy" Carpinello, Jim Cerny, Scott Charles, Russ Cohen, Charles Curtis, Brett Cyrgalis, Stan Fischler, John Foyole, Bob Gelb, Zach Gelb, John Giannone, Denis Gorman, Andrew Gross, Sean Hartnett, Patrick Kearns, Allan Kreda, Don La Greca, Dave Maloney, Gil Martin, Joe McDonald, Joe Micheletti, Pat Leonard, Brian Monzo, Ira Podell, Howie Rose, Dan Rosen, Sam Rosen, Ashley Sarge, Adam Skollar, Arthur Staple, Colin Stephenson, Jesse Spector, Justin Tasch, and Steve Zipay.

Thank you to the New York Rangers PR department—John Rosasco, Ryan Nissan, Lindsay Hayes, Michael Ali, and Michael Rappaport—for all their help during this project and over the past 15 years. This project would have never happened without you. Thank you to Réjean Houle of the Montreal Canadiens Alumni Association, Karen Davis of the Columbus Blue Jackets public relations department and Wendy McCreary of the NHL Alumni Association, who were instrumental in helping me find so many former players.

Thank you to my WLIE *Sportstalkny* interns Ryan Sherman and Mike Capece, who were a huge help in transcribing hundreds of hours of interviews for this project.

A note of gratitude to the scores of authors who have appeared on WLIE 540am *Sportstalkny* who have inspired me over the years as well as our loyal sponsors Leith Baren, Neil Cohen, Robert Solomon, David and Andrew Reale, and my co-host AJ Carter as without them none of this would have been possible.

A stick tap to our editor, Ken Samelson, who allowed Howie and I to complete our Rangers hockey hat trick with him.

Thank you to Hadley Barrett and Valerie Fabbro of The Topps Company who were instrumental in allowing to use the Topps® trading cards on the cover

Last, but not least, my writing partner in this project, Howie Karpin, as writing a book with him is like winning the Stanley

Cup.

Mark Rosenman

With the number of books that I've written or cowritten, it's been customary to thank my wonderful wife of 40 years, Kathy Block Karpin, for her support and her love. I wouldn't have had this career without her support. I want to acknowledge my son Danny and his fiancée and soon to be wife, Emily, along with my other son, Jake, and his wife, Anita. We have two boys and now we have two wonderful "daughters" to join our family.

My sister, Carol Shore, and her husband, Barry Shore, have been staunch supporters throughout my career. My niece, Wendy Shore Rosano and her kids, Alex and Rachel and Sharon Shore. We will always have the memory of Sharon's daughter and my great-niece, Melanie, in our hearts.

My family is most important to me and I love them all. Thanks for your support.

To all my friends (and I'm blessed to have a lot of them) I think you for your continuous friendship.

Howie Karpin

FOREWORD

You never forget your FIRST!

Those five words resonate in your memory banks, particularly the first time you do something. No matter how long your career lasts, there are some moments that will always stand out. Most times, it's the first time you have a personal accomplishment amidst the team concept.

If you're a baseball player, you don't forget your FIRST hit. A football player will never forget their FIRST touchdown, a basketball player, his FIRST basket.

For a hockey player, your FIRST training camp, your FIRST game as a player, your FIRST goal, are all memorable moments that stand out, but there are some firsts that are unique and hold a special place in a player's heart.

Mark Rosenman and Howie Karpin have amassed a collection of former and current New York Rangers players who talk about their "firsts," and the anecdotes that go along with those memories.

In September 2011, I was lucky enough to be named the 26th Rangers captain and I can remember the first time that I saw the

"C" on my jersey. My first Winter Classic in January 2012 was a blast and so was the first hat trick of my NHL career. Of course, there was the emotional first time that I returned to Madison Square Garden as an opposing player in November 2014.

The players who have been interviewed in this book talk about their experiences with their first Rangers coach, their first game as a Ranger at Madison Square Garden, and in some cases, their first fight and their first hockey idols from the time they were first being exposed to hockey. For a goaltender, it's his first win or first shutout, which are all memorable experiences.

How a player gets to experience his first is also profiled in this book. The players provide a look into the life of a professional hockey player with their stories and recollections. Starting with when they were kids and then as they progressed into manhood and a career in the NHL, the players in this book all bring something to the table that will enlighten any hockey fan.

Mark and Howie have helped me recall some of my firsts that are listed in this book.

For you Rangers die-hards and hockey fans, no matter who you root for, this read will jog your cherished memories as well.

Ryan Callahan

Ryan Callahan joined the New York Rangers in 2008 and served as the team's 26th captain until being traded to the Tampa Bay Lightning in March 2014. He also represented the United States in the 2010 and 2014 Olympics. Callahan retired in 2019 and currently serves as a studio analyst for the NHL Network.

1
MIKE ALLISON

Left wing Mike Allison was a promising goal scorer whose career was curtailed by injuries. Allison, who played six seasons with the Rangers, scored on the first shot of his first shift. In his second game, Allison scored a hat trick, but a series of knee and ankle injuries took away from his offensive abilities. He was able to alter his game to a more defensive style and he ended up playing 10 years in the National Hockey League.

FIRST CONTACT WITH THE NHL:

"Growing up, *Hockey Night in Canada* was always the thing that we would watch. I can remember we had a basement downstairs and my dad would always watch the games. I would always go downstairs in the basement. It's just a plain cement basement with washer and dryer. I would be shooting tennis balls and pucks down below and my dad would yell up because there was a goal of something fancy and I would run upstairs, watch the replay of the game or the intermissions when they used to have "Showdown" [a skills competition] all the time in the intermissions back in *Hockey Night in Canada* and that would be my introduction, really, to the NHL. It was really just sharing that time with my father in particular, just watching, who I thought were fabulous athletes, play this game. Then, the next day we'd go out on the outdoor rinks and try to emulate what they did. I can remember many a day I'd been out there by myself. Even though we used to get Toronto [games] 'cause I'm from Ontario, Toronto was the main team, I more or less cheered for Montreal. So it was more so that Montreal players. [Guy] Lafleur was such a good player. Henri Richard, I used to love him. Pete Mahovlich, those are the kind of players. I started to follow the Islanders and [Denis] Potvin, and [Bryan] Trottier are two of the biggest heroes for me, even though they're only five, six years older. It wasn't until I became a Ranger that I began to hate them."

FIRST REACTION TO BEING DRAFTED:

Mike Allison was chosen by the Rangers in the second round (35th overall) of the 1980 NHL Entry Draft.

"I was fortunate. My brother had been signed by Montreal a couple of years before that. His agent was Bill Watters, who would split with Alan Eagleson at the time. I'd played junior in Sudbury with the OHL. After the season, I came back to finish my school. Bill Watters, who was trying to recruit me as his client, flew me down the draft, it was in Montreal. I went to the draft. Bill Watters has member clients and we met the night before the draft and he said, "You're going to probably going to go in the first round.' Well, I didn't, I dropped down to the second round. I was sitting up in the Montreal Forum and I was sitting up there with a guy by the name of Dan Daoust, who played with my brother in Cornwall [the undrafted Daoust played more than 500 NHL games for Montreal and Toronto] and he never even got drafted that year, but he and I were just sitting up there. Then, I got drafted and was lucky enough to get down to the floor. You never, ever thought you were going to get to the stage where you had opportunity to play in the NHL. You dream about but you never think it's going to happen and all of a sudden, it did. Getting drafted now, you have to start the process of trying to make the team, but really, the reward for me that day was getting drafted."

FIRST RANGERS TRAINING CAMP:

"I come from a community of 8,000 people and I remember I was flying from Sudbury to New York. I don't if it was Kennedy or LaGuardia I flew to but remember, 'cause it was my first training camp, flying over the cemetery that seemed to go on [for] ever. That was my introduction to a really humungous city. I landed. Back then, they just gave you instructions, you had to figure out how to get to the airport, so I think it was Kennedy. Since I was flying from Sudbury, Ron Duguay was from Sudbury, he was actually on the flight and he saw me getting my equipment, picking up the equipment as it comes off the carousel. I had a Sudbury Wolves bag. He said, 'Oh geez, are you going to training camp, are you going to the Rangers?' I said, "Yep.' So he told me how to get there. I go to my first training camp, here it is. I have to catch the van to White Plains (New York). That's where we stayed and we're practicing. It was just overwhelming. I mean there was no doubt it was all overwhelming. It went by so fast. We had a rookie camp. You get to training camp, you get to exhibition games. Things just fell into place for me. I was in good shape, in fact, veterans never came in good shape ever. The second-to-last exhibition game, they said, 'You won't be playing them all but you'll be staying for the start of the season. We're gonna set you up in Steve Vickers's house, he was married. He took me under his wing and let me stay in their basement. Phoning my parents and telling them I was staying and making more that first year than my father, who was a 25-year veteran of teaching, will make. It wasn't a lot of money, but it was sure a lot of money back then, so it was sort of surreal when you look back on it."

FIRST RANGERS COACH:

In his first season, Allison played for Fred Shero, who was fired after 20 games and replaced by Craig Patrick.

"Freddy was very quiet, almost didn't say anything. The odd time I would catch him, I'd be at the rink in Rye (New York) and he'd be back in the trainer's room talking with one of the trainers, just kind of sitting there off by himself, and he'd say very astutely something about my game or about life. Here I was, a 19 year old. Everyone was at least three years older than I was, and he could see the struggle I was having. He had a way to just really just see what I was feeling and verbalize what I was feeling and making it okay. Whether I was homesick or whether it was missing my girlfriend or my parents. He just had a way to just say, very briefly and not very often, something that really hit the nail on the head. That really meant a lot and really was very kind to me. The perception I had back then was that some of the older fellas didn't want to play for him, but I thought he was fabulous.

"The other coach was Craig Patrick, who was probably the savior of my career. Craig believed in me as a person and kept me around when probably a lot of other people wanted me gone earlier in my career with the Rangers. I was so very fortunate that I had those two men. One that took a chance, Fred, to play and then one to believe in me as Craig did. I couldn't ask for more. I was always growing up. My father was somebody I had tremendous respect [for] but those two men filled that void that my father, who was still working, was only able to get to a couple of games. They provided me with a direction, made me feel safe, secure in an environment you don't feel safe and secure that professional sports, they ate their young, those coaches if you didn't fit into them. So, I was very fortunate to have both those men take such an interest and show some kindness to me and I'll always remember that."

FIRST RANGERS CAPTAIN:

In his first season, Allison played for three captains including Barry Beck, Dave Maloney, and Walt Tkaczuk.

"Bubba [Beck] was the guy that sticks in my mind as the captain through my years in New York. He was the guy that ultimately, I think, everyone was looking for to take that role, to be that guy. All three men were very, very different. Dave, I can remember in the going to one of the exhibition games early in the season, he would have been the captain then. He came in, introduced himself and tried to make us feel comfortable going to our first exhibition game, which is always wonderful. Walt Tkaczuk was a hard-nosed, quiet, unassuming person. Didn't say a lot but when he said something, it was listened to. Played the same position. Had that tragic accident and got hit in the eye. People don't even think about him as a great Ranger. Barry, he was the guy everyone really looked up to. He didn't say a lot to me. I ended up staying with him again in LA. I thought he was very astute. He said something, people listened."

FIRST TIME PUTTING ON THE RANGERS JERSEY:

"You never think it's gonna happen. You always have this dream as a kid. When you were a Canadian kid back in the '70s, to make the National Hockey League, you get the storied franchise, the New York Rangers. You're playing with Phil Esposito who set all these records. You're coached by Fred Shero, you go to play your first game, it really is just overwhelming Me, personally, I had some quick success right off the bat. We were in Boston, had went to Toronto, our first two games of the year. I scored some goals. The game in Toronto was on Saturday so we came back Sunday and played our first home game. That's really when you realize how special the Rangers are, is when you're playing in front of your home crowd that first time. The Garden is going crazy and the chills run down your spine as the national anthem is going. First time you step on the ice."

"That first game, I don't know the way it is now but we used to drive across the street, parked our cars and walk across into the Garden. Now, I would've gotten a ride with Steve Vickers. All the fans recognize him and they're tryin' to figure out who these guys are. They're coming up to you, when they ask your name. After the game, you'd go to the bar down below here and I'm a 19-year-old kid, sneaking into the bar so it really doesn't even seem real. It just happened so quick. One moment, you're a kid going in high school and next minute, you're playing in the National Hockey League with this wonderful franchise. It's really hard for me to describe. Most of what I look back is the friendships and the people that I met, both in and outside the game that make that whole journey, such a wonderful journey, and only such a small part of your life. When I look back on my career, even though I played three teams, the first six years were with the Rangers and they were the ones that stick with me probably because of the people I met there outside the game."

FIRST GOAL ON FIRST SHOT: October 9, 1980 @ Boston Bruins, 7–2 loss.

Allison scored a goal on the very first shot of his very first shift against Hall of Fame goaltender Rogie Vachon.

"Well, they call your name, you go out. It was a 4-on-4 situation, faceoff was the left of Rogie Vachon. Phil [Esposito] won the faceoff. He had lined me up behind him, so there was two defensemen and Phil and I and I took a weak backhand shot from the top of the circle and it was a weak shot and Rogie let it in. To think that you're in your first game, your first shift, and then you get your first goal assisted by Phil Esposito. It's surreal every time you think of all these memories that you really think that really happened. I was fortunate enough, when I got traded to LA, Rogie was the GM at the time. I think I was playing with Tom Laidlaw, I'm sure it was Tom Laidlaw that said, 'Rogie, you probably don't remember this, but Mike Allison scored his first goal and it was a terrible shot,' so that was always the joke with Rogie and I later on. Unfortunately, I didn't have too many, after my first year, I didn't get too many goals. I think I used them all up that first year but wish I had a few more."

FIRST RANGERS HAT TRICK: October 11, 1980 @ Toronto Maple Leafs, 8–3 win.

Allison scored his first and only career hat trick in his second NHL game.

"Well, it was a special moment. To have this success very shortly into my career, I think it helped me stay around longer, gave me opportunities with the coaches and the management. It was so special because that was the first *Hockey Night in Canada* game back in Canada. Saturday nights were the only time you could watch hockey back then and that was the first game of the year for the National Hockey League against Toronto. I'm from Ontario, so it was really big for my friends growing up. They all sat around and watched this kid from this small, little community playing. My parents were fortunate enough they were able to come to the game. It's a thousand miles so they got to the game and then you score a hat trick. You're playing with Anders Hedberg and Ulf Nilsson and winning in Toronto Maple Leaf Gardens. Being brought out, ended up being one of the stars of the game. Somebody had sent a sign from my hometown to the game. So it was just a wonderful moment in a young hockey player's career. It was wonderful to be able to share it with my family, my parents. We hopped on the plane right after and it was the first time we had taken a charter. We played the next night in New York and I'm a 19-year-old kid, probably had five steaks his whole life and they bring a steak in the airplane, and the lady said, 'Do you want another one?' I said, 'Yeah.' I mean, who wants two steaks right after the game. The game was done, got in the airplane. I thought, *This charter is exciting.* Flew back to New York and played the next night. I think we lost that next night, but, yeah, I had a successful start as far as goals and really very fortunate. Just way things had fallen out that first year. When you talk about first, my first season was by far my best."

FIRST RANGERS PLAYOFF EXPERIENCE: 1981 preliminary round vs. Los Angeles Kings. Rangers won the best-of-five series in four games.

"Never realized, you know how people say things change in the playoffs and they do that first playoff. LA had a very successful season with the Triple Crown Line and no one had given us a chance. I can still remember Craig Patrick saying, 'Hey, we can beat these guys.' We had a tough team, they had a tough team, and

I can remember how that started off. We had a brawl at the end of the first period. Barry Beck, our leader, his other talents were fabulous also but he got into a fight with Rick Chartraw. They were looking at each other and Barry popped him, knocked him down, cut him. Anyway, they had Dave Taylor, who is classy and hard-nosed and is one of the three greatest players that I played with, he was on the Kings at that time. He went after the end of the first period and started a huge brawl. I thought we physically beat them up, even though I got beat up in the brawl. I thought, as a team, we physically pounded them and then the playoffs are so intense. Every moment seemed like that. Even though that was the only game with a brawl, every game in the playoffs seems like a brawl 'cause you're just a do or die. I mean, obviously that's an embellishment, but it was exciting."

The brawl referred to by Allison took place in Game 2: April 9, 1981 , 5–4 loss.

"Eddie Hospodar was just going crazy. He was slapping Marcel Dionne, he was slapping Mario Lessard, I think was their goalie. Kings had a lot of tough guys. They had Chartraw, they had [Jerry] Korab. Anyways, Korab was coming after Eddie Hospodar from behind in that brawl and I could see it happen. I was tied up with some guy and I just lunged at Korab right before he was going to sucker Eddie Hospodar, deservedly so, I hate to say because Eddie was going crazy, but I ended up in the bottom of the pile and I ended up with this guy. Danny Bonar was his name. Danny Bonar ended up on top of me. He's like five-eight, I'm six-two and he had me pinned and I couldn't get up. It's hilarious when I think back on it and that's how strong he was, but I said, 'I can't breathe.' He was on top of me and there were six people on top of me. That's why I remember that one so distinctly.

"It was an eye-opener for me to realize that these players that had been through the playoffs before, even though they told me it was going to be different, there was no way I recognized it. Ron Duguay came alive in the playoffs if I remember correctly. He was just fabulous. He really had a mediocre year but come playoffs, he said this is a totally different time and he took his game to a whole different level and something you have to learn once you're there."

FIRST EXPERIENCE OF RANGERS-ISLANDERS PLAYOFF RIVALRY: 1981 Stanley Cup semifinals. Rangers lost in four games.

"The Islanders had won the year before and they seemed to take it to a different level. We weren't expected to get where we were. We got there and we were pretty good. They seem to be able to come up, rise up at the right moment. We lost a game on the Island. I can remember after the game I had caught right near the end of the game. Denis Potvin and I were going behind the net for the puck and we both going to hit each other, and I caught him. He was almost knocked out, but he was so tough, he was still playing. I can remember some of our guys that weren't playing were more excited about me hitting Denis Potvin, then upset about us losing. I thought after I hit him, I knew I did bad. He took my knee out the first year and I thought, *Man, he's going to club me now*. They were focused on getting to that Stanley Cup Final. They were about winning, not standing up. We played well, but really weren't mentally in it, where they were at the time. I understand that they were defending champs."

FIRST TIME SEEING HIS BROTHER PLAY IN THE NHL: March 25, 1984 @ Madison Square Garden vs. Montreal Canadiens, 3–2 win.

Mike's brother Dave played a total of three NHL games with the Montreal Canadiens. The game vs. the Rangers was his final game. Mike was injured and did not get a chance to play against his brother.

"The wonderful thing I remember about that game, even though we didn't get to play it, I took the warmup for that game. I went to the coach, Herb Brooks at the time and said, 'Would it be all right if I went in the warmup. I'd really love to get a picture of my brother,' and he said, 'Go for it.' So we got the Rangers' photographer, at the end, to take our picture. So that will always stay with us, this picture we have together. Him, in his Canadien jersey and myself in the Ranger jersey. It was sad not playing him. He was always the tough guy too."

FIRST REACTION TO BEING TRADED FROM THE RANGERS:

In August 1986, Allison was traded to the Toronto Maple Leafs for Walt Poddubny.

"I hate to throw Phil Esposito under the bus. He was the general manager. I found out, I phoned the Rangers, the trade had happened. I never talked to Phil about it. He said he tried to call my parents' home; I wasn't there. I never heard about it. I called and talked to the Rangers' trainer and he said, 'I got some news for you, Mike, you've been traded.' Phil came up to me a few years later and said, 'Jesus, I'm sorry I never talked to you about that.' I think he tried, but just wasn't able to track me down. It was sad. You think you're going to be there, this organization, you want to be a Ranger for life, but you can understand why they did make the trade. They had to make moves. Walt Poddubny came in, I think he scored 40 goals that year. I went to Toronto, I was playing for a guy that coached my brother for five years, John Brophy, but it wasn't something I was looking forward to. I was always wanted to remain a Ranger. I was a young teenager coming to New York and was treated so wonderful, even though I had a sporadic, up and down type of career. I was always treated very well by the fans. I had a lot of injuries, a lot of struggles but I loved my time in New York. Just loved it."

FIRST TIME BACK AT THE GARDEN AS AN OPPOSING PLAYER: October 26, 1986 @ Madison Square Garden. Rangers and Maple Leafs played a 3–3 OT tie.

"The people in Madison Square Garden were always so kind, always so wonderful. People that worked the visitors' locker room, you see them when you're with the Rangers. They come in and you meet them, and they were always very kind. You come back to this place and you're going to a different dressing room. I was always treated well by the fans. I'm sure a lot of them wanted to say, 'Allison, get moving here,' but they were always kind to me. We always had that space where you had to park your car across the street, walk back and forth both before and after the game. People were just wonderful. The Ranger fans were like no other. Obviously, hockey is huge in Toronto, but Ranger fans were something different. LA was a whole different thing, even though I was there when [Wayne] Gretzky came, so there's lots of fans. The Ranger fans were a special place. I grew up with some of the fans. I was the same age as they started to watch the Rangers. They came to the games, getting cookies. There wasn't a thing about it, I haven't a negative experience and so I just remember it so fondly. I'm sure some of the Ranger fans were saying, 'Allison's a bum.' I never heard it, never saw it, so it was a special six years in my life."

FIRST EXPERIENCE WORKING AS A TV COLOR COMMENTATOR FOR THE LA KINGS:

"As a player, you have some sense that you're somewhat competent on the job. As the broadcaster, when you're not prepared for it, that's not where you ever thought you were going to go. You are completely unprepared for what goes in the course of a broadcast. I give my partner at the time, Nick Nixon, who is still with the Kings and a Hall of Famer, just a wonderful man, but man, I could see him sometimes just cringe over there until I figured out the cough button and the different things that go on and I'm getting in and out. Always come in good and go out, good. Be concise, coming and clear and concise and clear going out and you'll be fine, but it's a difficult job. People don't realize the prep work that goes into it. Nick Nixon, after about three games, said, "I'm getting you a coach, a broadcast coach,' and I worked with him for the next ten games just to get ready and better prepare for the broadcast. So it was a tough job.

"We'd [him and the broadcast coach] tape all the broadcasts and then we'd go through them. He would send me home with some homework. I have a tendency to butcher names, especially when the Europeans started to come in. Nick, I could see him just shudder, you know, look at me and I would get the giggles and then he couldn't help but get the giggles. It added to our broadcast, I thought. This banter we had back and forth, especially about Eastern European names that I had such a hard time with."

FIRST EXPERIENCE WITH BEING INDUCTED INTO THE NORTHWESTERN ONTARIO SPORTS HALL OF FAME:

Allison was inducted in September 2003.

"It meant more a couple of years later when my brother joined. He and I both went into it, so at the time, it was a wonderful honor. Somebody thinks I belong in there; all I could say was thank you. That wasn't anything that I ever thought was going to happen. Never even thought about it. When I got the phone call, I said, 'Okay, who is this? This is a joke.' Then, when you actually get inducted or when you're in the ceremony, all you do is say thank you. When my brother came in, I was there at the ceremony for that. I still think someone's going to take it away, some sort of mistake. All I can say it was a nice moment and a thank you to Northwest Ontario for thinking of me."

The Allison brothers on the ice at MSG. Photo courtesy of Mike Allison.

2
HARDY ASTROM

Goaltender Hardy Astrom played 83 games for two teams during his modest career in the National Hockey League. Astrom was signed by the Rangers a free agent, playing a total of four games during the 1977–78 season. He also spent time at New Haven [of the AHL] where he played in 27 games. In July 1979, Astrom was traded to Colorado.

FIRST TIME PUTTING ON THE RANGERS JERSEY:

"It was great. Just a dream to get that name, over the years, and play for the Rangers at Madison Square. Ron Greschner and Dave Maloney, they took care of me before training camp."

FIRST RANGERS COACH: Jean Guy-Talbot

"He was okay. For me it was a big different then the coaches in Sweden and that time in US. they were very hard [John] Ferguson was screaming and yelling like that.and in Sweden that was not happening. In Sweden the coaches had more feelings. But I had no problem with Don Cherry because he played me a lot of games. He played me 48 to 49 games and they had no problem at all. I can tell you, I don't know why he is yapping about me now,I had never said a bad word against him and I never will"

FIRST RANGERS CAPTAIN: Phil Esposito

"One of the best team friends I ever have. Super guy. He'd take care of me. I remember one time, we were in the dressing room and I wasn't that good to speak English and some guys were speaking French. Then, he stand up and just yelling, 'Don't fuckin' speak that French because we are an American team. You're going to speak American so everybody can understand it.'"

FIRST RANGERS GAME: February 25, 1978 @ Montreal Canadiens, 6–3 win.

Hardy Astrom became the first European goaltender to start an NHL game as he ended Montreal's 28-game unbeaten streak

"Just a game for me. I had a good feeling and I was in good shape, played well in New Haven. I feel good. It's nice to have a win when you make your first game.

"I was proud I was one of the first Europeans, that's true."

3
SEAN AVERY

Left wing Sean Avery played for four teams during his ten-year NHL career. Avery had two separate stints with the Rangers and ended up playing six years on Broadway. Avery was a controversial figure throughout his pro career, but he was a spark after arriving in New York in February 2007 as he scored 20 points in 29 games to help the Rangers make the playoffs. Avery returned to the Rangers in March 2009 and played three more years before retiring after the 2011–12 season.

FIRST NHL GAME ATTENDED AS A KID:

"First NHL game was [the] St. Louis Blues against the Toronto Maple Leafs at Maple Leaf Gardens. I think it was 1992. Brett Hull was my favorite player. My Dad took me [to] my first game."

FIRST HOCKEY IDOL: Brett Hull

"Growing up it was Brett Hull for sure. I think only because I read his book, Shootin' and Smilin', I think I got it for Christmas, whatever year it came out. I'm not sure what year it came out, but I got the book for Christmas and that was like the first book I'd ever read and it was Brett Hull's book. That's kinda what hooked me, for sure. I found out 25 years later that he said he hardly wrote [it];

he hardly did anything. He didn't write the book."

FIRST PLAYER TO BE COACHED BY SOMEONE WHO ALSO COACHED HIS FATHER:

Longtime junior hockey coach Dave Siciliano, who coached Sean Avery at Owen Sound, also coached his Dad, Al Avery, at Lakehead University.

"It was very interesting because I'm the complete opposite of my Dad, from just a personality standpoint. From a player standpoint, my Dad was like a more skilled guy when he played juniors at Oshawa and he went and played collegiate. When I was 17 in Owen Sound and since Siciliano came to the team, I was totally fucking out of control, so I think it took him a while. Until he saw my Dad at a game, I don't think he believed that I was the son of a guy that he had coached, probably 20 years earlier, but he [Siciliano] was a very mild-mannered man, like a professor that was also hockey coach. He was a good guy. I haven't heard that name in a long time. I wish I could bump into him at some point and just kind of have a laugh and tell him I'm sorry."

FIRST CONTACT WITH NHL:

Avery was an undrafted free agent who signed a contract with the Detroit Red Wings in September 1999.

"I didn't get drafted. I had a big year in junior, like a big year pointwise (84 points for two teams). I was definitely one of the better players in the league for my age for sure. I was definitely in the top five, so I didn't get drafted because I was five-eight and maybe 170 pounds. Everyone thought I had attitude problems, so I didn't get drafted, but I had an opportunity. It was kind of like an open invite. I really had that opportunity to grow. I could pick whatever NHL team I wanted to go to camp with. Joe McDonnell, who was a coach for the Kitchener Rangers when I was growing up, he had become a scout for the Red Wings. I was like a die-hard

Ranger fan and I used to go to all the games at Kitchener Auditorium, so I knew who he was. He called me and he came in and met me for lunch one day in the summer. He talked to me a little bit about Detroit and he thought that I was an interesting player. The thing that was most interesting was he was essentially vouching for me saying, 'I think you should come to our camp and I trust that you could be an NHL player.' On paper, Detroit's camp was probably the worst place that I could go. Fast forward a few years later to that 2002 team, there really wasn't a lot of opportunity to come up through the system with that team at that point, but it was Joe McDonnell. He was the guy that definitely made me choose Detroit, because it was either Detroit or Montreal."

FIRST REACTION TO BEING TRADED TO THE RANGERS:

On February 5, 2007, Avery was acquired by the Rangers in a trade with the Los Angeles Kings.

"It wasn't completely unexpected because I'd come to New York on All-Star break a few weeks before. I also believe the Kings played the Rangers in a game and Shanny [Brendan Shanahan] had told me, 'Make sure you have a good game tonight 'cause they're going to be watching.' I think I ended up scoring and I had a pretty good game, I think a really good game against them. When I came to New York for the All-Star break, it was sort of this very unusual situation where I went and met Shanny after the game. There was a bunch of players, Ranger players there. Essentially, it was like this interview process a few weeks before I ended up getting traded, where I met some of the guys on the team. I think it was just a way for J.R. (Rangers VP of Communications John Rosasco) and Shanny to be able to say to [GM] Glen [Sather] 'Yeah, this is going to work out. Sean met some of the guys and they hung out and it seemed like all good.' So when I got the call, I was just walking around a shopping mall with my grandmother and my mother, 'cause my mother lived in Sarasota. That was like one of the times every year that I would get to see her. I remember it was [LA Kings GM] Dean Lombardi [who called him] it was a very, very quick phone call. I think it was one of those times where a GM probably knew that I was going to be happy on the other end of the phone. It wasn't this weird satisfaction that maybe GM's sometimes get when they can trade a guy that they just wanted to trade. It was a very quick phone call and then he gave me Glen's phone number and I remember calling Slats. He said, 'We're excited to have you. We need you to come in here, do your thing, don't hold back. We need you to get these guys going. That was kind of basically the extent of that."

FIRST RANGERS GAME: February 6, 2007 @ New Jersey Devils, 3–2 shootout loss.

"I don't know if it was the next night [after the trade] across the Hudson into New Jersey. That was where the infamous [Devils goaltender Martin] Brodeur relationship started. I played against him a few times, but it was just one of those games. I ended up on a line with [Jaromir] Jagr and we're having a really good game. I got into the front of the net and it's kind of a scrum and Brodeur didn't like me kind of poking at him a little bit. So he kinda gave me a cross-check with his blocker and his stick. I don't think he expected to get what I gave back to him. Remember, I've seen the video, I kinda went at him full bore and his helmet came up and then Colin White jumped on my back and Jagr was in the pile. That was the birth of, yeah, a pretty fun rivalry for a few years for sure."

FIRST REACTION TO SEEING HIS NAME ON A RANGERS JERSEY:

"Even growing up, you think about teams in the NHL, like a Red Wing jersey and a Ranger jersey are two of the most iconic in my opinion. The Leafs won a lot of Cups, but Gordie Howe and then, Detroit. Then you think of the Rangers in New York City. Even at that point, I had remembered I had heard the stories of [Ron] Duguay, and [Ron] Greschner and obviously, Mess [Mark Messier] in '94, you knew what the Rangers was all about. I'll tell you what's interesting, the moment where it kind of really hit me was, I think, after our second or third shift. Jagr, I ended up beside him on the bench and he kinda gave me a pat on my right leg. He was on the right side of me and he says, and Jags is like weird, broken English, but good English. 'Nice pass.' He just kinda looked at me and said 'Nice pass,' and I just kind of snapped out of it and I was like, 'Holy fuck.' I played with some good players, obviously unbelievable players in Detroit and then in LA, Ziggy Palffy, but sitting beside Jagr in a Ranger jersey and on his line and we were like totally in sync and him looking at me and saying that. Yeah, that's definitely one thing that I'll never forget, that's for sure."

FIRST RANGERS CAPTAIN: Jaromir Jagr

"An unbelievable captain. Obviously won Stanley Cups, but the type of captain, very similar to a Steve Yzerman. Very quiet, not a rah, rah type of captain but the type of guy that'll go out on the ice and just put a team, literally just put a team on his back and it was pretty amazing. He's one of the most memorable players I've ever played with. Everything from his sticks to his skates to the size of them. I don't think people understand how big of a man he is. Just huge. He kind of became like this Canadian-European. We all loved him, even though Don Cherry told us we shouldn't like him, but he was so cool. He was a great captain. I loved playing with him."

FIRST RANGERS COACH: Tom Renney

"People have this bad rap that Tom was like a bit of a pushover, but I think it's the complete opposite. First of all, he's just a great guy. He treated his players like they were his peers. There was never like, he was just happy to see the guys. He was always friendly and interested in what you had going on and he's just absolutely the most down to earth, respectful coach that I'd ever played for. That was definitely a breath of fresh air, coming from LA with Marc Crawford. Then we had Andy Murray who was like the most unpersonable coach I've ever played for.

"Tom, I loved him because it was also the first time that I ever had a coach who just kind of like embraced the role that I was bringing to a team. His way to discipline me was, he would call me into his office after a game the next day. It was always the next day. He'd always let it simmer over and he'd just have a conversation with you. Like it was man to man and he would tell you why I did something. Whatever I did wasn't a good thing to do and why it was hurting the team. That was the first time somebody had ever really kind of just talked to me and really told me like, 'I'm not saying that I don't like it. Like, I think this is effective, but I don't think it's effective at this time.' It was funny because Scotty Bowman did the same thing with me. He left the guys alone. The only time I ever got called in Scotty's office was once he called me in and he taught me about when I should fight and when I shouldn't fight. He was the first coach that told me never fight when we have a lead, unless it's a player that somebody has taken a cheap shot at one of our guys. You never fight when you're winning. It just doesn't work like that. The momentum shifts, so coming back to Tom, Tom was amazing 'cause I loved him because he just let us play but he was stern. If you fucked up or if you did something stupid, he'd sit you on the bench.

"I remember [him] benching Jaromir Jagr. There's not a lot of coaches that would have had the guts to do that and Jags and Tom loved each other. They had a great relationship. I think if I had stayed and not gone to Dallas, that Tom would not have lost his job and Tom would have been coaching a pretty good team down the road like that. The team that went to the Finals a few years later, every player loved him. I've never been on a team where all the guys liked the coach as much as they liked Tom. I think that kinda came to bite him in the ass a little bit towards the end when they started losing. I remember [they] started blaming Tom, saying he was too nice. It was the first time I'd ever heard that a coach was getting fired because he was too nice. So yeah, I loved playing for Tom. I, like the other guys on the team. Like the Ryan Hollwegs, Colton Orr or Jed Ortmeyers, guys that were not NHL superstars. They would take a bullet for Tom Renney and that's the type of team that you need. When coaches have players that'll take a bullet for them, they play harder. That's just a fact, so yeah, I loved playing for Tom."

FIRST GAME AS A RANGER AT MADISON SQUARE GARDEN: February 9, 2007 vs. Tampa Bay Lightning, 5–0 win.

In Avery's first home game as a Ranger, he scored his first goal in a Rangers uniform. Michael Nylander and Brendan Shanahan got the assists.

"What I remember more about the goal, I remember skating into the pile where everybody congratulates each other. It was like I was on the other side of the ice and I skate across the ice. The whole time I'm staring at Shanny and he's got a big ear-to-ear grin on his face. There was just irony and memories and so much built into that moment. It's probably one of the best moments of my career just from a single place standpoint. It was pretty fun. I also remember during that game, maybe right after the goal, I went to the bench and I just realized how good of a player Michael Nylander was. I was like, this guy's fucking good. He was an interesting combination of a Jagr, Ziggy Palffy kind of putting into one type of player. He's such a beautiful player to watch, but I'll never forget that moment of looking at Shanny and I think we definitely had a chuckle after the game on that one for sure."

FIRST RANGERS FIGHT: February 17, 2007 @ Madison Square Garden vs. Philadelphia Flyers, 5–3 loss.

Avery fought Philadelphia's Mike Richards in the first period in what was considered a good NHL fight that lasted nearly a minute. According to hockeyfights.com, Avery was the winner by a slight margin. Brendan Shanahan was taken off on a stretcher after a hard hit from Philadelphia's Mike Knuble.

"I think about all the fights I had in the NHL, that was definitely the best fight that I ever had. What you can't really understand from being in the stands or watching on TV. That arena, we're talking pre-renovation, the arena moved. Like it just had this energy where the walls shook and the ground moved and there was something so special about it. I remember I was on the ice when Shanny ran into Mike Knuble. First of all, it was like the loudest, heaviest thud I had heard on a hockey rink. It was like a tremble, like a silent bomb went off. I had never seen Shanny in that type of situation. He's always been a guy that was like kind of just Superman to a certain extent. So it was a crazy game and Mike Richards was the perfect guy for me to fight that night because I didn't like fighting guys that were bigger than me and I didn't like fighting guys that were tougher than me. I think Richards was just, it's like me looking at me in the mirror to a certain extent. I'll never forget the feeling of skating from where we finished the fight to penalty box. There was just like an energy in the air. I just knew that this was probably going to be the only team that I was ever going to be able to play for at that point. I think right then and there, I knew this was home for sure."

FIRST STANLEY CUP PLAYOFF EXPERIENCE AS A RANGER: 2007 Stanley Cup playoffs. Rangers beat Atlanta in a four-game sweep in the Eastern Conference quarterfinals but lost to Buffalo in the semifinals.

"I'll come back to the building again because I've never been in an NHL building in the playoffs with Detroit, in Detroit or on the road. I've never been in an NHL building that can create the type of energy that Madison Square Garden creates, and it starts the moment that John [Amirante] would finish singing the national anthem. There's just an energy in that building that they lost it when they did the renovation. I'm lucky to say I'm so thankful that I had the ability to experience it because it's the most electrifying arena in the world when it really hits that moment where everybody's rocking and rolling. It's just like an adrenaline shot into your veins, like literally the hair standing up on the back of your neck during the national anthem.

"There's such a scene. I don't think the hockey world really understands how powerful Ranger fans are when they get going. I had never experienced anything like it. I mean, it's the greatest arena in the world. I just remember that first couple of series. Two or three times I remember sitting on the bench, kinda looking down at my skates and then saying to myself, This fucking place, I can feel this arena moving, like the arena's swaying right now. There was probably, I don't know, maybe five or six times that [it] happened on that level and I'll never forget the feeling ever."

FIRST TIME PLAYING THE RANGERS AS AN OPPONENT AT MADISON SQUARE GARDEN AFTER LEAVING AS A FREE AGENT: October 20, 2008 for the Dallas Stars, 2–1 Dallas win.

In July 2008, Avery signed a free agent contract with the Dallas Stars.

"It just felt unusual and it felt very weird for everyone. It's easy to say now but I knew going into that game that I was going to be back there at some point. I didn't know how quickly but it was a weird, weird feeling. It was like the type of thing that I also felt looking at the guys on my bench on Dallas, thinking like you're wearing the wrong jersey. Even at that point, everyone kind of knew like I should be on the other team. So yeah, it was very unusual. I am sure there's not many NHL players that have that type of feeling. At the end of the game, we won the game and I didn't have a great game. I just didn't play well. I was so relieved that we won, just for the simple reason of like I needed to feel something other than how weird and uncomfortable it felt. That was the little bit of saving grace, but yeah, that was the weirdest NHL game I ever played in for sure."

FIRST GAME BACK AT MADISON SQUARE GARDEN AFTER COMING BACK TO THE RANGERS: March 8, 2009 vs. Boston Bruins, 4–3 win.

Avery was claimed off waivers from Dallas on March 3rd, 2009.

"New York fans are very rough and tumble fans. It's New York City; it's the way that this city was built. I was like on probation by the NHL and there's all this crazy shit going on between the league and me and Slats. They sent me down to Hartford first to make sure that I wasn't a serial killer, there was just that whole thing. I was so nervous, I can remember, I think I threw a big check my first shift and after I got to the bench, I don't think I'd ever been so tired in my life from an NHL shift, 'cause I just went out there and I tried to hit everything that went by me. I don't even know who I hit, I just hit everything. Yeah, that was the most nervous I've ever been for a game for sure. Coming back, that was like a wild, wild night. I remember that first check. I think I put every ounce of energy; it was the hardest I ever tried to hit somebody in my life."

FIRST TIME SEEING HIMSELF IN A MOVIE:

In the French-Canadian biopic, The Rocket (about Montreal Canadiens Hall of Famer Maurice "the Rocket" Richard) Avery played former Ranger Bob Dill, who was known as an intense, aggressive type, who wasn't a dirty player, who tries to intimidate the Montreal star.

"I don't [think] people understand the depiction of hockey games in the movie that are actually incredibly well done. That was like the first time I'd been on a movie set and had done any sort of acting whatsoever. I didn't know really who Bob Dill was and then you understand the story of him and Richard and Richard ends up coming back and kind of taking them out. You look back on it and it's so ironic and serendipitous and there's so many interesting elements to that. It's like fate was kinda knocking on my door before I even knew that fate was gonna be a thing, yeah, it's pretty funny. I guess one thing about movies that's great is like they never go away. You always have them, you have the ability to kind of go back and watch them. The fact that I did that, I'm pretty lucky. After putting the jersey on and now watching that movie, it gives me personally a whole new perspective on that crest on the front of that jersey. I remember filming and we actually used old skates. Normally, they would just paint them or do something. The movie didn't have that much money, so they made all the guys use old skates. It definitely did something to the way we skated and moved even. You put on a pair of skates from the late fifties, early sixties, those skates, you could only move a certain way in them. It's definitely the reason the guys skated the way they did and look the way it looked because of the skates. That's kind of an interesting movie tidbit. It's so authentic because you only have the ability to move a certain way in those types of skates. It's just crazy how life works. Like me playing him two years before I end up coming to the place I would call home. It's pretty wild."

FIRST TIME WORKING IN THE FASHION INDUSTRY:

In the summer of 2008, Avery worked as an intern for the famed fashion magazine *Vogue*.

"When I got to New York, I started to educate myself on the history of the team and started to read about the [Ron] Duguay and [Ron] Greschner days with the Rangers and Studio 54 and like the old Sasoon commercial. It's so unique, especially hockey at that time. It was so out of the ordinary and the fact that when you looked at it, it looked like it was just the way it should be. Like New York, it's Broadway and this organization. There's something inherently in the bones of the organization where there's freedom and you have freedom in the city to kind of make choices that, only the strong last in this city, certainly on the teams. Good players on Ranger teams have the ability to kind of embrace the city, and I just kind of ran with it. The world was my oyster at that point. It's like if you're a New York Ranger, you kinda can do whatever you want. So yeah, I just kind of went with it and I remember everyone outside of the team thought it was really weird and unusual. That was a fun summer, it was a fun summer. Like I was an intern at *Vogue* magazine and I was this New York Ranger hockey player. It's definitely something that somebody's going to make a movie about at some point.

"It gave me an interesting perspective on the honor that any

NHL player has. Like, to have the ability to wake up every single day. It sounds clichéd but going to work and your job is the thing you've loved doing since you were two years old and not many people get to do that. I don't know how many people do, but not many. That was the thing that kind of hit me the hardest, which was like it was the first time I understood what real work was like. It was the first time I had been in an environment where you saw working people that work nine to five and they had families and they had to go home. It wasn't a hockey player's life. It was funny because up until that point, fuck, I don't know, ten years, I've always taken a nap in the afternoon 'cause that was just what you do. Even in the offseason, you'd work out in the morning, you'd come home, eat lunch and take a nap. It was so hard for me to get through a full day because I had never done it before. There's so many interesting, eye-opening experiences that I had doing that internship. It just kind of showed me how lucky I was. The value of doing something you love, how special it is. It was everything that I got from it was everything that I didn't expect I was going to get from it. It was all gravy."

Sean stirring the pot in pregame skate.(Photo courtesy of Mark Rosenman)

4
STEVE BAKER

Goaltender Steve Baker played his entire four-year NHL career with the Rangers. Baker was the Rangers' goalie when they upset the Smythe Division–winning St. Louis Blues, 4–2 in the 1981 Stanley Cup quarterfinals.

FIRST CONTACT WITH NHL:

Steve Baker was a third-round selection of the Rangers in the 1977 NHL Amateur Draft.

"I was in college and I believe I was in my dorm [room] and I got a call from John Ferguson, who was the general manager at the time. Fergie just wanted to touch in, informed of the draft and wanting to welcome me to the organization. That was about it; I mean that's that's kinda how things were done back in the day. It's not quite as big of an event as it is now."

FIRST REACTION TO GETTING THE PHONE CALL FROM THE RANGERS:

"Obviously, I was walking on cloud nine. For a kid that grew up in Boston, and obviously through the [Phil] Esposito-[Bobby] Orr era when they were winning some championships. That was kind of the stimulus for me to wanna play the sport. To be drafted by the Rangers, it was like, okay, that used to be the Bruins' nemesis, but now it's gonna be my friend."

FIRST RANGERS TRAINING CAMP: Before 1979-1980 season

"My first Ranger pro training camp was in Richmond, Virginia. I guess Mickey Keating [assistant GM] who was relatively new to the position, forgot to secure ice time for the training camp so they were kind of scurrying and they found this Richmond opportunity available. That year, the Rangers were gonna to support an ECHL [actually, EHL] franchise in Richmond. They were called the Richmond Rifles. So we went down there for camp. I had an outstanding camp and you talk about taking advantage of an opportunity. They wanted to try and promote the Richmond Rifle franchise for the local public. So they staged an exhibition game and they put, basically, the New Haven Nighthawks, the American League farm team, that had lost the year before in the Calder Cup Finals. They put us in the Richmond Rifle uniforms and the Rangers were in their full regalia, having come off losing the Stanley Cup Final the year before. I started the game and when I left the game, we were winning 3–0 halfway through and everybody's up in the stands going, 'Holy cats, I'm buying my season tickets, our Richmond Rifles are unbelievable.' Of course, that didn't settle well with the big boys on the bench and they were giving me the "razz" all night long.

"After camp was over, I had an outstanding camp. Danny Summers, who was the chief scout, came down to me and pulled me aside and he said, 'Stevie, we know what you've done here. Just go down to New Haven, play well. You're gonna get your chance.' So I was pretty excited about that. We started off like a house on fire, I think we were 9–0. The Rangers were really struggling out of the box and that's when I got my call up, which I think was around the 27th or 26th of November."

When Baker was playing in New Haven in the spring of 1979, he got to scrimmage against the NHL squad.

"We were going to the Calder Cup Finals (AHL championship), the Rangers were going into the Stanley Cup Finals, and we both had a little window where the teams were waiting to see who was gonna play who and before Montreal had won their series and we were getting ready to go on and play Maine. Freddie Shero called us all up to Elmsford, New York, which is where their farm place used to be. We jumped into our New Haven Nighthawk uniforms and the Rangers, they're '79 finalist team were in their uniforms and we played a three, 20 minute [period] game. I started the game and basically stood on my head and I believe we were leading 3–1 halfway through the game. I know I stopped Espo on a breakaway, Dave Maloney was up hollering at me from the bench, 'You know, pull the horseshoe out of your ass,' but it was fun. Then, I gave way to Lindsay Middlebrook and nothing against Lindsay, you know you're playing against pretty good competition. They ended up coming back, storming back and I think they won the game, 6–4 or something like that, but it just speaks to, you know you've got to step up when you're given the opportunity."

FIRST TIME PUTTING ON THE RANGERS JERSEY:
November 1979

"I walked in the room, they had me in the very back of the room. If you remember the old configuration of the Garden, you walked in and back in the left corner [where] the stalls started. They ran along the back wall and then at the very end, there was about three or four more stalls. You had your entrance into the shower and the lounge that we shared with the Knicks, but they put me at the very back of the room and I was seated between Carol Vadnais and Phil Esposito. For a kid to grow up in Boston, two ex-Bruins and especially Espo. You know how many times I was Espo as a kid playing ball hockey in front of my house, I was starstruck.

"I remember a buddy of mine who was a restaurateur in Boston had sent me a post office box. You know what you would have at the end of your driveway, painted in Rangers red, white, and blue. I think it said 'Broadway Baker' on it and then my number, 35, and I opened it up and inside was a note that said, 'America's Best Champagne for America's Best Goalie.' I pulled out the bottle of Champagne and he had stuffed about 60 inner jocks. Fortunately, they were new to secure it inside the box when [it] shifted."

FIRST RANGERS GAME: November 28, 1979 @ MSG vs. Minnesota North Stars, 4–4 tie

"As you go out and go to your warm-up process, you know it's a place that I always wanted to be and the stage that I always wanted to perform at. Fortunately, we got out of there without losing. We ended up tying. I remember it was a late third-period goal that was kind of a fluke. A slapper from the point that came in end over end, hit somebody in the back, bounced off and hit somebody in the shoulder and the next thing you know, it jumped over my shoulder and into the net. So they secured the 4–4 tie and that's how it ended."

FIRST WIN: December 1, 1979 @ St. Louis Blues, 2–0 shutout victory

"I believe I had 38 saves and ended up winning the game, 2–0."

FIRST RANGERS PLAYOFF GAME: April 8, 1981 @ LA Kings, Game 1, preliminary round, 3–1 win

"The Kings had a phenomenal year but the Triple Crown line really kind of led the way but they had a good supporting cast and Mario Lessard, their goaltender, had a great season. It was a best three out of five series, so the goal is to at least take one win out of their building and we did, the first night. We played the next night. That building, the Fabulous Forum was hotter than blazes at that time of the year. I remember Game Two, which of course is when all the hijinks started with all the fights [a playoff-record 229 penalty minutes in the first period].

"That first period, I remember being so dehydrated. I recall they had like 18 to 22 shots on me in the first period. I mean they just poured it on and I was starting to cramp from the dehydration. The first thing I thought of at the end of that period was to make a beeline off the ice to the locker room. They had a TV monitor inside the locker room and I was down there drinking Gatorades and I'm looking up at the monitor and I see everything starts to break out like crazy. So I stayed in the room and avoided any of the insanity."

Steve Baker adjusting his signature mask. (Photo courtesy Mark Rosenman)

5
BARRY BECK

Defenseman Barry Beck played seven of his ten NHL seasons for the Rangers. The native of British Columbia was a two-time All Star who finished second in the voting for the 1977–78 Calder Trophy and was a top-10 finisher three times in the voting for the Norris Trophy.

Beck was acquired from Colorado in November 1979 in exchange for left wing Pat Hickey, right wing Lucien DeBlois, defensemen Mike McEwen and Dean Turner, and future considerations.

FIRST CONTACT WITH NHL:

Barry Beck was the second overall selection by the Colorado Rockies in the 1977 NHL Amateur Draft as well as the second overall selection in the 1977 WHA Amateur Draft by the Calgary Cowboys. Later that year, Calgary ceased operations.

"They didn't take players to the NHL draft, they sat at home and they would call you. Ray Miron [Colorado GM] had called me and I had discussions with him before the draft on playing in Denver. Montreal, during that period, had tried to move up in the draft and tried to make a top choice and would trade it as it did to Colorado the prior year. So they had called me about and I sort of want to stay in Colorado because I thought I would get a chance to play and play power play. I would probably make the team and really get to know the league and become a better player that way."

FIRST REACTION TO BEING TRADED TO THE RANGERS: November 2, 1979

"Well, that was a big shock to me because I was just buying a house and I had gone in and I talked to Ray [Miron] and Ray had said that no matter about the rumors of the team moving to New Jersey, that we were gonna stay in Colorado. I know that it wasn't his fault that the team was gonna move. I wanted to practice one day and [Rockies coach] Don Cherry called me in before practice and he said, 'Congratulations, you're a millionaire,' and I said, 'Well, what happened?' He says, 'You have just been traded to the New York Rangers.' I was shocked, I mean we had a good, young team in Colorado and we wanted to keep growing that team. When I did come into Manhattan, when we come in with the Rockies, the older players would take us to these old bars where I would go home. Once the deal was made, I just moved my equipment to the Rangers' dressing room because we played the very next night against the Rangers, excuse me, against Colorado, I was playing for the Rangers.

"Fred Shero had given out the lineup and he had said, 'Okay, Espo [Phil Esposito] you're starting and [Pat] Hickey, you're on right wing. Then, everybody has to tell him [Shero] nonetheless that he's [Hickey] not here anymore.

FIRST COACH: Fred Shero

"Freddy was sorta like, I think like a professor. I think everybody respected him and knew that he already had success and he didn't ask a lot from you. One of the things that I can remember is that he stuck up for me one game when the media was on me and the fans were on me. One game, he came in and he stuck up for me and I'll always remember that. He told me I can be a good player, he says I can be a great player and says, I got this, put the time in."

FIRST TIME PUTTING ON THE RANGERS SWEATER: November 3, 1979 @ Colorado Rockies, 7–2 loss

"Well, it's one of the first, you know, original six teams, so there's a lot of background with me growing up as a kid, you know all the hockey cards. I used to collect the players and growing up in Vancouver and playing at Madison Square Garden, greatest sports arena in the world, so it was a big honor and it was just, I had a difficult transition. The transition was difficult for me to make right at first. I think there was some players that resented me being there of the former players that were there. They had gone to the finals and now how was I going to take them to the finals."

FIRST RANGERS CAPTAIN: Dave Maloney

"I thought he was a good player. Good offensive player, a player who could play good defense, could move the puck well, could skate well and I thought he was a good captain at that point. They did come and tell me that they would be using three captains that year and that Walter Tkaczuk would be the second captain and I would be the third captain. I was told that was sort of my role was once I would remain captain, then I would remain throughout the next year when they came back. That's just the way they decided to do it that year."

FIRST RANGERS GOAL: November 7, 1979 @ MSG vs. Los Angeles Kings, 8–4 win

"I remember Phil [Esposito] pushed the puck ahead and I sorta had to jump over the goalie [Mario Lessard] to lift the puck over him, then I landed up on the crossbar. I was going pretty fast and I think that was the only way I could stop. I enjoyed that and it was much more after the game because Don King was at the game and [Madison Square Garden chairman] Sonny Werblin. We went down to "Charlie O's" after the game and that's where the players used to go. We stayed down there for a while, maybe have something to eat. Don King was down there with Sonny Werblin and they were on the other side of the crowd. Coach [Shero] would always go and say hello to Sonny and his wife. King started yelling at me, 'Too Tall wants you, Too Tall wants you Beck. That's right, Too Tall Jones.' You know Jones was the defensive end for the Cowboys. He was trying to set up a match already, so you know this is like a night in New York."

FIRST RANGERS PLAYOFF GAME: April 8, 1980, Game 1 of preliminary round series @MSG vs. Atlanta Flames, 2–1 win. (Beck was a plus-2 in the game.)

"It was a pretty rough series. The Rangers still hadn't won the Stanley Cup [since 1940] and that's all that was on my mind, just to win the Cup, there wasn't anything else. That's all we were trying to do and that's what we tried to do."

FIRST ALL- STAR GAME AS A RANGER: 1982 All-Star Game in Washington, DC

Beck was previously named an All-Star for Colorado in 1978.

"Well, I guess there's a little bit of a difference. I was proud to play in Colorado, but I think just the difference between being in Colorado and playing for the Rangers is sort of like night and day. I mean it's everything is just cranked up ten, twenty notches. I do remember playing with [former Islanders] Mike Bossy and [Clark] Gillies and [Bryan] Trottier. We won the All-Star Game; I think Bossy won the car. It was good playing with those guys, and I had played with them a little bit before early on in my career, actually my rookie year, 1978 in the "Challenge Cup" I played with them. I think there's a big difference between playing on the East Coast and the West Coast. It might've changed over time now, but playing on the East Coast, you're playing in Boston, you're playing in New York, you play in Philly, those are die-hard cities. I mean the other fans wanna kill ya and that's the way it is. When you go to LA, there's nobody leaning over the boards saying they wanna kill ya."

Don King was on hand for Barry's first Rangers goal. (Public Domain)

6
RICK BENNETT

Left wing Rick Bennett played college hockey at Providence where he was a Hobey Baker Award finalist in 1990. Bennett played a total of 15 games for the Rangers over parts of three seasons and scored one career goal. Bennett was inducted into the Providence College Athletic Hall of Fame in 2012 and is currently the Union College hockey coach.

FIRST HOCKEY GAME THAT HE ATTENDED:

"My first going to an NHL game was as a college player. I went to go see the Bruins and I can't even tell you who they actually played. I never was fortunate enough to go see an NHL game as a kid. It was pretty exciting. The fact that it was the old Boston Garden, 'cause I'd heard so much about and how small it was. The ice surface was the first thing I guess I noticed. Some of the players they had for the Bruins that we had followed just going to school at Providence College, so I was more aware of the Boston Bruins than I was the opponent. Just to see some of those players was pretty special."

FIRST HOCKEY IDOL: Bobby Clarke

"I know he was a Flyer and being a Springfield, Mass. guy, but just the way he played, played hard and he was a winner and I always liked the fact that he had a couple of Cups behind him. Facing adversity, being a diabetic along with being captain, his leadership and then the fact that he just absolutely played hard, to me that was really impressive."

FIRST CONTACT WITH NHL:

Rick Bennett was chosen by the Minnesota North Stars in the third round of the 1986 NHL Entry Draft.

"I remember being with grandfather and my father. We were roofing in Granby, Connecticut, at my grandfather's girlfriend's house and I didn't even know that I had got drafted until I got home. There was a note left by my sister saying, 'The Minnesota North Stars drafted you, blank round, and number pick.' After the news came out, did an interview on the front lawn and then I went out with my friends."

FIRST REACTION TO JOINING THE RANGERS:

In October 1988, Bennett's rights were dealt to the Rangers as part of a six-player trade.

"Not too emotional. I found out after study hall. We had the study hall at Providence College from, I think it was 7 to 9 p.m., so I found out after study halls. It could've been anywhere after 9 p.m. and that was it. No calls really. It was basically an 'Okay' and that was the end of it."

FIRST RANGERS TRAINING CAMP:

"The first thing was having a choice of a five-mile run, or 25-mile bike. If I ever had to do that one over again, I definitely would've taken the bike. Of course, you know, college kid, I took the five-mile run, so the first couple of days of training camp were a treat, but it was a different format. I think there's 80 guys there. Then, the format was, you know, it wasn't much practicing. It was just games, intrasquad scrimmages throughout training camp. I do remember the run and I just remember playing a lot of games and exhibition games that first camp."

FIRST RANGERS COACH: Roger Neilson

"Very detailed. I wouldn't say a lot of video, but video was necessary 'cause he was a little bit before his time with videos so that was really impressive. Pretty no nonsense. He talked to you when you needed to be talked to and it was kind of business as usual as you went along. I do remember Wayne Cashman (Rangers assistant coach) a lot, I had a little more of a relationship with Wayne Cashman than I did with Roger Neilson. Maybe it was because of the Bruins thing, too, but I knew of his name much more than I did Roger Neilson. Wayne always had a lot of words of encouragement as I was going along too. So that was helpful, especially just being there for the first time."

FIRST RANGERS CAPTAIN: Kelly Kisio

"A personable guy. I can't really tell you I recollect of when I walked in that dressing room the first time coming right from college 'cause I had signed right after our season, but just going into the locker room, he was one of the first guys to come over and say hello and how you're doing. Just basically a lot of short talk, but he was nice enough to come over. I had known Mike Richter and Brian Leetch from some of those USA hockey stuff in the summer, so that made it a little easier."

FIRST RANGERS PRACTICE:

"I can't tell you how long it actually took to sign but I know we were on spring break at school and I stayed home. I did not go on spring break 'cause I wanted to sign with the Rangers and it did happen. To sign that one night, probably like a Wednesday night or something like that and a limo was basically there the next morning at like 5 a.m. I remember hopping in it with my equipment and going to practice that morning. It was pretty funny.

The driver, on the way, had a New York station on as we were entering New York and it was Howard Stern and I'll never forget that, and Howard Stern was bashing me about, that's all the Rangers need is another goon, so I thought that was pretty funny. It was pretty funny, that's all we need is another goon. I thought that was interesting.

"Then, we got there, got practice and it took maybe two practices, then I think Randy Moller got hurt or someone got hurt and I was lucky enough, it was all timing, got to play six straight games."

FIRST RANGERS GAME: March 21, 1990 @ Madison Square Garden vs. Toronto Maple Leafs, 5–5 OT tie.

"I just remember actually going in for the first game, having a pregame nap at the hotel right across from, I believe it was at Madison Square Garden, one of the hotels and having the best pregame nap before that. The guy that I was with was Mark Janssens, who was a super guy and I didn't even know who he was outside this. We napped and then got up and we went to the game, but it was the best pregame nap that I've ever had in all my pro career. As far as the game, I don't really remember that game a ton, outside of a big hit. I remember getting back to the bench and I was like, 'What the heck are you doing?' and I guess it was one of their tough guys but that's really all I remember is a big hit behind the net."

FIRST RANGERS FIGHT: March 27, 1990 @ Quebec vs. Quebec Nordiques, 7–4 win.

Bennett's first fight was against Quebec's Steven Finn.

"One of the previous games, I think we played Washington, I got hit by Al Iafrate in the leg and he was a big man. Just playing through that, it was like playing on one leg for those games. I did not want to tell anybody. I didn't want to sit out and it was one of the more painful injuries that I had in my time. Then, having that fight that night for the first time. I think I got one lick in but it didn't look good after that. Eventually, it's one of those, you gotta show up and that's what I tried to do."

FIRST RANGERS GOAL: March 29, 1990 @ New Jersey Devils, 6–4 loss.

"I believe it went off my back and in the net, so as we tell our players here (Union College) being in the coaching profession, get around that net. Good things are gonna happen, so what was special about that is the college coach that I played for, Mike McShane, was at the game, so he was able to see that. To me, that was just as big as scoring the goal and it was pretty special.

"It's just nice to get a goal in the National Hockey League, but that's really about it for me. It was just the experience of and just being fortunate enough to make the NHL, you know coming from Springfield, Massachusetts, was huge for me. I never thought I was going to be able to do that and to be able to do, I know it was a 'cup of coffee' and with a few games, but that had meant a lot."

FIRST TIME BEHIND THE BENCH AS A COLLEGE COACH:

"Nate Leaman, who is now at Providence College, I worked for him here at Union for six years. When he left to go to Providence, our athletic director Jim McLaughlin waited all of about one second to offer me the job and I took it within another second. It was a pretty seamless transaction. That's kinda how it basically happened. As far as our first game, it was against Army at Army. This is what I do remember that they had scored first and I was just thinking on the bench, this is going to a short coaching career if we keep this up, so it eventually worked out. We went on to win the game and it was pretty special, but I don't know where the puck is or anything like that, but I have the memory of that first game. That's all that matters."

FIRST NATIONAL CHAMPIONSHIP AS A COACH:

In 2014, Bennett led Union College to the national championship, beat Minnesota, 7–4, in the championship game.

"It was, I'm sure people have used this word, surreal, but I have to say, I wish I would've enjoyed it more. That whole experience, because it was just, you're so dialed in, just the coaching aspect. I didn't have enough fun, but like watching and going through it and it was just like a blur. I didn't really appreciate it until after, it was the after effect more so that actually going through it. I was kinda like, basically naïve to it, which I kinda liked. If I'm ever put in that position again, I'd like that, not knowing the whole magnitude of it and you just play and that's how our guys played. So I'm just grateful to those players, our coaching staff and support staff, for the efforts that they put in that year were pretty, pretty special. We had some really special players and again, any championship team that you've talked to obviously has special players and people."

On being inducted in the Providence College Athletic Hall of Fame:

"Unfortunately, I had a decision to make that night, to either go to the Hall of Fame dinner or attend our game with Union College. I just decided to stay with our team and I never made it, but a special individual spoke for me. His name is Joseph D'Antonio and was our student manager at the time. In our four years, he's one of the best people that I've ever had a chance to meet, so he had spoken on my behalf and he sent me his speech and it was really special. I guess that'd be the only regret that I never was fortunate enough to thank the people that helped me along the way at Providence in my four years there."

You Never Forget Your First: A Collection of New York Rangers Firsts

Heard Howard Stern talking about him on way to first practice. (Photo courtesy of New York Rangers)

7
MARTIN BIRON

Goaltender Martin Biron played the final four years of his 16-year NHL career with the Rangers from 2010–11 to 2013–14. Biron was a solid backup goalie for Henrik Lundqvist. He finished his Rangers career with a 22–15–3 record with two shutouts.

FIRST CONTACT WITH NHL:

Martin Biron was the 16th overall selection by the Buffalo Sabres in the 1995 NHL Entry Draft.

"It was 1995 and it was in Edmonton. The '94–95 season was a lockout season in the National Hockey League and they played just like a half year. Our draft wasn't until July; it wasn't at the end of June like it usually is. So it was kind of a weird summer with free agency and draft day and all of that kind of happening all at once. So I met with a bunch of teams. I went to Washington, I visited some teams in Montreal, some teams came to Quebec City to visit, but I did a lot of meeting in Edmonton the week before. The way the draft worked back then is it was all in one day. We were there early in the morning and the draft starts and I sit in the stands with other guys that are going to get drafted. My family, my Mom and Dad and my brother were there and my agent is there.

"At number four, I believe the Mighty Ducks of Anaheim were drafting and I had a really good meeting with [them]. I thought, four is a little high, but who knows, maybe they want a goalie and maybe that's me. They picked [left wing] Chad Kilger, so I was like, 'Aw, man,' but then, my Dad and I kind of figured that there's prospects on both sides of the arena. Dave Keon Jr. worked for the National Hockey League and he was the one meeting the prospects down on the arena floor when they were being drafted. So we're paying attention to Dave and seeing what side of the rink he was going on. So if you went to the other side of the arena, I knew I wasn't getting drafted, but if he came to this side, ooh, there's a chance I may get drafted. So we had figured out the system how that all works. I want to say number 12 or 14th [actually 13th] overall was Jean Sebastien-Giguere, and that was the first goalie to be picked in that route, so I was a little disappointed because I wanted to be the first goalie picked and I was the top prospect that year. Now I'm thinking, okay, now that there's a goalie drafted, there's going to be a few goalies right after that and you know the trend will start. So the next few picks, Keon only went to the other side of the rink. So, I'm sitting there like kinda getting mad, now come back to my side, like it's my time to get drafted. When they got to 16 for the Sabres, he came over to our side of the rink. I don't remember them calling my name, I don't remember who called my name. It was a big blur until I got on stage. When I got on stage, I had [director of player development] Don Luce on one side, John Muckler was the GM at the time. There as a lot of people and Don Luce looked at me and he says, 'How about you give the fans a wave.' Then I wave to the fans from the stage and that's when it set in a little bit, like, holy crap, I just got drafted in the first round in the National Hockey League."

FIRST TIME PUTTING ON THE RANGERS JERSEY:

Biron signed with the Rangers as a free agent before the 2010–11 season.

"My first year with the Rangers, we were still in the old Madison Square Garden. They hadn't done any renovation my first season, so we're still in the old locker room. Everything is the way it was in the '90s. So I remember sitting in my stall the first time thinking, Wow, this is MSG and it had a really cool feel to it."

FIRST RANGERS COACH: John Tortorella

"I knew Torts from back in the days from when I got drafted with the Sabres. He was in the Buffalo organization and I knew Torts because my brother [Mathieu] had him as a coach with the Tampa Bay Lightning as well. So, I knew exactly what to expect with his training camp."

FIRST RANGERS TRAINING CAMP:

"I remember being, extremely, extremely, nervous. My first training camp for the fitness test because Torts is known to just put you through the ringer in the fitness testing. We had to do a two-mile run. We had to do a ton of physical things, some on ice things. I remember being very, very nervous for that. Getting older at the time, so I was thirty-three years old when I was there and it's not like I had it easy to get ready for camp and testing like I was twenty-three, so I was extremely nervous for that. As soon as camp started, I remember once again working with Henrik [Lundqvist], working with Benoit Allaire [goaltending coach], getting on the ice, just us, the two goalies and the goalie coach and really making me feel like this is the place I needed to be, this is the place I wanted to be. This was the first time that I was on a team that had their own private training facility."

FIRST RANGERS GAME AT MSG: October 27, 2010 vs. Atlanta Thrashers, 6–4 loss

"It didn't go well, we lost 6–4 and it didn't go well. I think a lot of it was I was in awe of the building and playing as the home team in New York, and they announce your name in Madison Square Garden. 'And starting in goal, number forty-three, Martin

Biron,' and it's like the fans are cheering. That feeling really cannot be duplicated anywhere else in the world. That's Madison Square Garden, that's the most famous arena in the world and your name is being announced as the starting goalie and the fans are cheering. I think that alone, I got so star struck that I didn't play well that night and got called out by Torts the next day, but I was able to enjoy Madison Square Garden and play well at Madison Square Garden after that."

FIRST SHOOTOUT WITH THE RANGERS: December 16, 2010 @ MSG vs. Phoenix Coyotes, 4–3 win

"I remember a game that I played at MSG and in the first five minutes, we're down 2–0 and the fans are yelling, 'Henrik, Henrik, Henrik,' like they want Lundqvist to go into net. I'm like, 'Jeez, this is not a good start,' and I remember we went through a shootout that game. By the end of the game, the fans are yelling, 'Mar-tee, Mar-tee,' and usually a 'Mar-tee' chant at MSG was reserved for [Martin] Brodeur and it's a negative chant. So the fact that the fans were yelling my name and that we had won in the shootout, and at the beginning of the game they were yelling Henrik's name, was really cool. I remember thinking, Yeah, I finally got you guys on my side now."

FIRST RANGERS SHUTOUT: November 6, 2011 @ MSG vs. Winnipeg Jets, 3–0 win

"I do remember my first shutout [against[Winnipeg. I thought the building was gonna explode. I do remember coming off the ice and thinking, I got a shutout as a New York Ranger. That is really cool."

Martin Biron on Heritage Night wearing a Gilles Gratton tribute mask. Photo by Mark Rosenman.

8
BOB BROOKE

Center Bob Brooke was a defensive-minded forward who began his NHL career with the Rangers and played in New York for parts of four seasons. Brooke was a member of the 1984 United States Olympic Hockey Team. Brooke also represented the United States in the Canada Cup and World Championships. The Massachusetts native had his best Rangers season in 1985–86 when he scored a career-high 24 goals and 44 points.

FIRST NHL GAME ATTENDED AS A KID:

"It's Boston Bruins. Take the train in, see the Bruins games. Bobby Orr, [John] McKenzie, and Johnny Bucyk. I think Derek Sanderson was probably a character on that team. I mean it's just eye opening."

FIRST HOCKEY IDOL:

"Well, growing up in Boston, it had to be Bobby Orr. He controlled the whole game when he was on the ice. From penalty killing and circling his own net, standing behind the net until someone flushed him out. I don't know if you remember this, but he would stand back there when they were shorthanded and he'd have the puck. When somebody came to chase him out, he would just circle the net and come right back behind the net."

FIRST OLYMPIC EXPERIENCE: 1984 Winter Olympics in Sarajevo

"I'll tell you how it feels to me to represent USA and put on a USA jersey. I'm somewhat opinionated on the national anthem and our flag and our military people. I didn't serve in the military, but I've had the opportunity to represent the United States and I'm really proud of that. We could've done a whole lot differently and a lot of things differently, but it does make me think of how fortunate, how maybe once in a lifetime, the 1980 results were, given what we've seen since then."

FIRST CONTACT WITH NHL:

Bob Brooke was chosen by the St. Louis Blues in the fourth round of the 1980 NHL Entry Draft. His rights were dealt to the Rangers in March 1984.

"Didn't even know the draft was happening. Didn't think I'd be that high in the draft. Nobody was talking to me about it. I was kind of in my own little world at Yale. I think the way I learned about it was by Tim Taylor, the coach at Yale, telling me I got drafted and you can expect a call from [Blues GM] Emile Francis."

FIRST REACTION TO BEING DEALT TO THE RANGERS:

"I had come back from the Olympics and was kind of working through an agent to get a deal worked out. He was working out a deal, conversations between Emile Francis and him. Next thing you know, he calls me up and says they want you in New York and I think this is a good deal for you. I said, 'Great,' and I flew to New York and signed the same day James Patrick did."

FIRST ROAD TRIP, GETTING ON THE BUS:

"I remember my first trip getting on the bus. I wanted to be respectful and let other people sit down. I went on the bus and grabbed an open seat, wasn't all the way in the back of the bus, wasn't up front. Though I was okay, next thing I know, Barry Beck comes back and goes, 'There's my seat.' I said, 'Okay,' and I forgot who I sat with, but I moved across the aisle or up one seat. 'Mind if I sit here?' he said, 'No, come on.' So, Barry was great about it and he treated me fantastic as a rookie, my second year there and so forth, all the way through my second year there. He was a first-class guy and a first- class leader. So that was my FIRST experience with the Rangers and in any road trip. I don't really remember."

FIRST RANGERS GAME: March 9, 1984 @ Winnipeg Jets, 6–5 win

"I think I was 23 years old and figured this isn't anything different than I'm supposed to do. You're an athlete, you get dressed, you get prepared and you go do what you're [supposed to], I wasn't even thinking about it as this is what you're paid to do. It's more like this is what you're supposed to do. I don't know that I thought too much about this being my first professional game or anything along those lines. I just got in the locker room and kinda stayed to myself."

FIRST RANGERS COACH: Herb Brooks

"When I stepped into the Rangers, there was a sense of friction between Brooks and Barry Beck and some of the other more senior guys on the team. I think they had gone through a stretch where they hadn't done very well. Maybe that made me more quiet and just kind of observant, just put my shirt on and my jersey and do what I'm supposed to do. Go out and do my job without high expectations or causing anything as a newcomer in the locker room."

FIRST RANGERS PLAYOFF: 1984 Patrick Division semifinals vs. New York Islanders. Rangers lost the series in five games, including a 3–2 overtime loss in the fifth and deciding game at Nassau Coliseum.

Games 3 and 4 were played at Madison Square Garden:

"Trying to understand what Madison Square Garden was yelling, you know, 'Potvin sucks,' or whatever, you know Madison Square Garden in the playoffs. You and I could sing the national anthem because it doesn't matter. Nobody can hear it anyway, so that was fantastic."

Overtime of Game 5:

"What I remember about the Islanders was two things. I had an opportunity coming in late in the game, if I could only get the puck up faster on [Islanders goaltender] Billy Smith, might've scored the game- winning goal. Right after that I remember the next shift, I think I passed the puck to Mikko Leinonen, wide open with an open net and I, like slow motion as I think of it now. The puck kind of slowly went up on edge and went right to his stick as he went to shoot. Shortly after that, Ken Morrow scored on a little wrist shot towards the net that went through three people's legs and through [Ranger goaltender] Glen Hanlon. He never saw it."

FIRST RANGERS PLAYOFF OVERTIME GOAL: April 23, 1986 @ Madison Square Garden, Game 4, Patrick Division finals, 6–5 overtime win. Rangers won the series in six games.

Brooke scored the tying goal late in the third period and the game-winner at 2:40 of the extra session.

"There's two things to that game that come back to me. One, it was late in the third period and I was playing with [Wilf Paiement]; he was tied up with a defenseman in the offensive zone. I left the front of the net to go help him and as soon as I left where

I was, he reached over and passed the puck right to there and I missed golden opportunity. I think he was a 14 or 15-year veteran, he let me have it on the bench. 'I'll do my job, you stay where you can, right.' It was the very next shift, almost the exact same thing happened and I said, 'I am not moving,' and he passed it to me and I scored the game-tying goal and then gave us an opportunity to get to overtime in the first place. I think it went off somebody's skate in the net for the winner. It's one of those, you get your 15 minutes of fame one way or another. I was in the right place at the right time and got a lucky bounce."

FIRST RANGERS HAT TRICK: November 20, 1985 @ Madison Square Garden vs. Toronto Maple Leafs, 7–3 win

"I never considered myself a big scorer by any means. Throughout my college days, I was more of a set-up guy, certainly got a lot more assists than goals."

FIRST REACTION TO BEING TRADED FROM THE RANGERS:

In November 1986, Brooke was traded to the Minnesota North Stars.

"I think I understood very quickly that day, that it is a business and you're one of the assets that helps the business run and you're going to provide some value in the NHL. Other people might see your value higher than the team you're playing for. That was probably the biggest realization and it was nice to go to Minnesota and [North Stars GM] Lou Nanne and a really good and younger team than we had in New York. I guess I really didn't think too much of it, other than, this is part of the business and I want to maintain my contract and my earnings, I'm on a flight at one o'clock."

FIRST TIME PLAYING AGAINST THE RANGERS:
December 15, 1986 @ Madison Square Garden, 4–3 Rangers loss (Brooke assisted on the go-ahead goal in the second period)

"You have a professional competitiveness is probably the best way to put it. You don't hold anything against any of the players. I was always treated really well by the players in New York and from the organization as a whole. So there wasn't any ill feeling towards anybody on the team. Certainly, you want to do well and kind of prove to them that maybe they made a mistake."

FIRST COLLEGIATE BASEBALL NCAA REGIONALS: 1981

Brooke, who was a teammate of Ron Darling on the 1981 Yale University baseball team, played in what many call "The Greatest College Baseball Game Ever Played." On May 21, 1981, Darling faced future major-league pitcher Frank Viola and St. John's in the NCAA Northeast Regional. St. John's beat Yale, 1–0, in 12 innings. Darling tossed 11 no-hit innings and gave up his only hit and only run in the 12th inning. Viola tossed 11 scoreless innings. Brooke was the starting shortstop and was 1-for-5, a double in the first inning. St. John's Steve Scafa led off the 12th with a bloop single just past Brooke at short. Scafa scored the game's only run on a double steal.

"Just a dramatic game where you knew one run was gonna make the difference. I can remember hitting a ground-rule double off Frank Viola early in the game to right-center field, one bounce over I think the 400 foot mark. I didn't see another fastball all game. Darling was just spectacular on the mound. They got a bloop hit, just out of my reach, just out of the left fielder's reach, just out of the third baseman's reach. That was basically the only time they got the bat on the ball and hit it anyplace. We still should've won that game. I think we played well enough. We didn't get to Viola and we didn't get to their second pitcher either.

"Without a doubt [best college baseball game he ever played in]. Some of that comes from looking back on it. Knowing what Viola and Darling went to do in their professional careers. I sit there and watch the playoffs. I'm a big playoff fan in a lot of different sports, baseball in particular. You see the playoffs where a mistake when the throw's not right on the money, past home plate, the guy scores instead of getting tagged out. A hit and run or a signal to steal at a certain time, these are coach's decisions that make the difference in any tight playoff game, especially baseball. I truly enjoy baseball from the 'mano-a-mano' type hitter [vs.] pitcher competition. That really excites me, and I look at these guys throwing upwards of 100 miles an hour now. I remember hitting Ron Darling in batting practice, if I connected on it, that was as good as it was going to get. That was as fast as I could come around. I really respect the hitters and the pitchers in baseball right now."

9
RYAN CALLAHAN

Right wing Ryan Callahan played parts of eight seasons with the Rangers. A fan favorite, he left it all on the ice and would do whatever it took to help the Rangers win. Callahan played 450 games with the Rangers and was named the 26th captain in franchise history in September 2011.

FIRST CONTACT WITH NHL:

Ryan Callahan was chosen by the Rangers in the fourth round of the 2004 NHL Entry Draft.

"I didn't attend the draft that year. I knew I probably wasn't going to be a top round pick, be in kinda the second round. I stayed home; it was actually the morning of the second day and I was downstairs on the computer, walked into watching the draft and the phone rang. I ran up to the phone thinking maybe it's my agent or somebody calling to let me know I got drafted. It ended up being a phone call for my Mom's doctor's appointment. The phone rings again. You know at that point I was bit disappointed because I thought that [first call] was the call, so I answered the phone kind of casually. It was my agent letting me know that, I don't know if it was the next pick or in two picks, that the New York Rangers were going to select me in the draft. I remember running outside, my

Dad was outside doing yard work, running outside to him and telling him. My family threw a little bit of a party, put something together really quick to have a little celebration."

FIRST RANGERS TRAINING CAMP:

"I remember walking in and being terrified. You know not knowing what to expect, being the first camp. I think my first camp, I didn't have that great of a camp and it hurt me because my attitude going in, I almost felt like I didn't want to get in the way. I just remembered had a lot of nerves and excitement about the camp, it was a challenging one for sure because I was so excited and so nervous."

FIRST TIME PUTTING ON THE RANGERS JERSEY:

"It's a tough feeling to describe to be honest with you. You work so hard your whole life to get to that moment and to actually see your name on an NHL sweater in a stall that has your name on it. It's kind of an eye opener to just sit there almost in awe like, you know this can't be real. So, it's special when you do actually see that jersey with your name on it. I think even more special for me being a New York Ranger jersey. Such an iconic organization, Original Six team, so much history. It's hard to put that into words, exactly how you feel, but it's overwhelming, for sure."

FIRST HOCKEY IDOL: Brendan Shanahan

"Brendan Shanahan and, I guess, Pat LaFontaine are the two. Obviously, being a Sabres fan, it was Pat LaFontaine that I loved to watch, see play, but the guy's game I loved the most was Shanahan, and the way he played it."

Callahan got to play with his idol in his very first NHL game:

"It was incredible. I still remember the first time we met going into the room. He [Shanahan] introduced himself and I kinda laughed at myself. 'You don't need to introduce yourself, I know who you are.' It was pretty special for me, just to be able to be in the same locker room with him and eventually become friends with him growing up. It's kinda surreal walking into that room for the first time, and then getting dressed in the same dressing room as him. I think what I loved about him and it was a little bit when I was older and could understand the game more, just what he did. He did a little bit of everything, which I thought was awesome. He was physical, he could fight. He obviously filled the back of the net. I really thought he was an all-around player, something I tried to model my game after when I was a teenager."

FIRST RANGERS GAME: December 1, 2006 @ Buffalo Sabres, 4–3 shootout loss

"That was special. I was really, really lucky to have my first game in Buffalo. When I got called up, I looked at the schedule and I was like, there's no way your next game's in Buffalo. I can't remember who it was, but someone was injured and debating if they were going to be able to play in the game or not, right when I first got called up and I was like, man, this is pretty special. It could be Buffalo, but I didn't know. Ended up finding out, a day or two before that I was gonna play in the game. Right away, I called my family and friends. Lucky enough that we were able to get a box for that game, so we had everybody come down. The biggest thing I remember about that game was going out for warm-ups. It literally felt like I wasn't even touching the ice. It's just so much emotion and energy and excitement I've ever felt skating around in warm-ups. I didn't even feel like I was moving my legs, obviously I was. Such a surreal feeling. It's one of the highlights of my career. I think I only played maybe just over three minutes of that game but to be able to do that in Buffalo, growing up a Sabres fan, going to the "Aud" with my family, then having them watch me play Buffalo, it was pretty cool."

FIRST RANGERS GAME AT MSG: December 19, 2006 vs. New York Islanders, 4–3 loss

"I grew up a Sabres fan, but still being from New York, you're so aware of the Rangers and you're aware of Madison Square Garden and how special a place that is. That was really big to know that I was gonna play at MSG, not knowing if I'd ever get a chance to do that again. The Ranger-Islander rivalry. You can tell right from the first shift, how intense it was and how involved the fans were from warm-ups. All of them lined up around the glass. That's something I really wasn't used to. About six rows deep around the glass, screaming, yelling. The energy in that building was something that I'll never forget. Lucky enough that the first game was against the Islanders in the Garden."

FIRST GOAL AND FIRST RANGERS FIGHT: March 17, 2007 @ MSG vs. Boston Bruins, 7–0 win (Callahan also scored his second Rangers goal)

"Assisted, I think, by Blair Betts and Sean Avery. I remember driving the net hard, the puck came in front and went off my stick, went off my shaft. Me and my hand also, shoulder, went into the net. Obviously, just extremely excited and they had to review it to make sure that I didn't put it in and obviously, I was little bit nervous during that. It was against Boston, another Original Six team, lucky enough at the Garden. My Dad was there, which was really cool. On Saint Patty's Day, which was cool, being an Irish kid as well. Couldn't ask for a better night to do it. Lucky enough to get another goal, a little bitty breakaway, got a first one out of the way too. A lot of firsts in that game."

With the Rangers leading 7–0, Callahan fought Boston's Chuck Kobasew early in the third period.

"I think it was a little scrum. Obviously, emotions were high right then. My first two goals at the Garden, playin' Boston. I said, 'Why not,' dropped the gloves and make a mark a little bit."

FIRST RANGERS PLAYOFF GAME: April 12, 2007 @ Atlanta Thrashers, Game 1, Eastern Conference quarterfinals, 4–3 win

Callahan scored his first two playoff goals in Game 3 as the Rangers went on to a four-game sweep.

"The biggest thing I remember, I guess two things. One thing is how intense playoff hockey gets. Not knowing that previously, how cool that is to experience that. The other thing I remember is scoring a goal at the Garden. Being on a two-on-one with Brendan Shanahan, I ended up looking Shanny off and shooting the puck and scoring. I still have the paper back home. In the *Post*, it had me celebrating with Shanny right in the background, chasing me, celebrating also. Him being my favorite player growing up, it was a pretty special moment for me in a picture that I'll always cherish."

FIRST RANGERS HAT TRICK: March 6, 2011 @ MSG vs. Philadelphia Flyers, 7–0 win

Callahan scored four goals and added an assist for a career-high five points.

"Just seemed like everything was going in. We're playing Philly; it was an afternoon game. I was talking to my agent the night before. We were just talking about the year-end totals because it was getting close to the end of the year. I remember him saying, 'You know, be great if you could hit that 20-goal mark.' I forget the number was at the time where I was but the next night, I go out and score four and then he called me afterwards. He goes, 'Oh, that 20 mark is a little more reachable now. I just know you're gonna have four tomorrow night.' Scored 'em all different ways. My first one was from the goal line, went short side. Had one of my foot, another one stole in front so that was a cool night, definitely."

FIRST WINTER CLASSIC: January 2, 2012 @ Citizen Bank Park vs. Philadelphia Flyers, 3–2 win

Callahan assisted on Brad Richards's winning goal in the third period. HBO produced a reality show leading up to the game titled

24/7: Road to the NHL Winter Classic.

"I remember watching the shows. I guess the first week or so, all the cameras are around and things like that but I thought it was awesome. I almost appreciate it more now, knowing that I have that footage to show my kids someday. They could go back and watch 24/7 to see what Dad did and what it was all about.

"The game itself, being in Philly stadium. I had family come in for that. That was a really tight game, [Daniel] Briere with the shootout [Briere was stuffed by Rangers goalie Henrik Lundqvist on a penalty shot with 20 seconds left in the third period] at the end there so there was a really cool atmosphere. You get mixed reviews sometimes about those outdoor games. I know as a player, I really enjoyed playing in that one. With all the hype, the lead up and the HBO series going on, there's so much hype and lead up to it that it almost feels so much more than just a regular season game."

FIRST RANGERS COACH: Tom Renney

"He was great. He was very approachable, honest, he was straightforward with me. What they saw in me, why they drafted me, what they expected of me. He kinda gave me my first crack when I got my first call up there and things like that. Helped through the process of trying to be a pro, he was great with me."

FIRST RANGERS CAPTAIN: Jaromir Jagr

"He just had a presence about him. He was Jaromir Jagr, he started [in] the league when he was like five years old. He's winning Stanley Cups right away with those Pittsburgh teams. He had a presence about him. He spoke in the room, he had everybody's attention. When I got to that team, he was the team. Offensively, he created a lot of things. Him, [Michael] Nylander and [Martin] Straka, I remember that line completely dominating games. He was a guy that got your attention right away and he led by his play because he was the best player on the team. He didn't speak up a ton, but when he did, you listened to him. I mean it was

Jaromir Jagr, future Hall of Famer, at that point, you already knew. So it was pretty cool to have him as a captain."

FIRST TIME SEEING THE "C" ON HIS JERSEY:

"It meant everything. I said it previously, when I was named it and then during it and I'll say it now. It was just an absolute tremendous honor to wear the "C" on the Rangers sweater. So much responsibility comes with that, an honor that was not taken lightly. So to see that stitched on a Rangers jersey is so special. I'm extremely lucky to have the chance to wear the "C" there."

FIRST STADIUM SERIES GAME: January 26, 2014 @ Yankee Stadium vs. New Jersey Devils, 7–3 win (Callahan had an assist in the game)

"That was really cool because I'm a big Yankees fan. My Dad's a huge Yankees fan. My Grandpa was a big Yankees fan so when I found out they were playing at Yankee Stadium. I was kinda pissed to be honest with you because we were in the visiting room, but to find out it was there was really, really cool. To be a part of the press conference before, the euphoria of the excitement for it, to be on the field, you kinda had the ice staked out and where it will be, but you still see the full baseball field. That was really neat."

FIRST GAME AS AN OPPONENT AT MSG: November 17, 2014 with Tampa Bay Lightning, 5–1 Rangers loss

Callahan scored two goals in his first game back since being traded to Tampa Bay the previous March.

"Very, very strange. You're going there as a visitor, be in the visiting room. Playing against all the guys that I've battled with for eight years. It was a very, very strange feeling. Luckily enough, I scored pretty early on in that game and I think that calmed my nerves quite a bit. The thing I remember too is a lot of appreciation signs in the stands and the cheers I got from the fans. That's a boost too that I would expect at the Ranger games, which put a little bit of a smile on my face as well. The fans, you hear them yelling, coming off the ice. 'Captain Cally,' saying things like that. It was pretty special to go back there and play as a visiting player. My time there meant so much to me and if you got to go back and play on that ice again for the first time as a visitor, it was special as well."

Captain Cally. Photo courtesy of Sarah Connors [CC BY (https://creativecommons.org/licenses/by/2.0)].

10
DANIEL CARCILLO

Left wing Daniel Carcillo played on five different teams over a nine-year NHL career. Carcillo played 31 games with the Rangers during the 2013–14 season. The 6'0", 200 lb. winger scored three goals and accumulated 43 penalty minutes during his brief Ranger tenure.

FIRST CONTACT WITH NHL:

Daniel Carcillo was chosen by the Pittsburgh Penguins in the third round of the 2003 NHL Entry Draft.

"I was actually at the draft because I was projected to go in one of the first three days, probably third round and I believe I was the 73rd overall. We were in Nashville; I had my parents there and my grandparents. It was cool, a culmination of trying to achieve something of a dream. That was kind of where the journey started as far as the professional journey, professional training camps. To be drafted after playing only a year in the OHL, everything was kind of happening really quickly for me, organically as well. Yeah, it was a great day. I think my parents too, me being a parent now to be able to watch your son or daughter succeed in a dream they wanted to achieve, I think that must have been a pretty, pretty cool moment for them."

FIRST REACTION TO COMING TO THE RANGERS:
January 4, 2014

Carcillo was acquired by the Rangers from the Los Angeles Kings for a draft pick.

"I got two calls from unknown numbers and I flipped them and they were both LA numbers and then a third call right away. I knew what that phone call was all about because a couple of weeks earlier, I expressed that I didn't want to be there anymore. Myself and coach [Darryl Sutter] didn't see eye to eye or weren't getting along. Everything was kind of serendipitous, the way it happened. Derek Dorsett got hurt and the Rangers were in need of somebody like me and LA had too many players like me. So, it was perfect and I was actually, really, really, really excited.

"To become a Ranger, selfishly, because of MSG. I'm a big music guy so watching so many concerts and just being in awe of the way the arena used to look. Actually showering and being in the dressing rooms of all of those legends that have their pictures up there is really nostalgic. Actually coming to the city and feeling the energy, embarking on a journey with the fans and then the run that we had. We ended up meeting LA in the Finals that came full circle. A really interesting year for sure."

PUTTING ON RANGERS HOME JERSEY FOR THE FIRST TIME: January 10, 2014 @ MSG vs. Dallas Stars, 3–2 win

"I started my career in Phoenix, Arizona, so anytime you go to an organization that's Original Six, you know you're gonna have to up your level of play and up your level of attention and focus just because the fans are so passionate. You want to play harder and it definitely gives you some extra incentive of walking into that new building after the renovation.

"It was great. It was getting towards the twilight of my career and I was just trying to cherish every moment and the room there, it was really, really special. Like with the guys. I didn't know a single person on that team, which was kind of rare for me in the hockey world, and everybody embraced me from the very start. Everybody was really welcoming and really nice. I think that showed up in our run, just how the guys in that room came together and rallied around Marty [St. Louis] and what happened with that situation, and then really, around the city and around the passion that the fans bring to every game. I'll never forget it. I'm pretty sure my first born was conceived in New York."

FIRST RANGERS COACH: Alain Vigneault

"First impression was just that he was upfront and honest to be pretty blunt. It didn't seem like he was the guy to play mind games, like the former coach [Tortorella], like the coach in LA did like Sutter. Vigneault would just tell it right to your face. For example, when I was suspended for those ten games and then it got reduced, I was able to come back against my former team and I really wanted to, but we had open discussions and he was just very forthright in saying that he had concerns about putting me in 'cause he didn't want to rest to hold it against the team. I was like, all right, I get that, I could swallow that, rather than tip-toeing around me and not telling the truth, which seems to be a common theme in the NHL, where it's fear based and they want you walking on eggshells. They don't actually want to communicate with you face to face. It was really refreshing, really, really refreshing and other than Joel Quennville, I think he [Vigneault] was by far, the best professional coach that I've had."

FIRST RANGERS CAPTAIN: Ryan Callahan

"Me and him [Callahan] battled a lot when he was in Guelph and I was in Sarnia. We had a first- round playoff, pretty, pretty, intense battles. So I was familiar with him and his game and how hard working he was. To learn about how great of a person he was and how great of a leader he was in the room and how he can communicate. He communicated through his play, more so than talking. I really resonated with people that did that. He just kept the room tight and loose and fun, really. It was a really fun team to be a part of, like a really, really fun team where it was actually fun. It wasn't like that, for example, in LA, they wanted you to walk around on eggshells. Like they wanted to be scared, so it was just really cool to see that dynamic."

FIRST RANGERS GOAL: January 12, 2014 @ MSG vs. Philadelphia Flyers, 4–1 win

"I remember scoring, yeah, wrap-around on Ray Emery [Flyers goalie] and then I remember getting chased around by everybody on Philly because I just recently put on a visor. I remember correctly taking it off in the second intermission and then fighting. I think it was Luke Schenn. So yeah, it was a good game, a good debut. It's something that really, New York, Philly, the game of hockey and that's what they want to see. They wanna see violence, they wanna see that rivalry. They want to see the hate and I was very willing to provide that and get the fans on my side."

FIRST OUTDOOR GAME WITH THE RANGERS: January 26, 2014 @ Yankee Stadium vs. New Jersey Devils, 7–3 win

"That was great. I remember playing with our line, Dominic Moore and I think it was fast. We ended up scoring the game-winning goal. I think that was my third or fourth outdoor game. I don't know why I was lucky enough to play that many. Cool to be in that stadium and in that city, the New York teams going at it. I always enjoyed those games because your family can come in and you can enjoy with them, so it was a pretty cool day. That Stadium Series is a lot of fun."

FIRST RANGERS PLAYOFF GOAL: April 22, 2014 @ Philadelphia vs. Philadelphia Flyers, Game 3, first round, 4–1 win

Carcillo rounded out the scoring with his first Rangers playoff goal, but he would score a more significant goal in Game 7 as the Rangers went on to beat the Flyers.

"I'll always cherish that run and then putting it back in Philly's face. Scoring in Game 7 and really fucking sticking it up their, 'you know what.' Can't get any better than that. It was on my late friend, rest in peace, Ray Emery. What a rivalry. Even like in 2010, we made that run in 2010 with Philly, I was in Philly and we had to beat you guys [Rangers] in that last game to get in so it was kind of cool how that all comes full circle."

Carcillo in one of the many outdoor games he has been in. (Photo by Mark Rosenman)

11
CAM CONNOR

Right wing Cam Connor was a rugged forward who began his professional career in the World Hockey Association. Connor was with the Phoenix Roadrunners for two seasons before joining the Houston Aeros for the 1976–77 season. Originally, a first-round draft choice of the Montreal Canadiens, Connor joined the Habs after the Aeros folded and he was a member of the 1979 Stanley Cup–winning team. On April 21, 1979, Connor scored a memorable goal in the second overtime of Game 3 of the Stanley Cup quarterfinals to beat the rival Toronto Maple Leafs. Connor played parts of three seasons with the Rangers.

FIRST CONTACT WITH THE NHL:

Cam Connor was the fifth overall pick by the Montreal Canadiens in the 1974 NHL Amateur Draft. Connor was the fourth overall pick in the 1974 WHA Draft by the Phoenix Roadrunners.

"I was sitting in my backyard in Winnipeg and my agent called me. It was in the paper that I was gonna be a first rounder in the World Hockey Association and a first rounder in the NHL. I think there was 18 teams back then. So does that mean you're going to be top-five or does it mean you're going to be fifteenth or sixteenth? You don't know what that means. Even if the reporters are saying you're going to be a first rounder, you never know until you get your phone call. So my agent, he phoned and he just said, 'Congratulations, you're the Montreal Canadiens number one draft choice and you went fifth in the league.' And I said, 'Okay, thank you very much,' and that was pretty lucky."

FIRST REACTION TO BEING ACQUIRED BY THE RANGERS FROM EDMONTON: March 11, 1980

"A couple of weeks before we played the Flyers with the Edmonton Oilers, we're busing back into New York City and I'd never really ever spent any time in a place like New York City. Back in those days, it was a little bit on the dirtier side. I remember, I was sitting on the team bus with [Edmonton GM] Glen Sather and I'm watching all of these people. Even though I'm sure they're not late, they're all in a hurry to get from A to B. I remember thinking I would feel like an ant in an ant colony if I was ever to play [in New York]. So I told Glen Sather, if you ever trade me, please don't trade me here. We go back to Edmonton, we go back on the road and the trade deadline, whatever that date is at twelve noon, is a big day for all players.

"We're on the road in Montreal, in the visitor's dressing room and it was 10 minutes before 12. We had a twelve o'clock practice, we had the sports [news] on and I had a bucket of pucks, all my gear on. I was gonna go out 10 minutes early and shoot some pucks. As I as just about to leave the dressing room, the sports came on, so I told the boys. Messier was on my team, Gretzky was on my team, Kevin Lowe was on my team, they're all 18 year olds. So I said, 'Hey, let's get the scoops.' So the first thing they said, 'Cam Connor was traded to the Rangers for Don Murdoch,' and [Dave] Semenko said that my jaw just dropped because nobody told me, didn't see it coming, and heard it on the radio when I was in this uniform when I was in the Oilers dressing room.

"When you are a Gretzky or a superstar, you could miss a couple of days of ice time and your timing is not off, but the average hockey player, when you're given an option, would prefer to go to the rink. So I said, 'Oh man, I got my gear on, I'll go practice with you guys' and the trainer just said, 'Get your effin' gear off right now, you're not an Oiler and you're not allowed to [practice].' I almost started crying.

"I think my wife Cheryl had got the impression of New York City based upon what I told you. I phoned her up; she was visiting her folks in Winnipeg and I said, 'Well, I got traded.' She said, 'Where?' and I said, 'Well, guess.' So, she named all the cities she'd like to live in and I said, 'Nope,' and then I said, 'New York,' and she said, 'New York?'

FIRST TIME PUTTING ON THE RANGERS JERSEY:

"It's the exact same feeling as when I put the Montreal Canadiens jersey on. This is an Original Six team. I didn't follow hockey when I was a kid but I played with Gordie Howe when I think Gordie was forty-seven, forty-eight in the World Hockey and he told me stories about the Original Six teams. So when I made that jump, I was proud to put on not an expansion team's jersey but to put on one of the Original Six in Montreal."

FIRST RANGERS GAME AND FIRST FIGHT: March 12, 1980 @ MSG vs. Colorado Rockies, 6–0 win (fought Colorado defenseman Rob Ramage)

"Being the fighter, this is a lot of fun. Like it is because they never run. When I would fight, they'd say, 'Well, you're dead next time. We're bringing so and so up from the farm team.' Like you never run out of opponents. When you go to negotiate your contract, they say to you, "Oh well, you only got so many goals.' So yeah, you got limited ice time and you look at a guy like Dave Semenko, for example. I was Semenko's first fight and first shift in pro hockey. He was my third fight, that shift. Semenko and I were talking. When he had to negotiate with Sather, just so they didn't have to pay him very much, they only focused on the value that he brought. It's pretty tough going into the Flyers with all the Broad Street Bullies and you've only got one or two guys at the most on your team that will be willing to fight. Even then, some of the fighters don't fight very much and if they're against a tough team, it's kind of interesting. You go to old Boston Garden and it's so tiny and you can't help but get in a physical game. So being the fighter, it's nice to be a crowd favorite and it's nice to win your fights but I think any fighter would rather be a Wayne Gretzky or an Esposito any day of the week."

FIRST IMPRESSION OF THE GARDEN AS A RANGER:

"There's no other rink like it and I can say that from the heart. There's always something going on in the stands. Where there's two people going at it or somebody makes the mistake of wearing the Islander jersey in there and you see fans run down or rip it off 'em. You see people that wear an Islander jersey get beer thrown all over. You see cops grab 'em. Madison Square was unbelievable and playing for the Rangers, having that opportunity. There's no other rink like it because the circus would be in town. They got everybody out by four or four-thirty, then they'd have to change and put the ice in there and take the boards out. Then warmups, you skate behind the net, you'd be on concrete. So they had so many activities going on at Madison Square Garden, unlike anywhere else I've ever played."

"Madison Square Garden, unlike anywhere else I've ever played." (Public domain)

12
TONY DeANGELO

Defenseman Tony DeAngelo was a first-round pick (19th overall) of the Tampa Bay Lightning, in the 2014 NHL Entry Draft. While playing for the Sault Ste. Marie Greyhounds, the Lightning's affiliate in the OHL, the 19-year-old DeAngelo was named the 2014–15 Max Kaminsky Award winner as the OHL's most outstanding defenseman. DeAngelo was traded to Arizona in June 2016 and was acquired by the Rangers in a trade with the Coyotes for center Derek Stepan and goalie Antti Raanta in June 2017.

FIRST HOCKEY IDOL:

"I was a big Jeremy Roenick [fan] when he was with the Flyers so that was probably my first guy I remember liking. Just the way he played the whole game. He was tough, he scored, I think he was the best player at the time. He did everything, good personality too."

FIRST REACTION TO BEING TRADED TO THE RANGERS:

"I found out on Twitter. It took a while to get the call so maybe things weren't done, just leaked obviously. I did not expect to get traded; I thought I was gonna play a good spot in Arizona. Sometimes the big deals come to that. Then, my GM called me and told me he was trying everything not to move me, but at the end of the day, they thought it was the best move for the team. Go to New York a couple of days later and got the full tour in New York and all that stuff, pretty excited about that."

FIRST RANGERS GAME: October 5, 2017 @ Madison Square Garden vs. Colorado Avalanche, 4–2 loss.

"Started the season with the home opener against Colorado and it was a crazy building. We ended up losing but it was a good experience."

FIRST RANGERS GOAL: October 28, 2018 @ Los Angeles Kings, 4–3 loss.

Tony DeAngelo scored his first Rangers goal in the second period against Kings goalie Jack Campbell.

"I didn't score the first season [with the Rangers]. I scored in LA, my first Ranger goal. Terrible one, threw the puck almost behind the goal line, hit the goalie and just rolled across the line. It was lucky."

FIRST RANGERS HAT TRICK: January 9, 2020 @ Madison Square Garden vs. New Jersey Devils, 6–3 win.

DeAngelo became the first Rangers defenseman to score a hat trick since Brian Leetch in the 1995 Stanley Cup playoffs and the first Rangers defenseman to score a hat trick in the regular season since Reijo Ruotsalainen in 1982. DeAngelo also had two assists for a five-point night to tie Leetch for the most points in a single game by a Rangers defenseman.

"That was cool. I hadn't had a hat trick. I was telling all the reporters that I never even had a hat trick since, probably when I was a kid. I didn't have one in junior. I had two games in junior where I had two goals and missed empty nets, I shot them wide. It was cool."

13
LUCIEN DeBLOIS

Center Lucien DeBlois was a highly touted first-round pick of the Rangers in 1977 who had two stints on Broadway. After two full seasons, DeBlois was sent to Colorado as part of the blockbuster deal that brought defenseman Barry Beck to New York. DeBlois was signed as a free agent before the 1986–87 season and played three more years with the Rangers.

FIRST CONTACT WITH NHL:

Lucien DeBlois was the eighth overall pick of the Rangers in the 1977 NHL Amateur Draft.

"The first call I got is from [Rangers GM] John Ferguson and he told me that I was being drafted by the New York Rangers in the eighth spot in the first round. So that's how I found out I was drafted by the Rangers. I talked to [Rangers public relations director] John Halligan after and talked to Jean-Guy Talbot who was the coach. Talked to a couple of reporters after, which my English was not really good at the time and I couldn't really communicate that well, so I cut it short."

FIRST RANGERS TRAINING CAMP: 1977

"My first rookie camp we had in Montreal, I had Mike Eruzione as my roommate. The big camp was first of all meeting Phil Esposito, Carol Vadnais, and Rod [Gilbert], and all these guys. The veterans, Steve Vickers, Walter Tkaczuk, Nicky [Fotiu] Ron Greschner, all the young guys, Dave Maloney, Mike McEwen, we also had Greg Polis who was one of the veteran players in the NHL. There were a lot of older guys that I'd seen play."

FIRST TIME PUTTING ON THE RANGERS JERSEY:

"I was so proud because it's such a big event for me. The Rangers were always one of our team because Rod Gilbert and Jean Ratelle played with one of my cousins. He was the left wing and he was a little bit older and he played with them. So just the fact that Rod was still there, so we always kept the Rangers one of my teams that I'll always follow. It always was the Rangers because Rod Gilbert was so popular. So it was a tremendous feeling to be part of the Rangers."

FIRST RANGERS COACH: Jean-Guy Talbot

"Good thing for me, no language barrier. When he had to say something to me it was always, well, I was trying to make sure that everybody understand, but he looked at me and there was something I didn't understand, he would tell me in French, so that was easier for me. He would try to give you your confidence as a player, as a young player, and all that. So, for me, it was good because he gave me a lot of ice time and I played my first year."

FIRST RANGERS CAPTAIN: Phil Esposito

"He was like not only big as a person, but you know the aura that he had. He's been like one of the top players in the NHL for years.

He was like something really special. A quiet leader, but when he had something to say, like step up and all that or working in practice. I learned a lot from Phil."

FIRST RANGERS GAME: October 12, 1977 @ MSG vs. Vancouver Canucks, 6–3 win

"The crowd, the chant, the Rangers fans are just tremendous. I got hurt just a couple of days [before] and I played anyway. I played the first few games injured but I remember the introduction and the chant. The Ranger fans are just so great."

FIRST RANGERS GOAL: January 7, 1978 @ Colorado Rockies, 3–1 loss

"I scored my first goal in Colorado against Doug Favell. I think I ripped a wrist shot or a slap shot right under the crossbar which was a surprise because I was shooting low those years and I kinda surprised him. I got on a little bit of a tear for a while."

FIRST RANGERS FIGHT: November 4, 1977 @ Vancouver Canucks, 5–1 win

"The first fight was in Vancouver, it was Harold Snepsts. I thought I did okay at him while he was a big, big and he was pretty tough also. I know we squared off in the middle of the ice. I remember I didn't lose it badly."

You Never Forget Your First: A Collection of New York Rangers Firsts

Lucien's first Rangers roommate was Mike Eruzione. (Public domain)

14

BRANDON DUBINSKY

Center Brandon Dubinsky played his first six seasons in the NHL with the Rangers. After playing six games in 2006–07, Dubinsky played all 82 games in a successful rookie season that saw him finish 10th in the voting for the Calder Trophy. Dubinsky was named the winner of the Steven McDonald Extra Effort Award in his rookie season. He was one of 16 rookies who were tabbed to participate in the YoungStars competition at the 2008 NHL All Star game in Atlanta, where he was named the MVP. In July 2012, Dubinsky was traded to the Columbus Blue Jackets as part of a five-player deal that brought Rick Nash to New York.

FIRST MEMORY OF THE NHL:

"I lived in Alaska when I was growing up and then, when we moved to Denver and then we were leaving [again] I was obviously a big fan of the NHL and actually a big fan of the Rangers because my Dad was a fan of the Rangers growing up since the early '60s. I remember him coming and talking to our family about moving 'cause we were going to get transferred to his job. I remember him mentioning going to Washington as one of the places, one of the two places. I immediately remember saying, 'Let's go to Washington, let's go to Washington.' I just remember him being like, 'Why are you so adamant or so excited about

Washington.' I remember just saying, 'Because the Capitals play there.' Little did I know, he was talking about Washington state, so that's the first thing I remember specifically in regard to being a fan of the NHL. That was probably when I was about six years old when that happened."

FIRST HOCKEY IDOL: Adam Graves

"I think it was a combination of being my Dad's favorite player. Like I said, he grew up as a Rangers fan and he was a Rangers fan all the way through. He was in that era when I was a young kid playing and obviously with '94 and stuff. I would've been eight years old so I asked him who his favorite player was and it was Adam Graves. Looking back, I just know he just played the game the right way. I loved how he protected his teammates and obviously he scored 50 goals. He was a talented guy too and a well-rounded player. Outside of that, I would say Wayne Gretzky, Mario Lemieux, Pavel Bure, those guys, but my true first favorite NHL player was Adam Graves."

FIRST CONTACT WITH THE NHL:

Brandon Dubinsky was chosen by the Rangers in the second round (#60 pick) of the 2004 NHL Entry Draft.

"I was with my parents. We actually went down and made a little vacation. Obviously, coming from Alaska is a long way to go, so we went down to Florida, had a little vacation before and then came up to the draft. My draft was in Carolina. I remember my agent telling me to be prepared for something. We didn't know if there's going to be some testing at the time. Used to be able to do like physical testing at the draft. They don't allow that testing anymore, but I remember being on vacation for a few days and then you're coming to Carolina, having to do a bunch of physical tests. The Rangers, believe it or not, were one of the teams that do like the worst testing. I had to run a shuttle run beep test for 'em and do a few things like that. Most of the other teams were doing like some jump tests and some other stuff like that. Like short and sweet stuff in the hotel and other places that you'd have these meetings. I wasn't one of the top prospects that go on all the media tours and all this other stuff. They all wanted to meet with me and talk to me before the draft. So, yeah it was kind of a crazy situation. I was kind of on vacation. All of a sudden, I had to do a bunch of physical testing and then I have a bunch of meetings and after that, I remember going and buying a suit. My parents took me to buy a suit for the draft and we got it tailored in time. They did the first three rounds on day one so I was happy to get drafted on day one and not have to worry about after that."

FIRST REACTION FROM HIS RANGERS FAN DAD ON BEING SELECTED BY THE RANGERS:

"I was excited, but I think he was more excited than I was. It was a pretty special moment. I remember looking back and there's three or four teams that I felt like I had a really strong chance to get drafted by and New York was one of them. Believe it or not, Columbus was one of those teams as well. So when Columbus had the 59th pick, I thought there was a chance I went there and they ended up picking this guy from Ottawa [Kyle Wharton] and the next pick, we kinda of looked at each other and sure enough, it happened. There was very surreal moment I think for both of us but him even more than me at the time because he was a lifelong Rangers fan and he was super excited. I remember when we got home, he was pulling out all his old pictures and all sorts of stuff. He was just really excited about it."

FIRST RANGERS TRAINING CAMP:

"It was definitely a surreal moment for me. I remember there was not just the superstars, you know we had like Marty Straka and [Jaromir] Jagr and Brendan Shanahan. At the time, we had Michael Nylander amongst others. You know there was just some of the guys you just grew up watching, like so many of these guys. When I came into the league, I wasn't even in the league yet but when I got drafted, it was such an older league then. A lot of these guys have been in the league for 10, 12 years. Being an 18-year-old kid, that puts me back all the way to being six or eight years old. I mean it was just my whole life watching these guys play and being in the NHL, it didn't matter if they were a Hall of Famer, fourth-line guy. It was just kind of crazy, sharing a locker room with a bunch of NHL guys. At the same time, I had a chip on my shoulder, and I felt I had always had something to prove. Even my draft year, being ranked low by the scouting system and having such a strong season in the WHL, felt like I always had some to prove. I went in there trying to prove something. I ended up having a really good training camp and playing really well. I remember being sour when they sent me back to the juniors, but it was obviously, the right thing for them to do. It was definitely a 'Ah-ha' moment, followed by 'Okay, let's try and prove people wrong and show that I belong here.'"

FIRST RANGERS COACH: Tom Renney

"He [Tom] gave me a lot opportunity my rookie season. The year that I made the team full time, 2007–08. I had a pretty strong year in 2006–07, had a cup of coffee there at the end. That summer, he called me and said, 'Are you training hard and ready to go?' I remember saying, 'Yeah,' and it was right after they signed [Scott] Gomez and [Chris] Drury and I'm thinking like, Shit, I don't fit in here anywhere, 'cause we had Drury, Gomez, now we had Matt Cullen still and Blair Betts there and being like there's nowhere for me to really fit in here. Ended up trading [Cullen] back to Carolina and Tom called me and said, 'I hope you're taking care of yourself and getting your work in because the third line job is yours to lose.' That was unbelievable, coming from him and he obviously gave me that opportunity right away. I came in, had a really good pre-season training camp that year. I made the team full time, so I felt good about that. I was in great shape and ready to go. We had some ups and downs. He was a player's coach and I think he deferred to a lot of the veterans.

"I think there's some young guys and I'll probably speak for a few of us. Sometimes you'd get frustrated with a guy like Jagr and instead of telling him about it, he would take his frustrations out on us sometimes. Knowing the way that world works now and how the game works, that's pretty typical. The veterans get the benefit of the doubt. The rookies get [picked on] a little bit. I got an opportunity to play with Jags on a line for a majority of that season and ended up having a good rookie season with the Rangers. A lot of good things happened. I owe a lot of my early career to him; he pushed me along the way. He helped me along the way. I look back and I have nothing but good things to say about Tom and how he helped catapult the start of my career into where I've gotten to be."

FIRST RANGERS CAPTAIN: Jaromir Jagr

"It was amazing, the things that he taught me the most. He was a really quiet guy. He didn't say a whole lot. He went about his business, he was always a guy who worked and put in extra work, comin' in at night, staying after practice. For me, it seemed like he cared more about practicing on his own instead of practicing with the team. I remember him pulling me aside after practice ended, it was like practice was just starting. We would shoot pucks, we'd skate lines and we would get on the bike, especially the playoffs the first year, we gotta be ready for games five, six, seven in the playoff. Pretty much after I got onto his line, obviously he wanted to have success, so he wanted to help mold me into the player that he wanted me to be, especially being on his line. That's when he really kind of took me under his wing and started doin' extra. We had good communication and we talked a lot about things and how to have success and how to play and showed me a lot about work ethic and stuff like that. He was really special to me and I think part of that was because I played on his line. He was another guy that really helped me build that extra work ethic and find out what it took to be a good NHL player."

FIRST RANGERS GAME: March 8, 2007 @ New York Islanders, 2–1 win.

Dubinsky's first NHL game featured an infamous incident in Rangers history. In the third period, Islanders left wing Chris Simon hit Rangers center Ryan Hollweg with a vicious, two-handed slash across the face. The NHL suspended Simon for 30 games.

"You can just imagine being in my first game in the NHL and seeing that, it was absolutely wild. I just remember being extremely nervous for the game. The whole memory of it isn't always there because I feel like, in that moment, you're so excited. It's like there's so many things running through your head. Like, you almost don't take the time to enjoy it. You hear that with a lot of significant moments in people's lives. You never really sat back and took the time to enjoy it because you were nervous or you're worried about it or you had so many different things going through your mind. That was sort of that moment for me. The only thing I remember about the game was having a pretty good game in the faceoff circle. I think I played about eight minutes. I don't know if there [were] any good minutes in there. It was a pretty special moment honestly, the moment you dream about your whole life. I remember getting ready for our game but the Chris Simon and the Hollweg thing, I remember thinking, Holy shit, what am I getting myself into? It was a pretty wild way to start my NHL career, nonetheless."

FIRST IMPRESSION OF THE RANGERS-ISLANDERS RIVALRY:

"That's one of the things I loved the most playin' in New York was just the rivalries, the away buildings, the Atlantic [Division] and the boos. Obviously, the amount of Rangers fans that traveled and all those other things. That history with the Rangers and some of those other Atlantic teams made it really special to be a part of."

FIRST RANGERS FIGHT: October 13, 2007 @ MSG vs. Ottawa Senators, 3–1 loss.

Dubinsky's first fight was against Senators defenseman Luke Richardson.

"I remember before it, I'm not sure if I remember after it quite well because I got knocked out by Luke Richardson, so yeah, I remember it. It wasn't the prettiest moment. It was one of those things that needed to happen. I feel like I was getting a little cocky, getting a little tall for myself. I think I probably had three or four or five fights during the preseason. Andy Sutton was one of them and he was a big boy, so I felt like I could take on the world. I learned pretty quick to not take a 240-pound guy that had been in a league for 15 years, not pick that fight. Again, it was all about lessons and being a young player. I learned that lesson pretty dang quick too."

FIRST RANGERS GOAL: November 8, 2007 @ Madison Square Garden vs. Pittsburgh Penguins, 4–2 win.

Dubinsky's first Ranger and NHL goal came in the third period against Penguins goaltender Marc-Andre Fleury.

"I remember waiting a long time for it, that was the first thing. Wondering if it was ever going to happen. Comin' over the blue line, Nigel Dawes gave me a good pass and [I] went to the backhand and beat Fleury. Petr Prucha was right there first to congratulate me on that one. It was a pretty damn good feeling, that's for sure."

FIRST EXPERIENCE WITH THE YOUNGSTARS COMPETITION AT THE ALL-STAR GAME: 2008 NHL All-Star game in Atlanta.

"It was an amazing weekend. Obviously, being able to be a part of that and sort of really getting a taste of the good life in the NHL. The Rangers, first of all, always do it in first class, so all your family was invited. They got you your own car and it's kind of like you had your own staff for the weekend. It was pretty amazing. Just being a young guy and going out there and having fun with some of the other young stars of the game. I remember the game being a lot of fun, Atlanta being a lot of fun. I had my brother there and my Dad there with me and we really soaked in the weekend, had a good time. I really didn't know what to expect from the game but just had fun with it. When I got the MVP, that was a really, really cool feeling, especially you looked back at the other names of the players that were on that roster."

FIRST STEVEN McDONALD AWARD:

"That's one of the more special awards I've ever got as an athlete. First of all, it's sort of the award that epitomizes New York and the blue color. Everyone always thinks about the glitz and the glam and the money in Wall Street and all that stuff. New York is just to me is, it's a blue-collar place where people appreciate hard work and work ethic and going above and beyond, as the award states, in order to do your job the best you can. That was something I tried to do. I never took a day for granted, especially my rookie season [in the] NHL because I didn't know, being on that entry level, when I was going to be on the next [train] to Hartford, so to speak. I really tried to make sure that I prepared myself and played the right way and did everything that it took. Little things, blocking shots, fighting, scoring, all the things I took in order to help up be a good team. To get recognized for that with that amazing award and some of the guys that have won the award and multiple times, that was a really special feeling. I think it was a little bit of validation, having that chip on the shoulder and always had to prove something to somebody. People were recognizing the effort and being a gamer and being the guy that you could count on and rely on every night to show up and give you his best. That one means a lot, a lot to me, if not the most in my career as far as awards go."

FIRST WORLD CHAMPIONSHIPS:

Dubinsky played for the United States team in the 2008 World Junior Championships. Dubinsky scored a hat trick in a 9–1 qualifying round win over Norway in Halifax, Nova Scotia, that put Team USA into the quarterfinals.

"Halifax was awesome, obviously being in North America. I went over to one in Germany, was pretty fun, but not the same as being over here in North America. Being a 21-year-old kid and going out and playing with a lot of the guys. Sometimes they don't always get the greatest teams for those events, but that year we had a really strong team, even though we lost in the quarterfinals to Finland. We had a really strong team, it was playing with a bunch of stars around the league and guys that went on to play a few Olympics with the U.S., so it was a pretty special moment. For me it was a really special moment 'cause that was actually the first time that I played for Team USA. I had gotten cut for under-18s in World Juniors, twice or three times so that was the first time I wore the USA sweater. Really special memory for me and had a lot of fun over there."

FIRST "GORDIE HOWE HAT TRICK": November 24, 2008 @ Madison Square Garden vs. Phoenix Coyotes, 4–1 win.

Dubinsky's scoresheet totals from this game: goal, assist, fight (aka Gordie Howe hat trick) with Daniel Carcillo less than three minutes into the game.

"I just remember Tom Renney saying something that I thought was really stupid and I don't really understand why he said that to this day. I don't remember what the quote was, something about me not doing very well in a fight. I ended up getting a couple of those along the way. It was cool, you know those are always fun. I think my favorite one always has to be against [Alex] Ovechkin in the Garden against the Caps. When I think of Gordie Howe hat tricks, that's the one I think about."

FIRST PLAYOFF EXPERIENCE: 2008 Eastern Conference quarterfinals vs. New Jersey Devils. Rangers won series, 4–1.

"You have a couple of things on your side when you're that age. You don't really, care is not the right word, but you almost don't care. You're out there, you're enjoying yourself and you're just playing. You're not really focused on how big the moment is because maybe you're too naïve to realize how big the moment is.

I looked back and I remember thinking about going out and playing my game. Again, we had such a veteran group of guys, there were so many guys to lean on. Jags, he prepared me for that moment. He talked about how the intensity was gonna rise and stuff like that and playing one of our big rivals across the river. I just remember it being very exciting. Playoff hockey in the Garden, it's unbelievable. The crowd's unbelievable. The city's unbelievable. You can't go down the street without, 'Let's Go Rangers.' It was pretty amazing. Having played as long as I've played now, you realize how tough it is to just get into the playoffs, so having that opportunity and actually winning a playoff round in five games my rookie year, I think now it sort of sinks in more than it did then. When you're that age or when you're going through it, it's sort of the way that it always is but you don't sort of appreciate the moment as much as you do now."

FIRST WINTER CLASSIC: January 2, 2012 @ Philadelphia's Citizen Bank Park vs. Philadelphia Flyers, 3–2 win.

Dubinsky had an assist in the game that was featured as part of an HBO documentary series, *24/7, Road to the 2012 Winter Classic*.

"When the cameras get around, they [the players] clam up and get shy, they're not used to it. I just remember one of the big things I was thinking about during that time was how amazing the HBO crew was and how professional they were. It wasn't very long before you forgot they were even there and they did such a good job blending in and becoming a part of the team, which was a lot of fun, even as we traveled around before we got going. So that was amazing.

"The game itself, Mike Rupp with the two big goals. The penalty shot [stopped by Henrik Lundqvist] at the end with like seconds left in the game, ended up winning, 3–2. I got an assist on the winner. It couldn't have gone any better. I had my grandparents, my parents, my brothers, I had everybody in town, and we did a huge dinner the night before. It was an amazing experience and one that I'm really thankful that I got to take advantage of 'em."

FIRST TIME BEING ON THE ICE WHEN HIS IDOL'S NUMBER WAS RETIRED: February 3, 2009 @ Madison Square Garden vs. Atlanta Thrashers. Before the game, Rangers retired Adam Graves's No. 9

"I saw a few different retirements at the Garden. Each one of them was, obviously, really special but, obviously, Adam Graves holds a really special place with me because of being such a big fan of his growing up. Looking back at those moments, that was so early in my career, and things are going well you sat there and it was amazing and you almost couldn't help but to dream, maybe one day this could be me or that would be amazing or whatever. If not getting my number raised, hopefully I can spend my whole entire career here and I can be here forever. Hopefully, we can just sort of freeze this moment in time and it lasts forever. That's just not the way the world works, but I think those are some of the things that you're thinking about as a young player when you're sitting in those moments. Having those feelings allows you to realize how special those moments are. Not only playing for the team, but for Adam, and the rest of them while I was there."

FIRST TIME SKATING AT THE GARDEN WHILE HIS WIFE'S GREAT UNCLE'S NUMBER HANGS IN THE GARDEN RAFTERS:

Dubinsky's wife Brenna's great uncle is New York Knicks basketball legend Dick McGuire, whose No. 15 (along with Earl Monroe) has been retired.

"She [Brenna] comes from a very special family, basketball royalty type of family. With her grandfather [Al McGuire] and obviously her great uncle. Her dad [Allie McGuire] was a star at Marquette playing basketball there and she played. It was obviously a different sport but that was really special. After, things got a little more serious for us as well. About a month before I got traded, we got married. For a year before that, we were engaged. It started taking on more special meaning knowing that she and her family had such a history. Her father played for the Knicks for parts of two years as well, so between that and her great uncle having his number raised there, got to hear a lot of cool stories about the Knicks back in the day, through her uncle and her father, so it was definitely cool. I took a moment to look up there every time we stepped on the ice, that's for sure."

FIRST REACTION TO BEING TRADED FROM THE RANGERS:

"My brother-in-law actually was the one that told me I was traded. I think I went online and found out and then, maybe a matter of minutes later, either Scott Howson or Glen Sather called me. I'm not sure which one first. I can't remember, I just remember being shocked that I got traded. It was a tough moment for me obviously. You play in a place. My 2011–12 season wasn't the greatest. My worst season to date up at that point in my career and right off the heels of signing a four-year contract. It was tough. I was devastated and especially going from a team, we had just missed the President's Trophy and gone to the conference finals, to a Columbus Blue Jackets team that had 60 points. Kind of going from the top all the way down to the bottom and switching conferences. This is before the realignments and thinking to myself, Oh shit, I'm going to be flying from Ohio to California all the time. Things are gonna get a lot harder and more difficult, so the two things didn't exactly make the day any better. At the same time, I felt like there were certain points throughout my last season there that, there was obviously a lot of rumors and a lot of things going on that I was one of the guys that could've been traded and they were looking at some of the guys in particular, obviously Rick Nash. I just remember having a conversation with Slats [Glen Sather] before the deadline. He told me to start playing better and he said, 'Listen, I'm not going to trade you,' so 'I won't trade you at the deadline,' is what he told me. So you don't get traded at the deadline and the team ends up finishing well. I feel like we should have won that series against New Jersey [Rangers lost in six games] that's always a tough pill for me to swallow. Just 'cause I think we had a good enough team to go to the finals. I know the Kings were on a hot run that year, but I feel like we had a really good chance that year. So that was tough. After you hear those words from your general manager, you start looking at some deadlines. Like the end of the year comes and nothing happens and then the draft comes, nothing happens and then the UFA [unrestricted free agency] comes and nothing happens. You sort of feel like you're in the clear and then, all of a sudden, the third week of July, you get that call. I was caught a little bit off guard. I went through a period where I felt like there was a chance I was going to get traded. Some dates and some expectation that it might happen to, I think I'm gonna have another chance, another kick at this thing to have a better season and just show that was just an anomaly and everything will be fine. Obviously, I got traded but everything happens for a reason.

"Things worked out really good for me personally here as far as my role with this team. Couldn't be happier living in Columbus and this is home forever. I've built some lifelong relationships here and friendships. New York will always hold a special place for me, but this is home now. Everything, like I said, happens for a reason and I definitely miss my time playing in New York. I loved it, but at the same time, I had some really amazing years there and got to have a lot of fun in New York. I was a young player in New York and got to really enjoy New York City and all the things that came with it. Now, I'm a father of three and New York City's not the most conducive place to have a family of five. I'm in a great place and I looked back with nothing but fond memories of my time in New York."

FIRST TIME AT THE GARDEN AS AN OPPOSING PLAYER AFTER BEING TRADED: December 12, 2013, Rangers lost, 4–2.

"We'll start with the fan reaction first, 'cause that was amazing. There's a lot of Dubinsky jerseys in the stands. There's a lot of signs. I got a really good response and reaction. As far as playing, I don't think I've ever had a good game at MSG as a visiting player, not one. I think I've scored there; I've had a couple of points and stuff. Me, being a realist, and being honest with my game, I don't think I've ever played a good game there. It was always a weird feeling for me to go back and play there, especially being on the other side. A feeling that never really went away, even after playing like ten times there or so, I don't think I've ever had a good game there. There's been some games that we've won, some games that we've lost but it's just always been a weird feeling. The fans gave me such a great reception and it's always fun to come back there. To come back and visit friends and have dinner the night before and check everything out. When it always came time to get ready and go to the games, there's something that felt a little bit different and I can't put my finger on it. Some people thrive in that situation, going back and playing in front of their old [fans], and having that familiar feeling. To me, it was always a foreign feeling. It was just weird being on the other side of the arena. It was just always a little bit awkward for me."

Brandon was a big Adam Graves fan growing up.
Photo courtesy of Resolute [CC BY-SA (https://creativecommons.org/licenses/by-sa/3.0)].

15
BILLY FAIRBAIRN

Right wing Billy Fairbairn was an underrated player who spent parts of nine seasons in a Rangers uniform. Fairbairn, who was undrafted, signed with the Rangers in 1964 but didn't make his NHL debut until the 1968–69 season when he played one game. Fairbairn, who was nicknamed "Bulldog" for his tenacious play, scored 23 goals in his rookie season of 1969–70 and finished second to Chicago goaltender Tony Esposito in the voting for the Calder Trophy. Fairbairn scored career highs in goals (30) and points (63) during the 1972–73 season. Fairbairn was traded to the Minnesota North Stars in November 1976.

FIRST RANGERS CONTRACT:

"Growing up in Brandon [Manitoba] Emile [Francis] came out and scouted the team once when I played junior. I started playing junior at 16, I guess I was and he came out and I did sign a "C" contract. I didn't know anything about contracts or anything else and I had nobody to look to, to sign, but signing that "C" contract meant I was owned by the Rangers and got $100 for signing it. So that was big money to me at 16. I had lost my Dad when I was 11, so I was kind of on my own."

FIRST RANGERS COACH: Emile Francis

"He was one of the only coaches I had, except in Minnesota and St. Louis, but starting off with him, he was scary. He was a little guy, but he was scary and he made you scared and made you play better and did everything. You didn't want to make mistakes 'cause he had a voice you respected and everybody on the team respected that guy. He was small, but you didn't want to make a mistake when you were out there which helped a lot of players. They think he made them play harder and work harder just because of the way he was. He was serious all the time on the ice, off the ice. I couldn't have had a better coach than him. The funny thing was, I started with him and when I finished in St. Louis, he was there when I finished my career. So it was kind of a funny set-up starting with him in the 60's and then finishing up with him in the late '70s. I can't say enough about him. He was a good coach, real good coach."

FIRST RANGERS CAPTAIN: Bob Nevin

"Nevy" was a good captain. You followed the way he played. He played hard all the time and demonstrated that you've got to play hard to stay on the team. The funny thing was, I ended up taking his spot with Walter [Tkaczuk] and that was hard to do because I respected maybe two, but if you want play on the team, you've got to outplay other players, so, that's what happened."

FIRST RANGERS GAME, PUTTING ON THE JERSEY FOR THE FIRST TIME: February 15, 1969 @ Toronto Maple Leafs, 6–2 loss

"It was pretty exciting but what I recall in that game. I was more or less a checker. He [Francis] sent me out to watch [Paul] Henderson. He scored one goal when I was on and he scored a second goal when I was on and I thought, *Oh, that's the end of my career already*. The Cat had a lot of confidence in me, so I was lucky he kept playing me.

"Just awesome [to put the jersey on] that's all I can say. The thing that I never realized to go that far and to be with New York, the big city team and everything else, it was quite a thrill. Quite a big thrill."

FIRST RANGERS PLAYOFF SERIES: 1970 NHL quarterfinals vs. Boston Bruins, Rangers lost in six games.

"The big thing about that is you always remember you lost. You always think, could I have played a little harder, could I have done something to make you win. You only get one or two chances at the Cup. To finish off your career and not getting it."

FIRST RANGERS STANLEY CUP FINAL SERIES: 1972 vs. Boston Bruins, Rangers lost in six games.

"You always go back to play in Boston. The games we could've won, we've won games that we shouldn't have won and we could have won, then I didn't like losing in the Gardens (MSG). When you lose the Cup, the final game in the Gardens was hard because of the fans. The fans were the greatest fans in the world and you want badly to win for them. You always think back 'cause there's something you could have done to maybe have won that game."

FIRST RANGERS HAT TRICK: October 23, 1974 @ MSG vs. St. Louis Blues, 5–1 win

"One of the goals went off their players, one of them was a missed shot, and they're all sort of garbage goals. I didn't really get a good one in there because this one bounced off the player and goes in, one off a skate and went in. It wasn't a fancy hat trick 'cause it was all garbage goals.

"I don't really think that often about the hat trick. There was a lot better goals that I had scored and goals that I remember. Like the one in Boston, we killed their longest winning streak in Boston. I remember that one 'cause I was coming down with Walter [Tkaczuk] and myself. Bobby Orr was the only one back and he faded more towards Walter, thinking I'm gonna pass 'cause I do pass usually and instead I let a wrist shot go and got the top corner on Eddie Johnston."

FIRST REACTION WHEN HE LEARNED HE WAS TRADED FROM THE RANGERS:

"That was the low part of my career. I think I was called into the office by John Ferguson (Rangers GM and coach) and I really didn't get along with him. He was coach, GM and I don't think he liked me and Walter too much 'cause he kind of split things up there. I just knew it was a matter of time before I'd be going out there but it was hard to leave the team that you'd played for all your NHL career and you love playing there with the fans. Like I said, the best fans in the world and going to Minnesota, which was a team that wasn't gonna make the playoffs. A lot of college kids on the team but it was the lowest part of my NHL career, getting traded out in New York."

FIRST GAME AT MADISON SQUARE GARDEN AS AN OPPONENT: November 28, 1976 @ MSG with Minnesota North Stars, 4–1 Rangers win

"It was nice to come back to play in the Gardens but playing against a lot of the players that I had played with were traded too. There were new guys there. I played with Espo [Phil Esposito] when he came there, but they weren't there that long. So the team was kind of half the players I knew really well and half that I just got to know before I was traded. It was a funny feeling playing in New York, but only half the team that you used to be with were there. Other ones were gone. [Brad] Park was gone, [Jean] Ratelle was gone. Eddie Giacomin was gone so you just felt like that team had just completely changed."

16
THEO FLUERY

At 5'6", right wing Theo Fleury played bigger than his lack of a physical stature would dictate. Fleury had a 51-goal season in 1990–91 while playing with the Calgary Flames. He signed with the Rangers as a free agent in 1999 and played three seasons on Broadway. In 2000–01, Fleury had a 30-goal season for the Rangers.

FIRST HOCKEY GAME ATTENDED AS A KID:

"It was probably my Dad playing [in] my Dad's game. It was exciting to watch my Dad play. My Dad was a really great hockey player, so it was just fun to go and watch him, support him. They were called the 'Russell Rams,' like Los Angeles Rams."

FIRST HOCKEY IDOL: Mats Naslund, 1988 Lady Byng winner and 1986 Cup winner with Montreal.

"He was vertically challenged (5'7") and was playing in the NHL, so gave me hope."

FIRST CONTACT WITH NHL:

Theo Fleury was chosen by the Calgary Flames in the eighth round of the 1987 NHL Entry Draft.

"I was home in Manitoba, so the first year I was eligible for the draft, I didn't get drafted. I wasn't really even expecting to be drafted and phone rings at about, I don't even know, five o'clock in the afternoon. It was one of the scouts from Flames basically said, 'Hey, Ian McKenzie. Just want to let you know we drafted ya. We drafted ya in the eighth round.' Hung up the phone and yeah, it was like jumping around excited, you know, dream come true."

FIRST REACTION TO SIGNING WITH THE RANGERS AS A FREE AGENT:

"They [the Rangers] really didn't give me a choice. They sent a contract and I was out at my lake property. You remember the old fax machines. I got a fax that was like a mile long 'cause it didn't cut the pages. It was just one big, long thing. So I looked at the salary portion of it and they gave me, I think, two hours to decide. So who doesn't want to go play for an Original Six team? Yeah, that's how it happened."

FIRST RANGERS TRAINING CAMP:

"It was a new team, a whole brand-new set of teammates. I think we went to Vermont, University of Vermont for training camp. The thing that blew me away the most was, when I played for the Flames, we traveled commercial the whole entire time I was in Calgary. When I got to New York, they had their own plane. I remember seeing one of the guys, I was like, 'Man, that's really cool that the Rangers owner is flying us up to Vermont on his private jet.' He said, 'What are you talking about?' I'm like, 'Well, this doesn't happen all the time,' and he's like, 'This is our plane,' and I was holding back the tears of joy that I didn't have to fight through an airport anymore. That I thought was the coolest part, that we had our own airplane."

FIRST RANGERS COACH: John Muckler

"He's an old school, kinda hardass tough kinda guy."

FIRST RANGERS CAPTAIN: Brian Leetch

"He's a pretty quiet guy but I think he just led by example. He worked hard in practice every day, worked hard in the gym and he was a super nice guy, really nice guy, and an unbelievable talent, unbelievable talent."

FIRST TIME SEEING HIS NAME ON A RANGERS JERSEY:

"There's a few iconic jerseys in the NHL and that's one of them."

FIRST RANGERS GAME: October 1, 1999 @ Edmonton Oilers, 1–1 OT tie.

"Well, that night was the night that they retired [Wayne] Gretzky's jersey, not only in Edmonton but the whole league. Not only was it awesome to put the jersey on, but Wayne Gretzky's in the house, you have this big ceremony for him, so yeah, it was cool."

FIRST RANGERS GAME AT MADISON SQUARE GARDEN: October 5, 1999 vs. Ottawa Senators, 2–1 loss.

"Well, Madison Square Garden is one of the iconic buildings in the world, and I'm standing at center ice going, you know Muhammad Ali fought here and the Rolling Stones and all these iconic, you know Billy Joel, Elton John. It was like, here I am, a little guy from Russell, Manitoba, town of 1,500 people, got this red, white and blue jersey on, you know playing for the Rangers. So I don't think it gets much better than that."

FIRST RANGERS GOAL: October 8, 1999 @ Madison Square Garden vs. Carolina Hurricanes, 3–1 win.

"That's the reason why I went to New York. They wanted me to score and produce points. I'm sure I really felt good at the time but it's not one of those sort of iconic things that happened in my career. I was expected to do that and I was probably pissed off that it took three games for that to happen."

FIRST TASTE OF RANGERS-ISLANDERS RIVALRY: October 11, 1999 @ Nassau Coliseum, 4–2 win.

"After playing in the battle of Alberta [against the Edmonton Oilers], it was pretty much similar. Both teams do not like each other and I was a perfect character for that situation. I think I scored every time we played in that rink."

FIRST RANGERS HAT TRICK: November 1, 2000 @ Madison Square Garden vs. Tampa Bay Lightning, 6–1 win.

Fleury's last of 16 career hat tricks came as a member of the Rangers. His first career hat trick came against Mike Richter and the Rangers in December 1990.

"I have the greatest hat trick ever scored in the history of the game. Three shorthanded in one game [against St. Louis in March 1991]. How does a guy get three shorthanded goals in one game? Must be a really shitty power play that I'm playing against. I was lucky 'cause Adam Oates was playing the point and he's probably one of the slowest guys ever to play the game, So he served up a couple of pizzas that night. I went in on breakaways and scored. I remember the last goal [of his Rangers hat trick] 'cause I think I shot it and went five-hole."

FIRST OLYMPIC EXPERIENCE: 1998 Winter Games in Nagano, Japan

Fleury was a member of the Canadian Olympic Team, scoring a goal with three assists in six games. Canada finished fourth.

"As a kid, you don't dream of all playing in the Olympics because we weren't allowed to back then when I was a kid. It's the ultimate in sports, playing in the Olympics. That first experience was pretty wild. It was in Japan and when we arrived at the airport, there had to be like 2,000 cameras and reporters and it was wild."

FIRST GOLD MEDAL: 2002 Winter Olympics @ Salt Lake City, Utah

In his second Olympics, Canada beat the United States in the gold medal game, 5–2.

"I don't know if it gets any bigger than that. They're [winning a Cup and a gold medal] very similar, yet very different. I think the reason why we do what we do is to win, and you know, it's hard to explain. You know that when you're standing on the blue line listening to your anthem, wearing your flag on your chest and you have a gold medal around you, I don't think it gets any better than that. I look at that team and all those amazing players that I got to play with. It's hard to explain, it really is, and it's in Salt Lake against our biggest rivals at the time, the American team and we beat them, right in their own barn."

FIRST REACTION TO WINNING THE STANLEY CUP:

Fleury won a Stanley Cup as a member of the Calgary Flames in his rookie season of 1988–89.

"I got it [the Cup] from Al MacInnis and I was the youngest guy on the team. I was a rookie, so I got the Cup last, right before we were going to do the picture, etc. I just had it for a brief second, but you know, at that point, it didn't matter. "

FIRST GAME OF PROFESSIONAL BASEBALL:

Fleury made his pro baseball debut in 2008 as a member of the Calgary Vipers of the Golden Baseball League. He singled as a pinch-hitter in his first at-bat.

"I was just at an event with Mike Soroka, the pitcher for the Braves. He was a Canadian and I was telling him that I was actually a better baseball player than I was a hockey player. The whole entire week leading up to that game, I was like, you what man, I picked the wrong sport. That whole week I took batting practice, I was shagging fly balls, I was taking ground balls. I was like, this is awesome and to go up in my first at-bat and get a base hit was like, I don't know. It doesn't get much better than not either."

FIRST TIME SKATING ON A REALITY TV SHOW:

Fleury was partnered with former Olympic champion Jamie Sal on the CBC's figure skating reality show, *Battle of the Blades*.

"It was the hardest thing. One of the hardest things I've ever done in my life 'cause the skates are different. I have to lift somebody; I have to be an actor. You want to talk about being vulnerable. That's it.

"I loved every second of it. It was one of the hardest things, but it was also one of the funniest things."

FIRST ALBUM HE RECORDED:

In the fall of 2015, Fleury released a country single, "My Life's Been A Country Song," and a debut album, *I Am Who I Am*.

"You just hope that somebody listens to it and somebody buys it but it was a really fun project. I grew up around music. It was kind of a tribute to my grandfather and my Dad and my uncle who sort of introduced me to music. It was so much fun. It was really cathartic for me to sort of get all this stuff out, get it off my chest and turn it into something that was really cool. Yeah, it was amazing, and I was shocked at how many interviews that I had to do around this music album. So, yeah it was a lot of fun. The whole project was great and I think we sold like 10,000 copies, so that's pretty cool.

17
ADAM FOX

Defenseman Adam Fox was a local kid who grew up in Jericho, New York. Adam's dad was a longtime Rangers season ticket holder. Fox played collegiately at Harvard and was chosen by the Calgary Flames with the 66th overall pick of the 2016 NHL Entry Draft. Fox's rights were traded to Carolina in June 2018. One year later, the Rangers acquired the rights to sign the 21 year old, who made his debut during the 2019–20 season.

FIRST HOCKEY IDOL:

"My dad was a big Brian Leetch fan when he was on the Rangers, so I was always watching highlights of him and stuff like that. He was a guy that I definitely looked up to growing up, obviously being a defenseman. He was one of the best skaters, obviously could create a lot of offense, which I certainly liked, so he was a thumbprint."

FIRST RANGERS TRAINING CAMP:

"It was pretty intense. I mean, I've never really been part of something like that. It was a new experience for me and something that I really enjoyed. I knew it'd be intense, guys competing for a spot on an NHL roster, so everyone is going to give it their all and it was definitely a good experience for me."

FIRST RANGERS COACH: David Quinn

"He's been good. Obviously, fielding a young team and coming from college, he understands the transition I'm trying to make, so it's been good and a lot of good communication as well."

FIRST RANGERS GOAL: October 29, 2019 @ Madison Square Garden vs. Tampa Bay Lightning, 4–1 win.

Fox scored his first NHL goal late in the third period.

"That was special. I always thought about what celebration I do if I scored. The moment you just black out and I was super excited and I got a nice picture to go along with it. It's just pure joy [when it goes in the net], I think it's one of the happiest I've ever been. I know you can't really control yourself so it's definitely nice to get that. Everyone says they just wanna get that out of the way, so it was nice to get that kind of settle in."

FIRST TASTE OF RANGERS-ISLANDERS RIVALRY AS A PLAYER: January 13, 2020 @ Madison Square Garden, 6–2 win.

Fox scored a goal and added an assist in his first game vs. the Islanders.

"It's really awesome. Obviously, saw a lot of games and went to a few at both rinks. You kind of see how the crowd is now a little split and it's really awesome to be a part of on this side and you feel the intensity when you're out there."

On scoring a goal against the Islanders:

"I don't know of too many to have a real favorite but a big goal and scoring against a team that was 10 minutes from my house is pretty cool."

Scoring against Islanders "was pretty cool." Photo courtesy of New York Rangers.

18
BOB FROESE

Bob Froese primarily served as the backup goaltender to John Vanbiesbrouck during his four-year Ranger tenure from 1986 to 1990. Froese's best Rangers season was his first in 1986–87 when he won 14 games and finished fifth (just ahead of Vanbiesbrouck who was sixth) in the voting for the Vezina Trophy. In his last full season with the Philadelphia Flyers, Froese (along with Darren Jensen) won the 1985–86 William Jennings Trophy for the fewest goals allowed as a team. Froese retired after the 1989–1990 season after a shoulder injury limited him to 15 games.

FIRST NHL GAME THAT HE ATTENDED AS A KID:

"I was in Buffalo. I had been voted goaltender of the year in a minor hockey program in Niagara Falls, I believe it was. I got to go see a game, my dad and I went, I was probably 11 at the time. We saw Buffalo play my favorite team, the Boston Bruins. We were in the gold seats, right behind Boston's net, probably four or five rows up. I can tell you everything. My dad and I got there way early. We walked around the entire arena. I don't think I blinked during warm up, but so disappointed because my hero, who was from my hometown [St. Catherines, Ontario], Gerry Cheevers, didn't play. You know Eddie Johnson played and I was so disappointed, but I just remember watching Bobby Orr and what a great player he was. So that was my first game and I know that Boston won and my dad bought me a program. I spent so many mornings getting up early, having my breakfast and reading that. That became, I hate to say that became my bible, you know what I mean. I knew that program from front to cover, everything I knew about [the] Boston Bruins."

FIRST HOCKEY IDOL: Gerry Cheevers

Bob Froese said Cheevers's mask with painted-on stitches is why he was his idol.

"I don't know if it sounds quirky, but I think a lot of goaltenders, in fact, two of my sons are goaltenders and you love the equipment. I think that's why I fell in love with the Boston Bruins because of Gerry Cheevers' mask."

FIRST CONTACT WITH NHL:

Froese was selected by the St. Louis Blues in the 10th round of the 1978 NHL Amateur Draft.

"I was kind of a wild card. I'd played for poor teams in junior. I played four years, 16, 17 in St. Catherine's and the team moved from 18 to 19. I played in Niagara Falls and then I got picked up by the Toronto Marlboros for the playoffs with George Armstrong. While I was there, I made some poor decisions, lifestyle, you know playing for them and it was very obvious. I missed the team bus going to the last game of the playoff series. Had to drive my car to Kitchener to play and I wasn't right and my value dropped, incrementally. I didn't know what was going to happen because I'd been touted a lot higher than that. When the news came that I had been drafted, I was disappointed that it was the tenth round, but I was pleased that I'd even been drafted. At that point, I don't even know if I really had a plan. I mean, I was basically living on my own with a wonderful couple in Niagara Falls, but my life was not on the track. At that point, I can't even remember a whole lot about what my plans were or anything like that. I went from, I understand I'm digressing here, but I went from playing for the Marlboros to go to Saginaw, Michigan, to be like the third goaltender for them for the playoffs in the IHL. I got to meet Don Perry there and that's eventually where I landed to play in the IHL initially, then loaned out to Milwaukee that year to come back to Sag and eventually win the championship. That was kind of like my calling card to get on my way to Philadelphia."

FIRST EXPERIENCE PLAYING AGAINST THE RANGERS AT MSG: January 16, 1983 @ Madison Square Garden. Playing for Philadelphia, Froese recorded his first career shutout in a 4–0 win.

"I came up as a wide-eyed rookie, just happy to be on the team, but everything's falling into place. I had tremendous confidence from a guy named Tom McVie, who coached me in the minors in Portland, Maine, before I got up to the Philadelphia Flyers. I was extremely confident, and I wasn't in awe of playing in the NHL. Now I was in awe of seeing Clark Gillies, you know different players, [Bryan] Trottier, even Ron Duguay, who I played against with the Rangers. Ironically, I stopped Duguay on a breakaway in the third period of that shutout in Madison Square Garden, which was great.

"I do remember, near the end of the game, there was a couple down the other and I was standing like any goaltender would stand and I got hit with an apple in the head. I don't know if it was from the blues [upper deck] or what but I just think from then on, anytime I was in New York, I scatted back into the net because I remember reading Gerry Cheevers's book where he said he was in Madison Square Garden and a knife [was thrown] from behind in the net over top of him. So I figured, from now on when there's a tussle and we're in New York, I'm just going to back right into the net for safety."

FIRST ALL STAR GAME: 1986 NHL All-Star Game

While playing for the Flyers, Froese was chosen for the Wales

Conference All-Stars and was the winning goaltender in a 4–3 overtime win over the Campbell Conference at Hartford.

"I was scared to death because you're looking around the locker room and just seeing all these great offensive players. You're wondering 'cause when I played in Philadelphia, we had a defensive-minded team with some great defensemen. There were great offensive defensemen but I'm wondering who's going to help me? I just told someone recently, that they asked me when I was nervous, I said that's the most nervous I ever was before the game. I will say in overtime, I stopped [Wayne] Gretzky on a breakaway and then we went down and scored, like off the faceoff. The year before, my goaltending partner, Pelle Lindbergh, had been lit up at the All-Star ame and nobody wants to do that in front of everybody."

FIRST REACTION TO BEING TRADED TO THE RANGERS:
Froese was acquired from Philadelphia for defenseman Kjell Samuelsson on December 18, 1986.

"We were playing that night, but Mike Keenan did not have me dressing. Ron Hextall was there obviously, and Chico Resch was the backup. I knew I was going somewhere and the whole team knew. I was a big part of the team in the locker room, the camaraderie and the team spirit. I got along with my teammates extremely well but that morning we went in and there was huge stereo in front of everybody's stall from the Prism TV Network, but there wasn't one in front of my stall. Everybody has one in front of their stall, but not me. I'm thinking, This is unbelievable, I mean how low can they go, but then eventually Brad Marsh went and got it. They had hid it, as a joke, because it was obvious I was going to be traded very soon. I thought that was pretty funny."

FIRST RANGERS COACH: Tom Webster

"Tommy was there for a little bit. Tommy played junior, I played junior so we had a little bit of a relationship. I really like Tom, but he was going through vertigo at the time."

Phil Esposito took over the coaching reins for Webster midway through the 1986–87 season.

"I loved Phil Esposito. I can understand why the Bruins loved Phil Esposito. I thought he was a team-oriented guy. Now, two guys had a great effect on my life, Bobby Clarke and Phil Esposito. Totally different guys, but both put the team first, both champions but I can't say enough about Phil Esposito. I thought the world of him. I really appreciated playing for him. He was a guy that could give you confidence, so is Clarke. They were both guys that gave other players props but didn't put up with lackadaisical attitude and I liked that about both.

"When you first meet people, you see them as an icon in your life, but when you start to build a relationship with them, a personal relationship with them, you get to know them as the person, rather than the idol or whatever you want to say. I just really liked the way Phil interacted with people and I believe that he genuinely cared. I remember coming off of a game in Madison Square Garden where I had been the star of the game and coming off there stood Bobby Orr just outside our locker room. He kicked me on the pad and said, 'Great game, great game, Frosty, which was my nickname and I was like in seventh heaven. There's certain things that you remember in your life. That's one thing I remember."

FIRST RANGERS CAPTAIN: Ron Greschner

"Great guy, one of my closest friends on the Rangers. I remember the time my locker at MSG was right next to Gresh. It was at the one end and there was this big pillar, I don't know what its like now, but there was this big pillar in front of us. When things were going well, we would slide over and so that coach could see us. If things weren't going well, we would slide the other way so that he couldn't see us. I thought Gresh could do it all. I would say the one word I would use for him was underrated. He was a lot better than everyone thought he was. Not only that, I thought he was a great guy and I really appreciated my time with Ron Greschner."

FIRST TIME SEEING HIS NAME ON THE RANGERS JERSEY:

"Your name is sewn in, it's not on a patch. It's ominous and hey, let's be serious, Madison Square Garden is an ominous place to play also. Fans, who, if you work hard and you play tough, they'll appreciate you, but if you dog it or if you don't do well, you'll know it. I mean, it's there in some ways you could say fickle, but aren't fans generally that? So it was surreal. I just remember George McPhee, who I also have great respect for, him telling me he came up to visit us at Lake Placid, our summer place we had back then. He came up and he said he remembered me coming into the locker room and just how confident or even how brash I stood in the middle of the locker room, taping my sticks. That was the one thing that I think you had to have as a goaltender is you had to have confidence. If you got caught up in being odd, you'd be out of the league. So you had to have confidence in your ability. As a goaltender, I don't think it's any different than a quarterback in football. You can't be in the corner, sucking on your thumb in a fetal position. You know what I mean? I appreciate it, being there in the locker room, looking at it from, now this is my home team in MSG but you've got a job to do so there's not a whole lot of time to sit back and just think of all these things. You're focusing on your job."

FIRST RANGERS FIGHT: March 1, 1987 @ Washington Capitals, 7–3 loss

Froese fought Washington right wing Dave Christian in the first period but, for some unexplained reason, was the only one assessed a fighting major penalty.

"Remember, I came from a team [the Flyers] where they were tough and we were, as much as they said, okay, we're playing differently back then when you know when Keenan came in and said, 'We've been telling everybody publicly and we're supposed to say it publicly, we're going to play differently. We were playing the same ol' way the Flyers always played. By the time I got to the Flyers, I was brainwashed. Not in a bad way, but I was trained that that's the way we played. When I went to the Rangers, it was a little bit different. All right, let me put it this way. In the Flyers locker room before a game, this is no lie, okay, 'Watch out for this guy, he's a lefty. Watch out for this guy. He likes to punch this way.' That's what's going on in the locker room, I'm not kidding you. Back when I played, when I went to the Rangers, we were actually talking about plays. You know, power plays and stuff like that. So I came in there, I had no problems sticking up for myself. I do remember one time playing in Toronto. We won the game and I was the first star and after being interviewed, I had gotten in a tussle that night and I forget who it was with, but they said, 'Boy, where did you learn to fight?' and I said, "I had two sisters growing up.' Matty Loughlin, who was our traveling secretary, said, 'You know, don't say that again. That's a politically incorrect statement."

FIRST RANGERS PLAYOFF EXPERIENCE: 1987 Patrick Division semifinals vs. Philadelphia Flyers. Rangers lost in six games.

Froese relieved starting goaltender John Vanbiesbrouck in Game 2.

"In that game that we played, there are some of my closest friends dressed in orange. Rick Tocchet, Ronnie Sutter, Dave Poulin, Timmy Kerr, my closest friend, right? The trainers, we have a son named after my trainer there in Philly, but in the second period, and this has been on videos, Lindsay Carson comes and runs into me, alright. Runs me over because I'm playing well. The rule in Philadelphia if the goalie's playing well, you run over him. They tried to take him off his game, so I knew what was going on. So I skated up, I lost my stick as he ran over me, but I got up and started skating after Lindsay and I yelled at him like as I got close, I yelled at him, it was a delayed penalty. I was going to the bench and I think he thought I was chasing him and I was just going to the bench for the delayed penalty, but I said, 'Sucked in Lindsay,' and at that, he turned around and took a swipe at me. Well, he missed me, alright, but I went into this Billy Smith dive. Then, when I got to the bench, [Rangers assistant coach Wayne] Cashman said, 'Drop again, Frosey,' so I dropped down again. Now, Espo was behind the bench and he's saying nobody laughed, nobody laughed. So, our trainer, who's like four-eleven gives me smelling salts 'cause I used to always tell him that I loved him for that and he's saying, "You still love me Frosey, you still move me Frosey,' and I'm sitting on the end of the bench. Well, I picked up my mask, grabbed him and kissed him. At that point, Espo starts laughing behind the bench. So now the whole bench is trying not to laugh and if there's one thing I did when I was playing was I had a good time. I got back onto the ice and they're trying to sort out what's going on and all this because there was a little bit of a melee. Tony McKegney, I think was involved in all that went on. So, I'm on the ice in front of the goal and I dropped down onto one knee and I turned my goal stick around and I'm shooting my stick like a rifle at Mike Keenan. My buddies on the bench, because this is the Flyers, you would never laugh on the bench, they've got their hands over their face and they're laughing so much at this and there I am. I dunno, I don't think I ever got a picture of that, but there I am, like a sniper with my stick resting on my one knee that's upright and I'm like kneeling on my other knee shooing my stick. I played the best when I was having fun. Not like a class clown but just when I was enjoying myself. I don't know what came first, maybe 'cause I was playing well, I was enjoying myself."

FIRST GOAL "SCORED" BY A RANGERS GOALTENDER: November 29, 1987 @ Madison Square Garden vs. New York Islanders, 3–1 win.

Froese was originally credited with becoming the second goaltender in NHL history to score a goal. In the second period, Islanders goaltender Billy Smith left the ice on a delayed penalty. Denis Potvin came in on a breakaway, but he hit the post. The puck bounced out to Brent Sutter, who tried to pass it back to the point, but the puck went all the way down the ice and into the net. Officials ruled the puck hit Froese's skate and since he was the last Ranger to touch it, he was originally credited with the goal, but it was eventually changed to David Shaw.

"I didn't know whether it [the puck] hit me or not. If you take a look it's Potvin on a breakaway, he moved to my stick side and my skate was there up against the post. I didn't know if I touched it or not, but the puck didn't go in. I think it was Sutter who went to put it back to the point where Billy Smith had gone, you know, it's a delayed penalty on us. So he goes to the bench and all of a sudden you just see the puck going down. The first thing, my first concern, 'cause Gresh was there with me in the net. Our concern was that was it going to count? Was that goal going to count because I'd never seen anything like that before. I see Gresh, he goes over the penalty box and he's talking to the ref and he's looking back at me and I'm not catching on. I'm a little sick, so I'm not catching on what's going on, then all of a sudden, he's pointing at me again and I realize I'm going to get the goal here until they announced it. Beezer [John Vanbiesbrouck] could play the puck, Hexty [Ron Hextall], he could play the puck. They could shoot the puck to scare ya. You know what I mean? I couldn't shoot the puck. If I ever shot it over the glass, it was a miracle, but for me to get a goal, that was funny. After the game, they brought me in because, once again, believe it or not, that game, I was the star of the game and we won, I think, 3–1. They show me on the clip and I think on the clip, that's not my goal. It didn't touch me and Espo catches me after and he said, 'You tell them that's your goal, this is good for PR and all that,' and I said, 'I'm not going to lie, I'm not gonna say that,' so the press came all around and I said it wasn't my goal. Then, Billy Smith was all upset because he said he didn't touch it and I didn't touch it, but I never said I did, so it was really funny. Eventually, Espo came back and said, 'I appreciate your honesty.' I mean, that was Espo. That's the kind of guy Espo was or is. That was funny because there was a big brouhaha because Espo was telling me, 'You've gotta say this,' and I'm saying, 'I'm not going to say I touched it if I didn't touch it.' Whereas, there'd be a lot of forwards that say they touched it when it didn't come near them so they could get the goal. I told the press that Shaw had a bonus for goals, like maybe two or three goals. I said he had a bonus for goals and he needed this goal for his bonus so I just decided to give it to him."

FIRST INTERNATIONAL EXPERIENCE AS A MEMBER OF THE RANGERS: 1987 World Hockey Championships as a member of the Canadian team. Froese became the first Canadian goaltender to blank the Russian team in 32 years as he keyed a scoreless tie in the first game of the medal round.

[What struck him was] "How dirty the Russians were? For being the star of the game, they gave me an envelope with money, and I had no idea how much money it was. I gave it to the trainer, I ended up giving him a lot of money. I didn't know that so he made up a plaque of this. It says 'Froese the Rambo in Canada's net.' In that game, I knew I had a few set-tos with the Russians because they had set plays where they would come in. One guy would be slashing your glove hand down and the guy with the puck would be shooting it, you know trying to shoot it over your glove. International play is different because it's a wide ice and stuff like that. I just remember before the last game that we did play there, we lost handily to the Swedes. I was sicker than a dog, I should've probably bailed but you know I never wanted to bail out on a game, but that game against the Russians was pretty intense."

FIRST EXPERIENCE AS A GOALTENDER COACH WITH THE RANGERS:

After his playing career ended following the 1989–90 season, Froese was hired by the Rangers as a goaltending consultant and worked primarily with Mike Richter and Corey Hirsch.

"Work ethic, physical specimen, attitude, everything about him. I just didn't want to screw him up, and we'd been roommates. I mean, back then, I don't know what it's like now but goalies always got their own room. Well Roger [Neilson, Rangers coach] put me with him [Richter] to protect him and to mentor him and that's when I was still playing. It was Beezer and Richter were playing, and I was always the regular backup. I just remember what I wanted to do is to not change him. I wanted to really always give him confidence and to improve on the things that he could already to just get better at that. I'll tell you what, Mike Richter is as wonderful a young many, now an old man, but he's as wonderful a guy as he was a goaltender. I'd like to say there are more guys like that but that's a rare thing. I always hold it in high regard that I got to work with a guy like Mike Richter."

FIRST DAY AS A PASTOR:

In 1995, Froese became the youth pastor at Faith Fellowship Church in Clarence, New York. A year later, he became the senior pastor.

"We [he and his wife] moved to Buffalo and we started attending a church here. My life drastically changed when Pelle Lindbergh [Flyers goaltender who was tragically killed in a car accident] died. That day, my life had changed forever for the good. I gave my life to Jesus Christ that day and it's never been the same since. So my wife and I always knew that we were going to do something in the ministry."

Froese said the senior elder approached him about joining the pastoral staff.

"I remember thinking, just a super nice guy this guy is, but I can't believe that he's smoking crack because there's not a chance that I'm ever going to join the pastoral staff. I've got a great job in hockey [Islanders goaltender coach], I've got my credentials in hockey, I just wanna help out."

Froese decided to leave hockey and join the pastoral staff.

"Hockey was my identity as a man. I went on the Sunday following [the decision] and they announced it at the church. Then I came home, and I was going to call Mike Milbury [Islanders GM] who was my boss in the Island. I wasn't looking forward to this call a whole lot, but just then Mike called me and he informed me that he had let go of a number of guys in the organization, but there was three guys that he was keeping and that he had big plans for me in the organization, and I said to Mike, 'Let me just interject, I need to step away from my contract, I need to resign from my contract,' and there was probably 30 to 45 seconds of dead air, which, if you know Mike, it's a long time. Then he said to me after that 45 seconds, he said, 'How much are they offering you?' and I remember being taken aback because I said to him, 'Mike, if you knew, if you knew what they're going to, what they're offering me, you'd think I was absolutely insane.' Well, the draft was two weeks later in St. Louis and I thought there's no way they're going to bring me to the draft, but in fact they did. When I got there, he had all my cronies, Gordie Clark and guys that I really appreciated spending time with, guys that I'd played with, tried to talk me out of what I was doing, you know, to think about my family. Then, Al Arbour took me out for lunch and I had like anybody, I have great respect for Al Arbour but he said, 'You know Bob, I don't really understand what you're doing so much, but I know that you're doing what's right.' He said, 'I've watched and I know you and I would say, I've been told to talk you out of this, but I'm telling you, you do what you're doing and I see that this is the biggest part of your life,' and I really appreciate that. Initially, it was a tough decision, but I've never regretted it. Even on the tough days, it's still great. We've been at the same church for almost 24 years now and my wife and I just love ministering here to these people."

Bob Froese initially was credited with a goal against the Islanders.
(Public Domain)

19
MIKE GARTNER

With 708 career goals, Hall of Fame right wing Mike Gartner is seventh on the all-time list. Gartner played for five teams during his 19-year NHL career. Gartner scored 173 of his career goals in parts of five seasons with the Rangers. Gartner had four of his twenty-one career hat tricks with the Rangers and became the first player in franchise history to score 40 or more goals in three straight seasons. During the 1992 Stanley Cup playoffs, Gartner led the Rangers in scoring with eight goals and 16 points in 13 games. In March 1994, Gartner was traded to Toronto.

FIRST HOCKEY GAME ATTENDED AS A KID:

"I can't remember, I think I was about 13 years old. It was at Maple Leaf Gardens and it was against the New York Rangers. Oh wow, pretty cool, how appropriate. It's funny because I only attended two NHL game before I actually played pro. My first recollection, I still actually remember seeing all the sticks, you know how you kind of have snapshot memories. I remember seeing all the sticks lined up along the wall as I kind of went down to watch warm-up and the stick that's stuck out in my mind was Rod Gilbert's stick. He had, I think, three sticks on the side of the wall. I just thought, wow, imagine that, three sticks.

"The second time that I attended a game, I think I was about 18 years old. I was just playing junior hockey and the season finished up and my dad and I went to watch a New York Islanders game. I remember saying to my dad after the game, I said, 'Dad, I really want to play in this league,' and you know, two years later, I was playing in the league."

FIRST HOCKEY IDOL:

"I remember my mom's favorite player was watching the Chicago Black Hawks and watching Bobby Hull. So I kind of took that on, but then as I got a little bit older, I started watching the Toronto Maple Leafs because that's really the only team that we could watch back then and Darryl Sittler was a player that I always used to love watching. I had a great opportunity to play with Darryl and Team Canada over in the World Championships and ended up having a cottage just a few down from him so I got to know him really well.

"The other guy that I used to watch when I was growing up as well when I watched the game, believe it or not, was Gary Dornhoefer. I remember Gary Dornhoefer when he played for the Philadelphia Flyers and they used to really appreciate how he used to stand in front of the net and kinda get the crap kicked out of him in front of the net in order to score goals. You kind of look back and you think, Bobby Hull, I get, Darryl Sittler, I get, Gary Dornhoefer doesn't quite fit in there, but that's what I remember."

FIRST SEASON IN THE WHA:

Mike Gartner scored 27 goals while playing for the Cincinnati Stingers of the World Hockey Association in the 1978–79 season. Gartner finished second to Wayne Gretzky for the WHA Rookie of the Year Award and played on the same line with Mark Messier.

"We had a really good hockey team in Cincinnati, a lot of players that went on to play in the NHL and have great careers including Mark Messier. Mark and I were teammates and roommates. Back then, I was 18 years old and he was 17, and we're just trying to find our way, just having fun playing hockey. Certainly, you could see with Mark, he was such a great skater and a strong, strong player. He thought the game, even though he only got one goal that year, you could see that Mark was going to be a great player. I remember we had a great group of older players as well. We had Robbie Ftorek, Barry Melrose was there. We had a really good group of veteran players and it was actually a great year when I look back at it, a great stepping-stone because when I got drafted in the NHL the following year, you kinda come in sort of ready to play, so I have very fond memories of the WHA."

FIRST CONTACT WITH NHL:

Mike Gartner was selected by the Washington Capitals with the fourth overall pick in the 1979 NHL Entry Draft.

"Back then, was just coming off the merger with the WHA, so in 1979, I played in the WHA as an 18 year old, when it was a 20-year-old draft. The following year, four teams from the WHA merged into the NHL and they had the '79 NHL entry draft, which is considered by many to be the best draft ever, but it was also because there were two years of players getting in the draft because they went from a 20-year-old draft, back to an 18-year-old draft. They didn't even have it live; it was done over the telephone. I wasn't anywhere. I was sitting at my mom and dad's farm, we lived at a farm just north of Toronto. I remember kind of waiting around for the phone call and I got a phone call from Max McNab [Caps GM] saying that the Washington Capitals had drafted me. I remember grabbing a big atlas out of our bookshelf and figuring out where exactly is Washington, D.C? Is that way on the West Coast or is it kind of on the East Coast?"

FIRST PENALTY SHOT GOAL AGAINST THE RANGERS: December 10, 1980 @ Madison Square Garden in

a 6–2 Rangers win.

Gartner's first career penalty shot came in the second period against the Rangers and goaltender Wayne Thomas.

"Wayne Thomas. I'm pretty sure I scored over his glove, so I had three. I think the other one was Mike Liut, I also scored over his glove. The other one was Glenn 'Chico' Resch and I got Chico through the five-hole. Why you remember those things? Like that's stupid, right? To remember penalty shots from 35 years ago but you kind of do. I guess I always looked at it, when I was going in on a penalty shot, and I don't know if the guys look at it the same way now, is I had two things in mind. I had two spots that I wanted to shoot. I had to look at it like if I have too many thoughts in my mind, then I'm going to get really confused, but if I have two things that I want to do or two spots that I wanna shoot, I'll just take a look and see which one is open. If my favorite one was open, which is top glove, I'd take that and if the second one was open, which was five-hole, I take that. So that's the way I looked at it and make sure I get a shot on net. I think it's a lot more complicated now when the guys are going in on penalty shots, they look like they're thinking about a lot of different things."

FIRST REACTION TO BEING TRADED TO THE RANGERS:

Gartner was acquired from the Minnesota North Stars in exchange for Ulf Dahlen and a draft pick in March 1990.

"It was one of those things where I was pretty sure I was going to get traded. I was having some contract issues with Minnesota and it looked like they weren't going to re-sign me. I started to hear a lot of rumors that I was going to get traded right close to the trade deadline. I had heard the Rangers were one of the teams that were interested. I had never played on an Original Six team, so I was actually pretty excited about it. When I did get traded to the Rangers, I was actually very excited about it."

FIRST RANGERS COACH: Roger Neilson

"I had heard of Roger Neilson a lot. As a matter of fact, Roger Neilson wanted to draft me with the Peterborough Petes, back [as] a junior player, probably 13, 14 years prior to me going to New York, when he was coaching the Peterborough Petes in the Ontario Hockey League. I really wanted to go play with Roger, but the Niagara Falls Flyers had the pick before Peterborough and they ended up taking me. I was very familiar with Roger, I was very familiar with what was happening with the Rangers and the success that they were having under Roger. I've been asked the question many times, 'Who was the best coach that you've ever had?' and I say without hesitation, it was Roger Neilson. [Roger] was a quirky, funny, endearing man. He was extremely well prepared. He knew the game well and we were so prepared as a team, so I was really looking forward to it and everybody had a role within the team. Whether you were on the top line or whether you were on the fourth line, everybody knew exactly how they were going to contribute to the team's success. I think that was one of Roger's great strengths and also kind of being ahead of the curve. When you look at what teams do now, with all of their video and their analysis, you know Roger was doing that 25 years ago."

FIRST RANGERS CAPTAIN: Kelly Kisio

"Kelly was a good captain because Kelly just did his job. He wasn't a guy to stand up in the middle of the room and say anything, but Kelly just led because you knew he was a terrific guy. He worked hard, he worked hard in practice. He was respectful for everybody and that's how Kelly was as a person. That's how Kelly was as a captain."

FIRST RANGERS GAME: March 8, 1990 @ Philadelphia Flyers, 7–5 win.

In his first game as a Ranger, Gartner scored two goals.

"I remember coming in and just being pretty excited about

putting the Rangers uniform on and you know you're going into Philadelphia, that was nothing new, right? I probably played, I don't know how many games in Philadelphia up till that time, maybe 30 or 40. Who knows? So going in, wearing a different uniform didn't really seem that different, so playing against the Flyers was very comfortable from the standpoint of kind of knowing that to expect. Yeah, I do remember I got a couple of goals in that game and I think I had a breakaway in the third period and probably should have scored that goal too. Anyway, that's what I remember is that I should have had a hat trick in my first game, not two goals."

FIRST RANGERS PLAYOFF EXPERIENCE: 1990 Patrick Division semifinals vs. New York Islanders. Rangers won in five games. Gartner scored a hat trick in the series- clinching win.

"First of all, knowing and realizing, I mean, I had heard how big the rivalry was between the Islanders and the Rangers but experiencing it was quite different. I realized the extent of that rivalry and the dislike for Ranger fans with Islanders fans and Islanders fans for Ranger fans, so that was the first thing that struck me. The second thing was just how excited Ranger fans got about their hockey and I loved that. I've always said, when asked what I loved about playing for the New York Rangers was that, you know when you did well, they appreciated it and when you didn't do well, they let you know right away, so we knew exactly how you stood with Ranger fans before you even got into the dressing room, which I always appreciate it because you didn't have to win all the time, but you certainly had to put it an effort. I thought that really kept you very honest and certainly when you're playing against the Islanders that comes through for sure. Having the ability to score a hat trick in the clinching game was pretty cool as well."

FIRST TIME HAVING HIS NUMBER RETIRED:

In December 2008, Gartner's No. 11 was retired by the Washington Capitals. Gartner was on ice when the Rangers retired Eddie Giacomin's No. 1.

"It's different because you're watching when you're watching it, when I saw they retired Eddie's jersey, I mean, you're looking at it, you think, 'Hey, I know Eddie Giacomin and what a great career that he had.' How cool is that, to get your jersey retired, that you've played long enough and you've had this success and the touch points with the fans, in the community, in the city that they decided to retire your jersey. I dunno how many years later, being in the same position with Washington. When I got my jersey retired in Washington, it was a lot of years after I played there because I had another, almost ten years of my career that I played after I got traded from Washington. There were a number of years after that, before they made the decision to retire my jersey, so there was a lot of time in between there. A lot of time to think and what I can remember is that I certainly appreciated it a lot. From the standpoint of knowing that, this is something that doesn't happen very often and that the Capitals thought that much of my career, not only in Washington, but finishing up with different teams and then having a chance at getting inducted into the Hall of Fame. Then, having them retire my jersey was just kind of a surreal feeling. I had my whole family there. My youngest son, Dylan was about two, almost three years old by the time I retired, so he never really watched me play. Then all of a sudden, he's on the ice out there with me. Our other two kids that did watch me play and my wife, having my jersey retired was certainly something that seemed a bit surreal at the time."

FIRST PLAYER TO SCORE HIS 500TH GOAL, 500TH ASSIST, AND 1000TH POINT IN THE SAME SEASON:

"It was this strange type of thing. Those are all big milestones in a player's career and having them all happen in the same year was pretty unique, right? I mean, it's something that coming up in your thousandth game, I was about a point-a-game player. I was about a goal every two games, so it all just clicked in and all just happened in one year. I actually don't think it's ever been done, just the coincidence of having it all happen in one year. What's so cool and what was really kind of neat about it too is being a New York

Ranger, because in my opinion, the New York Rangers have the greatest organization in professional hockey and they always treated their players so well. When I hit those milestones, they brought my family in. They presented silver sticks on the ice and all the things that you remember so much. You remember the milestones, but you remember sharing it with your teammates and your family and the Rangers were always great about doing that."

FIRST NHL ALL-STAR GAME MVP: 1993 NHL All-Star Game at the Montreal Forum

Gartner, representing the Rangers, scored four goals to lead the Wales Conference to a 16-6 win over the Campbell Conference at the historic Montreal venue. Gartner also won the Fastest Skater competition.

"I wasn't selected to the All-Star game. Mess [Mark Messier] was supposed to go and so Mess couldn't go so I was selected to go so I was kind of a late addition to the game. Then it all just kinda fell into place. With the goals in the fastest skating competition and being at the Montreal Forum and that kind of stuff, just all kind of happened at that one time and it was a lot of fun."

ON BEING TRADED FROM THE RANGERS:

In March 1994, Gartner was traded to the Toronto Maple Leafs for Glenn Anderson.

"It was tough. I had heard kind of rumors about a week before that something was in the works, but I thought, Oh no, I mean we're in first place overall. I mean why would you make any changes now? I was part of the Rangers for four years prior to that and we could just see it building. Right from the beginning of that year, like we knew that there wasn't a team in the entire league that we couldn't beat and didn't beat. We all felt that way. First of all, going to Toronto, if I had to be traded, that would have been the first place that I wanted to get traded to because [it's] where I grew up but I really didn't want to get traded. Then watching the Rangers go on, my teammates that I played with in some cases for a number of years, it was kind of bittersweet because I was very happy for them that they won the Stanley Cup, but man, it hurt a lot not being part of it."

FIRST GAME AT MSG AS AN OPPONENT AFTER BEING TRADED FROM THE RANGERS: April 8, 1994 as a member of the Maple Leafs. Rangers won, 5–3, but Gartner had a goal and an assist and was the third star of the game.

"The fans' reaction was really good. As Ranger fans do, they gave me a good ovation and then I was on the other teams' bench, which is the way it should be, but it was weird. It wasn't the first time that I had gone back and played against a team that I formerly played with, but it was pretty fresh and it was kind of raw. The Leafs had a good team too, we went to the semifinals that year. We were only a couple of games away from actually meeting the Rangers in the Final, which would have been kind of ironic to do but it is always strange going back. It's always strange sitting on that other bench, instead of the one that you've been so used to sitting on and playing with your teammates and wearing a different color jersey and all those things, but you get through it."

FIRST REACTION TO BEING INDUCTED INTO THE HOCKEY HALL OF FAME:

In 2001, Gartner was inducted into the Hockey Hall of Fame.

"When I was a young kid, I dreamed about playing in the NHL and that dream is realized when I started playing in 1979, so you kind of live out your dreams but I never dreamed about being in the Hockey Hall of Fame. That's something that is you don't dare dream about. It's something that, you go through your whole career and you don't really think about it until you're finished playing, it's all over. You do realize that you're going to be eligible in three years for induction. I could still remember getting the call in 2001. I was working for the NHL Players Association at that time and I was just in my office in Toronto and the phone rang about twelve or one o'clock in the afternoon and Jim Gregory just said, 'Mike, I just want to let you know that the selection committee has selected you to go into the Hall of Fame Class of 2001,' and I was just absolutely speechless. I just really didn't even know what to say. It kind of came as a surprise. I think that was my feeling about that particular time in my career. I'm actually really glad that there was a three-year waiting period because it gives you an opportunity to realize just how fortunate you were to play. Sometimes when accolades come, when you're playing, you just kind of get on with it, right? But when you have that waiting period afterwards and you have time to reflect and appreciate it. It's something that I appreciate even now because every time you're introduced, I'm introduced as a Hall of Famer and that doesn't go away and it still feels good hearing it."

FIRST REACTION TO BEING NAMED ONE OF NHL'S 100 GREATEST PLAYERS:

In 2017, the Hockey Hall of Fame named Mike Gartner as one of its 100 Greatest Players.

"It still sounds weird. I remember going out there with my Colleen. I said, 'I thought these were all over, Colleen,' so she said, 'No, I guess they're not over.' So we went out to LA. I can still remember I'm on a bus and we're there at the hotel. We're going to one of the events that they had for and I'm sitting beside Bobby Orr on the bus. Bobby says, 'Mike, this is pretty cool,' and I said, 'Bobby, this is unbelievable.' He said, 'I am having so much fun. I'm just so honored to part of this group,' but I'm looking at him and I was thinking, Come on, you're Bobby Orr, how could you think that way? Bobby was like genuine, like he was just thrilled to be there and I'm thinking, Oh man, Bobby Orr is thrilled to be there. I am just beside myself with that honor. When I actually went out on the ice, I went out on the ice at the same time that Bobby Hull went on the ice. Bobby was struggling a little bit physically. I think he had some hip problems and he said, 'Michael, do you think I could get a hold of your arm as we walk up just to make sure I'm okay?' and I said, 'Of course you can,' so I can remember things like that, during that time and being a part of that group. Once again, it's just quite an honor and I'm very humbled by it."

Mike Gartner was named one of the NHL's Top 100 all-time players.
(Public Domain)

20
ROD GILBERT

Hall of Famer Rod Gilbert is considered by many to be the greatest player to ever wear the Rangers uniform. Gilbert played his entire 18-year NHL career with the Rangers. He is the franchise all-time leader with 406 goals and 1,021 points and is third with 1,065 games played. Gilbert, center Jean Ratelle, and left wing Vic Hadfield made up the the famous GAG (Goal-A-Game) line that combined for 139 goals during the 1971–72 season. In October 1979, Gilbert became the first Ranger to have his number (7) retired and displayed in the rafters of Madison Square Garden.

FIRST EXPOSURE TO AN NHL GAME:

"When I was a kid, I grew up in Montreal. We were too poor and the Canadiens, we couldn't get tickets to go there. My dad was a blacksmith and we didn't have much. We couldn't do that as a kid, go to a game. When the first TV came out, probably 1952 in Montreal, there was a hardware store. I used to go in the window. They would leave the TV on after closing, you know, six o'clock, and then I would sneak in and sort of get to watch it on TV."

FIRST HOCKEY IDOL:

"That was easy for me [as a kid] because now I'm a big fan. I listen on the radio and then watch a little game in the hardware store on TV. My dad was a blacksmith and he had a forge. In the winter, three, four old men used to come and play checkers. One of them was [the uncle of Bernie] 'Boom-Boom' Geoffrion. He was a rookie at the time of 20 years old. He brainwashed me about his nephew and then he said, 'Boom Boom this,' and 'Boom Boom that.' I'd been doing this for two years, idolizing him, then my dad said, 'If you get good grades, I'm gonna take you to meet him.' Wow, that was exciting. I was arranged by Maxim Geoffrion, his uncle, so he had a chalet. This was in July, so my dad and I went to church and then, after church, we drove 50 miles to his cottage in the north of Montreal. I was so excited I was going to get his autograph and I was gonna meet him. I must be ten by then, so as we were nearing his cottage, it started to rain really hard. It didn't matter, I mean, the weather, I'm going to meet my hero. As it turned out, we show up and there's no car in the driveway and there's a big padlock on the door. Oh my God. Knock at the door because the weather wasn't any good. He went back to Montreal, I guess and he forgot he was supposed to meet me. It broke my heart big time that I didn't get to do that. It stayed with me a long time. That stayed with me until I said, 'One day, I'm going to play against him and I'm gonna kick his ass.' You can't do that to a kid, so I was really hurt. Then, I came to the Rangers and then I got to play against him. He was on the ice my first shift and I just checked him in the back and I had him lying down, face first on the ice. He came back swinging, I mean he wanted to kill me. 'Who the hell are you to do that?' Every time I played against him, I looked for him and I just wanted to kill him. Would you believe, he gets traded to the Rangers and now he's my teammate. He says to me, "What the hell is the problem, why you don't like me?' I said, "Because you broke my heart you jerk. I was like, 11 years old. You didn't wait for me to sign an autograph and meet me and I was always upset.' You know what, I carried that for a long time. Maybe he'd give me incentive to make it. He looked at me and he said, "Well, when are you going to get over it, for cryin' out loud.' I said, 'I got over it, now you're my teammate, you're a good guy.' We had lots of fun. After that, he coached me." (Geoffrion coached the Rangers for 43 games in the 1968–69 season.)

FIRST RANGERS CONTRACT:

"There was this scout that was starting a team in Montreal and he asked me to play for the junior B team in Montreal. My brothers said, 'Well, you have a chance to go through Ottawa with the Canadian junior for training camp, you were invited then.' My brother was my mentor. He's six years older, Johnny, and we asked [the scout], I said, 'I'll play for the junior B Ranger in the new league.' I was independent because every kid was signed by the Canadiens then. If you lived in Montreal and played in the park, you had to sign with the Canadiens. Not me, because I went to an independent school and we weren't involved with the park and recreation. I didn't play in the park.

"We asked the scout to send me to Guelph. I insist that I go to Guelph for training camp. I'm 16 years old and I go to Guelph, no English, they said in Ontario. I make the team; I love to come back to Montreal. I wind up playing for Guelph, the Guelph Biltmores, which was sponsored by the Rangers. It was a Rangers farm team where Andy Bathgate and Harry Howell and Dean Prentice, they all had played there in Guelph, so in order to make it to the NHL, you had to play junior. So I stayed there for four years and then they brought me up for one game. I was 18 years old. They brought me up and I played with Bathgate and Prentice on the line, got my first assist, my first point. I was pretty impressed by the national anthem. The old Garden was built for basketball and boxing. It was straight up and there was a balcony above the bench and there's a guy who used to yell and curse. Right after the national anthem, they were still standing up and I hear this loud mouth voice yelling, 'Harry, hit him with your pocket book.' I said, 'Geez, this is a tough place,' I'm a kid. I better play hard if I don't want to get booed over here.

"Everything was about Andy Bathgate with the Rangers, so I started emulating him. He was a right wing, I was a right wing. I did receive a lot of handling from him. When I did come with the Rangers, I played with them for three years and it was a thrill to play with Andy Bathgate. My first contract was negotiated by my dad, who didn't speak English. It was Muzz Patrick (Rangers GM), you can imagine what I got. He said, 'You know he's going to play for the Rangers, and he has to sign a contract for two years.' First year, I made seven thousand five hundred and the second year, $7,500 and I was named the best player in the junior league in Canada. I was probably the best player in Canada. I would've been a first-round draft choice. I led the league in scoring, scored like over 100 points in my last year. Then, I got injured, I broke my back and that slowed me down."

In the 1961–62 season, Gilbert played one regular season game (his second career NHL game) for the Rangers.

FIRST RANGERS COACH:

"I certainly remember Muzz Patrick and I certainly remember Doug Harvey. I mean he was unbelievable at it. Red Sullivan, I remember he was a feisty little guy and he was a disciplinarian. He gave me all kinds of chances to do what I did. He put together the "French Canadian" line. I played with Jean Ratelle, he came up from Guelph. I brought him to Guelph. My second year there, he played one year in Montreal and I said to Eddie Bush, the coach in Guelph. I said, 'Bring this guy up. He's better than me,' and they did. So Ratelle and I played in Guelph together for three years and then I got injured and I didn't play for awhile. Now, I'm playing for the Rangers and Ratelle is up. So we play with Camille Henry. It was interesting. The 'Canadian-French' line."

FIRST RANGERS PLAYOFF EXPERIENCE: 1961–62
Stanley Cup semifinals vs. Toronto Maple Leafs. Rangers lost in six games.

"The playoffs are so exciting. They had played the first two games in Toronto. We won the third game, I think I had five points in that series. We won both games in New York, that was exciting. Then, we go to Toronto and its 2–2 and we're going to overtime and I hit the post. We would've won the game and they make it 3–

2 and come back to New York. Gump Worsley (Rangers goaltender) made about 60 saves, Toronto had a good team then. Red Kelly scored the winning goal in that overtime. We're down three games to two. Instead of coming back to New York, the circus was there, we played a sixth game in Toronto. We lost 7–1."

FIRST RANGERS GOAL: April 3, 1962 @ Madison Square Garden. Game 4 of the Stanley Cup semifinals vs. Toronto Maple Leafs. Rangers won, 4–2, as Gilbert scored the first two goals of his career. The Rangers lost the series in six games. Gilbert had not scored a regular-season goal before scoring in the playoffs. He also had an assist in the game for a three-point night.

"The second [NHL] game, I had gotten my back finally fixed after ten months. I started to play for Kitchener. Started playing there, I got better and then they called me up for the playoffs. They were in the playoffs against Toronto. The first two games were in New York. Doug Harvey was the coach. What happened is they bring me up. Ken Schinkel had gotten hurt, broke his toe or something, so I'm playing with Johnny Wilson and Davy Balon on the line. The first time they started the game against Toronto in the playoffs, they scored a goal like my first shift against [Leafs goalie] Johnny Bower. The period wasn't over and the end of the first period, I got another goal. So now, we get two goals in the first period. I finally found my league, right? So then I go and ask [Rangers GM] Muzz Patrick, 'You better come over here. I think I'm dreaming, pinch me or something.' Anyway, I wound up getting an assist and the first star of the game and the people had been waiting for me from Guelph because I was nominated as the best player from Guelph. They were waiting for me and I got injured seriously and now I come in the playoffs and scored two goals and an assist. They thought I was all right.

"After that, I see Johnny Bower, I was friends with him forever. I'd see him in Toronto, All-Star games, I said, 'Johnny, thank you so much, Mr. Bower for letting me score my first goal against you.' He said [jokingly] 'Everybody scores their first goal against me, that's my thing.' I said, 'Yeah, what about the second one, did you let me score that one too?' He said, 'Not that one.'"

FIRST ALL-STAR GAME: October 10, 1964 @ Toronto's Maple Leaf Gardens. NHL All-Stars beat the Stanley Cup champion Toronto Maple Leafs, 3–2.

"It was just a dream come true. To be with these guys, chat with them. You're talking about Gordie Howe and Ted Lindsay and those guys, which were the dirtiest bastards that I played against. Now I'm playing with them. Gordie Howe knocked me out my first game in Detroit. I never knew who hit me, Gordie Howe. I was unconscious on the ice. He elbowed me at center ice and I was out. My two teammates are carrying me back. They're dragging my feet back to the bench, no stretcher. So I get close to the bench and the linesman skates by and he says, 'Number NINE.' I said, 'I'm gonna get him, I'm gonna get him.' I played ten more years before he jumped to the other league and I never got him.

"I was in Minnesota, now I'm in the alumni and I go to the alumni game and Gordie Howe is there. He's being honored. The dinner before, I'm at the table with ten people and I tell them that Gordie Howe did that to me and I was going to get him back and I never did. Now I'm waiting until he gets in the 'old age home.' We're in a wheelchair and I'm going to go behind it, flip his chair and tell the nurse, "Go tell them it's number seven.' They laughed, thought it was really funny. The next day, I'm sitting for breakfast and he's across the table from me. He's looking at me and he's winking. He had a plate in his hand, he says, 'Tell me, hey Rod, did I ever get you?' 'Hey, Gordie, who did you not get.' He used to get everybody, he's a dirty bastard. So I said, 'Yeah, you got me.' He says, 'Well, you intend to get me back.' I said, 'What do you mean?' He says, 'Somebody told me last night that you were going to get me back when I'm in the old age home.' 'Not yet Gordie, I'm not getting you yet."

FIRST RANGERS PENALTY SHOT: November 27, 1963 @ Madison Square Garden vs. Detroit Red Wings, 3–2 win.

Gilbert was awarded a penalty shot late in the first period when the Red Wings' Larry Jeffrey fell on the puck in the crease. Gilbert's shot beat Detroit goalie Terry Sawchuk on the right side tie the game, 1–1.

"I think I panicked and I think I slapped the puck from about 20, 25 feet when I scored."

FIRST OUT-OF-BODY EXPERIENCE:

Gilbert underwent a spinal fusion operation in 1962. Approximately three years later, Gilbert needed a second operation and while he was on the operating table, he says he had an out-of-body experience.

"I was in the hospital for my second operation. This Japanese doctor which had supervised the first one, he wasn't happy with the results. He said, 'I'll do it in about four or five years.' He cleared me for the first one and said, 'We're going to do it again in about four years,' and all that. They didn't do it right. So, one day, it happened. When it happened, I couldn't cross the street. I was so hurt. The Japanese doctor said, 'I told you.' 'Okay, let's do it.' So then he performed a spinal fusion and then he didn't feed me solid food for seven days because in the Mayo Clinic, I had developed staph infection.

"Now, I'm in the St. Claire's hospital in New York and he performs the operation and he wants to prevent the infection so he doesn't feed me solid food, only intravenously and he's giving me seven pills every four hours to prevent the infection. Emile Francis is in the room with Bill Jennings [Rangers president] visiting me, 2:30 in the afternoon. I start choking on the pills, the esophagus was totally closed up. So, I started coughing and all of a sudden, like I passed out and I turned blue. Now, I hear Francis calling the nurse, they keep panicking. He's looking at me and I'm totally blue and I'm out, I'm dead. So, she comes over and she said, 'Oh no, I can't find his pulse. I think we lost him.' Then in the corner of the room I hear Francis tell the nurse, 'Well, bring him back, he's my best player.' I could hear it, I'm done. If I didn't want to come back, I'm too young, 25 [years old] right? So, then they shocked my heart, they restarted it and they give me a blood transfusion and then I'm okay, I came back. I've been back in my body, this lasted about five minutes, this whole procedure that I was out of body. Then I came back and I'm looking at Francis and I said, 'Listen, if I'm your best player, how come you're not paying me like your best player?' He freaked out. For years, for years he freaked out when he saw me. He said, 'You were dead and you heard all that stuff.' I said, 'Yeah, that's right.' He didn't pay me, anyway."

FIRST FOUR-GOAL GAME: February 24, 1968 @ Montreal Canadiens, 6–1 win.

Gilbert scored four goals on 16 shots. Linemate Jean Ratelle assisted on three of the tallies.

"I scored four goals in Montreal. My parents, my sister, I probably had 15 people there. I wasn't supposed to play the game, I had 103 fever in the afternoon. That said, that meant much. I got all these people come in and they've come to the game and watch me. I went in and I got into the warm-up and I can't believe I played. I got all my energy and I says, I'm playing. You know how many shots I had, sixteen shots."

FIRST RANGERS STANLEY CUP FINAL: 1972 vs. Boston Bruins. Rangers lost in six games.

"It was exciting. We were pecking at it for a couple of years. We were good enough to win the Stanley Cup. We had a full team, a complete team. Eddie Giacomin was a superstar, our goalie. We had Brad Park and Jim Neilson and Dale Rolfe. We had the whole package, you know, Rod Seiling and three lines. We had our lines, the G-A-G line, we were one of the best lines in the league at the time. We had the second line. Walt Tkaczuk was an All-Star and Billy Fairbairn. The third line was Pete Stemkowski, we were really, really a complete team. We didn't win in '68, '69, '70. It was disappointing, we're losing the playoffs. I remember like making the playoffs the last game of the year. That was nine goals. [In 1970, the Rangers needed to outscore Montreal by five goals for a tiebreaker on the final day of the regular season to make the playoffs. Rangers beat Detroit, 9–5, while Montreal lost, 10–2.] From that time on, we made the playoffs every year. We felt we had a really good team to make it and '72 was no different except we played Bobby Orr, that's the problem. When it comes down to it, we didn't play our best against the Bruins, I think we had the superior team. The next year, we beat them in '73 in the playoffs, but we could've beaten them the year before as well."

FIRST SUMMIT SERIES VS. USSR: 1972, Team Canada beat USSR in eight-game series, 4–3–1.

"That was my Stanley Cup. That was so intense. I played all the games in Russia. It was like nothing that was ever challenging to me in the NHL. This was really, really challenging and I'd been playing for ten years by then. Ratelle and Hadfield and I were the only line which was broken up after the first game. Vic was mad. Ratelle and I persisted and we played there a couple of more games in Canada and then we played the four games in Russia. The challenge was like nothing I ever experienced. The Russians were really good and we didn't expect that. We came together, the team, we were figuring out what they were and we played well. We had to win three out of four. We won the last three and we did win, but they [the Russians] were upset at us. Off the ice, they used to wake us up in the middle of the night. They stole our food that we flew in from Canada they were following us everywhere. They didn't give us the right practice time. Turned the lights off and we were practicing. They were like cheating bastards and I think they were blood doping too at the time, so we had a big challenge against it. That's why it was so rewarding to win."

FIRST RANGER TO HAVE HIS NUMBER RETIRED: On October 14, 1979, the Rangers hoisted Gilbert's No. 7 to the rafters at Madison Square Garden.

"That was quite an honor. You're sort of blown away with the whole ceremony. There was no numbers retired. There was no Knicks, there was no Rangers. So what's the meaning of that? I mean, nobody fussed around it. I felt that the number of seven being retired for all the number sevens that had been played for the Rangers, they were all there. Again, it was quite an honor, but it was still a humbling experience when I saw all these other numbers. Red Sullivan wore number seven. It was just another acknowledgement, which was great and I had to make another speech."

ON BEING SELECTED TO THE HOCKEY HALL OF FAME IN 1982:

"It's special and that was what you didn't expect when you start playing hockey, even when you make the NHL, you play for the Rangers. That [Hall of Fame] never crossed my mind. [That] I went in with Emile Francis and Yvan Cournoyer was exciting. It was quite an honor, but it meant more after, when I wore the ring, when I showed the kids, that I made it to the Hall of Fame. It did seem like later on in life it was great. You look back on your accomplishment and you say it's a Hall of Fame career and I'm really excited and proud but you always stay humble about it. There's so many great people there and you're happy to get mentioned in there with them. I mean, the greatest players ever. I guess that's the sign that you had a good career."

Rod was first Ranger to have his number retired.
(Public Domain)

21
DAN GIRARDI

Defenseman Dan Girardi was an undrafted free agent who played 13 NHL seasons, 11 of those with the Rangers. Girardi was eligible for the 2004 NHL Entry Draft but was not selected despite posting 39 points in 68 games with the Guelph Storm in the Ontario Hockey League. Girardi contacted a number of teams and was eventually signed by the Rangers. Girardi was known as a solid backliner who eventually became an alternate captain with the Rangers. The defenseman signed with Tampa Bay as a free agent in 2017 and announced his retirement in September 2019.

FIRST TRYOUT WITH THE RANGERS:

"My actual first tryout was with the Washington Capitals. It was like one of the rookie camps, but I just went for the rookie camp and that was it. My first NHL camp was with New York. I'm pretty sure I tried not to get in a close quarter with Jaromir Jagr anywhere. Wouldn't even know what to say. Watched him growing up when I went early '90s, he's playing and I'm in training camp with this guy and it's like, what's going on right now. I probably was in shock the whole time, not really knowing. I think I knew "Cally" (Ryan Callahan) there, he got drafted there and that's the only guy I really knew that was at the camp."

FIRST RANGERS COACH: Tom Renney

"I thought Tom was a great coach. Very, very, easy to talk to. Laid out the game plan very well, like nothing was too complicated. Very, very good teacher with the video and it helped me out a lot. I believe I had Perry Pern, assistant coach, "D" coach, and he showed me a lot of stats, like game sheets. I remember distinctly showing me my shots on goal per game, that's one thing I learned. Like, we don't shoot the puck on net, you're not going to score a goal. I remember he showed me like three game sheets in a row. I had zero shots on net. I'm like, 'Well, that's not gonna help.' So, I'm like, 'Gotta shoot the puck a little more and hit the net.' Like I said, I thought Tom was a great coach. Obviously, didn't work out for him but I really learned a lot from Tom."

FIRST RANGERS CAPTAIN: Jaromir Jagr

"I didn't know what to expect, to be quite honest with you. You see this elite NHL superstar on TV all the time. You don't really see him in the media too much, watching the games. I don't really know what to expect, but he was an amazing guy, amazing teammate. I'm not sure how much I talked to him but when I did, he was very, very kind and nice. He signed a stick for me after, I think my second year. I still have that in my basement. Very nice for me to get a stick from him.

"I sat kind of near him on the plane. It was me and Cally and all the Czech guys up in the card tables. So me and Cally didn't say much for our first couple of years there. Like I said, they were nice to us. They did talk to us and include us sometimes but there was a lot of Czech talk going on We didn't really know what was happening but he was a great leader, amazing player and very, very lucky to be able to play with a guy like that."

FIRST TIME PUTTING ON THE RANGERS JERSEY:
January 27, 2007 @ Philadelphia Flyers, 2–1 win

"First time it was in Philly. My first game, walking into the rink, honestly I think I probably felt like I was walking from above. I'm sure I was just floating on air the whole time. Kind of just trying to take it in but not get too excited, you know what I mean? Like get too overwhelmed and I probably didn't say much. I was looking at number 46. I'm like, 'Oh, what's this crappy number?' I'm like, 'What is this garbage?' Generally I didn't care what number it was. I remember one thing for sure that Brendan Shanahan told me. He's like, 'Hey, play like you belong here. Don't like you're here for just one game or just try to survive. Play like you deserve to be here and like you've been here a while.' So I just went out there and played like I did the last year or so in the American League and it seemed to work quite fine."

FIRST GAME AS A RANGER AT MADISON SQUARE GARDEN: January 31, 2007 vs. Toronto Maple Leafs, 2–1 loss

"It was pretty crazy. The dressing room back then, before the renovation, it was kind of like the stalls were all kind of broken up. It was all weird. It was still nice, but it wasn't the greatest room in the world until they all renovated it. I was like, 'Oh man, I've got a lot of people watching at home,' 'cause every Leaf game is televised. No matter what day of the week or where they're playing, it's always on CBC or TSN or stuff like that. Like it was always on TV. That was kinda in the back of my head. Like, 'Oh crap, it's going to be everyone watching me tonight.'"

FIRST RANGERS POINT: February 17, 2007 @ MSG vs. Philadelphia Flyers, 5–3 loss

Girardi had two assists including a shorthanded assist late in the third period.

"It was probably quite a relief. I'm not sure how many games it actually was, but I know for a fact, that season I actually didn't score [a goal] so I think I had six assists or something like that. It was nice to get a point and get on the scoresheet a little bit more.

Every time we played Philly, you check the game sheets, you have your career stats. I played like 60 games, had like 30 assists or something like that."

FIRST RANGERS GOAL: October 18, 2007 @ Atlanta Thrashers, 5–3 loss

"I believe it was a power play. I just remember kind of exchanging, I think it might've been Chris Drury or someone at the top. I pull up the clip all the time for my son. It's on like the tribute video for me and stuff. I point my stick over for like Drury to move and I'm telling Chris where to go, it's kinda funny. I find the seam and [Jaromir] Jagr feeding me for a one-timer and I'm like, this is not real. It wasn't like it was a deciding goal in the game or something very important, but you don't want to celebrate too much. I kinda gave a little like, stick in the air a little bit. Kind of a little, little point but I think it was a pretty cool moment. It was in Atlanta of all places, a team that probably my son, honestly, he probably has no idea that existed. It's funny, it was not that long ago either."

FIRST RANGERS FIGHT: January 16th, 2009 @ Chicago Blackhawks, 3–2 overtime win

"Cam Barker, it was against the Black Hawks. It might have been like a dads' trip too. It was decent. It wasn't anything crazy. I think I kinda like fell on the ground, kinda like a little stunned, something like that. I remember the next day, I think we're going to Pittsburgh. I was like kinda riding the bike. I didn't feel great but I think I'd still play because my Dad was on the trip. I'm like I got to play."

FIRST RANGERS WINTER CLASSIC: January 2, 2012 @ Citizens Bank Park vs. Philadelphia Flyers, 3–2 win

HBO's *24/7, Road to the NHL Winter Classic* was a documentary that showed the teams on and off the ice as they prepared to play the outdoor game.

"The whole year itself was a big year personally for me. It was a really good year, had a great year. All-Star Game and we do the Winter Classic, HBO *24/7*. My son kind of got a little famous during that. People see him at the game say, 'Hey, can I take a picture of your son?' I'm like, 'Maybe not, he is two.' It was all not serious but I think that was really, really cool. It didn't start too long before that, so it was nice to be able to be part of one. It was in Philly, you know, a lot of family members there. My son, my wife [was] there; we done a family skate which was really fun, all that stuff. There's a ton of video evidence, my son ever asked I played an outdoor game, like 'Hey, buddy, let me show you something.' Show them the HBO, show him this and that. Those are career highlights that are always nice to where your family can be part of something like that."

FIRST RANGERS STADIUM SERIES GAME: January 26, 2014 @ Yankee Stadium vs. New Jersey Devils, 7–3 win

"That was very special. Yankee Stadium, the new one but it was a very, still historic building and historic areas. The Yankees are probably the world's most well-known team to anyone in the world. You know you say New York Yankees, everyone knows about then. To be able to play in that stadium was very cool. Obviously, against both our rivals [Rangers played the Islanders at Yankee Stadium three days later], Islanders and Devils. Those are really cool games too. I could picture like Hank's [Lundqvist] pads and his blocker and like to put the "pinstripes" on him. That's all super cool stuff. Once again, family being a part of that. I remember the game got delayed a little bit 'cause the sun was shining too much. I'm just sitting in the family room in my full gear, talking to my family. Those are really, really fun games to play."

FIRST ALL-STAR GAME AS A RANGER: January 29, 2012 @ Ottawa, Canada. Girardi represented the Rangers as a member of "Team Alfredsson."

"It meant a lot really. Not really known for my overall flashy play, so to be recognized of being a solid "D-man," that plays the right way but can contribute offensively. I can't remember if it was J.R. (John Rosasco, Rangers VP of Communications) or I forget who told me; I thought they were joking. I went, 'Good one.' My agent called and I'm like, 'Really,' and he's like, 'Yeah, you're going to Ottawa for the All-Star Game.' I'm like, 'Are you kidding me?' Obviously, I was like so excited. My parents were losing their mind and my son was only two, but he got to go there. I still have an autographed jersey. All those memories and keepsakes. Got to meet Drake in the dressing room. Like, you kidding me?

"I remember sitting beside Scott Hartnell [Flyers winger], you know a guy I think I fought during the year, with Flyers-Rangers just killing each other every night, right? Trying to bury him, he's trying to bury me. I'm sitting beside him at the All-Star Game and it was just kind of funny. Then he was like buddy, buddy. Right? Like nothing happened. That's the cool thing about the All-Star Game. It doesn't really matter what happens. You go there, have some fun, enjoy your time. They get back to reality after that."

FIRST STANLEY CUP FINAL GAME: June 4, 2014 @ Los Angeles Kings, 3–2 overtime loss

"Once we beat Montreal, I think all the guys were excited, maybe anxious is the word I'm looking for. 'Okay, what's going on now?' Like you got the media stuff, the whole week of stuff before in LA. A lot going on, a lot of distractions but I think it was a really cool experience. I didn't get a chance to get back there but I'm hoping the guys that were there, that are still playing, that maybe have a chance to get to the next level; it wasn't the best Finals for us. We were close, you know overtime games, couple of goal leads, that first game was something special. You know you've got the huge beard on, your body feels like crap, no one feels great, but you know that you went four more games, you got the ultimate prize but just didn't happen. It's a tough way to lose but even though we lost, it's gonna be an experience that I'll remember forever."

Even though he was on losing end, the 2014 Stanley Cup Final is something Dan will remember forever. Photo courtesy of Robert Kowal [CC BY-SA (https://creativecommons.org/licenses/by-sa/2.0)]).

22

TONY GRANATO

Tony Granato's career in hockey has gone from being a solid player to becoming a coach in the NHL and at the collegiate level. The right wing played for the University of Wisconsin before joining the Rangers for parts of two seasons before being traded to the Los Angeles Kings for Tomas Sandstrom and Bernie Nicholls in January 1990. Granato was the winner of the 1997 Masterton Trophy. He went on to become the head coach of the Colorado Avalanche in December 2002. Granato is currently the head coach of the Wisconsin Badgers hockey team.

FIRST CONTACT WITH NHL:

Tony Granato was chosen by the Rangers in the sixth round of the 1982 NHL Entry Draft.

"I didn't find out until Sunday after the draft, so it wasn't publicized and there wasn't TV coverage. So, I read it in the paper the next day. I didn't get a call until Sunday from Chuck Grillo actually, one of the Ranger scouts. He called and told me I was drafted. Later that week, I get a call from Craig Patrick [Rangers GM]; I believe Craig called later that next week. So I found out Sunday, read it in the *Chicago Sun Times* or *Tribune*. They had the draft list and one of the Blackhawks' personnel guys, a guy named Wally Gunzo [Walter "Gunzo" Humeniuk], who was their equipment manager, called my Dad and told us that he wished he knew I was eligible for the draft because he would've helped the Blackhawks select me. So that's how I found out.

"Obviously, you get drafted by an Original Six team and being drafted by the Rangers was really, really cool. I remember my parents got me a Ranger hat, my sisters and brothers were all fired up. It was very exciting to be recognized by an NHL team that potentially, you could play for them."

FIRST RANGERS TRAINING CAMP: Before 1988–89 season

"I remember I was number 39. The Olympic year, 1988, Mike Richter, Pete Laviolette, Kevin Miller, Corey Millen, and Brian Leetch were all on the Olympic team together and we all six were Ranger draft picks and we had played the Rangers in an exhibition game. I started to get to know the organization 'cause Phil [Esposito] started hanging around the Olympic team a little bit. Brian, obviously was a first-round pick, Mike was a second- round pick, so those two were real high-end prospects. The rest of us, were pretty good players 'cause we made that Olympic team and all of us, we're now NHL prospects. So we started to get noticed a little bit more by the Rangers and there's some more conversations with the Rangers during the Olympic year. I signed with the Rangers right after the Olympics and went straight to Denver with Pete Laviolette and with Mike Richter. Brian signed and went right to the Rangers. Corey and Kevin, I believe both of them went back to school, neither of them signed. So I started with the Colorado Rangers and played a couple of months there.

"My first Ranger training camp was at Trois-Rivieres (Quebec, Canada) and that was Guy's [Lafleur] return to Quebec and to the Rangers. Michel Bergeron was the coach and it was an unbelievable experience going to your first NHL camp with guys like Guy [Lafleur] and Marcel [Dionne] Ron Greschner, Chris

Nilan, John Vanbiesbrouck. Lots of players you watched on TV and admired for being NHL stars and I had the chance to be in the same training camp. Brian [Leetch] had already played up there so he was really helpful in me feeling comfortable and kind of being the guy to introduce me to the rest of the big club, even though it was still probably a long shot that I made the team that training camp, but camp went well. Had a really good start to the camp, worked, won a chance to play some exhibition games. The games went well, the exhibition games, and I was fortunate enough to make the team out of that camp."

FIRST RANGERS COACH: Michel Bergeron

"I was his type of player. I think he loved the energy and I think he didn't mind smaller guys, then he wanted some younger blood into the mix. He was like a spark plug, a real energetic, emotional coach. I think I fit the style of player that he was looking for. I was fortunate that he appreciated what I did in camp to give me a chance to play and make the team.

FIRST RANGERS CAPTAIN: Kelly Kisio

"Kelly was outstanding and I felt they made me feel comfortable and part of it as a rookie, which sometimes in those days was hard to do. I was nervous as a rookie and back then it was different to be a rookie. Those guys including Guy Lafleur, including Marcel [Dionne] Ron Greschner, Chris Nilan, the older players, John Vanbiesbrouck, David Shaw, Brian Mullen, Lucien DeBlois, Donnie Maloney, they were all unbelievable to me as a young player. I was fortunate from the standpoint that I started at 23, not 18 or 19. I played four years of college. I played on three US [national] teams where I played with some pro guys in those tournaments, so I was a little bit more mature, I guess would be the right way to describe it, so the older players treated me great."

FIRST RANGERS GAME AND FIGHT: October 6, 1988 @ Chicago Blackhawks, 2–2 overtime tie

"I remember not sleeping when I found out I made the team. I didn't sleep until the time that puck was dropped. I was so excited. That was the building I grew up watching hundreds and hundreds of Blackhawk games, so to start your first game and the building that you dreamed of playing in someday, made it that much more special. My first shift, I got a major for boarding, so it didn't take long for me to find a way to the penalty box. It was almost like you felt like is this really happening? Like, almost the way it happened so fast. I remember early in training camp, recognizing the fact that first game was October 6th, and Chicago Stadium and I'm thinking, Oh my gosh, if I make the team, wow, that'd be unbelievable. Play your first game in front of your family, Chicago Stadium, and it happened.

"I was leading the league in penalty minutes after the first game. Ten penalty minutes in the first game, which wasn't kind of the way it was drawn up but I think it was something Bergy appreciated just from the standpoint that I wasn't intimidated, wasn't scared. I don't know what kind of impact I had on the game, but it was noticeable from the standpoint I was in a fight, got a major for boarding, was pretty involved in the game. I was a little nervous after the game, you know getting a major penalty on your first shift probably wasn't the right way to break in but Bergy loved it. I got big pat on the back and big smile after the game, a big handshake with it. I knew he appreciated the energy and how hard I, or at least thought I played hard enough to hang around for a little while."

Granato fought Chicago's Trent Yawney, who was known to drop the gloves.

"I got jumped. That was from the first year, like they were all after me. I mean, I get it. I ran Steve Larmer, not because I wanted to run Steve Larmer; it's just 'cause I was so wound up and so excited to be in a game that I was going to run into whatever was in my way. I was on the ice for probably four seconds when it happened. I beeline straight to where the puck was and Larms

[Larmer] turned his back on me and I ran him over. Next thing you know, I got jumped, eye gouged and everything else. Period later, I'm out on the ice. I know everybody's coming, they're chirping me the whole game. 'You're gonna get it, you're gonna get it.' I know it's coming. I was behind the net and I got jumped from behind from Larmer and I rolled around and I don't really know if I even threw a punch but the first NHL game, you get your first NHL fight so I guess it was kind of a memorable start."

Making debut in Chicago was a dream come true for Tony Granato.
Photo courtesy of NY Rangers.

23
GILLES GRATTON

Goaltender Gilles Gratton played 47 games in the NHL, 41 of those with the Rangers. Gratton began his pro career in the World Hockey Association in 1972. After a six-game stint with the St. Louis Blues in 1975–76, Gratton signed with the Rangers as a free agent for the 1976–77 season. During his playing career, Gratton was known as "Gratoony the Loony" for his outspoken character and eccentric personality.

FIRST CONTACT WITH NHL:

Gratton was drafted by the Buffalo Sabres in the fifth round of the 1972 NHL Amateur Draft but signed with the WHA's Ottawa Nationals.

"I was drafted by Buffalo, they offered me like $5,000 to sign, $8,000 for the first year and $10,000 my second year. I don't know why but I wasn't so serious about hockey. Then, when I got the offer, I just told [Buffalo GM Punch] Imlach, 'You know, I can make more money with my band.' So I just said, screw this. I'm not going to do this. You know what happens, the World Hockey [WHA] came that summer. I was drafted by Edmonton and ended up in Ottawa."

"My grandfather died, so I buried my grandfather like early afternoon and then I drove to Ottawa, not very far, about 40 kilometers from there, I drove to Ottawa to sign my contract with the Ottawa Nationals. They gave me a $20,000 bonus and 25 my first year, and 30, my second year, so fuck them, might as well keep playing you know. I didn't have any money and then you get a $20,000 check when you're like 20 years old. So I signed with Ottawa."

In 1975, Buffalo traded Gratton's rights to the St. Louis Blues.

"I had a five-year contract with the Toronto Toros [after the Ottawa Nationals moved there]. I only played one year; what happened was they fired [coach] Billy Harris and Billy Harris was kinda father figure for me. He had been my coach for three years with Ottawa and Toronto and they fired him. I just kind of went off the deep end, I just started acting really crazy. When [Toros owner John] Bassett called me in the summer to patch things up, I said, 'Screw you, I'm not going back to Toronto.' So he sold my rights to the St. Louis Blues.

"When I was sold to St. Louis, the draft that year was in Montreal. In those days, when I trained, I would smoke pot and I had long hair and play tennis and screw around the pool. My agents had called me and they said, 'You should come to the hotel for the draft and meet the owners of the St. Louis Blues.' So, I get there and I have long hair and I've been drinking and smoking all summer, I don't look that good, you know. I get to the hotel and in the lobby, I meet Garry Young. I knew Garry Young from Oshawa because I played three years in Oshawa. I'd known him because he worked in the Oshawa organization but I didn't know that he had been named the coach of the St. Louis Blues. So we get in the elevator and he says, 'How do you feel about coming to St. Louis?' I said, 'I don't give a fuck about St. Louis. All I wanna do is get my money and get the fuck out of there.' Fuck, man. The guy went like white and I didn't understand. I said, 'What's wrong with him?' We get up in the elevator and about 10 minutes later, I learned that he's my coach.

"I had a car accident in the summer and my leg wasn't so good. We get to St. Louis and he gave me a hard time, the whole time. At one point, we played on Long Island and the first shot of the game, I get hit in the arm. I went to the bench, said my arm hurts and I'm not playing anymore. So he sends Eddie Johnston in and we lose 8–0 [actually 8–2]. The next day in the room, he calls me out and says I let the team down and I said, fuck you, and I went to hit him and I went after him. The players held me back and then I left and never came back. I was going to beat the shit out of him."

After the game vs. the Islanders, Gratton was placed on the voluntary retired list by the Blues. St. Louis refused to place Gratton on waivers so he could not go back to play with Toronto of the WHA. Gratton secured his release from St. Louis and that enabled him to become a free agent and sign with the Rangers.

FIRST RANGERS TRAINING CAMP: Prior to 1976–77 season

"The camp was in Montreal. So I stayed at home, but the guys were staying in a motel not far from my place and we played in Pointe-Claire, a suburb of Montreal. We didn't train those days, we got to camp to get in shape. Today, guys get to camp and they're in shape. I remember missing the year I didn't play in St. Louis and I remember coming to camp and I was completely out of shape. I didn't have a very good camp. In those days, if you didn't have a good camp, they didn't give a shit. I wasn't sharp, I was out of shape and I thought to myself, *Ooh, this is going to be a tough year*. I was hoping that [John] Davidson would carry the load and I'd only play like 15 or 20 games and maybe I would slowly get back and then Davidson got hurt and I had to play and I wasn't playing well."

FIRST TIME PUTTING ON THE RANGERS JERSEY:

"It's always special because it's the six original, you know, either Detroit, Chicago, New York, Boston, Montreal, Toronto, it's always special."

FIRST RANGERS COACH: John Ferguson

"I just remember he didn't have a clue. No one would practice with like two-on-one, three-on-two. Coaches today, they have a system. There was no system. There was just a three-on-two, two-on-ones and breakaways and just fucking shit that you did when you were a Bantam (a level of hockey played by 13 to 15 year olds) and the guy didn't have a clue, didn't have a clue. All he did is fucking scream and try to get the guys, he was like a cheerleader and the other guy there, Jean Guy Talbot, I call him 'rent a coach.' That guy didn't have a clue either. Jean Guy Talbot, you could tell he fucking hated me because he'd come into the room and instead of saying, 'Come on you guys,' he would say, 'Come on youse guys,' and I'd always make fun of him by mocking him. 'Come on youse guys' and at practice, he always tried to shoot at my head but he had a real poor shot and he never got me."

FIRST RANGERS CAPTAIN: Phil Esposito

"We played in Providence, an exhibition game. After the game, we're just sitting there. Maybe, there's three or four guys left in the room. There's me, Esposito and a couple of guys. I'm really slow when I'm done. I think we tied Washington 3–3 in Providence, something like that. This Italian guy comes in and starts speaking Italian to Esposito. He [Esposito] says 'I don't fucking speak Italian,' and he turns to the trainer and said, 'Get that fucking guy outta here.' I was shocked and I couldn't believe it. You know, he could've said, 'Sorry, I don't speak Italian' and maybe sign an autograph. I thought to myself, *You fucker. If you ever fucking cross me, I'll fucking drop you. You don't treat human beings like that*. I was in shock, I'm telling you I couldn't believe it. I come to New York and this fucking prick, an Italian guy comes to him and he says, 'I don't fucking speak Italian, get that fucking guy outta here.' From that day on, I thought to myself, he was like 'King

Shit' in the room anyway.

"There was a day in practice that he came to me and I was leaning on the boards and he said, 'Are you playing on Saturday in Toronto?' and I said, 'Yeah.' He says, "If you don't play well, you're going to hear about it from me.' I said, 'Fuck you' and I said, 'Get the fuck out of here. I'm going to break my fucking stick on your head.' He was in a state of shock, nobody ever talked to him like that and I was waiting for that moment. Then, in the room, he tried to suck up to me, but I said fuck you and then I went after him but [Bill[Goldsworthy and Rod Gilbert held me back. A couple of days later, Gilbert told me, 'You're fucked. You're not gonna play anymore.' I guess they had a meeting and stuff and I didn't play in Toronto that Saturday. He [Esposito] was not a very nice guy."

FIRST RANGERS GAME: October 6, 1976 @ MSG vs. Minnesota North Stars, 6–5 win

(On October 12, 1976, Don Murdoch became the first Ranger and the sixth NHL player to score five goals in a single game in a 10–4 victory over the North Stars at Minnesota.)

"I thought to myself, *Fuck am I lucky they score nine* [ten], *I couldn't stop a football.* I was grateful to Murdoch scoring five.

24

MIKE HARTMAN

Left wing Mike Hartman was acquired from Tampa Bay in March 1993 and played parts of three seasons with the Rangers. Hartman played in 35 regular-season games but no playoff games during the Stanley Cup–winning season of 1993–94, but his name is etched onto the Stanley Cup.

FIRST CONTACT WITH NHL:

Mike Hartman was chosen by the Buffalo Sabres in the seventh round of the 1986 NHL Entry Draft.

"The year before was my draft year when I was 18 and I was rated in the first three rounds, which is exciting. I was rated really high before going into my OHL year. Turned out that, I went from the second round to the third round to the being rated in the seventh round to not even getting drafted. My father knew Jimmy Devellano [Detroit GM] from the Detroit Red Wings and he told my father, because my father took pictures and he told my father, 'Mike isn't doing anything really well. He's not hitting, he's not like big enough to be the tough guy. Like he went from a guy that can kill penalties and play all positions to playing a little defense in junior,' so I was figuring out what I was going to do with my life.

"I was ready to be done with hockey, and I'd go back to school, which I did anyways. I went back and got a degree but I said I'm done. Then Jimmy Devellano talked to me and told me to work on a few things and I met with him. It was great, after the draft, he called me down to meet with the Red Wings. I was so excited, I thought he was bringing me to training camp. He didn't really bring me to training camp, he sat down to tell me, 'Listen, you need to do these seven things. Number one, you need seven shots on net in a game, you need to finish your checks, you need to pick your spots and fight for a reason. Fight for your teammates. Like, he really was my life coach and was great to me."

As an 18-year old, Hartman was with the Belleville Bulls of the OHL but was traded to the North Bay Centennials.

"I went to North Bay, played with Darren Turcotte and Nick Kypreos. We had a stacked team. Troy Crowder's our tough guy. We had a helluva team. Dave McLlwain who I got traded for [in 1991 after five seasons with Buffalo]. I ended up killing penalties and scored, 20 goals maybe (he scored 19) but I played physical, played really well and the Buffalo Sabres drafted me in the seventh round."

FIRST REACTION TO BECOMING A RANGER:

"My grandfather was born in Brooklyn and he's a big Brooklyn Dodgers fan and a big Rangers fan. He'd say, 'Why can't you play in New York?' I said, 'It doesn't work like that.' The day he passed away, I was playing in the Garden [with Tampa Bay] and Tie Domi, I got in a fight with him and hurt my shoulder and I found out after I flew home to Detroit. Then, that same year I got traded to the Rangers and Phil Esposito called me and said, 'It's a deadline deal.' I was in New Jersey like, 'You've been traded to the New York Rangers.' You know, you don't think about it at the time but it's kinda weird. I mean, my grandfather passed away that night when I was in the Garden and then I got to New York."

FIRST RANGERS PLAYER HE MET WHEN HE CAME TO THE TEAM: Adam Graves

"We grew up training together so we were friends way before the NHL. He would help me with my hockey school. I think he's one of the greatest people I've ever met in my life. He would come down, and a lot of guys would ask for money, to run the hockey school. He would come down and just be with the kids. When I got here, he greeted me right away along with Ed Olczyk, 'cause Eddie and I were great friends in Winnipeg. Those two guys were the first two."

FIRST TIME PUTTING ON RANGERS JERSEY:

"Well, it really hit me because, growing up, my favorite team was the Oilers. So even when I played the Oilers, I go like, 'Holy cow, we're playing, look who we're playing against. You're playing against, you know all those guys that I loved watching growing up.' So the first thing I saw was we got Mark Messier, we got Kevin Lowe, we got [Jeff] Beukeboom, we have [Esa] Tikkanen. You have all those guys that won championships elsewhere but it was like, 'Look at this team, it's stacked.' The amount of talent we had was great. So it was a really cool feeling. I always wanted to play on an Original Six team so to come to New York, it was really exciting."

FIRST RANGERS COACH: Ron Smith

"He was fine. He just said, 'You know we brought you in here, we were gonna use you in and out of the lineup. We want you to play physical,' and he was fine with me. I mean, I didn't really know him that long. I mean, I got here and the season was done, after three weeks or so back then. That was fine and the next year was [Mike] Keenan."

FIRST RANGERS CAPTAIN: Mark Messier

"He was very quiet, but when he said something that mattered and then you would watch him practice, watch him play and he would walk in the room and the atmosphere of the room changed. It was crazy. He cared about everybody; he made sure I was taken care of. He came up to me, 'Anything you need, can I help you with anything, welcome to the team.' Talked to me privately, 'Where are you staying, where you living,' and I tell him staying in the hotel. He said, 'Hey, if you ever need anything, I'm here,' and it was really welcoming. Here am I coming into the best leader in hockey in my eyes. So it was an honor and a privilege to play with him."

FIRST RANGERS TRAINING CAMP: Before 1993–94 season

The Rangers brought in Mike Keenan to be their new head coach and Hartman's first Rangers training camp was under Keenan.

"Everything was different with him. Like you were never comfortable, I could tell you that. Then a guy like me, who's on the bubble, it was stressful. Like, okay, so what's going to be. Then you got to remember, at the time, we carried, I think we had 20, 25 players. You never knew when you were going to play, even if you were told you're not going to play in the morning, I played at night. He would say, 'You're not playing tonight but go for warm-ups,' and I'm thinking, okay, I'm not playing, still need a good warm- up, I'm gonna ride the bike. Then he told me I'm not gonna play a lot and I played a lot. The other games, you just never knew. I liked Mike Keenan, I respected Mike Keenan and I'm one of the guys that really liked him. I think I understood him and he just wanted to maximize everybody's ability and get the most out of what you can bring, whether you think you could bring more or not, it didn't matter."

FIRST GAME AS A RANGER: April 12, 1993 @ Philadelphia Flyers, 1–0 loss

"You can't forget it because the team was three points out of a playoff [spot] and I got traded from Tampa and I played against the Flyers in Philadelphia. That's not always a fun game to play when they have, you know six or seven guys. You know you're going into that game, 'Oh they got [Craig] Berube, they got Dave Brown. Played on a line with Joey Kocur and Paul Broten."

FIRST RANGERS GOAL: March 14, 1994 @ Florida Panthers, 2–1 loss

Nine days before, Hartman claims he should've been credited with his first Rangers goal but it was awarded to Jeff Beukeboom.

"Yeah, they didn't give it to me. I scored on the Island when I wasn't supposed to dress. We ended up winning that game. They pulled Glenn Healy and I deflected it in. I think [Jeff] Beukeboom shot and I scored. They didn't give it to me, I didn't care. The first goal I got credited was the only goal in Florida and I wasn't supposed to dress that night.

"We were in Florida and I mentioned to Mess [Messier] that I'm going to be leaving, I know you have a dinner but I'm going to be a little bit late 'cause I'm going to see my mother. 'Your mother's here?' Yeah, my mother had lived in South Florida, so he said 'No problem, we'll just see you when you get here.' So I got there and he asked me how my mother is, 'cause he asked me, this is my favorite story. The next day, they told me I'm not dressing and I'd been playing well and Mess says, 'You're not playing uhh, tonight.' I go, 'Nope, I'm not playing.' Mess says, 'Don't go anywhere, stay here.' So Mess goes to the back and talks to Mike Keenan and the next thing I know, [assistant coach] Colin Campbell said, 'You're playing tonight,' and that's the game I scored in Florida. Mess was the one that went back there and he knew my mother was there. I can't believe the guy did that, I'll never forget that. He [Messier] went back, talked to Mike and the next thing I know, I was dressing. They pulled somebody else out and they said, 'You're playing tonight,' and I played a lot, scored a goal. On John Vanbiesbrouck actually and it was thanks to Mess."

FIRST RANGERS FIGHT: October 28, 1993 @MSG vs.

Montreal Canadiens, 3–3 tie

Hartman fought Montreal's Mario Roberge in the first period.

"I was never a heavyweight guy going out there to fight; I didn't love to fight, I did it because I'm gonna run around and try and create some energy for the team. I wasn't the guy that was like Joe Kocur or even in Buffalo was Kevin Maguire, there was always that other guy. I wasn't the guy to go and be the heavyweight but I did it, I fought a lot of the guys. It was against Montreal actually, it was against Roberge. I think it was a four- minute fight. Back in those days you could swing and punch and there's only a few punches and they gave us four minutes.".

25
PAT HICKEY

Left wing Pat Hickey played parts of six seasons as a Ranger in two tenures with the team. Hickey joined the Rangers for the 1975–76 season before being traded to the Colorado Rockies in November 1979. Hickey played one game for Toronto in 1981–82, then was traded to the Rangers, who sent him to the Quebec Nordiques later that season. Hickey scored a career-high 40 goals for the Rangers in 1977–78.

FIRST GAME ATTENDED AS A KID:

"My father went to St. Mike's High School in Toronto. You are probably aware of the tradition where they brought in, like Frank Mahovlich played there, David Keon, all these guys. Allan Stanley was a teammate of my dad's because my dad played for the Boston Olympics way back when in the American League. Then he went off to the Canadian Air Force in the war, but they remained buddies. So Allan Stanley played for the Toronto Maple Leafs and I think I was about 10 or 12 years old. Allan got my dad two tickets to Maple Leaf Gardens and we went there for warm-up. Allan came to the glass and we had a chat and threw me a puck. I guess this was all part of the process in believing in your dad that he was the most special guy in the world. As far as him playing pro hockey, I never knew that until I was 14 or 15 years old that my dad even played professional hockey. I knew you played at St. Mike's, which is a prestigious hockey-related school. They called him 'The Sniper,' so he was a center-man, but anyway, that was my first NHL game going to Maple Leaf Gardens in Toronto and meeting Allan Stanley and sort of looking at my dad, being amazed that he'd actually arranged this."

FIRST HOCKEY IDOL:

"Bobby Pulford, because he scored 20 goals a year for the Toronto Maple Leafs killing penalties, it was like his forte in my mind. That was something my dad always taught me that not everybody gets to play on the power play, so become a specialist killing penalties. Bobby Pulford was that guy. He was kind of the second team penalty killers for the Toronto Maple Leafs. Davey Keon would've been the first, but Pulford, from my recollection, kind of unseated Keon from like killing the first minute, which is the most important minute of a power play. Remember, back then, these guys stayed on the ice for more than a minute and Pulford always scored like four or six shorthanded goals and he always ended up with 20. When I watched the NHL, 20 goals was the benchmark. If you had 20 goals, man that was something special. So he was my guy."

FIRST CONTACT WITH THE NHL:

Pat Hickey was chosen by the Rangers in the second round (30th overall) of the 1973 NHL Amateur Draft. Hickey was also chosen 18th overall by the Toronto Toros in the WHA Amateur Draft.

"The NHL draft came and two days later it was the WHA draft. I'd already been contacted by the WHA through a fella that also played for the Toronto Maple Leafs, Billy Harris. He coached me in my second year of the Hamilton Junior Red Wings. At the time, the draft was [for players] 20 years old, so basically, you spent three years in OHA, the Canadian Junior league. Harris had coached for a year coaching the Swedish National team, which I thought was pretty impressive. He came back and then he coached me in Hamilton for that year. That was also the year that I was the only guy on the junior team that went to a university. I went to McMaster University. That was kind of like a rule from my father and the discipline that we had, but Harris coached me there. So by the time I played on and I was a captain of the Red Wings the next year, word got out that the Toronto Toros were hot on my trail.

"The word was that I'd be drafted fairly high in the NHL draft and the Toronto Toros were going to draft me first. The morning of the draft, I went golfing with my brother, which we kind of grew up doing. I came home and called my father and said that, you know, sort of the news that the Rangers had drafted me 30th overall, first in the second round, so that was great. I think at the time, lawyers and agents were getting into it. It was about a week later where Emile Francis got in touch with us and had a chat and said [a] welcome to the club type of thing, but the structure at that time, which everyone knew was, in the NHL, you got drafted and you went to their American [League] team or their minor-league affiliate and that's where you learned to be a pro. In the WHA, they promised that you'd be sitting in the locker room learning from guys that we were going to sign like Paul Henderson, Frank Mahovlich, Vaclav Nedomansky from Czechslovakia, who was, at that time, the 'Frank Mahovlich of Czechslovakia.' So my dad and I sat around the kitchen table and he said, 'Son, you can go to work every day and pick Frank Mahovlich and Paul Henderson's brain, you might become a better, better forward.' I kinda liked that idea and sure enough, although the Rangers offered me, at the time, like a one-way contract as far as the money goes, but the process was that I'd be going to Providence. The Toronto Toros were the team that kinda broke the rule and started trusting at 18 years old. It was very soon after, 1973? I'm not sure when the NHL changed the rules, but on the way to '79 when the leagues merged, but they drafted a fellow named Wayne Dillon who was 18 and my teammate on the Toros.

"When I signed a contract with the Toros, it was kind of an interesting story because it goes back to my father again. My father played with a fellow named [Tom] Windy O'Neill at St. Mike's. Windy O'Neill went on to play two years with the Toronto Maple

Leafs and they won two Stanley Cups, but he retired immediately because he was a lawyer in Toronto. My dad got the call and thought that maybe I was going to get drafted and in this day and age, you needed a lawyer or an agent. My dad didn't think we needed an agent because we had a little bit of an IQ, but you need a lawyer or an accountant, so he called up Windy O'Neill and we went to see him before the draft and introduced me. At the time, Windy had one client, it was Terry O'Reilly and it was the same kind of relationship. The fathers knew each other when you said, 'I'll do that.' The key behind it was that Windy O'Neill was also [the] personal lawyer of a fellow named Punch Imlach, so we had a little bid of inside information in terms of contracts and salary payment for this or that, so I felt pretty comfortable at the time. What happened in the following year, was Windy actually passed away, but he had two older brothers, who were also fancy Toronto lawyers, so we just sort of passed the dossier over to Paul O'Neill, who represented me on my WHA contracts and ultimately coming to the Rangers. So the point of the story is they [the owners] were going to build a new arena in downtown Toronto, so we put a clause in there. They said they were going to build a building within two years, so we said, put it in the contract, and they didn't, so I had an out and I think Emile Francis knew that. I had two years in the WHA, learning from the best and I guess Emile sort of scouted that and recognized that. Then I signed with the Rangers in '75 because I had that out in my contract."

FIRST RANGERS TRAINING CAMP:

"I felt pretty comfortable going to New York. I was greeted at the door by Rod Gilbert and I guess that's why we became a little bit like brothers, but Rod said 'Hi, how are you' and everything else. He says, 'They tell me you're fast,' and I say, 'Yeah, that's what they tell me too.' He says, 'I'll race you down the ice for a hundred bucks.' I said, 'Let's go,' and we had to hand a hundred bucks each over to Pete Stemkowski. He was the referee and we lined up. I'm a rookie and I'm sort of intimidated, but I wasn't intimidated by the whistle going and me racing down the ice against Rod Gilbert, so I raced him down the ice and I beat him by about ten lengths. We skated over to Pete Stemkowski and Pete sorta held out the 200 bucks and Rod grabbed it and said, "Thank you, that's payment for the privilege of racing,' and I looked at him and I wasn't gonna argue. I was with a good group of guys right now, so I better keep my head up for the practical jokes. I had learned and you can see them coming at you, so for a hundred bucks, I thought, *Well, this would be a good day*, and then we went on scrimmaging.

"The training camps back then were pretty tough. It was twice a day, the morning was basically drills and wind sprints and stops and starts. They basically just tried to tire you out so that when you scrimmaged in the afternoon for two hours, they could really see the people that had talent or that were in shape. You're never in shape when they beat the body up like that in the morning. They were tough and it was a highly competitive camp. I had to earn my spot; I didn't play a lot. We had a guy named Derek Sanderson there and he had my number. It's one of my little trivia questions. Like, what was your first number with the New York Rangers? I wore [No.] 14. Derek got traded to St. Louis, so I jumped on number 16 really quickly. They gave it to me but I didn't play too many. I didn't get too much ice time, you really had to earn your spot there. Be ready, somewhere along the line the coach was Ronnie Stewart. He was a legacy NHL player, again with the Toronto Maple Leafs, I think he won Stanley Cups and things like that. As far as I was concerned, he wasn't very personable and I don't think he liked me too much. It's like everything else. Everybody had to do it, you just had to earn your way on there. He made the mistake of throwing me out there to kill a penalty, you know, one game when I was sitting on the end of the bench. Pete Stemkowski and I sat on the end of the bench a lot that year. I learned a lot from Stemmer. Stemmer would do the play-by-play and I would do the color commentating on the end of the bench, but one time [Stewart] said, 'Go out and kill the penalty.' We went out there and I don't know if we scored or had some chances, but we killed it and then they put me on a line with Walter Tkaczuk and Billy Fairbairn. It's pretty hard to have a bad game with those two guys, so I just used my speed and opened up the ice and we moved the puck around pretty good and I never looked back. I had a regular spot."

FIRST RANGERS COACH:

Hickey first played for Ron Stewart. After 39 games, Stewart was replaced by John Ferguson.

"When I got to the Rangers, I'd been beaten up on coaches and watched those transitions over and over again. I don't want to say anything bad about anyone but with Ron Stewart, I had to prove my way, either way as the toughest tests usually come from your teammates. So getting acclimated to the Ranger locker room and kind of proving yourself and becoming one of the guys, it was not easy. In my first year, we go to California and Rod Gilbert, a friend, not a brother yet, but we're roommates together and the phone rings at five in the morning and it's the day they traded for [Phil] Esposito and his good friends, Jean Ratelle and Brad Park get traded to Boston. I'm sitting there and he runs down to the lobby and I came down about an hour later and everybody's crying. I'm going like, Hmm, seems like an opportunity to me, because I'd been through this before with the Frank Mahovliches and the Paul Hendersons and their careers and other guys that I played with, it's a tough business. Emile Francis kinda cleaned house a year before, 'cause my understanding was the Islanders beat the Rangers in the playoffs in the first round the year before. I understand these guys are all brothers and I'm a stranger. You had to be accepted by your teammates, let alone be accepted by the league and earn your stripes and earn your time and space that was there. So it was a little bit more difficult in those days as far as WHA guys. A lot of the stars in the NHL left for money and the perception was that we got paid well in the WHA to go there first. I think Emile Francis caught on to that and he started to pay and re-signed Tkaczuk and all kinds of guys, sort of that level of money. I was comfortable because I had Punch Imlach sort of behind the scenes letting me know what was proper and what was not. I would never ask for anything more than I deserve but they paid well, now it's on me, now I have to 'earn it,' so everybody was crying. There was a cleansing of it, there was other things going on I guess because by January, John Ferguson came in. I just thought it was just a great opportunity to you know, 'pitter-patter' as they call it now, they didn't call it back then. It's a rebuild. Smarter guys than me can see this, but I better get off my ass and I better play well and better contribute where I can, on the ice, off the ice, so I took it as an advantage. I thank Ron Stewart for making it tough for me but he made it tough in a negative way and I could figure that out but John Ferguson was the toughest guy I ever had because you always hurt the one you love. I think he loved me and it was more in a positive way. Whatever comment he had for me, like, 'Take off that helmet,' or 'Tie up your laces tighter,' I just wanted to do it. I wanted to shove it right down his throat, but that's how you succeed. So John Ferguson was one of the best coaches for me at a time in my career to earn acceptability and become a real player and become a pro. He was the first guy that really made it tough on me."

FIRST WHA COACH: Billy Harris, Toronto Toros

"They signed me to a contract, I'm here at camp, I'm going to play on the power play the first game, right? Well, it was 22 games in, and I went to him after about 12 games and I said, 'Like, what's going on here. I'm working my butt off, I'm trying to prove to you.' He says, 'You've proved to me, but you don't see those 20 guys out there. They also proved it to me last year in the playoffs,' because the Toros had a good playoff. They were in Ottawa actually, the Ottawa Nationals, they moved to Toronto. Then he says, 'I have to show them the loyalty back. You have to earn your spot and be better than them.' So it was about 22 games into the season. We're playing the Houston Aeros with Gordie Howe and his son, Marty. It was the first night that I played on a regular line that we practiced two days before and I played the whole game, I scored four goals. I was pretty tickled. Everybody come up and pat me on the back, the press and the whole bit but all I wanted was for Billy Harris, the coach, to come in and I wanted to know what he had to say. He walked up to me, he stuck out his hand, we were getting on a plane to Chicago to play the Chicago Cougars, like right after the game. This was a Saturday night we played there. He stuck out his hand, he said, 'Good game, I expect the same thing from you tomorrow.' Yeah, I'm going to do that again tomorrow. Well, I had my five minutes of fame and joy and everything else, but the coach just laid it on me. You see how that was kind of a teaching moment. There was no kind of teaching moments with John Ferguson but they're all teaching moments. He just made a better player and a better man."

FIRST RANGERS CAPTAIN: Brad Park (who was traded during Hickey's first season) and Phil Esposito

"There was the type of camaraderie that they had like Brad Park, Walter Tkaczuk, Billy Fairbairn, I can go on and on. They made sure that you had someone to go out to dinner with them, someone to have a beer with them, someone to chat hockey and that kind of stuff, but [the Park trade happened] so quickly. I think it was November 7, that's the big trade. The big trade happened. We're in the West Coast and then when we came back, I can't remember exactly, but Phil joined us right away. There was a game or two on that road trip that he played, yeah, there was a lot of sunglasses going on in the eyes 'cause like Neil Young said, 'A man's a man who looks at a man right between the eyes.' There was a lot of not looking a man right between the eyes going on at the end of that road trip. I remember the first practice we had back then. It was like the guys wanted to get to practice early. There's the stretching and all that was sort of coming down the pike. We always went out early and fooled around and the coach came on the ice and then you're in the drills and everything else. Everybody, by then, was sort of tired after practice because you worked hard. We're walking off the ice and there's Phil out there with a bucket of pucks in a slot and he's doing some sort of a drill all by himself. I kind of went into the locker room and guys are trash talking or whatever and I said, 'Screw this,' and I turned around and went back out. I joined in with Phil and just became his buddy and started working on these little drills. I asked him, like I used to ask Frank Mahovlich and Paul Henderson, I'm like, 'What the hell are you doing? Teach me something, I'm listening,' right, and we had quite a little relationship going.

"Then, the next day, by the time guys showered and were leaving the building, Phil and I were still out there doing some little drill, catching passes, playing catch with whatever we were doing. The next practice, all of a sudden, Mike McEwen joined me, [Dave] Maloney joined me and so Phil had three guys out there working with him. The next day, was ten guys and that's what I remember. Phil had great leadership skills and he drew you in and he always had something to say. So I sat on a plane with him, my first exhibition game, we flew into Sudbury, Ontario. He didn't like to fly. He was sweating and his hands were tight on the armrest, but as our conversation went on, he said, 'Patty boy, do something for me.' He said, 'Do what I say, don't do what I do.' He was bit of a nut and a practical joker, but he gave me really good advice and it was kind of the same thing. Phil kind of said the same thing. He said, basically, 'Listen to what I have to say. Do what I say and don't do what I do.' Phil was a little bit affluent and arrogant and we were all just building ourselves, becoming the pros that he wanted us to be we were destined to be. He was a good leader. I mean [Jean] Ratelle and Park and these guys, I would've loved to spend six years with them too, but it wasn't to be and that's what we had. Four years later, we kinda went to the dance and the Stanley Cup Final, so it was all good."

FIRST RANGERS POINT: October 8, 1975 @ Madison Square Garden vs. Chicago Black Hawks, 2–2 tie.

Hickey assisted on Billy Fairbairn's goal in the second period on Opening Night and was the first Ranger goal of the season.

"The Fairbairn assist, it's consistent with the way I wanted to play. I wanted to give it all in the first period because after that, adrenaline drives you for the rest. It's like getting in a fight in the third period after the game got [out of hand] I think it was John Ferguson that said, 'That was a great playtime or that was a great aggressive forecheck, Pat, why the heck don't you do that in the first period.' You know what I mean. We're down 5–2 and now you decide to play really good, so I always took those types of things and tried to incorporate them. It's not easy to do. You can't do it every game, but if you go in there like the first shift of the game, I'm just going to turn it on and then take it from zero to sixty when everyone else is just doing zero to 30 to warm up."

FIRST RANGERS FIGHT:

During his rookie season, Hickey fought Chicago Black Hawks defenseman Keith Magnuson. The fight took place on the first shift, just 12 seconds into the game.

"John [Ferguson] probably said something to me that really upset me, but he'd already trained me, like if you're going to do something, do it in the first period, so I did. There is many, many times when people in that day and age. It would come out of your mouth, the code was like, 'Do you wanna go?' My dad taught me long time ago, like in junior hockey in Canada, you either learn how to play, you learn how to protect yourself, learn how to instigate or you go home. So, the NHL it wasn't, it wasn't scary or a surprise or anything. It was just the way it was. Yeah, Magnuson and I had some history. I was going to be checking for 60 minutes on him. So why don't we get squared like right away. My dad always taught me, the guy that wins the fight is always the guy that throws the first one. So you, either, better throw the first one of you better keep eyes in the back of your head because someone else is going to throw the first one and after the first one, just learn how to run really quick.

"Nobody has really never wanted to fight, but it was understood sooner or later, you're going to do it. I remember I was playing with Walter Tkaczuk and Billy Fairbairn and this is like learning to become a pro. Bobby Clarke was who Walter always played against and he had the scorers on his line. Usually a [Dave] Schultz, [Don] Saleski or [Bob] Kelly, whatever. So probably Clarke's giving me, the rookie, you know, stick between the legs. The slash on the thigh pad, the poke from behind and this was only 12 games into the season. We go into the locker room and I always was a guy that stripped down and I sweated a lot and Walter followed me into the washroom and he grabbed me. He almost picked me up in the air and he says, 'What the hell are you doing with Clarke?' I said, 'What am I supposed to do? Fight him?' He says, 'No, you whack them back and then you drop your gloves and you turn around and you fight Schultz, Saleski, or Kelly. I said, 'Okay, I got it.' We go to the second period and I see Walter just get thrown out. I go in, Bobby "The Pitchfork' and I turn around and drop my gloves. I shouldn't say the name but one of them comes and I said, 'Do you want to go?' and he said, 'Don't you touch Bobby Clarke ever again.' I said, 'You want to go?' 'I'm telling you, don't touch him again,' and he skated away and I went, 'Holy shit, I won that fight.'

"It's not just Philly. Philly has the reputation, but those are the things that you learn in junior hockey in there along the way. People don't really want to fight and especially, they don't want to fight the guy that wants to fight. So you have to stand up for yourself. If they know that you're going to go, I think I'll take a pass, let's do it later, but you're not going to intimidate me or the teammates, but sooner or later, it's kind of like brotherly love. I remember Mario Tremblay. Every time we play against [Montreal], it just happened like three, five, six years. We just lined up together. I had some pretty good tussles with my brother [Greg] too. If you whack me twice, the first time I might let it go. Second time, we're going to go or we're going to even it up. They just become wrestling matches and premeditated stuff. I always said there's rough and there's tough. Rough has premeditated, tough is a well conditioned athlete that can give it and take it."

FIRST RANGERS HAT TRICK: February 23, 1978 @ Madison Square Garden vs. Chicago Black Hawks, 6–2 win.

During the first of a home-and-home series against Chicago, Hickey had his nose broken by Black Hawks defenseman Keith Magnuson. The following night at the Garden, Hickey got some payback by scoring a hat trick to lead the Rangers to a win.

"Kind of what Johnny Ferguson taught me. Take your lumps, shove it down my throat, so I took my lumps and I guess I shoved it down their throat the best way that I knew how. I played well and scored three. I play a lot of games where I thought maybe three pucks of going to the net also for good plays by my teammates, but if you're telling me that's what happened following like someone smashing my nose then that's probably the mentality that I had at the time as I just shove it down their throat, shove it down their teams' throat. I already did my business with Magnuson. You do things that you gotta do at the time. I just hope that was Magnuson on the ice for all three goals.

FIRST TIME PLAYING WITH HIS BROTHER AS A TEAMMATE ON THE RANGERS: April 8, 1978 @ Nassau Coliseum vs. New York Islanders, 7–2 loss.

Pat's brother Greg played one NHL game in his career.

"That was like a dream come true. Jean-Guy Talbot was coaching, "The Sweatsuit," and it was like the 80th game of the year or the 78th game of the year, something like that. Greg is a very personable guy. He'd been around training camps and things. The guys knew him. I think he ended up playing on a line with Walter Tkaczuk and I want to say, Steve Vickers, but I don't know. They were checking [Bryan] Trottier, [Mike] Bossy, and [Clark] Gillies. So I remember Jean-Guy came up to my brother well in advance before the warmup. We went out and again, just before the game [Talbot says] 'Greg, your job is Bossy. You watch that Bossy, that Bossy guy doesn't score,' and he goes, 'You got Bossy.' Then, Jean-Guy walked out of the room. I think Walter was first and he walked over to Greg and said something. I don't know what it was, but I gave Greg the fingers, 'Let's go to the can,' and I said, 'The way you watch Bossy is like skate, he'll chase you, get the puck ahead and forget that bullshit and just go play your game. I think Greg went out and did it.

"I watched my brother, he was there, I trusted he knew what to do. He could whatever he wants to do with my advice. When the game started, I never really had too much on my plate at the time 'cause I was emerging, I think, that time as one of the leaders. I think the game was important to us at the time, for playoff positioning or whatever, so I don't really remember about him, how he played or anything, or how the game turned out but I know he minimized Bossy and we had a good game. It was a fun time and even my brother tells the better story of his idol growing up was Stan Mikita and we came back the next night to play at Madison Square Garden. You know how you're warming up and you're circling and both teams are going in opposite directions. He [Greg] timed it, to meet at center ice and Mikita came by and they had some sort of conversation like, 'Hi Stan,' and then, the next time around, 'I'm going to be watching you tonight,' and Stan said something to him. We got back in the locker room and that was the highlight of my brother's career and Jean-Guy pulled him from the lineup. He didn't play, he was so disappointed."

FIRST TIME SCORING 40 GOALS: April 9, 1978 @ Madison Square Garden vs. Chicago Black Hawks, 3–2 win.

Pat Hickey's 40th goal in the third period proved to be the game-winner.

"I think the assist came from [Ron] Greschner, so it was kind of like a well-rehearsed goal that I scored. My father was there. I remember dancing for the puck and skating over and throwing it behind our bench to my dad. I remember sitting on the bench, catching my breath and then looking up to that long scoreboard at the Garden there. Then, it said, 'Pat Hickey, 40th goal, assisted by Greschner.' I just remember turning around, 'cause my dad was four rows up, just turning around to my dad and kind of had the puck in his teeth. I just looked at him and he winked at me and I winked at him. It was sort of a point of accomplishment and a relief and celebration. Yeah, it was a really good night."

FIRST GAME AGAINST THE RANGERS AS AN OPPONENT AFTER BEING TRADED: November 3, 1979 @ Colorado Rockies, 7–2 Rangers loss.

Hickey was dealt to the Colorado Rockies on November 2, 1979, as part of a five-player trade that brought Barry Beck to the Rangers. The very next day, he played against his former team and scored two goals while adding an assist for a three-point night.

"I'd met my wife at the time and I'd spent like four or five, high level, high tension years in New York. I think I became a pro. I started thinking about what's this all about and what do I want to do? It's the future and that's when, I was kinda like, I'm going to marry this girl. I'm going to maintain the level of my career and this got thrown at me. I just thought, *Well, this is what it's all about.* That game that we played, I scored two goals and my perception of the Rockies was always that they weren't in contention and maybe I can just continue on down this path and make the playoffs. We had a good coach there in [Don] Cherry, the franchise was stable. Cherry, I knew him from Boston and other areas. He was the kind of guy, maybe going backwards a little bit like John Ferguson had a style, Cherry's was similar. I learned it wasn't all that consistent with the younger guys type of thing. Don was a guy you loved to love and you loved to hate. That's just the reality and everybody has their own opinion. I got shipped out of there rather quickly for whatever reasons. I think I found out later that Punch Imlach made the trade (seven weeks later, Hickey was traded to Toronto) for me."

FIRST GAME BACK AT MADISON SQUARE GARDEN AS AN OPPONENT: February 17, 1980. Rangers lost, 6–4.

"Well, most of all I remember the reception I got from the Zamboni drivers. They had an office down there by the visitor's room. I don't know if too many people know that the bus comes in and they always have to come up the ramp there and they have to walk right by the Zamboni driver's office there. There was a little office where they had the coffee machine in the morning and I always strategically sat in there and had my game chat with them as they had a nice coffee for me with the door open. I'd sit there as the visiting team walked by and all of that was about basically stating that this is my building and this is our game tonight and keep your head up. When I came back with Toronto, I was very comfortable and that's where I went. That's representative of the fans there. The recollection of the game but as a professional athlete, you can't live in the past and you got to get over it but when you get a chance to shove it down their throat the best you can."

FIRST REACTION TO BEING TRADED BACK TO THE RANGERS:

In October 1981, Hickey was traded from Toronto back to the Rangers. Hickey played one game for the Maple Leafs that season before he returned to New York.

"Painful. Craig Patrick and I had a great relationship and I think it was the right move, but I didn't think it ever could happen again but what I walked into was a fellow named Herb Brooks. He had the reputation, he was progressive and we all did it. Things were changing then, right? Diet and exercise and knowing the body and the whole bit. I'm pretty well read and he [was] coming off the 1980 Olympics, the miracle and the whole bit. He had a very strategic plan for training camp and conditioning. I'm not sure what the date was but I just remember when he said, "You didn't go through my camp. You're going to have to prove to me. So, we'll see you on Monday at 10 o'clock and we'll go through a routine. It all comes to bear later. It was in the movie, right? When they send the team down, down and back and stops and starts. He said, 'It'd be about 45 minutes and I'm going to make you puke.' You know what, I would say, 'I'm not going to puke. I'm going to shove it down your throat like, let's go.' So he started blowing the whistle. We had a little technical practice before, for like about 30 minutes, 45 minutes. He put me through the pace, but I'm not going to puke. Back and forth and back and forth and back and forth. We talked a little bit through it, I was breathing out of my butt for sure. Finally, whatever it was, I accomplished it in 45 minutes. He said, 'Okay, thank you very much, you're done,' and I skated straight through to the locker room, straight through. All the guys were waiting to see and straight back to the can and puke my guts out, but I didn't do it in front of him."

Hitch won the race but lost the race against Rod Gilbert.
(Public Domain)

26
DARIUS KASPARAITIS

Defenseman Darius Kasparaitis began his 14-year NHL career with the New York Islanders and finished it with the New York Rangers. The Lithuanian-born Kasparaitis was known for his physical, aggressive style. Kasparaitis is credited with creating the postgame salute after a Rangers win. The entire team goes to center ice and raises their sticks to salute the crowd. Kasparaitis played four seasons with the Rangers. In 2016, Kasparaitis was inducted into the Russian Hockey Hall of Fame.

FIRST EXPOSURE TO NHL:

"I wasn't exposed to the NHL until the late '80s. Soviet team [was] going to play a series against NHL teams so I started watching more and get to know the players more at the time. Basically, I didn't really get too deep into the NHL until I was drafted in 1992. I didn't really follow the NHL at all because the games were not televised at that time, so we had no opportunity or chance to watch on TV except when the Russian teams travel to Canada or the States to play against NHL teams.

FIRST HOCKEY IDOL:

"I grew up during an era when Slava Fetisov and his generation were playing so good so I basically idolized them. Guys like Valeri Vasiliev [Russian defenseman]. As a kid, whoever was hot at that time, I tried to pretend I was them. As a kid, you don't really watch the game. The winning, that's what made them very appealing. I remember anytime you watch USSR play, I don't think they ever lost a game since I watched them. It was easy to root for them. I was living in the Soviet Union, so they were the one team I knew."

FIRST CONTACT WITH NHL:

Darius Kasparaitis was chosen fifth overall by the New York Islanders in the 1992 NHL Entry Draft.

"It was very cool to actually go to the draft. I felt a little off because I felt old [he was about to turn 20]. I guess that was a '73 born draft. I was born in '72 and a year before, nobody drafted me, so I was kind of feeling left out and I really didn't expect to go that high. I had no expectations because I didn't really know how big the draft was. Now I realize how big it is to be drafted fifth overall. I got drafted; I didn't speak English at that time. I got the jersey and a hat and then just hung out with my guys who traveled from Russia. I remember I traveled the first time without the team, you know abroad without anybody checking on me. My ticket back home, I threw it in the garbage and when I was as at the airport flying back, they asked me, 'Where's your ticket?' I said, 'I don't have it, I threw it away,' so I have to buy a new ticket because those days we actually had a paper ticket. I didn't realize I had to save it. It was a round-trip ticket so I didn't realize I had to save it. That's the biggest memory I have of the draft."

FIRST CONTRACT WITH RANGERS:

Kasparaitis signed a free agent contract with the Rangers in July 2002.

"I always wanted to go back to New York. I played for the Islanders so I loved being in New York. I remember I was driving on Long Island to go see Alexei Yashin. My agent called me and told me how much the Rangers offered. I had some kind of ballpark [figure] but once I heard the numbers, I told my agent it's too much money, I don't think I deserved that. He told me, 'Are you crazy, just stop at Alexei's house and sign a contract.' I didn't really think about other options. Toronto and Boston had the same numbers, but I chose New York because I always wanted to play at Madison Square Garden. I knew the Rangers from being an Islander, how cool it is to play there so it was kind of, not a dream come true, but I always felt like I'd be a Ranger one day."

FIRST RANGERS COACH: Bryan Trottier

"I feel bad for Trots because he didn't have much time to have any success. We had a good team, but I think we had a lot of superstars and I don't think it clicked right away. We had some major injuries on our team, and I think Bryan had no chance. I still have a relationship with Bryan. I respect him as a person; it wasn't good as a coach. Maybe expectations were very high, I don't think he had much time to prove it. He reminded me of Al Arbour, he loved taking guys' weights all the time. How much they weigh and things like that. Trots didn't care how you play, he was worried more are you in game shape and, you know, preparing yourself for the game. I deeply respected him. Sometimes he would get mad at you and sometimes he had a good talk with you, let you feel you belong here and that he wants you to do good."

FIRST RANGERS CAPTAIN: Mark Messier

"Mark was their voice. He was not really emotional because he was at the end of his career when I got there. He was a true leader. He always spoke as we needed him to speak. He organized events and he was very involved. Even in his leadership role, he was just very humble. A cool individual. I had a lot of captains in my career and most of them are like Mark. Mario Lemieux was the same. He was a really screaming captain, but he did things by example and Mess was the same way."

FIRST RANGERS TRAINING CAMP:

"We moved to a new facility in Tarrytown. I guess it was one of the NHL practice facilities with a beautiful setup in the locker room. All the other things that comes with the locker rooms, you know, medical staff and I think this was one of the new ones in the NHL. I felt very special to be a part of the organization. I still had a couple of preseason, not games, but practices in Rye, so I realized how advanced the Tarrytown facility was, so it was cool. I also realized how important it is to be a Ranger."

FIRST RANGERS GAME: October 9, 2002 @ Carolina Hurricanes, 4–1 win

"When you play the game, you just go and try to be the best. It's a new team and it didn't feel as weird as [if] I played, for example, the Islanders. I knew how much the Islanders hate the Rangers and I played for Pittsburgh; it was different too. Carolina was fine, but I wasn't really nervous and played against Pittsburgh and Rangers and Islanders because I knew when I was [an] Islander or a Penguin, I hated the Rangers. No matter how big you play for the team, if you step on another side, you know they really didn't like you. I think that I understood that I had played for the Islanders, I lost a lot because I signed with the Rangers. I knew how much they loved me in Long Island, but now, every time I go back there, I don't really feel they have some kind of grudge against me that I played for the Rangers. I've seen some people even telling me, 'I wish you never played for the Rangers, I would love you more.'"

FIRST RANGERS HOME GAME: October 11, 2002 vs. Montreal Canadiens, 4–1 loss.

"We played a preseason game there but playing a regular-season game and the support we had. It wasn't still the old Garden [before renovation] but you know the smell, the beer and that stuff when you go into the Garden, it was different, but it was cool playing there."

FIRST RANGERS GOAL: December 28, 2002 Florida

Panthers, 2–1 OT win.

Kasparaitis's first Rangers goal was a game-winner in overtime.

"You know why I remember that? Because my daughter was there, sitting in the stands. She lived in Florida and she came to watch me play. I remember scoring the goal. I remembered that because she was so excited. Not only 'cause I scored a goal, I scored it in front of my daughter."

FIRST TIME FOR THE STICK RAISING TRADITION: November 26, 2005 @ Madison Square Garden vs. Washington Capitals, 3–2 15-round shootout win. (At the time, longest shootout in NHL history)

"It was a game against the Washington Capitals when we had the longest shootout and Marek Malik scored the beautiful goal. I was the next guy, last guy on the bench. I remember [coach] Tom Renney, he looked at us and Marek Malik, he didn't want to do anything with that. I told Tom, 'Let me go.' I remember Tom Renney telling me, 'I'd rather go before you go,' and he put Marek on. When he scored a goal, I was so relieved that the pressure was off. I skated to Jaromir Jagr, I said, 'Jags, let's go ask all the guys to go come in the middle of the ice and we raise the sticks to thank the fans for basically supporting us because there was the lockout [the previous season]. We did similar things in Europe, so I told the guys, let's go in the circle and just raise the sticks. A lot of guys were looking skeptical at me, like I was crazy, but we did it and the people went crazy. We started doing it after every home win, now it's cool to see that it's still going on and a lot of other teams started using it."

FIRST OLYMPIC EXPERIENCE:

At the 1992 Winter Olympic games in Albertville, France, Kasparaitis won gold as a member of the Unified Team (composed of players from six of the fifteen former Soviet republics).

"I was not invited to the training camp after my world juniors. I was very upset because we won the gold medal for the juniors and I was the best defenseman in the tournament. Then I was invited to training camp before the Olympics, but after a couple of days, they told me to come. I just tried to make the team and when I made the team, I was so shocked that I'm gonna go and play in the Olympics. I'll be participating in Olympic games. We had no expectations, we had a young team, except a couple of guys, some were from the former Red Army machine years. Winning the gold was unbelievable. I remember the last three seconds and knowing that you're going to be Olympic gold, Olympic champion, you're gonna have this the rest of your life. It's just a dream come true for any athlete I think, even if we didn't have a country."

Legendary Russian defenseman Viktor Tikhonov was the Unified Team's coach.

"I watched Tikhonov since I was a kid. I knew he was tough and a very successful coach. He was expecting us to win because I felt the atmosphere was so relaxed on that team. We had a lot of guys that were young and non-experienced. I have only good memories about him."

FIRST GOLD IN THE IIHF WORLD CHAMPIONSHIPS:

At the age of 46, Kasparaitis was a member of the Lithuanian team that won the gold medal in the International Ice Hockey Federation World Championships.

"When I retired from hockey, was in 2009, it was because of the injuries. I always had this unfinished business, deep down in my soul. What happened. I started thinking, maybe I should represent Lithuania in one of the tournaments. Eventually, when I knew my biological clock was ticking, so I realized that I thought there's going to be five years and I can play. I didn't realize I have to play for Lithuania for four years. The last time I played for Russia was 2006, so I thought maybe 2011, I can play for Lithuania, but I was realized that was not an option. So I used to fly every year for like a week to Lithuania and play two, three games for 'Hockey Punk' to get qualification to represent Lithuania. In November, there was a friendly tournament of four nations. I said, 'Listen, let me go before you even make the decision if I want to play for Lithuania to see where I'm at now.' I played three games in November 2017 and I felt pretty good, so I said, 'Let's just do this.' When I was playing for Lithuania, the tournament was in Lithuania so it was very cool. I wished that I was 15 years younger and people would see the way I played when I was younger. I still felt good, the guys helped me out a lot. I was probably can be [sic] to some guys on my team, but at the same time, they respected me and helped me a lot.

"I'm very grateful that we won the tournament and I ended up winning the gold. Even better, it was like a good book story. I'm not who I am as I was playing in the NHL because I didn't have that, not mean, I didn't really feel hungry and that's why I didn't want to play again this year because I didn't feel hungry and I felt bad. I wanted to go home with my kids, and I didn't miss being nervous and not knowing what's going to happen before the game. I have to go to sleep, I have to prepare myself, I hated that feeling. I did what I did. I still think sometimes, like even today, I say, 'Maybe I should play a game,' but always bring back the memories and how I felt, how old I felt being on the bench. I felt like I should just stay home and be a dad."

27
MIKE KEENAN

Mike Keenan coached eight different teams over a 20-year career in the NHL, but he is mostly known for being behind the bench when the Rangers won their first Stanley Cup in 54 years in 1994. Keenan's Rangers won the President's Cup with 52 wins and 112 points in 1994. In 20 years, Keenan recorded 672 wins and a .551 career winning percentage.

FIRST COACHING JOB: Forest Hill Collegiate Institute, Toronto, Ontario, Canada

"I was a teacher at the high school and I was teaching history and Phys Ed. It's unlike the American system, it's completely voluntary, so I guess I was the obvious choice. I played junior hockey, played university hockey, played minor league pro hockey so when I accepted the job there, the principal asked me if I would coach the hockey team and I said, 'Of course I will.' Everyone that coached was a teacher at the school as well. I coached a few sports at Forest Hill. I coached the women's swim team and I coached the hockey team and I coached some of the basketball teams."

FIRST CONTACT WITH THE RANGERS:

"Rob Campbell was my agent and friend. I'm not sure who

contacted him first, whether it was Neil [Smith] or Bob Gutkowski [MSG president] or Stanley Jaffe [chief executive of Paramount, who was then running the Garden] or maybe John Davidson. I don't know who reached out to Rob. Of course, Rob contacted me and said there's some interest from the Rangers. I do remember that Bob Gutkowski and Neil Smith flew to Toronto to Rob's office and met us there to recruit me and then possibly negotiate a contract with Rob. So that's the genesis of how that transpired."

FIRST RANGERS PRESS CONFERENCE:

It was a hurried situation because I was on my way to Munich, Germany, to coach Team Canada and [former Rangers coach] Roger [Neilson] and I had recruited a number of players. I had been dismissed by the Blackhawks and Roger had been dismissed by the Rangers. Our affiliation went back to Peterborough, then Buffalo. Scotty Bowman was the first general manager in the league to hire me to coach [in] the American League [AHL] and Roger was an associate coach and I knew Roger from Peterborough, so they both recruited me to go to Rochester.

"I flew to New York and did the press conference. I believe we went on a private jet from Toronto with Bob Gutkowski, Neil Smith, and Rob Campbell. Then it was a hurried thing and I had several interviews and I actually ended up getting a bad neck infection because I was so rushed, I forgot to get the make up removed. I don't know enough about it, women know more about it, but if you're not careful, you get bacteria in that make up and then it can be a problem. That's exactly what happened to me on my flight over to Germany. I started to feel my neck was swelling and that's exactly what happened.

"The other thing I remember is they presented me with a beautiful leather jacket, and I took it off to be photographed with my suit on. I turned around and the jacket was gone. I never saw it again."

FIRST MEETING AS RANGERS HEAD COACH:

"It was in Rye, New York, and I assembled the group and spoke to them and I can remember what an impact that particular time was. That particular meeting was for Mark Messier, when I showed them, I think it's become pretty public, the [1986 New York Mets championship] baseball parade. Unfortunately, I can't show you a hockey parade because they haven't won, but this is what you can expect from the New York fan and what they'll give you as a winner."

FIRST RANGERS CAPTAIN: Mark Messier

"I coached him on Team Canada. He was an assistant captain on that particular team, but a real strong leader. Wayne [Gretzky] was the captain in 1987 when we beat the Soviet Union; it was the last Canadian team to play against the Soviet Union, which then became Russia. So that was a very eventful, historical series in the history of Canadian hockey. In 1991, Mark played for me again [for] Team Canada, so I knew of him well. Our series with the Chicago Blackhawks and Edmonton Oilers, I believe is also 1991, where Mark had a huge impact. So I was very familiar with Mark, coached him twice, saw him at his best against us, coaching, first of all Philadelphia and Chicago. I knew what a presence he was in the locker room with Team Canada, both on and off the ice, so I already built a bond with Mark before he even arrived in New York."

FIRST RANGERS STANLEY CUP FINAL GAME BEHIND THE BENCH: May 31, 1994 @ MSG vs. Vancouver Canucks, Game 1, 3–2 overtime loss

"We had set ourselves a goal that we would aspire to be in the Finals, to win the Cup, and when you come to that realization, when you win the series against New Jersey, you say yeah, now we're going to the Finals. I can recall that both times in Philadelphia and Chicago. You look at the out of town scoreboard and there is no out of town scoreboard. When you get to that point, it's a very significant impression because of the attention that's paid to your team, the series and the hockey world in general is watching and everybody can feel it, sense it, knows it. I think that's part of what that first game and any Final, and particularly in New York meant we had aspired, we won the President's Trophy, now we're in the Finals. We still had an opportunity to seek the goal that we were looking for from day one."

FIRST REACTION TO WINNING THE CUP:

"I was very, very surprised though because it hadn't happened before where the captain came over and gave the coach the trophy and Mark was approaching me. I don't know if it's too strong a word, shock or surprise, but he kept coming and then I realized he was coming to me. So that was an incredible, powerful experience, and then when I lifted it over my head, I know that the Garden exploded, like the roof was going to be blown off the building. So that was a very powerful moment. When I did lift it up, I said, this thing is so difficult to win, it was my ninth year coaching and I already had been to the Finals four times and I said, it's very, very difficult trophy to win."

Mike Keenan and Neil Smith at reunion of '94 team.
(Photo by Mark Rosenman)

28
TOM LAIDLAW

Defenseman Tom Laidlaw spent parts of seven seasons with the Rangers. In 1980–81, his rookie season, Laidlaw had six goals. 23 assists, and 29 points, which would all stand as career highs. The Ontario native was traded to the Los Angeles Kings in March 1987. After his playing career was over, Laidlaw became a player agent.

FIRST CONTACT WITH NHL:

Tom Laidlaw was chosen by the Rangers in the sixth round of the 1978 NHL Amateur Draft.

"It was 1978 that I was drafted. Nobody talked about the draft; you didn't get invited to the draft. There's nobody coming to you before, at least, to me anyways, to actually and do interviews or anything like that. On draft day, I was really unaware that there was even a draft going on. I was working on a friend's horse farm and I was cleaning out the stalls, I was cleaning the shit out of the stalls and my father got a call and we didn't even know who it was from the Rangers who called him. They called our farmhouse and some gentlemen told my father that I had been drafted in the sixth round by the New York Rangers. Then, my father called the farm where I was working and they take me up to the house and I got on the phone and my father said, 'You've been drafted by the New York Rangers in the sixth round,' and I said to him, 'Well, what do I do know?' and he said, 'Get back out there and finish putting the shit out of the stalls.'"

FIRST TIME PUTTING ON THE RANGERS JERSEY:
Spring 1980

Laidlaw was playing at Northern Michigan before joining the Rangers.

"They were gonna bring me in and have me go to New Haven to play in the playoffs, but they had me come to New York to sign my contract and it was game day. There was a transit strike going on, so it took me [what] seemed like two hours to get from LaGuardia to Madison Square Garden. I was like, I'd grown up on a farm in Canada, smallest university town, Michigan, so coming to New York was pretty overwhelming. I remember walking across 7th Avenue and I get my skates, dropping them on the street and all that kind of stuff, carrying my bags then I go into the Garden.

"Phil Esposito was still playing. His jersey was hanging up in the locker room. In the afternoon, I was in the locker room all by myself, trainers [are] there and Phil walked in and I'll never forget, because, you know growing up in Canada, going back to the '72 Series against the Russians, you know Phil was a god. I knew he was on the Rangers but I didn't know how I would get to meet him, wherever. He walked in the room and he starts whispering to the trainers. He was asking like who the heck is that guy? The trainers were saying nice things about me, whatever. I remember Phil walking over to me and it was the most amazing thing. All your life, you're dreaming of playing in the NHL, now you're in a NHL locker room and one of the most iconic players that's ever played the game was walking over to you and you think to yourself, you just couldn't believe it was happening. He was so nice, obviously he didn't know me, he had never seen me play but they [trainers] had told him who I was. He walked over to me and said, 'Tom, I've heard great things about ya, glad to have you on board and I look forward to playing with ya' and I just about could've died and gone to heaven right then, it was incredible what Phil said. So that was the first time, my interaction. They sent me down to New Haven and even though it was New Haven, to put the jersey on for the first time, a pro jersey with your name on it, pretty special. That whole couple of days there, your head is spinning because it's finally happening, your dream is finally coming true."

FIRST RANGERS TRAINING CAMP: Prior to 1980–81 season

"I remember coming in and doing the testing and I really worked hard on my conditioning that year and I was in really good shape so that was a confidence booster for me, knowing that, okay, I am in not just as good shape, but better shape than most of the guys here. That was the days that the old guys would come in totally out of shape and work themselves into shape during training camp, that's kind of the first thing I remember.

"I've gotta tell you the Phil Esposito story. Freddie Shero was coaching, you know I was a big, physical player, that's my game. I had to hit people and we were scrimmaging at Rye Playland. To me, I was going there to make the team, you know those old guys were there to get themselves in shape. I remember we had a scrimmage going on, Phil's carrying the puck through the neutral zone. I played against him and he had his head down. I thought, I mean I've gotta hit Phil, I just didn't think about it too much, I just stepped up and knocked him on his ass. Place went silent and Phil was pissed and he got up and he was swearing at me and everything. I was thinking to myself, what have I done, you know I thought I was doing the right thing but Phil is so mad at me. I'm like 'Jeez, I've ruined my career,' you know, socially knocked him down. Scrimmage gets done and we go into the locker room after and he comes walking over to me. I'm serious, I thought, *Oh God, he's gonna pull out of here, he's gonna send me home.* I know he's not 'Joe Manager' or coach but he's still Phil Esposito and he walked over to me and he says, 'Listen, I was mad that you hit me like that.' 'I said, Sorry, I just came to make the team,' and he said,

'You know what? I respect that a lot. That's exactly what you need to do' and he says, 'I really respect you for doing that,' and I was like, cool. It actually turned out to be a good thing."

FIRST RANGERS COACH: Fred Shero

"The stories were all true. I heard all the stories with the fact that he just hardly talked and he didn't talk on the bench very much. He'd kind of give you a look. I was in a restaurant during training camp and he walked in and I was sitting there by myself and he looked at me and nodded, you know, pleasant but that was it. With Freddie, communication was the big thing. It's like if you're getting played, obviously you must be doing something right. If you're not getting played, it means you're not playing well. I do remember he would come over sometimes during preseason games and he'd stand behind you and not say a word but put his hand on your back.

"I read his book later and I think I remember correctly, he felt he was doing that to, like send a message, that you send to like getting people to calm down or whatever. Like, at first when he would do it, it was like, Oh my god, you're getting cut, you know he'll throw you off the bench or something, but I remember him standing there and feeling like, after a while, okay, I guess I was all right."

FIRST RANGERS GAME: October 9, 1980 @ Boston Bruins, 7–2 loss

"It's Boston Garden, I'm supposed to be the physical player. They've got Terry O'Reilly, John Wensink, Stan Jonathan, Wayne Cashman, and all these guys are still playing. It was the Boston Garden, fans are right on top of ya. If you get kicked out of the game, you've gotta go through the rink past the Boston bench to get to the dressing room, so I remember thinking to myself, Wow, this is the real deal. You played preseason games and all that kind of stuff and this was the real deal."

John Davidson was the Rangers' goaltender in Laidlaw's first game.

"Even though he wasn't the captain, he was the kind of guy that you'd want JD's approval that you were playing well. I had the puck in our zone and I was to the left of JD. I was left defenseman and I was getting pressure, so I'm trying to shoot the puck around the boards to the right side and I shot the puck up JD's leg and into the net. I'll never forget it because it's so long ago, I kinda questioned myself. Did that really happen? I remember JD looking at me through the mask. You want his approval and he's looking me like, 'Shit, what kind of an idiot are you? Like what did you just do?'

"It wasn't like a coachable play. It wasn't like the coach could come to you and say, 'Tom, you shouldn't do that.' Well, no kidding, of course you shouldn't do it, so like nobody talks to you on the bench. So here you are, first game in the National Hockey League, you've just shot the puck into your own net. It's nobody else's fault because I did it but nobody's even talking to you because what are they going to say to you, you shouldn't do it."

FIRST GAME AT MADISON SQUARE GARDEN: October 12, 1980 vs. Pittsburgh Penguins, 6–3 loss

"I tried to explain to people now about Madison Square Garden and I didn't know it at the time, but Ranger fans, just like are die hard Ranger fans and they express themselves so if you're not playing well, they don't mind telling you, they can boo you. But you view it like, especially as a young player, when you don't know what's going on as much, you think, well, they don't like you or whatever. The exact opposite is true. They love the team. They love the players and they want you to do well so if you do something great, they're going to cheer you on. If you don't do something well, they're going to boo you or make comments or anything.

"I just remember that feeling, it's a special building I think, where you really feel that when you're playing. If something doesn't go well, you just feel it in the building. I think more than any other building in the NHL. At the same time, if things are going well, it's like, wow, this is incredible."

FIRST RANGERS GOAL: November 8, 1980 @ Vancouver Canucks, 6-4 loss

"I was in Vancouver and Freddie Shero had put me in front of the net. I think Phil Esposito passed the puck to Barry Beck at the point. Barry shot and I put in the rebound. My parents kinda made a little plaque with a picture of that, so I definitely remember that."

FIRST FIGHT AS A RANGER: December 30, 1980 @ Quebec Nordiques, 6–3 win

"The first one I had in the regular season is against Dale Hunter. I think he grew up in Quebec. He hit me in the cheek too in front of our bench. He was that kind of guy. I think I gave it to him pretty good and everybody, referees were coming in to break it up. So we're right beside each other and he hit me in the cheek. At that point, I couldn't do anything about it. That was Dale Hunter; that was the way he did things."

FIRST RANGERS PLAYOFF GAME: April 8, 1981 @ Los Angeles Kings, Game 1 preliminary round, 3–1 win

"We're ranked 1 through 16 back then and we didn't have that great of a regular season but I remember feeling like we really had a team there, like we were a bunch of team guys. They were really skilled, you know the Triple Crown Line (Dave Taylor, Hall of Famer Marcel Dionne, and Charlie Simmer who was hurt and did not play in the series) and all those guys. I don't think we ever necessarily talked about it but we knew that we could be more physical than them and then Barry Beck knocked [Rick] Chartraw down with one punch, cut him open and it's kinda like, okay, and that was my first playoff game."

At the end of the first period of Game 2, there was a wild brawl between the teams that netted a record 229 penalty minutes.

"At the end of the period, when the brawl happened, you could just tell it really scared 'em a little bit. I remember when one of the guys on LA who wasn't dressed was on the bench and grabbed Eddie [Hospodar] from behind and Nicki Fotiu came down in street clothes, grabbed the guy, and then threw him around a little bit."

FIRST RANGERS PLAYOFF GOAL: April 12, 1981 @ MSG, Game 4 preliminary round, series-clinching 6–3 win

Laidlaw's goal in the third period snapped a 3–3 tie. It was one of two playoff goals he would score for the Rangers.

You Never Forget Your First: A Collection of New York Rangers Firsts

Tom put the puck in the net in his debut but not in a good way.
(Public Domain)

29
BRIAN LEETCH

Brian Leetch is one of the greatest players in Rangers franchise history. The two-time Norris Trophy-winning defenseman played 17 years with the Rangers. In 1994, Leetch became the first American-born winner of the Conn Smythe Trophy as the Rangers won the Stanley Cup for the first time in 54 years. In 2008, Leetch was inducted into the United States Hockey Hall of Fame and in 2009, he was inducted into the Hockey Hall of Fame in Toronto. Leetch's number 2 was retired by the Rangers in 2008.

FIRST HOCKEY GAME ATTENDED AS A KID:

"The first one I can remember wasn't till Hartford and going to the Whalers. We had played the 'Brass Bonanza' [Hartford Whalers theme song] as Pee Wees in our locker room. Going to the first game with my dad and some of the teammates and some of their dads was a lot of fun for us to run around the arena. The song [was] going off and being in a big stadium for the first time, so it was all new. I can't remember who won or who they were playing, but I remember being in the big stadium and being so excited to actually be at an NHL game."

FIRST HOCKEY IDOL:

"I didn't watch a lot of NHL hockey when I was younger. We didn't really get a local channel. We watched 'Peter Puck.' When it was on CBS, we'd see the *Game of the Week*, but it always had different players on. My dad was a Bruins fan, growing up outside of Boston. I remember talking about [Phil] Esposito when I was really young but never seen him play. Just from listening to my dad and listening to the TV. It wasn't until I was really into high school that we started getting the Bruins games and I started watching Ray Bourque. I liked the way he played and never envisioned myself as an NHL player. Just the way he played defense and being able to score on the old Garden from the red line or from just over the red line with a slap shot because of how small the neutral zone was and what a good shot he had. Just the way he could do everything else, played the body, and moved the puck. Later on, it was, obviously, a big thrill to get to meet him at an All-Star Game and get to become friends with him later on."

FIRST CONTACT WITH THE NHL:

Brian Leetch was chosen by the Rangers with the ninth overall pick of the 1986 NHL Entry Draft.

"I guess we were just up there for a couple of days in Montreal and they had a bunch of expected first rounders into the second round, all in one room. It was really the first time you did a few interviews and there were certainly other players, Canadians, that were getting more attention. I do remember a lot of my friends, American guys, we were all together because that was gonna be one of the first times that more than one or two Americans were going to go in the first round, the first round and a half. So, there were others that were up there, and we were able to go through it together, which was nice. Then, just sitting in the stands at the Forum with my parents and watching the different players get up and go down and put their jerseys on and seeing the families' excitement on their faces and just kinda in awe of the whole thing. My parents were very excited, they didn't know what to expect. It was just kind of just people that were dropped into a situation and they had no reference point for nobody we knew had ever gone through this and could tell us anything that was going to happen next. I just remember my dad as we got the Rangers and he looked at me and said, 'Well, you never know, Brian.' They were one of the teams that checked you out for the testing and the off-ice testing and had me out to Rye Playland. So, we're just kind of going through our heads some of the teams I had interviewed for and done some of those written tests that they had then to try and figure out your personality. They didn't do the whole combine like they do now for individual interviews. It was just what teams and scouts in the area wanted to do. We still expected to be somewhere further down, you know, seven or eight, six or even further, so when the Rangers announced my name, it was just kind of shock. I can't tell you what I did after I stood up. I can't tell you if I kissed my parents, I don't remember. I've seen photos of me putting a jersey on, a video of me putting a jersey on, but, honestly, I don't remember sitting up there or standing up there with Craig Patrick and the other management people there. It's just such a blur. It was one of those moments that you don't expect. You don't know how to handle it and it just goes by in just a flash."

FIRST OLYMPIC EXPERIENCE:

Leetch played on the United States Olympic Hockey team in 1988, 1998, and 2002.

"It was great, it was a great experience all the way around. The eight months we traveled together, we were basically like a college team. We had a few guys that were basically just graduating from college and a couple that had been out for a year or so, but basically it was guys that were all 20 years or younger, 21 years or younger. I guess we might add a 22 or 23 year old here and there, but basically we were a college team, traveling around together and we didn't have to go to class and we skated every day. I guess the hardest part was just traveling for all that time, not having, really, a home base. Our white shirts were yellow by the end of that and our clothes, we weren't into washing the clothes like you did when you had one place. So, it was a motley crew sometimes when we pulled into different cities and went to some of the sponsors luncheons. Playing against better competition [was beneficial] playing against some of the NHL teams and training camps there and the NHL training camps. Going over to Europe for free tournament games and then playing in the Olympics and actually being there eight years after watching Lake Placid and learning, over the years, the bigger implications than just us winning a game. The Olympics, you learn about history and politics and what's going on in the world. Nineteen eighty just kept becoming bigger and bigger and eight years later, you're representing your country in North America trying to do the same thing, so it was really special. We had a really good team. We just were young and all our mistakes ended up going against us but a great, great experience. Made a huge jump in my career because of my development, because of the off-ice work we did, the on ice work we did and the quality competition that I played through that whole process."

FIRST TIME PUTTING ON THE RANGERS JERSEY:

"I remember when I was on the bench for the anthem and it actually felt bigger than the USA jersey. I had been wearing the USA jersey for eight months for all the exhibitions and then represent my country before and then world juniors, so I was used to that. For many years, I never thought about being an NHL player. Then, all of a sudden, I'm at Madison Square Garden and the fans there are strictly New York Ranger fans and it's all in house. Our Olympic games for in Canada, we had fans but not the numbers like Canada did. They definitely supported use but it's a different feeling when you move to a smaller area like that and everybody's behind you in a loud arena like MSG. It was something special, the whole thing, and I was so happy to get to that point and get through a couple practices and just get it started. I wanted to just try and get those first few games behind me, but it felt bigger to me than the Olympic games 'cause I was ready for that and I was accustomed to representing my country. It was special."

FIRST RANGERS GAME: February 29, 1988 @ Madison Square Garden vs. St. Louis Blues, 5–2 win.

Leetch had an assist in his first game, which was played just eight days after the 1988 Olympics ended. It was also "Marcel Dionne Night" when the Hall of Famer was honored by the Rangers.

"[I remember] Chris Nilan getting into a fight shortly after the drop of the puck. It was probably his first shift in like three shifts into the game or something and it came right over next to the boards near me and you know, it's just one of those where I laughed to myself and said, 'Boy, I'm in the NHL now. It's no more college, no more Olympics.' It was real men going at it and the crowd was going crazy. I remember some of the blue seats are chanting 'USA' early in the game and after warm-up, which I was kind of embarrassed about, but I was excited. It didn't last too long, but it was amazing. Like, those are really two of the biggest things that stick out about that game. I didn't remember Marcel Dionne Night, I can't really remember the score. I can remember making a pass and getting an assist but that was about it."

FIRST EXPERIENCE OF RANGERS-ISLANDERS RIVALRY: March 2, 1988 @ Madison Square Garden vs. New York Islanders, 3–1 win.

Leetch's first game against the Islanders was his second career game and the only time he faced Hall of Fame defenseman Denis Potvin.

"I remember that one even more than the first one because that was when you could bring signs into the arena. They had banners unfurling from the upper balcony and none of them were positive, obviously. There's all fans down on the glass at warm ups, banging on the glass and yelling at him [Potvin] and I'm like, 'What could this guy has done so bad, you know?' I knew what a great player he was, one of the all-time best players. I've seen him skating around with the Stanley Cups, All-Star and he's going to be a Hall of Famer. I really didn't know the background, specifically about Denis. The chants and everything else and have that be my second game. Actually, there was a play, I think I dropped it to Chris Nilan, and I went to the net and Denny gave me a jab in the back of the leg as I was going. I fell down and smashed into the goalie and into the net, right as the puck was going in. They called it back because they said I knocked the net off, so I remember that. I remember thinking that [it was] Potvin that did that, got me in the back of the leg. I had never seen a building that wound up, that against, liked singling out one player. I certainly became aware later of Ranger-Islander rivalries and Ranger-Philly and whatnot when those games were going on, but this was quite an experience to start."

FIRST RANGERS GOAL: March 24, 1988 @ Madison Square Garden vs. Edmonton Oilers, 6–1 win.

Leetch scored his first NHL goal (which was the game-winner) and had two assists on the power play.

"I remember [Tomas] Sandstrom coming around the net. First, I couldn't believe that I was playing against the Edmonton Oilers. I mean, all those guys that I read about and heard about and I'd watched half of them play in the 'Rendezvous Tournament.' [Wayne] Gretzky, [Mark] Messier, [Jari] Kurri, [Paul] Coffey and all these guys there out on the ice. Just to go into those first shifts, facing off and looking at weighing a face off five feet from me. Just in my head, I can't believe what's going on that Wayne Gretzky's right there. I could go over there and tap them in the pads right now if I wanted to. You know, he's right next to me. I remember Sandstrom coming around on the right side and I'm on the left point. There's a scene there and he puts it right on my tape and I look up and Grant Fuhr is giving me a little bit of the glove side. I still say to this day, it was my best shot that I've taken without a screen or anything where it's just me and the goalie. It went exactly where I tried to shoot it, I mean, we could only put it in the corner, up high, over his glove and it had to be a perfect shot. The puck actually went where I was trying to shoot it and went in. I was surprised that it's coming off my stick and going where I wanted it to. As it was, I just scored my first NHL goal. I just remember I throw my hands up and then it's a blur from there. I only remember that from seeing highlights when they look back on your career or something, but that one was a vivid one and that has not gone away and that will stick with me. I think it was because I just saw a spot to shoot it. It doesn't usually happen. Usually you're off by, you know, anywhere from an inch to 12 inches or more, but it's one line exactly where it has to go and against Grant Fuhr. It was a big deal for me."

FIRST RANGERS COACH: Michel Bergeron

"Yeah, I loved him. I loved his personality. I loved the way he treated me. He gave me responsibility right away. You were telling me, 'cause we need you, like if we're behind and we needed a goal or I wasn't playing as aggressively offensively or I was a little off my game. He had the French-Canadian accent in English and he'd be like [in a French-Canadian accent] 'Brian, we need you now. Wake up, let's go,' and then he encouraged me to rush the puck. Then, a forward had to back up if a defenseman was rushing it. They knew that was a strength in my game the team needed it as part of something they thought they were missing. Norm Maciver was really good at that too. The fact there was the two of us there and being able to add offense from the back side with James Patrick, they really encouraged that. So, for me, it was great. When I made mistakes, they were there to correct me and telling but there was never a way to demean you or to put you in bad spots. There was just a lot of encouragement that went on from him in that role, so I loved that. I was shocked when he was released and he came into the locker room and told us and I was really down. It's the first time I had seen really the business side of the NHL. I hadn't seen anyone traded yet. I hadn't seen anyone fired yet, so it was an eye-opener for me."

FIRST RANGERS CAPTAINS: Ron Greschner and Kelly Kisio

"The Rangers were always a veteran team and I had great guys around me and those two were great. Gresch was a defenseman, was always there to tell me what I was doing right and wrong. I loved listening to their stories. I sat next to Kisio in the locker room for games and he's always encouraging and always wanted to know how the young guys were doing and he was a friend. I don't know how much older he was, but he treated me like just another guy on the team. That's what you kind of realize as you go ahead, that we're all the same, like each guy is a part of the team and same values. They were great leaders and great examples of what it was like to be a captain. Never mind when Mess came obviously."

FIRST NHL AWARD:

Leetch scored 23 goals with 48 assists for 71 points in the 1988–89 season and was named the Calder Trophy winner emblematic of the top rookie in the NHL.

"It just was a nice thing to go through. Tony Granato had a good year that year as well, so we kind of went through our first year together after playing on the Olympic team and then the end of the year. So, you're disappointed when it doesn't end the way you want, so that was fun. We got meet guys like Gretz and other guys at the awards show that we never met before, but it didn't really do anything confidence wise and everything. It's just a nice thing at the end of the season but going through it with Tony was the real enjoyable part. Being able to go to the ceremony with them and his family was great."

FIRST RANGERS PLAYOFF EXPERIENCE: 1989 Patrick Division semifinals vs. Pittsburgh Penguins. Rangers lost in four games.

"It's not one and done. You've got to adjust from game to game and people can kind of single you out in different situations early in the series and how you adjusted as team and how you'd adjust to it as an individual. Every mistake is magnified and as you move along, it becomes more and more important. It was fun. You know those are the ones that are not like mid-January or mid-February. When you're worn down, this is a no-brainer. You've come to the rink, you're excited and you're ready to go."

FIRST RANGERS HAT TRICK: May 22, 1995 @ Philadelphia Flyers, Game 2, Eastern Conference semifinals. Rangers lost, 4–3, in OT.

"We lost 4–3 in overtime so it kind of took all the fun out of it. To be honest, the goals weren't great goals. They're just ones we had to have at the time and the puck found its way in, but we lost that game in overtime. That kind of was one of the ones that we felt we had to have, so it was disappointing."

FIRST NORRIS TROPHY:

In 1991–92, Leetch had 22 goals and 80 assists for 102 points as he won the first of his two Norris Trophies.

Just being able to go to those award ceremonies [was great]. I looked up to Ray [Bourque] and to be able to hang out with him there and be around all those players you see at the All-Star Games. Now, you're kind of in a non-competitive situation where everyone just gets to hang out and really have a night or two just having fun. The ceremony is nerve-wracking because I was never one to really get up there and give a long speech or anything. Part of you doesn't want to get up there, but a lot of you wants to get up there because you want to hear your name called."

FIRST RANGERS STANLEY CUP FINAL GAME: May 31, 1994 @ Madison Square Garden vs. Vancouver Canucks, Game 1 of the Stanley Cup Final. Rangers lost, 3–2, in overtime but won the series in seven games.

"We were a good team and we knew it. We were excited and we

expected to win that game and to play well. We did play well, but [Vancouver goaltender Kirk] McLean played great. The atmosphere in the arena [was electric] for an organization that hadn't won in a while. It was all those tickets had been handed down from family to family and year to year and they hadn't risen to a price where everybody was not able to go anymore. So it was still a very die hard group of fans at that time and they were excited too. They knew we'd had a successful year and we just had a big series against New Jersey and come through, so they were just as excited as we were. It definitely took the wind out of everybody, losing in overtime, but we'd gone through that New Jersey series and there was no panic. So we were really excited for that series to start."

FIRST REACTION TO HOLDING THE STANLEY CUP:

"Kevin Lowe handed it to me. Just every emotion, you've already gone through a ton of them and just the small ten-minute time frame or eight-minute time frame till they actually awarded it to Mark. You've gone through excitement, relief, kind of shock, like it all kind of hits at once. So that's kind of where you're starting to get over all that clash of emotions and just really start to enjoy it. I knew where my friends were sitting so I kinda tried to angle towards them briefly, but I think I was the third guy to get it. I just held it up very shortly. I knew the other guys wanted to do the same thing and were all as important winnin' that as you know, Mark, Kevin. and myself. There were a few pictures taken and gave it right to Gravy [Adam Graves] and went right down the line."

FIRST PARADE DOWN THE CANYON OF HEROES:

"We could hear a roar. It sounded like the subway getting closer and it was actually the fans getting to understanding on the big board and everything, that the procession started and we were near the front of the line so we could hear a wave of noise reverberating off the buildings as we started to go. We realized, pretty soon, that it was people that were excited and how many people were there, the excitement they were expressing as we started. It's still one of those most memorable experiences of any of the benefits of winning the Cup and the different things you get to experience."

FIRST EXPERIENCE OF HAVING HIS NUMBER RETIRED:

The Rangers retired Leetch's No. 2 on January 24, 2008.

"It's a great day, for, I mean, the whole organization. We had a couple of hundred tickets they gave me and we put it together with a friend of mine that passed away on 9/11, and had a bunch of people down from the Boston area that I had met through the Rangers. My night was on a Thursday night and that was a great time. Everybody stuck around 'cause we did a benefit for our buddy that passed away and we all stayed. I got to enjoy that on a more relaxed part of not having to worry about talking and making sure the tickets were all set up and everything was organized. So that was a tremendous weekend, a great honor."

The ride through the Canyon of Heroes was one of Brian's most memorable experiences of winning the Cup. Photo courtesy of Håkan Dahlström.

30
MIKKO LEINONEN

Finnish center Mikko Leinonen played a "baseball season's worth" of games in the National Hockey League. During parts of four seasons, Leinonen played 162 NHL games, 159 of those with the Rangers. In only his second career playoff game, Leinonen set an NHL playoff record (later tied by Wayne Gretzky in 1987) with six assists in one game. Leinonen played three games for the Washington Capitals in his final season of 1984–85.

FIRST HOCKEY IDOL:

"I think it was '74, when I was underage, I was 19 at the time and I met Mel Bridgman and some other drafted players, and I was playing in the World Juniors in Canada. I think that was in Winnipeg, that might've happened in '75. On the way to Winnipeg, I think we were in Minnesota. We saw the game of Boston-Minnesota and Bobby Orr was, at that time, my favorite player. I saw him live and he was a really good player. What I can remember is that there was, I think, one or two biggest fights."

FIRST OLYMPIC EXPERIENCE:

In the 1980 Winter Olympics, Mikko Leinonen played for Finland, the team that lost to the United States team in their final game.

"That was the dream of any athlete to get the chance to represent your country in the Olympics. I was really happy to make the team in '80 and the Olympics were in the states. It was a prison (laughs) where we got in the Olympic village, so we didn't know that before that we are going to live in the rooms after the Olympics too, which will be the prison (laughs) it was a really amazing thing. It's a small town [Lake Placid] but we played good hockey there too. You know, we were close to beat the Russians in the Olympics. The US, they beat the Russians. We could have won the first medal by winning USA in the last game. Anybody could've won in the tournament because the Russians were not that good. I don't know what happened, but they didn't play that well in the tournament. It's really important that the players get the chance to play for their country also in the future, in the Olympics of course."

FIRST REACTION TO SIGNING WITH RANGERS AS A FREE AGENT:

Leinonen signed with the Rangers as a free agent in 1981. A year prior, Leinonen received an offer from the Vancouver Canucks but decided to play in Finland one more year.

"I had an offer from Vancouver in Europe before the Rangers came in. I'm really happy that it happened. Vancouver is a nice city, but I think that it would be good for me to play one more year in Europe in Karpat [Finnish team] and we had our first child. So it was easier for us as a family to come over the next year if somebody would be interested in me. Lars-Erik Sjoberg, he was a scout for the Rangers at that time and he already know me playing in Sweden a little bit and that we played together with Rexy [Reijo Ruotsalainen] in Karpat. Rexy as a defenseman, he was a producer and a good skater and a good shot and could also use his strengths. I think that was the very influence of Lars-Eric, that you go play for the Rangers and I have been really happy about that. The Rangers signed me and Rexy at the same time. The chance to come over there as a pair and because the Rangers at that time, had Anders Hedberg and Ulf Nilsson. Herb Brooks was the coach, Craig Patrick was the GM, so they knew. They were a little bit ahead of the other teams about European hockey that we had in Europe."

FIRST RANGERS TRAINING CAMP: 1981

"The Rangers came over to play Helsinki that time. Me and Rexy went on training camp in Helsinki, so that was easy for us. We didn't fly over to New York, the Rangers came to Finland and then we went to play in Sweden couple of training camp games so it was a really easy way to adjust to coming to the team when the Rangers came over to Europe to play some games and it was easy for Rexy and me to jump into the team in Helsinki."

FIRST RANGERS CAPTAIN: Barry Beck

"Barry was a good captain of the team and he supported us all the time. There were some other guys also. Nick Fotiu, I played a lot with him on the fourth line. Nick was a really good guy for me. It doesn't matter nowadays, or even in that time, that when you are in the team, you know you do those same things for the Canadians or the US players so then you will be accepted in the team. Barry supported Rexy and me all the time and was behind us if we needed help. I think that you know it was tougher to play against Philadelphia or Islanders because they didn't like that much in Europeans in that time. You need to be tough; you don't give up or nothing like that. You use your skills and then beat up if it's needed. Sometimes there was small fights, the big boys fight them, the skill boys play skilled because that's how it works."

FIRST RANGERS COACH: Herb Brooks

"He liked the European style game and he tried to teach that to the Rangers too. We had a different style in Europe because we keep the puck moving more. We don't dump in that much, if it's needed, we do it. I liked the style of Herbie, how he handled the people. His passion for hockey, he wanted to win the championship for the Rangers."

FIRST RANGERS PLAYOFF EXPERIENCE: 1982 Patrick Division semifinals vs. Philadelphia Flyers. Rangers won best three-of-five series in four games.

"Madison Square Garden is so great a place to have a chance to play for that kind of arena. It's always filled, I couldn't understand [why] they were yelling my name. I didn't realize that, it was the end of the game that I realized that. I have been so happy that I didn't sign in Vancouver, I signed with the Rangers and the chance to play there [the Garden]. I learned the national anthem of the USA in Madison Square Garden, so it's really unbelievable. I almost got all the words [of the anthem] all USA. So I liked the atmosphere in New York, especially the games about the Islanders and the Rangers. It was not the same to play against the Devils. The Devils were a new team, and everybody respects the Rangers and the atmosphere in the old ways. I'd been there a couple of times and I like it every time when I come into Madison Square Garden."

FIRST NHL RECORD-SETTING PLAYOFF GAME: April 8, 1982, Patrick Division semifinals, Game 2 @ Madison Square Garden vs. Philadelphia Flyers, 7–3 win.

"I only remember the first one [assist] because that was so unbelievable a goal. Carol Vadnais, who was I think, 38 or 37 years old [actually, 36] D-man who didn't score goals, he shoot it from the blue line, it was so funny. That was so funny, the fact that he scored the goal. I couldn't believe it. Those other passes, it just happened so fast. I think they all happened in the first and second period so I could have made some more. I have the tape of that game at home, I got it from the Rangers but I haven't looked at the game yet."

FIRST RANGERS FIGHT: December 26, 1982 @ Pittsburgh Penguins, 4–3 loss.

Leinonen fought Pittsburgh's Mike Bullard in the third period.

"We were pushing each other during the game and then something happened. I don't remember but we were close to the boards."

FIRST EXPERIENCE WITH FREE AGENCY:

In March 1985, Leinonen signed with the Washington Capitals as a free agent.

"I was also starting to think about what I was going to do after my NHL career, so I didn't want to stay. I could have stayed with the two-way contract, but I didn't want to do it. To accept a two-way contract was not enough for me. I could have stayed there, but I decided if you're not going to get a one-way contract, then maybe it's better to go home and continue my university studies."

Mikko Leinonen and Wayne Gretzky are the only two players to record six assists in a playoff game. (Public Domain)

31
DON LUCE

Center Don Luce began his career with the Rangers but made his mark in the NHL with the Buffalo Sabres. Luce played a total of 21 games in parts of two seasons with the Rangers. Luce was chosen by the Rangers in the third round of the 1966 NHL Amateur Draft.

FIRST HOCKEY IDOL: Gordie Howe

Luce got to play with Howe during the 1970–71 season.

"The consistency, the skill. You get the same game every time. He was a great man, great teammate. Actually, he's probably the best natural athlete I've ever seen. He could do anything, plus he was mean. I have a story about him too because playing an exhibition game with the Rangers, we played the Red Wings and I got a chance to body check Gordie and I hit him. I hit him good. He went down and I remember I was playing with Vic Hadfield and there was an offside. So we go back to the bench and Vic said to me, 'Look, from now on, you have to know where Gordie Howe is.' I said, 'Why?' He says, 'Because he's coming for you.' So I heeded Vic's advice and I think four or five times, I remember Gordie coming in. I was aware of Vic telling me and he never got me. Two months later, I get traded to Detroit and we're in practice, you know take a shot and then get back in line kind of thing. So I come down, take my shot, I kind of skate to get in line kind of looking at the ice a little bit. I look up and Gordie's got his stick right on my forehead, and he says to me, 'You're the only guy I ever got back.'"

FIRST RANGERS TRAINING CAMP:

"The biggest thing was the excitement of playing with guys like Rod Gilbert, Jean Ratelle, Vic Hadfield, Teddy Irvine, playing NHL guys."

FIRST TIME HE SAW A RANGERS JERSEY WITH HIS NAME AND NUMBER ON IT:

"I got called up from Omaha. Bernie Geoffrion flew down to Omaha and then back with me. I walked into the room and I remember seeing my number 14. I met with [Rangers coach] Emile [Francis] and you know, I've worn number 12 up until that time but Ronnie Stewart was there. He had 12. So he [Francis] says, 'We're going to give you number 14.'"

FIRST RANGERS COACH: Emile Francis

"The first thing that comes to mind, what I remember was that he was so competitive. He was like a stick of dynamite, his energy, his desire. Also, he made you feel good about yourself. As a player, he respected you and was straightforward, honest, and just a great guy to work for. You knew right away talking to him that you were going to get the truth from him. There was no fudging it or anything. He was a straight shooter and that's all he wanted back was give the best you could."

FIRST RANGERS CAPTAIN: Bob Nevin

"Bob wasn't that vocal, but he was a player that seemed to me to be underrated because he played such a solid game. His effort was consistent, he enjoyed the game. He had fun while he was playing and he led by example."

FIRST RANGERS GAME: March 8, 1970 @ Madison Square Garden vs. Pittsburgh Penguins, 0–0 tie

"I remember skating out and seeing the crowd and the warm-up. Then we started the game and Bernie Geoffrion had told me, he said, 'Just go out and play your game. They don't change it. Anything you've been doing, just go out and play your game,' and I took that to heart and I went out and I was probably a little more physical than normal but I tried to play my game. I think I did a pretty good job. I remember it was a 0–0 tie, I believe."

FIRST RANGERS PLAYOFF SERIES: 1970 Stanley Cup quarterfinals vs. Boston Bruins. Rangers lost in six games.

"It was great. You play regular season, it's exciting too, but you get to the playoffs, it just amps up so much more. Everything's on the line, every little mistake is magnified, I guess. You think it is anyways and you're playing a very, very good team. It was like, 'I can't believe I'm here.'

FIRST TIME HE WAS TRADED:

In November 1970, Luce was traded to the Detroit Red Wings for right wing Steve Andrascik, who played one postseason game in his Rangers career. After one season with the Red Wings, Luce was dealt to the Buffalo Sabres, where he played ten years.

"I remember this vividly because we played a game and Emile [Francis] would call me and he said, 'I want to tell you we traded you to the Detroit Red Wings. That's something that we have to do 'cause we have a shot at going to the Stanley Cup and we're going with an older team.' He said, 'I didn't want to give you up, but it came down to getting veteran players back and stuff. It was very, very well done. I remember afterwards, he told me not to tell anybody. The funny part is [after the game] my wife and I rode in with the Egers [teammate Jack and family] going to be a party at Walter's [Tkaczuk] house and so we got in the car to drive back there. I told my wife, 'I've been traded,' and she started laughing because she spent the whole time getting the place we were renting in ship shape. It was just the final day that she had it ready to our standards. She said, 'Come on,' I said, 'No, I'd been traded,' and she says, 'Well, who for?' I said, 'Gordie Howe,' and then she laughed and I said, 'No, it happened to me, I've been traded.' So it was kind of funny but you know, I told Jack and Wendy [Egers] the same thing. It was kind of our first Ranger team party and it was my farewell party."

FIRST TIME PLAYING AGAINST THE RANGERS AS AN OPPONENT: December 26, 1970 @ Detroit, 7–4 Rangers loss.

"Well, it's funny but you have a little more confidence 'cause you know the players and you want to prove to the Rangers that they made a mistake, that they shouldn't have traded me, so you have a little more confidence and you have a little more proof kind of thing. It's strange, but you just play your game."

FIRST GRANDSON TO PLAY COLLEGIATE HOCKEY:

Don's grandson, Griffin, is a defenseman who plays for Michigan. In 2016, Griffin was invited to a Buffalo Sabres developmental camp where Don was able to watch him participate.

"It was really exciting; it was super because he's a hard working kid. It was great, it was a sensational thing. It was so rewarding to see that. My grandson works so hard and it got to the point where he could play at that level. Just an exciting time."

32
HENRIK LUNDQVIST

Henrik Lundqvist is putting the finishing touches on a Hall of Fame career. The Swedish born goaltender holds a number of franchise and NHL records. Lundqvist is fifth on the NHL all-time goaltender wins list and he holds the NHL record for the most wins by a European-born goaltender. Lundqvist is a five-time Vezina Trophy nominee and won the award in 2012. That same year, he was also nominated for the Hart Trophy. Lundqvist is the Rangers' winningest goaltender and has been voted the team's MVP nine times.

FIRST HOCKEY GAME HE WATCHED AS A KID:

"I was probably five or six years old and I watched Frolunda [Swedish Hockey League]. Traveled far to see them play. I think ever since that day, I wanted to become a hockey player. My big dream was to one day play for that team and I did and won a couple of championships and after that, went here. That team played a huge part of my life as a hockey player."

FIRST HOCKEY IDOL:

"I looked up to a lot of different goalies growing up. My first idol was Peter Lindmark. He was one of the best goalies in Sweden, late '80s. Then I started watching guys playing for Frolunda. My first idol over here was probably Patrick Roy, and Dominik Hasek."

FIRST CONTACT WITH THE RANGERS:

Henrik Lundqvist was chosen by the Rangers in the seventh round of the 2000 NHL Entry Draft.

"My brother [twin brother Joel] was ranked pretty high, second round or third round, so they want him to come over, so I went with him. I was at the draft hoping to go in the third or fourth round, but ended up in the seventh, so it was a long wait. That's what I remember."

FIRST RANGERS COACH: Tom Renney

"Looking back now with the coaches I've had here, Tom was the perfect transition for me as opposed to a European and the way he managed the players. Very nice man, he made it easy for me to make that transition. I think he was a very humble, nice man and I think a good start for me to have."

FIRST RANGERS CAPTAIN: Jaromir Jagr

"To play with the guy that's one of the best players to ever the game. At the time, he won the scoring title the first year so he was probably the best player in the league. It was exciting, interesting and inspiring to having him in the locker room. He was carrying this team, big star on Broadway, so it was very cool to get that opportunity."

FIRST RANGERS GAME: October 8, 2005 @ New Jersey Devils, 3–2 OT loss.

"In Jersey, it's not the sexiest building in the world. It's a lot of concrete. It's just a very cool feeling to play my first NHL game. I think I was even more excited to play my first home game, playing at the Garden, first time and also get the win [five nights later against the Devils, 4–1 win]. I just remember the first stretch when I started playing and I just remember really enjoying the moment. It was a cool moment for me. I think I felt like I was ready for it. When you come over, so many questions and you're really not sure, you still believe and then things started happening and you feel like you can play at that level. That's a very exciting feeling and you just keep on going."

FIRST PLAYOFF EXPERIENCE: 2006 Eastern Conference quarterfinals vs. New Jersey Devils. Rangers lost in four games.

"It was not a good experience to me. I was just not feeling well physically, and it was a disappointment just to not feel well, struggling with migraine headaches and just affected me way too much. That was the disappointing about that playoff. I didn't feel like I could play with my strength."

FIRST STEVEN MCDONALD EXTRA EFFORT AWARD:

"It was that whole first year, there was so much happening for me. A lot of it felt like a dream and a lot of it was just a very happy moment for me. I was very proud to receive that. I think back, it makes you proud as well. I remember being very happy and excited about the whole first year."

FIRST OLYMPIC GOLD MEDAL: 2006 Winter Games

Lundqvist led Sweden's Olympic hockey team to the gold medal in the 2006 Winter Olympics in Turin, Italy. Lundqvist went 5–1 and allowed only 12 goals during the games.

"It was just another dream come true. Same year, started playing in the NHL and then you get an opportunity to play in the

Olympics with guys they grew up idolizing. [Peter] Forsberg, [Mats] Sundin, [Daniel] Alfredsson, [Niklas] Lidstrom. First thing when you walk into the locker room is, Wow, this is cool. Two weeks later, [I'm] celebrating the gold medal. It was a high, for sure. Something I'll always remember."

FIRST GAME AGAINST HIS BROTHER: December 14, 2006 @ Dallas Stars, 5–2 win.

Joel Lundqvist was a center on the Dallas Stars.

"Yeah, that was nerve-wracking. I was nervous the whole day and very stranger feeling. I've been on the same team with my brother my entire life until my first game here. It was also a proud feeling. We both made it over here and we were both very happy for each other to get that opportunity again. Very nervous, but I had a good game, I remember that."

FIRST EXPERIENCE SEEING THE RANGERS RAISE A BANNER TO THE RAFTERS:

On January 12, 2006, Lundqvist watched as the Rangers retired Mark Messier's No. 11.

"You look at their emotions and you're happy for them and you can only imagine that impact. Obviously. you hear about it, but I was obviously not here when those guys played but real legends. You sit on the bench and you're just amazed what they accomplished and seeing them get emotional. It's a cool feeling, you know playing the game, how much they invested in the Rangers and their careers, so it's the ultimate reward to have that happen too."

FIRST RANGERS OUTDOOR GAME: January 2, 2012 @ Citizens Bank Park vs. Philadelphia Flyers, 3–2 win

"Kind of amazed how big the arenas are when you walk out there for the FIRST time and you hear that roar. I loved every game, but the first one was very special because it was the first for me but also playing in New York is very cool. It was such a build up to all these games. So much anticipation so when it's finally there, you're ready, you're excited. I think we all feel like we got lucky to play for but it almost feels like this is a once in a lifetime opportunity to enjoy this moment because it's so unique. You play so many games regular, so when you get that opportunity, if you ask all the players that play it, I don't think anybody said I did not enjoy it."

FIRST STANLEY CUP FINAL: 2014 vs. Los Angeles Kings. Rangers lost in five games.

"I was super excited. Obviously, go to the Final, but thinking back, its so many mixed feelings. It's the most excited I've been, but it's also the most heartbroken. You mix that together, you're not sure what to think, really, but it was a very good experience. That whole run we had, and you wish you could be there again. You know, it was such a fun feeling."

FIRST TIME PLAYING GUITAR ON NATIONAL TELEVISION:

In Sweden, Lundqvist played guitar for a rock band called, Box Play. In September 2014, Lundqvist jammed with former tennis star John McEnroe and a band called Noise Upstairs at the inaugural fundraising event for The Henrik Lundqvist Foundation at Refinery Rooftop. Lundqvist jammed on such tunes as "Sweet Child O'Mine," "Layla," and "Time of Your Life."

"A different type of excitement and being nervous, every time you're on stage and play music, part of you is relaxed, part of you is excited and you need focus, but it's just different, you know, sports and music. It's both entertainment, but it's a different type of focus that you require. I don't enjoy playing [with] just me. It's more like when you get together in a band and just jam for hours. That's what I enjoy the most."

The 2014 Stanley Cup Final was both the most excited and heartbroken Henrik felt in his career. (Photo by Mark Rosenman)

33
TROY MALLETTE

Left wing Troy Mallette was drafted by the Rangers in the second round in 1988 and played two seasons on Broadway. Mallette was a big, bruising winger who spent a lot of time in the penalty box. During his two seasons with the Rangers, Mallette scored 25 goals but accumulated 557 penalty minutes.

FIRST HOCKEY GAME HE ATTENDED AS A KID:

"One of the first games I've seen was the Los Angeles Kings and the Buffalo Sabres in Buffalo. I guess I was around 12 years old and we had a local player that played for the Kings named Dave Taylor. Levack (Ontario) is a very small town. One of the guys that was the editor of the local little newspaper knew him a little bit. My dad, the editor, and myself and my chum, we went down and watched the game and it was in a snowstorm where there was probably only 500 people (2,079 was the reported attendance) that attended the game. Crazy storm, it snowed over two and a half feet in like a 24-hour period. Needless to say, free hot dogs and very first hockey game. Got to meet a lot of the LA Kings and yeah, it was a really good experience, that's for sure."

FIRST RANGERS TRAINING CAMP:

"My first training camp, we were in Quebec. My roommate was Marcel Dionne, believe that or not. I was only there for five days. I was an 18 year old so it was pretty much just a cup of tea to get acquainted with how a camp goes. I got sent back to junior, but I guess the high point of that was rooming with Marcel Dionne, who was a linemate of Dave Taylor, who was the childhood hero of mine that was from Levack. I got to watch him, so it was kind of ironic that the first camp I attended, my roommate was Marcel Dionne."

FIRST RANGERS COACH: Roger Neilson

"The biggest thing with Roger that he gave me was, he instilled confidence in my game. He was just a super person, as everybody knows. A coach that gives you confidence in your capabilities, gets the most of ya. I've learned that through the years in different aspects of life, but that was his thing for me, he instilled the confidence that I needed to play in the league and to play a decent role in the league for me."

FIRST RANGERS CAPTAIN: Kelly Kisio

"He was super. Starting from training camp where I wasn't sure if I was going to get an exhibition game in. It just kind of snowballs where they kept throwing me in there for an extra game. The more I went on, the more I felt comfortable. After I played a couple of games, they had me in a hotel room and Kelly Kisio was the guy that would pick me up periodically at the hotel and drive me back and forth from Port Chester or Rye and I would commute with him. The talks coming back and forth again, instilled somewhat confidence in my game. He was a true leader."

FIRST RANGERS GAME: October 6, 1989 @ Winnipeg Jets, 4–1 win.

Mallette had an assist on the game-winning goal in his first game.

"All I remember is, when I skated on the ice and I had my first shift and I came on the bench, I had something that nobody could ever take away as I played a game in the NHL. Whether that was the only game I ever played, I had that under my belt. So all that hard work was paying off for that one game. Darren Turcotte scored a goal, I think I got an assist in the first game. So the fact that I got a point in my first game was another surreal experience. It was a very rewarding game, that's for sure."

FIRST RANGER GOAL: October 13, 1989 @ Washington Capitals, 7–4 loss.

Mallette tied the game at 4 in the third period with his first goal.

"It was a dirty goal. It was right in front of the net. I remember the goalie, Don Beaupre, 'cause I played with him in the past, I believe in Ottawa. I might've crossed paths and played with him for a bit, but the first goal was against Donnie Beaupre, who was another childhood hero, that when I played street hockey and I was in net, I was Don Beaupre. Scored a goal against one of my idols that I kinda cheered for as a kid. He made that big run with Minnesota prior to me playing in the NHL and he was like a star for them. I got my first goal against Donnie Beaupre on Friday, the 13th, a date I'll never forget."

FIRST RANGERS PLAYOFF EXPERIENCE: 1990 Patrick Division semifinals vs. New York Islanders. Rangers won the best-of-seven series in five games.

Mallette scored his first playoff goal in game three. Mallette had an assist in Games 4 and 5.

"Just the intensity of playoff hockey and the fact that every little play, every shift is a difference maker, whether it's good or bad. It's just there's so much more on the line in playoff hockey. I just wish I had the opportunity to play more playoff hockey compared to regular-season play. I think I could excel but I do remember that series against the Islanders. I think it was Jeff Norton. It was, I guess, a controversial hit. I had a hearing. I think I had to do a phone call. I didn't end up getting suspended, but I remember on the Island. I believe I hit him behind the net. I didn't end up with this suspension but kind of ramped up the rest of the series, for me, anyway."

FIRST REACTION TO BEING SENT TO EDMONTON AS COMPENSATION FOR THE RANGERS SIGNING ADAM GRAVES:

"I was upset and in some ways, happy because Edmonton was a team that I cheered for, like most young kids from Canada when Edmonton had their glory years, so I was happy. When I went there, I got picked up by the trainer and I got brought to Glen Sather's office and basically was told he wasn't happy with the arbitrator's decision. 'Bide your time and we'll try to get you out of here as soon as we can.' From going from an organization that had a place for me and going somewhere where I was happy to get a chance to continue my career to getting slapped in the face and we don't really want you and we're going to try and get rid of you ASAP."

FIRST TIME PLAYING THE RANGERS AS AN OPPONENT AT MADISON SQUARE GARDEN: March 4, 1992 as a member of the New Jersey Devils. Rangers lost, 5-4.

Mallette had a goal and an assist in helping to beat his old team at the Garden.

"I always like playing on the Rangers' side at MSG, not the visitors' side. There's no doubt about it. I think the fans, there was somewhat of a connection when I played. My first two years were kind of a blue collar, hardworking player and I think they took to me, so even when I came back on the Devils' side, there was still a connection. Even though I was on the 'bad guys' team, I still felt kind of welcome 'cause I had that connection, so I still had the spirit to play hard at MSG."

FIRST TIME RESPONDING TO A FIRE AS A FIREFIGHTER:

Mallette is a firefighter with the Greater Sudbury Fire Department.

"That first fire I responded to, we had a guy on the coach with a kitchen fire. It was cooking french fries, so the kitchen was, I'm not gonna say fully evolved, but it was going pretty good. We were able to get in and he was sleeping on the couch, so the first time, I actually put my breathing apparatus on. I went in with two other guys and were able to get this guy out. I haven't had another real fire like that where we've had a clean save where somebody walked away with very minimal injuries, so that sticks out in my mind much like my first hockey game and the two guys that I went with are very much like Kelly Kisio and Roger Neilson. I went in with a captain and I had a fellow firefighter and we have this bond together of going in and saving somebody. It was something you never forget, much like your first goal."

34
DAVE MALONEY

Defenseman Dave Maloney was not only the youngest player to wear the Rangers jersey, but he was also the youngest captain in franchise history. Maloney made his Rangers debut as an 18 year old in 1974. In 1978, he was named the 17th captain in team history and wore the "C" for the Rangers in the 1979 Stanley Cup Final vs. Montreal. Maloney played part of 11 seasons with the Rangers.

FIRST NHL GAME ATTENDED AS A KID:

"It was the early '60 s, mid-'60 s and it's a good chance, it was the game that [broadcaster] Marv Albert debuted. Apparently, it was a Ranger-Detroit game at the Olympia. I had family in Detroit, and we went, my uncle Frank, one of my cousins, my father and I went, saw the Red Wings play at the old Olympia. Knowing Kenny [Albert] when I told my first story, he said, 'I think that's when my father,' whatever, so you'd have to follow up this case, but that was my first memory of a pro game. I saw Bobby Orr play as a junior when he played for the Oshawa Generals. Saw him play against the Toronto Marlies. We were able to go into the Marlie locker room and Brian Glennie, who was a defenseman who would end up playing the league, I got his autograph on the little programs we had. As a kid, we lived in a little town too, Lindsay, and the Junior

C team was the big team in town. The Lindsay Cleaners, they were sponsored by the dry cleaners and you could get like a ten-game pass for maybe two bucks, whatever it was.

"So, that was a way for me to get out of doing the chores on a Friday night. I'd go watch the game."

FIRST HOCKEY IDOL: Bobby Orr

"I was a Leaf fan, so where we grew up, everybody's a Leaf fan, except the outcast were Montreal fans. The Leafs were winning Cups in the early '60s. Davey Keon, I remember I got a wool sweater, one of those old wool Leaf sweaters and I put, with chalk, I put [number] 14 on the back of it. To me, he [Orr] changed the game. So, I was certainly not in his class, but I could skate and handle the puck a bit. You were more encouraged to do that when Bobby came up and opened up the game. I was fortunate. I went to his camp as a 12 year old and then I worked [there] the following summer, they had me back as a junior counselor. I worked for 11 weeks for 50 bucks and skated every night and Bobby would come out with us. So, I would work the next nine summers. I went from a junior, a camper, to a pro, on-ice instructor at the camp." One night of summer, he'd [Orr] come out and skate with us and it was like God came on the ice.

"One of my first games I got called up, there were four or five of us got called up to play the Bruins at the Boston Garden. Bobby was obviously in the lineup for Boston. It was December, probably '74, 'cause it was the first year. I'll never forget, he came through the neutral zone. You know that Boston Garden was smaller, so it was a smaller neutral zone, and I looked around. He's coming up, coming up through his right side, my left side, and he put a move on and three of his guys went offside. He skated by me and whacked me on the ass on the way back, almost like, 'There you go, kid.'

FIRST CONTACT WITH THE RANGERS:

Dave Maloney was chosen by the Rangers with the 14th overall pick of the 1974 NHL Amateur Draft.

"Draft day was unique. I was still 17 [years old] so I was going to St. Jerome's High School. I left early that day because [Maloney's agent] Alan Eagleson, who would go on to be an infamous character in this league, he had about six or seven of us ended up being taken in the first round and he had a little reception in Toronto. I was driving to the reception of the draft and I heard on [radio] I had just gotten drafted by the Rangers.

"The Bruins were gonna take me, Montreal was going to take me. Apparently, the Bruins had actually called two days before the draft and wondered if I'd turn pro. I didn't take the call. My mother took the call. I was running track at the time. I remember coming home and there was all smoke in the kitchen and stuff. She was cooking some meat up and left it on the pan as she took the call. Forgot it was there."

FIRST RANGERS COACH: Emile Francis

"It was August 10, 1974. There were a couple of things I remember because August 9, 1974, President Nixon had to resign. I followed the Watergate hearings and stuff like that. Emile came up for the signing. My family was there, and I remember him acknowledging my presence and welcoming me aboard. Then Gresh [Ron Greschner] and I got called up to play an exhibition game against Detroit. NBC was taping something that day at practice [and] that was when they had 'Peter Puck.'

FIRST TIME HE SAW THE RANGERS JERSEY WITH HIS NAME AND NUMBER ON IT:

"I do remember Derek Sanderson telling me that if your name is sewn on the back of your jersey, you're in pretty good shape, but if your name is on Velcro on the back of your jersey, it's probably not good."

FIRST RANGERS GAME: December 18, 1974 @ Madison Square Garden vs. Minnesota North Stars, 7–0 win.

Maloney's first NHL point was an assist on the first of Derek Sanderson's three-goal hat trick.

"My first game was here [MSG] we played Minnesota. I knew I had an assist. The next night we were in Boston. My Mom and Dad were here and then they went to Boston also. Of course, playing Boston, we talked about Bobby. It doesn't seem that long ago, but it was a long time ago."

FIRST RANGERS CAPTAIN: Brad Park

"I wasn't around Brad that much 'cause he got traded in November of '75. The guys who had the impact on me, it was Jean Ratelle and Rod Gilbert. We had rookie camp in Kitchener, my hometown, and they started filtering in at the end of rookie camp. I was having a bit of a groin issue and I was sitting on one of those old silver tubs, the rehab tubs, the whirlpool and they both came in to introduce themselves. I stood up in the whirlpool to shake their hands and they're goin' 'It's okay, you can sit down.' Jean, didn't have much of a chance to play with him, but he was everything that everybody knows about him. Of course, Rod was also everything that everybody knows about him. Rod was tremendous. He took a young guy, I was literally, four months before, I was wearing gray flannels and a blue shirt and a great St. Jerome's high school sweater. Now, I'm in Manhattan and Rod has me over to his apartment. He was on the East Side and East River and it was the best thing."

FIRST RANGERS GOAL: February 28, 1976 @ Minnesota North Stars, 5–3 loss

"[Against] Cesare Maniago in Minnesota. Phil [Esposito] and Greg Polis got assists. It was a shot, I'd like to say it was end-to-end, but it wasn't, if my memory serves me correct. It was kind of a shot from about the mid circle area. That was fun.

"You certainly know it was your first goal. I never kept anything and in our day, I'm not sure if anybody kept anything. It's another kind of validation, and maybe I'm speaking in retrospect. If you're on a score sheet, regardless of on your score sheet, whether you're there on the roster, a penalty or goal, you can actually say, you know what, I played in the league. I might not have played as many games as Gordie [Howe] or Wayne [Gretzky] or anybody but getting that first goal is pretty exciting."

FIRST FIGHT: February 25, 1976 @ Madison Square Garden vs. California Golden Seals, 6–4 loss

Maloney's first foray as a pugilist featured three fights against California defenseman George Pesut.

"The worst thing is it classified me, perhaps in a lot of people's mind as somebody that I really wasn't. I was game to be involved, I was pretty emotional, and I don't remember why. I guess I probably fought him three times 'cause he hadn't beaten the snot out of me the first two times. I might as well go round three. I remember we had a Ranger fan club dinner dance like a night or two later and all of a sudden, I just kind of cult hero of some sort. As far as the fighting goes, I know very few people like doing it and the guys that liked doing it, I kind of stayed away from, but you know you had to do it at a certain point and whatever. I would end up with all kinds of penalty minutes. A lot of those minutes were from yapping at referees and stuff.

FIRST RANGERS PLAYOFF EXPERIENCE: April 1978 vs. Buffalo Sabres, Rangers lost best-of-three preliminary round in three games.

"It was a bit of a 'Magical Mystery Tour' three-game series. We lost to Buffalo, two of three, but it was just a little bit of a taste of spring hockey. Life changed. The teams were better, you were better, but it had to start somewhere, and it started in Buffalo. Donnie Murdoch scoring Game Two in overtime. It was the first kind of kiss of springtime to realize that, it's a different time of year and so it was good."

FIRST RANGERS STANLEY CUP FINAL: 1979 vs. Montreal Canadiens. Rangers lost in five.

"It would be everything that anyone could imagine your best fantasy ever been. I scored a shorthanded goal against [Canadiens goalie] Ken Dryden. Fast forward, I'm doing this [working in the media] and we have Ken Dryden over on a Hockey Night show. He's here to watch Cornell play and we get to speaking about different things. Then, he starts talking about the Stanley Cup win in '79 for him, might have been the lowest point of his career. He went on to explain how he was as he was explaining why that was such. He was concerned about moving on his retirement, his relationship with [Canadiens coach] Scotty Bowman and I'm thinking that was a highlight of my life. We lost and I scored against him, a shorthanded goal. It was actually a legitimate goal. It's all perspective. From my standpoint, it really didn't get any better than that. Especially too, we're in Montreal and it would go back. One of my fond memories was being at the Montreal Forum with my father, seeing a game at 'Expo [67]' when I was 11, so it was great."

FIRST NHL GAME WITH HIS BROTHER DON: February 14, 1979 @ Madison Square Garden vs. Boston Bruins, 5–1 win

Don Maloney, who played with brother Dave for the first time, scored a goal in his first game on his first shot in the NHL.

"That was pretty special, especially the way he came on. I very quickly went from being his older brother that he looked up to, that he'd be my younger brother and I looked up to him. I'm like, what the hell happened here. That was pretty special because we grew up in a family of seven. The last time we played together, I played with my brother Bob. It's me and my brother Bob, in order, then Don. We played together on a squirt team for Lindsay; Moose

Lodge Squirts and we played 52 games that year. We lost four games. We won seven tournaments that we played in. My Dad was the kind of general manager of the thing. My Mom was a team mother and there were three Maloney boys playing on the same team. Then to be reunited, just the way it all worked out, we never had a chance to play again. They didn't really realize what a good player Don was. He was a great player."

FIRST GAME THAT HE AND HIS BROTHER SCORED A GOAL IN THE SAME GAME: February 21, 1979 @ Madison Square Garden vs. St. Louis Blues, 7–3 win.

"A lot of brothers would end up playing but not on a relative basis to the numbers. We grew up by and large in a little farming town in Lindsay, Ontario. We moved to Kitchener when Don was a first-year year Bantam or last year Pee-wee for a lot of our formative years. We were two kids from Lindsay, Ontario, that not only made it but ended up in New York and playing together. It's crazy how it worked out. Any kind of thing that validates one's past is kind of neat. So, he and I were roommates on the road at times and it was great. A lot of people think we sound alike and talk alike. So I say, 'You take that call in case it's for me, or if you want me to take it and they're looking for you, I'll just pretend I'm you, so it was good.'"

FIRST RANGERS HAT TRICK: March 9, 1980 @ Madison Square Garden vs. Minnesota North Stars, 4–2 win. (Only three Rangers defenseman have recorded a hat trick since Maloney.)

"There haven't been many since then. I think it's two [Tony DeAngelo became the third in 2020]. I played my first regular-season game against Minnesota, scored my first goal against Minnesota. I had my only hat trick against Minnesota. As life would take me into my second career on the street, my major account base was in Minnesota. So Minnesota was very good to me. It becomes bigger in my memory perhaps when someone asks me about it, but it was pretty fun. I did have some offensive ability and I can always say I scored three goals at Madison Square Garden."

FIRST TIME THAT HE FOUND OUT HE WAS TRADED FROM THE RANGERS:

Maloney was traded to the Buffalo Sabres in December 1984. Maloney played 52 career games for Buffalo.

"I came to the rink early and I got the message from one of the trainers that [GM] Craig Patrick wanted to see me upstairs. I had a pretty good relationship with Craig. Herb [Brooks] and I had kind of gone different ways. I know I got off on a tangent a little bit. When I went to retire, I thought Brooks was an idiot and I thought Scotty Bowman was an idiot and I thought, *Wait a minute. One guy is the greatest winner in the history of hockey. Other guys might still be winning Stanley Cups, so maybe I'm the idiot.* The point is, I went upstairs and it was tearful, both Craig and I. The most poignant memory will always be, by the time I finished talking with Craig, I came down and the guys were all out on the ice for practice. Ten years of my life as a Ranger was packed up in a little box. I went out and left a note on the board saying I'd buy beers after practice. A little gin mill we used to hang out in Rye [if] anybody wanted to show up. Most of the guys did show up, which was good, but it was such an empty feeling. Bobby Orr couldn't finish as a Bruin, Wayne Gretzky couldn't finish as an Oiler. The uniqueness is [Ron] Greschner finishing as a Ranger, so I had no expectations of ever thinking that I was destined to be a lifelong Ranger. It was that empty feeling of driving out of Rye Playland going, 'Wow, that's it.' So it was off to Buffalo.

FIRST TIME FACING THE RANGERS AS AN OPPONENT: January 16, 1985 @ Madison Square Garden, 2–2 OT tie

"There was a side of the building I didn't know existed. How you got in the room and the game went by so quickly, obviously I don't remember a lot. I remember [Rangers goalie] Glen Hanlon stopping me stone cold with the off hand on a shot that I had from the slot. I swore I never played against Don, but I guess, according to Kenny [Albert] pulled up the sheet and said, 'You played against your brother.' I said, 'Really?' I don't remember what it was, all a bit of a haze."

FIRST TIME APPEARING ON DAVID LETTERMAN'S SHOW:

"That was fun, that was unique. That evolved because apparently, according to Marv Albert. Marv was doing the Top 10 [list] with David Letterman. I had done some work with Marv along the way and apparently Wayne Gretzky either couldn't do it or wouldn't do it. My suspicions are he couldn't do it, and so Marv said to the producers, he said, 'Listen, I got a guy I know will do it.' So, that's how I got the call. I remember telling Letterman the whole 'Eddie Shore story'. He had a goaltender that flopped because Dave had put on the goal pads. We went down to Rockefeller Center and he put the goal pads on. I said 'Eddie Shore, in the old days, rumor has it, he had a goaltender that flopped and he chained him to the crossbar with a chain and I said, 'I got a chain in my bag here.'

"Six months later, we're in Minnesota again. I mean the back of a cab coming back to the hotel and there's this big, burly cab driver. A big, burly man with a big beard. He's kind of looking at us. He's looking in the mirror and he goes, 'Hey, were you just on the Letterman show?' 'Yeah, that was me.' So it was great. It was a great experience here. There's a lot of things happened in my life because I wasn't drafted in Montreal and I wasn't drafted in Boston, I was drafted here."

Dave is one of three Rangers defenseman to record a hat trick. (Public Domain)

35
STEPHANE MATTEAU

Right wing Stephane Matteau played parts of three seasons with the Rangers, but he will go down as the player who scored arguably the most significant goal in the history of the franchise. In the seventh game of the 1994 Stanley Cup Eastern Conference finals, Matteu scored the game-winning goal in double overtime that put the Rangers into the Stanley Cup Final where they finally ended their 54-year drought. Matteau scored six goals in the Rangers' run to the Cup. He scored 11 regular-season goals as a Ranger.

FIRST HOCKEY IDOL:

"I used to watch the Canadiens. I would say Guy Lafleur. In the '70 s, Lafleur was a mega-star in Montreal. I just remember his name. They were mentioning his name a lot. [Yvan] Cournoyer was probably at the end of his career, I think. So, Guy Lafleur at that time."

FIRST CONTACT WITH NHL:

Stephane Matteau was chosen by the Calgary Flames in the second round of the 1987 NHL Entry Draft.

"I had a few interviews before I went to Detroit. Actually, Neil Smith was there at the time with [Jimmy] Devellano, the GM. I think Neil was 27 or 28 and I went for an interview. They were gonna pick me second in the second round. They picked somebody else. I met the New Jersey Devils before the draft, but I had no expectation. I knew I was not going to be in the first round. There were only 21 teams at the time. Maybe, second and third round. I was so naïve and there was less media coverage at that time so I couldn't have read the ranking. Like today, they know the kid like [Jack] Hughes or a [Kaapo] Kakko, they know for the last two or three years, they're going to be number one and number two and we didn't have that.

"Pierre Turgeon went first overall, [Brendan] Shanahan went second, [Glen] Wesley, all those guys. For the rest of us, there was no pre-draft selection or mock draft, as they called it. I remember I was eating a pizza in the second round, Saturday I think, and I was eating with Pierre Turgeon's Dad. I didn't hear my name announced. I saw it on the big screen door. So I was not at my seat when the Calgary Flames selected me 25th overall. I was eating a pizza, but my parents, my sister, some of my cousins were there and they saw my name and they were excited, but they were asking, 'Where's Steph?' So they were looking for me. I got drafted and I'm not even near my seat. So I saw my name on the big screen and I said, 'Holy crap, I got drafted by the Calgary Flames.' Then I went downstairs and I went to hug my parents and my sister. I kept going downstairs and someone was waiting for me and I remember going to the Calgary Flames' table and they were all happy, but I couldn't speak English much at that time. I remember wearing that jersey, it felt so right. I became a Calgary Flames instantly and they were saying, 'We liked you from the day, we've been looking at you for the last two years.' At that time, the Calgary Flames were competing against the Oilers. So they drafted bigger and stronger and they said I fit right in their mold. I remember that [Flames GM] Cliff Fletcher was the GM at the time, was very nice and it was a magical day."

FIRST REACTION TO BEING TRADED TO THE RANGERS:

In March 1994, Matteau was acquired by the Rangers from the Chicago Blackhawks.

"[In] '94 we didn't have much media coverage. Even though we didn't have the internet, didn't have an iPad to read about rumors, but things were not going well in Chicago. Being in a dressing room, players, we don't talk rumors. I know I had some friction with coach Darryl Sutter and things were not going great. You almost feel it in the air that something's going to happen. So the day of the trading deadline, we didn't have a regular practice. At a quarter to one, Chicago time, I was the only one left on the ice. There was nobody else in the building. On the ice and in the stands, there was nobody.

"I kept skating and I said, 'Shit, I'm going to stay in Chicago and I have to deal with the negativity that was going through with Darryl.' We had a very good team, had some good friends on the team. One time when I went for a lap, Paul Baxter, the assistant coach came [by]. I was on the bench and he waved at me and goes, 'Steph, management wants to talk to you.' I knew that right there that I was getting traded but sometimes I can be a funny guy. I told him as a joke, 'Tell them I go talk to them tomorrow. I had a very stressful day, trading deadline is stressful for all of us and tell them I go talk to them.' So he puts his head down, he goes, 'No, they really want to talk to you in the next five minutes.' So, at that time, I really knew I got traded. Management don't want to talk to you on trading day just to say how are you and how's your family. Showered, I went upstairs and everybody has their head down. [Chicago GM] Bob Pulford goes, 'Steph, we just traded you to...' Seems to me there was like music 'cause I still didn't know where I was going. I could hear the drums, like where am I going? 'We traded you to the New York Rangers.' Didn't ring a bell because we played them a week or two weeks before in Chicago and they kicked our butt. They were the fastest team. My first thought was like, *Wow, I'm not going to play much. They're the best team in the league and they traded me for safety measure and that's all right.* They said, 'You get traded with Brian Noonan and Neil Smith will call you in like five minutes.' First, I was a little disappointed to be traded to New York, thinking that I was not going to play much. Sure enough, the next day in Calgary, when I look on the board, I was on the second line with [Steve] Larmer and [Alex] Kovalev. Things happen very quickly in hockey. It's never easy. It was my second trade in my career. It was not easy but going to a championship team, you turn your focus pretty quick. When I flew to Calgary, I found out coach [Mike] Keenan put me on the second line and I said, 'Well, I don't want to disappoint you guys.' So I did my best not to disappoint them."

FIRST RANGERS COACH: Mike Keenan

Keenan was Matteau's coach in Chicago.

"Chicago was a nightmare. He was a mad man; he was tough, things that he did in Chicago would not have worked in New York. Going to New York. Who's the coach? Mike Keenan. Holy shit, he was really hard on me my first time around and I had to fight and show him that I really cared and really wanted to play for him. After that, he left me alone. He was very tough on any players, not only myself. When I get to New York, my first [game] in Calgary, I missed a pass. Steve Larmer was in Chicago with me and Steve was an intense player. Both of them, I mentioned Steve Larmer because he was as intense as Keenan. When I missed my first pass with Larmer, I apologized to him and I said, 'Steve, I'm so sorry,' he said, 'Steph, different worlds here, just relax, do your best and have fun.' That really relaxed me and Keenan was the same way.

"We would talk before games and he would grab me by the neck and my shoulder and he goes, 'You know what Steph, always believed in you. We have a very good thing going here. Things are different in New York than in Chicago. I want you to be comfortable.' So that was like two different worlds. He was crazy in Chicago and in New York, Messier realized later on, [that] the leadership group that we had would not accept anything that

Keenan would have done in Chicago."

FIRST RANGERS CAPTAIN: Mark Messier

"Just to be next to him, just crazy. My first NHL game was against the Oilers when I was 18 years old. [Wayne] Gretzky was on the ice, [Jari] Kurri, [Paul] Coffey, [Grant] Fuhr, and the one guy that impressed me the most was Gretzky obviously, but Mark Messier, his glare, his flair, whatever you call that. His look and his behavior, the way he skated. When I get to know Mark later on, it was like he's the most humble person I've met. Ranger fans realize how sensitive he is, but he never talked bad against anyone. He would lead by example. People don't talk enough about the other leaders we had. Kevin Lowe, Craig MacTavish, Adam Graves and Glenn Anderson. Mark would take information from other players and the other players accepted their roles and Mark would communicate with all the information that he got from the other players, and then he would analyze the thing. His message was short, but precise. Not only was he a good leader, he was a performer. He was 33 years old, I think at the time, so he was still putting some very good numbers on the board. He surrounded himself with his soldiers, plus we won, obviously, that makes it even better. He performed one of the greatest games to me. Game Six in New Jersey was even better.

"Keenan would go crazy at times. I remember one time in Vancouver, we were on the way to practice. Mark went in front of the bus and I don't know what they said to each other, Keenan and himself. So, we ended up going to a restaurant bar and instead of all of us going to practice, we all went to the restaurant and had a few beers. To me that was like, 'Wow, we don't need to practice. We just need to relax,' and Mark had the guts to come up to Keenan and suggested that maybe we need, so maybe it was a set up. A lot of times, we don't know what's going on behind [closed] doors, but I was very impressed. When Mess said, 'Everybody out,' we all like, 'All right, Mess, thank you.' We all thanked him so he's got even more power out of it. Those little things that people don't talk enough or they don't see what us players, [notice] we notice those little things."

FIRST RANGERS GAME: March 22, 1994 @ Calgary Flames, 4–4 overtime tie

Matteau scored his first Rangers goal to tie the game with 14 seconds remaining in the third period.

"It was game time in Calgary. So, not only myself, but Brian Noonan, MacTavish, Anderson, we walked in and introduced ourselves. The next game we went to Edmonton, the next night we played. These players, I realized that are there, lost some very good friends like Tony Amonte was there. Everybody loved him as a teammate, so they lost him, but nobody made me feel like, 'While you take my friend's spot, you better perform' I never felt any of it. What I felt like was a humble group, a focused group and a very, very good group. Like we never felt like that in my career. Every single game we played we had a chance to win. We didn't lose too many games and when we did, practice time was amazing. Everyone was focused. A lot of people don't mention Greg Gilbert, Eddie Olczyk, Nick Kypreos, Mike Hartman, Mike Hudson, Dougie Lidster, or Jay Wells. All those guys, they took a step back and they accepted their roles. Greg Gilbert really helped me out. He didn't play much, he was on the fourth line, but he talked to me. He relaxed me a lot of times when players would have, maybe not jealousy, but they would have done anything to be in my position, being on the second line and second power play.

"We had an amazing group. We were rushing to the dressing room in the morning, having our coffee 'cause none of us wanted to miss any second of what we experienced. I learned to respect others. I learned to follow, like one of my greatest idols now as a human being, is Adam Graves. I've been fortunate the last 25 years I had been around Adam and what a beautiful human being that he is, but we had, maybe 15 of them in the dressing room. Was very powerful and what a great time. The way we won and the way we lost hockey games 'cause we lost a few hockey games in the second, third, and fourth round and the way we battled back, just incredible.

"We pulled our goalie out. Richter came in and Keenan kicked me in the ass and said, 'You're going,' 'cause it never happened before, but that was Keenan's style though. Those are the games you played the most with Keenan. When he wanted to showcase you, he would put you on the ice. That happened a few times in my career with Mike. Sure enough, I went on the ice. I remember it was a fat rebound. I got it on my chest and beat [Flames goalie] Mike Vernon, my ex-teammate, so that was pretty ironic."

FIRST OF HIS TWO DOUBLE-OVERTIME GOALS : May 19, 1994, Game 3 of Eastern Conference finals @ New Jersey Devils, 3–2 win. May 27, 1994, Game 7 of Eastern Conference finals @ MSG vs. New Jersey Devils, 2–1 win.

Matteau scored in double overtime of Game 3 to beat the Devils and give the Rangers a two games to one series lead. The second was Matteau's famous goal in Game 7.

"Game One. Once Stephane Richer scored the first double-overtime goal, I played my worst game in the playoffs. I was an up and down player emotionally and I went to play golf. We had a day off the next day and a friend of mine from Calgary took me to play golf because my mind was not there. I had my worst game and I thought I blew it. So that game was behind me. We won Game Two and Game Three. I remember it was so physical, there was ups and downs and I was physical. I got hit hard, paid the price in front of their net many, many, many times. Every time I went in front of the net. That's what I made my living. Even though I didn't score 20 goals a year, I did score some goals and it was all in front of the net, pretty much like ten-feet radius.

"It was a very good shift for us. I think Kovalev was on the ice with me and Anderson and we battled pretty hard. I just remember it was a weak, backhand shot. All my goals were pretty weak. Backhand and I saw the light go on, that's when I realized like I scored. My celebration was not the greatest one, but this time, I didn't give a crap because we're back [up] two to one in the series. 'We are up two to one, we are up two to one,' that's what I kept saying. When you scored, you realized, wow, this is pretty special because all of us kids, all of us players, we dream about scoring those goals. When that really happened as a professional, it's more special. I remember the crowd going crazy. I was impressed that there was so many Ranger fans in the audience. Something that I learned that when we played the Devils, there could be 10,000 people cheering for the Rangers. I know why they felt like there was 10,000 people cheering for us.

"Game Seven. I've learned over the years, that's the Rangers' way I guess when [Valeri] Zelepukin scored [to tie the game late in the third period] and it's 'never over until it's over.' You hear that a lot. They [Devils] scored all right. I had a few shots on net that game and I played pretty solid, nothing special. I was not an up and down player like Kovalev was but there was a lot of players you would notice when they have the puck. First overtime, I remember [goalie Mike] Richter stood on his head. The Devils went on a two-on-one a few times and the puck almost went in a few times and Richter was just incredible. That's what I teach the kids when they go to the Bronx. When I show them the video [of his goal] when I scored, inches away would have been somebody else, inches away would have [Esa] Tikkanen and Tikkanen swiped at it. He could have been the one and I would not be talking to you today probably.

"I felt very confident when it was time for overtime. First overtime, things went like pretty intense, but our whole group was very focused and we stayed on the ice for like a 45-second shift. We kept rolling the lines and then, when we went to the second overtime, everybody knows the story. When I broke my lace and I stayed in the dressing room. Keenan always started Messier, Anderson, and Graves, first shift and I knew my line was second. Every game that we start, every period that we start, Messier's line, he [Keenan] always starts with his best player. So when talking to Eddie Olczyk, that was a special moment. Eddie was not playing. I know he was not happy, he was suffering, but he never made us feel like that. As a proud person that I know him now, I asked him, 'Can you kiss my stick again?' because he kissed my stick in Game Three in New Jersey. In overtime, the extra players there are by the dressing room 'cause as soon as the game is over, the coaching staff has a quick meeting and they want everyone in the dressing room. You don't want to get caught in the press box or going down the stairs caught in traffic. So you learn very early that the extra players are close to the dressing room. So Game Three, I asked Eddie to touch my stick and he kissed it and it worked. Eddie came out of the dressing room and we were just alone. There was a quiet moment and I was very focused and I felt good that I was gonna go score. I'm a nervous person naturally and I felt very good and I focused I was going to score. Sure enough, I did it and it felt surreal. When you focus to do something, when you visualize to do something and it actually happened, the emotion, the tiredness, the fatigue all kicked in and said, 'All right, we're going to the Stanley Cup Finals.' I fed from the fans, from my teammates jumping on me. I wish I still be on the ice and just celebrate because that was the best moment in my professional career. Twenty-five years later, people still talk about it. The feeling was just incredibly high. I'm going to the Stanley Cup Finals. I know my parents, my friends, my wife, my kids. My son was only a few months old, but my friends were watching, what a great feeling. Finally my turn to shine in my career."

FIRST STANLEY CUP CHAMPIONSHIP: June 14, 1994 @ MSG vs. Vancouver Canucks, Game 7, Stanley Cup Final, 3–2 win

"We were winning, no matter what happened, we were winning. Great teams, they don't, even though it was the Rangers' style. We blew it in Game Five (6–3 loss with a chance to win the Cup) We worried so much about our party that we forget to, I even forget my passport just in case we lose and we ended up losing. I forgot my passport, so somebody had to rush to my house. I remember we stayed in New Jersey and flew to Vancouver and the next day, didn't think twice about going back to Vancouver. Just to show you the focus wasn't there. Game Six, Vancouver played their best game in the playoff. Game Seven, what saved us, there was a lot of controversy with Keenan's story [about leaving the Rangers for another coaching job]. What saved us was the two days off in between.

"We played pretty much every other night. I remember between [Games] Six and Seven, we had a few days off and then Kennan performed one of the greatest speeches ever. Whether it was a true story or not, I felt he meant it. We were focused. We jumped on the ice for the warm-up, the crowd, we felt the energy going in, that the Stanley Cup was in the building, we were going to win. We took the early lead when [Brian] Leetch scored, I think it was on the power play. He had a pass from [Sergei] Zubov and then "Zubi " to Leetch, he scored. Then we took a 2–0 lead, was even better. We didn't lose too many games with two goals. Then Trevor Linden (Canucks captain) scored to keep us honest. Then, we scored another goal to make it 3–1 at that time. It was just a matter of time.

"Once again, they scored. What's the word, resilience? Trevor scored again, [to] make it 3–2 to make it even more Ranger style. Then we just kept being on the ice, 40 seconds, 45 seconds. We kept it like very short, very focused. We had one of the best offenses in the league but also one of the best defensive teams in the league, including the Devils. We were just amazing with one- or two-goal leads late in the third, but nothing was taken for granted until the very, very last second. When they announced the final buzzer, [Brian] Noonan and I were on the bench. Everybody jumped on the ice and I hugged Brian and said, 'We did it.' That was my first thought. Brian was another key player of our team that nobody mentioned. Him and MacTavish and [Sergei] Nemchinov, we miss a lot of players from that team. They were just incredible but to share that with those guys. What a great moment."

FIRST TIME HE TOUCHED THE STANLEY CUP AFTER WINNING IT:

"I regret it. I apologize to Brian Noonan. He had the Cup for less than one second and I grabbed it from him. If I had to do it again, I would wait for him to take it for about 20 to 30 seconds. I took it from him, and he was laughing. Well, I have it on tape. I was so in a rush to get it. It doesn't matter if you got it, the 12th player or the 50 players, you're gonna touch the Cup, but what a great feeling. What a great feeling to lift that trophy over your head. Once you have it over, that means thank you to Mom and Dad. Thank you for Grandpa to take me. Thanks for my family's support. Thanks for my friends' support. We did it as a team and all of us players I think go through that. Thank you very much and finally, I'm going to have my name on the Cup forever."

FIRST REACTION TO HIS SON'S FIRST NHL GAME:

Stefan Matteau made his NHL debut for the New Jersey Devils on January 19, 2013 vs. the New York Islanders.

"Wow, that was a crazy first. Get the call, gonna play against the Islanders. It was a crazy season; it was a lockout season. I didn't understand the Devils bringing in an 18 year old was playing junior. He was playing in juniors. We went to the [Nassau] Coliseum with my daughter and my wife. In warm-up, I saw my son. It's weird, I'm going to describe it. So my seven-year-old son, first time skating on the ice. I'm emotional here.

"You see my six-year-old, five-year-old son, dreaming of playing in the NHL. Whether it's a Devils or a Ranger jersey, it doesn't matter. He's on the ice and playing with [Ilya] Kovalchuk on the same line and he almost scored on his very first shift. My wife and I cried for a moment. My daughter cried also. We couldn't stop. Then, the national anthem and his first NHL shift, the whole thing was just special. At the end of the game, [Devils goalie] Marty Brodeur, I think I met him once before, came into the stands. He had no business coming in, and he came in and introduced himself and congratulate the whole family. He said, 'We're very proud of your son,' and I really appreciate that moment. You could tell that he was happy as us knowing that he has his own kids and maybe one day he would experience the same thing. I thought that was very classy on his part."

FIRST REACTION TO HIS SON SCORING HIS FIRST NHL GOAL:

Stefan Matteau scored his first NHL goal on February 9, 2013, against the Pittsburgh Penguins.

"I was working on my junior team and I recorded the game. I was playing that night, made sure everyone would not tell me the score. When I went home, I didn't pick up any phone calls, nothing on purpose. I watched the game and then I would fast forward to every shift that Step was on the ice. All of a sudden, while I was fast forwarding it, everybody jumped. So I rewind it and I saw him getting the pass from [Andy] Greene and he got it on his backhand, forehand and he beat [Marc-Andre] Fleury on an empty net. I was surreal. I start jumping and I was by myself in the house. I was jumping up and down on the furniture, up and down, up and down and just so proud and happy for him."

Matteau! Matteau! Matteau! Photo courtesy of New York Rangers.

36
SANDY McCARTHY

Right wing Sandy McCarthy played 11 seasons in the NHL, four of those seasons in two separate stints with the Rangers. From 2001 to 2003 McCarthy missed one game as a Ranger. He returned to the team for the 2003–04 season, his last in the NHL.

FIRST CONTACT WITH NHL:

Sandy McCarthy was chosen by the Calgary Flames in the third round of the 1991 NHL Entry Draft.

"I was at the draft in Buffalo and didn't know if I was gonna get drafted. I ended up seeing Doug Risebrough [Calgary GM] in the lobby the morning of the draft and he was looking at me from head to toe a couple of times so I had a feeling that he might be interested. It ended up coming to be true that he drafted me in the third round. I was sitting with my Dad. It's a hard feeling to explain in words when you hear your name drafted to the NHL. It's almost like butterflies through my body when I heard that. As a kid playing the game from a young age, it's kind of a goal that I had always had and when I did get drafted, it was like, okay, here's my first step."

FIRST REACTION TO BECOMING A RANGER: Traded

from Carolina to the Rangers in August 2000.

"I was with Carolina at the time and I was living in Carolina with some personal trainers. I was doing some fitness stuff and Glen Sather [Rangers GM] had called me and said that he had traded for me."

FIRST RANGERS TRAINING CAMP: September 2000

"I remember that when I first came to the Rangers, I noticed that how they did things was all first class with everything that did. That was my first impression with being around the team."

FIRST TIME PUTTING ON THE RANGERS JERSEY:

"Anytime you're on one of the original teams, it's a feeling of, it's almost like I was honored to be selected to wear that jersey. I've had a lot of pride in it too. Knowing that their history in hockey went back to some of the starting days and it was something that I wanted to make sure that I showed everybody that I had pride wearing it in the way I played."

On playing for an Original Six team:

"It is a badge of honor because there's some of the teams that started the league. To be part of the organization and have your name in their logbooks is an honor as a hockey player."

FIRST RANGERS COACH: Ron Lowe

I loved Ron; I thought he was a good coach, a good old school guy. He loved the way I played and loved what I put out for them. I respected what he used me for."

FIRST RANGERS CAPTAIN: Mark Messier

"Mark was an awesome guy. Not only was he a good captain, he was a good human to his teammates and he made everybody feel like they were important and part of the team. As I got to learn later in my career, that was very important for especially the younger guys to make them feel a part of it. He was very easy to talk to and was a great leader for us."

FIRST FIGHT AS A RANGER: October 11, 2000 @ MSG vs. Montreal Canadiens, 3–1 win. McCarthy fought P. J. Stock early in the second period,

"Well, it's one of those things [reputation as an enforcer] that follows you around when you played the game the way I did and had the responsibilities that I did on the ice. You tend to become a pretty quick favorite of the fans. You know, I loved P. J. and he's a great guy and he was a great teammate when I played with him in Boston also. It was too bad that he had to draw my straw that night because I was ready to put on a show."

37
ROB McCLANHAN

Center Rob McClanahan spent parts of three seasons with the Rangers to finish up his five-year NHL career. The Rangers acquired McClanahan from the Hartford Whalers in February 1982, nearly two years after he was a member of the historic 1980 United States Olympic hockey team. McClanahan played for Herb Brooks when the United States team upset the heavily-favored Soviet Union team in the semifinals and then beat Finland to win the gold medal. Brooks was McClanahan's coach when he joined the Rangers.

FIRST HOCKEY GAME ATTENDED AS A FAN:

"Boston Bruins [vs.] North Stars. Bobby Orr, "Espo," all those guys. Kenny Hodge, [Gerry] Cheevers, all those guys. Boston was really good."

FIRST HOCKEY IDOL:

"Bobby Orr or Bobby Hull, they both revolutionized the game."

FIRST STEPS TO EARNING A SPOT ON THE 1980 U.S. OLYMPIC HOCKEY TEAM:

Rob McClanahan represented the United States in the 1979 World Championships in Moscow, Russia

"Playing in the world tournament in '79 was a huge opportunity. Candidly, it's what spearheaded my desire to really do whatever was necessary to make the Olympic team. That was the deal. It as my mission to do whatever it took in terms of training and preparation to make that Olympic team because I was not one of the guys that was guaranteed a spot.

"When I was selected for the Olympic team and then we went over the Finland to play for two weeks, I was a fourth line guy. I was not a frontline [player]. I did not play with Mark [Pavelich] until we got back from Europe and I was a fourth line guy at best. Herbie [coach Herb Brooks] switched lines around and when he put me and Mark together, we clicked right away. That was probably sometime in October or November. From there, we just ran with it."

FIRST THOUGHT THAT WENT THROUGH HIS HEAD WHEN THE UNITED STATES TEAM WON THE GOLD MEDAL:

"Just major pride, represented our country. Just huge pride. Just proud to be an American."

FIRST TIME GETTING THE NEWS THAT HE WAS TRADED TO THE RANGERS:

"I got called into Larry Pleau's office, the GM of the Whalers. He said, 'You're going to the Rangers.' Then I called [Rangers GM] Craig Patrick [and he] says, 'You're going to play at Binghamton for a while.' I was there for a couple of games, then I got called up to the Rangers. I was there from that point on and it was great. Pav and I became really good linemates and I was surrounded by some really quality players."

FIRST GAME AS A RANGERS WHERE HE SAW THE

JERSEY WITH HIS NAME ON IT FOR THE FIRST TIME:
February 18, 1982 @ MSG vs. Colorado Rockies, 4–4 tie

McClanahan had played in the Garden when the United States team played the Soviet Union in an exhibition game a few weeks before the Olympics.

"An opportunity to play for a storied franchise in a very cool building. A lot of people when they went to New York on the road, the old argument was the ice is lousy and it was not a great venue to play but Madison Square Garden, it's pretty good. I didn't have an issue with the ice at all."

FIRST RANGERS COACH: Herb Brooks

"Herbie taught not only me, but he taught a lot of players that they were capable, far, far, more capable of accomplishing far more than I thought or than any of us thought. That goes beyond the Olympic team. It goes up to any team that he coached. That's not without hard work of course, but the ability to be able to accomplish more than we ever dreamed of, first and foremost."

"Familiarity, he knew what he was getting. There were no surprises and I knew what I was getting. I was able to play for him three years at Minnesota on the Olympic team and play reasonably well so there were no deep, dark secrets. That gave me a level of comfort that perhaps I didn't have in other places."

FIRST IMPRESSIONS OF HERB BROOKS AS AN NHL COACH AS OPPOSED TO AN OLYMPIC COACH:

"Totally different. He refined his style. He realized that he couldn't be as stern with a professional player as he was with college. He realized that he needed to buy in from his leaders and if his leaders followed, the other players would follow as well. Herbie was not someone who was stuck in the mud in terms of his style of coaching. He was very progressive in his methods and in how he handled players as he continued to coach."

FIRST RANGERS CAPTAIN: Barry Beck

"Loved him. Came to play. He was passionate, worked hard, he was a guy you wanted on your team. Barry was terrific. He was respectful of not only me, he was respectful of all the players. Whether you were Canadian or American or Finnish or Swede, it didn't matter. You were a New York Ranger and that was first and foremost."

FIRST RANGERS PLAYOFF SERIES VS. THE ISLANDERS: 1982 Patrick Division finals, Rangers lost in six games

"I think we gave the Islanders their toughest series. So we didn't stretch it to seven, but we gave them really good games and they just had too much and we couldn't overcome that. They were just that good.

"Didn't like each other at all. When we played the Islanders when I was in Buffalo, but (Islanders goaltender) Billy Smith butt-ended Lindy Ruff, damn near took out his eye. That was when Billy Smith, the knob of his stick was actually an inch or two below the end of the stick and he damn near took Lindy Ruff's eye. That was not something that you want to be remembered for."

FIRST RANGERS HAT TRICK: November 24, 1982 @ MSG vs. Minnesota North Stars, 8–5 win

"I remember it vividly. I also remember that traffic was so horrendous going down to Madison Square Garden, that I was late and got fined. I was lucky to make the game; it turns out I got a hat trick. I'm very proud of it. If I recall Donnie Beaupre was the goalie. I'm very proud. I watched the North Stars growing up, so I knew a lot of those guys and it just put a little extra "oomph" in the fact that I was able to do that. It was a good day for me."

FIRST NY RANGERS TO APPEAR AS HIMSELF IN THE

CARTOON *AMERICAN DAD*

"They called me and I just did some voiceovers. What's ironic is I get these checks for like twenty bucks, all dependent on how often it's played on TV. It took me probably, I don't know, 20 minutes to do the voiceovers that was all it took. I mean, it's strange to hear my voice on it. I've only seen it one time, but I always get calls from people when they see it or e-mails or texts asking me, you know, talking about it.

Rob was fined the day he scored his Rangers hat trick. Photo courtesy of New York Rangers.

38
GEORGE McPHEE

Left wing George McPhee was an outstanding collegiate player at Bowling Green State University. In 1982, McPhee won the prestigious Hobey Baker Award as the top player in college hockey. McPhee was an undrafted free agent who played four seasons with the Rangers but made his NHL debut in the Stanley Cup playoffs. McPhee tied an NHL record by scoring three goals in a single playoff series before playing in a regular-season game. (Chris Kreider set a new record with five goals in 2012.) After his playing career, McPhee began a management career as the vice president and director of hockey operations for the Vancouver Canucks. Following a stint as the Washington Capitals' GM, McPhee became the first GM of the expansion Vegas Golden Knights who stunned the hockey world by qualifying for the Stanley Cup Final in their inaugural season of 2017–18.

FIRST HOCKEY GAME THAT HE ATTENDED AS A TEENAGER:

"Montreal Canadiens at Toronto Maple Leafs. I remember being way up in the gray seats and having a nice, high view which is what managers like because you can see everything obviously. The one thing that really stood out to me, Montreal was a great team with [Guy] Lafleur and that cast of players. The player that stood out the most to me was Bob Gainey. Just his incredible skating stride and how much ice he covered and how he just seemed to sort of dominate every shift he was on."

FIRST HOCKEY IDOL:

"Bobby Orr would stand out. I took a liking to the Philadelphia Flyers because I went to buy a hockey jersey one day. My parents, they gave me a little money to buy a hockey jersey and I saw this orange jersey that I liked. I wasn't even sure what the team was and got it. That team ended up, they got to be pretty good in one, two Cups. I liked [Dave] Schultz for all the shenanigans but Bobby Clarke would be the guy I think I ended up admiring the most, the way he competed and the leadership. You don't realize how important it is until later on, but he may have been one of the best leaders ever."

FIRST CONTACT WITH NHL:

"It was before I went to college and I have no recollection of it because I didn't really care or expected I would ever be drafted. I don't know what the draft was in those days. I don't even know when my draft year was, to be honest with you. I was playing two-tier hockey and loved the NHL. Like every kid, [I] fantasized about playing there someday but never ever thought it would happen for me, which is why I went to college."

FIRST REACTION TO WINNING THE HOBEY BAKER AWARD:

"Jerry York was our coach at Bowling Green, and I was certainly was aware of it because the ten finalists are named at some point, probably a month or two before the end of the season. Coach York was great. At the start of the season he said both Brian MacClellan and myself, there were going to be some NHL teams that are interested in you guys. Let's just play hockey. We're not going to talk to teams or agents until the season's over. You guys focus on school, focus on hockey, and it was great advice and we did that. Then, when the year was over, we were eliminated in the regional playoffs by Northeastern University. If we had won that series, we would go on to play in the Final Four. We lost that series. We tied the first and we tied the second game and then we lost in overtime in the second game.

"We were back at the hotel and Coach York told me then that I had won the award. I found it really hard to believe. Something like that happens, you don't feel like you deserve it and anything like that, but ultimately, you're really proud that you represented your school well enough and that you delivered something to your school. You know, we all would prefer championships over individual awards, but we didn't win a championship, but the individual award was nice. It was great recognition for the school."

FIRST RANGERS CONTRACT:

In July 1982, George McPhee signed a free agent contract to join the Rangers.

"I wanted the right opportunity and its stuff we still preach to all the kids today. It's the fit that matters the most. Might be lots of teams interested in, but you've got to get the fit right to make sure you succeed. I really thought at that time, it was two years after Lake Placid, I really thought a chance at signing with an organization that was managed by Craig Patrick and coached by Herb Brooks would provide the best opportunity because they were college guys. I was a college guy, [the] fact it was the New York Rangers was a big deal, you know Original Six team, but I was a college guy and I wanted to work for college guys."

FIRST RANGERS COACH: Herb Brooks

"Herb Brooks, I thought, was ahead of his time, a terrific bench coach. His practices were incredibly demanding. Fitness requirements were incredibly demanding in relation to other NHL teams. He was an intimidating presence. He was intelligent and obviously really demanding. Frankly, I enjoyed playing for him and he's one of the better coaches that I've ever had a chance to play for or work with."

FIRST RANGERS TRAINING CAMP:

McPhee went to training camp before the 1982–83 season.

"I thought it was a very difficult camp at that time. I think Herb was doing three-a-days on the ice, plus a session off the ice, some sort of strength and aerobics session off the ice. So we were in the hotel in Armonk (New York) so we had to get on the bus and go back and forth three different times to skate. I remember the weather, the New York weather being really hot and humid. I remember feeling the same way in the rink. I remember the equipment just being wet the second time we went back, the third time I went back, and they were just really long days. If you think about it, you go, you get down there, you get ready, you go on the ice, you do what you do, you come off, you take the bus, you go all the back to Armonk, have something to eat. An hour later, you're going back. Same routine, drive all the way back, have something to eat. An hour later, you're going back again. Went on what felt like a couple of weeks, it was a grind. It was hard in terms of what was going on on the ice. I only got on the ice a few times with the vets. It was mostly the vets were separated from the rookies and we had our rookie games and those kinds of things. I didn't get a chance to play in an NHL game that preseason."

FIRST RANGERS CAPTAIN: Barry Beck

"Barry was a real good guy, a smart guy, a good player. There was a lot on his shoulders as a captain. It's interesting. I think he's, in some ways, a quite guy, a shy guy. When he's with friends, he's real talkative and a great sense of humor, but his style of leadership was a little different. He would say the right things to people all the time, but he also enjoyed his privacy. He was not one to be out all the time with the team and everything else and doing extra things and looking after things with the players. He wanted to come to the rink, practice or play and move on, but while he was there, he was really committed and a good leader."

FIRST RANGERS GAME: April 5, 1983 @ Philadelphia Flyers, Game 1 of the Patrick Division semifinals, 5–3 win. Rangers swept the best-of-five series in three games.

McPhee made his NHL debut in this playoff game and had an assist.

"I was called up a couple of days before the whole group and met the team in Washington and watched the Rangers play Washington and then we got on the bus with the team. We were starting the playoffs in Philadelphia and I have no idea where we were. We were out in the country someplace [the Poconos] and we practiced up there for a few days. I remember Barry Beck's humor on the bus. He was a really, really funny guy. Then, I remember the day of the game skate. Craig Patrick used to like to skate after practice and get his exercise in and he was on the ice at the end of the morning skate. He came over to me and just said, 'You're in tonight,' and there's this jolt of electricity that went through me. I couldn't believe it. I was playing in an NHL game, playoff game against the team that I really liked as a kid. I remember going back to that hotel after practice. Most players take a nap before the game and that just wasn't happening.

"I was just so wired. The Flyers were introduced individually, and Herb insisted that our team be introduced collectively. So we were all on the blue lines for the national anthem. I can remember, I was so wired, just chirping at the Flyers 'cause they were facing us from their blue line and I was chirping at them during the anthem. It's just crazy. Then, standing in the hallway before we go out, I remember Ron Duguay was three or four players ahead of me and he was just jumping as high as he could, up and down, just to get his legs going and then you go play. It was about as physical a game that I'd ever played, but that's NHL hockey. It's one thing to play a game in the NHL. It's going to be bigger, faster, stronger than anything you've ever done, but to do it in a playoff game, I couldn't believe how physical it was and how hard it was to get to the net. I thought, Jeez, I know this is so good. I don't know that I'll ever be able to keep this up but we're gonna try."

On his assist on Eddie Johnstone's goal in the second period:

"It was a nice one. I was really happy with that one. We were battling for the puck on the boards on the right-hand side of the rink in the offensive zone and came up with it. I remember looking out to the point and sort of facing that way with the puck. I had seen Eddie Johnstone off to the side of the net on the other side of the rink all by himself, just peripheral vision, I guess. I sort of fake the pass out to the point and then in just one motion, to slide it the opposite way down to the other side of the net through one of the Flyers' legs, I think and right on Ziggy's tape and he put it in."

FIRST PLAYOFF GOAL: April 7, 1983 @ Philadelphia Flyers, Game 2 of the Patrick Division semifinals, 4–3 win.

McPhee scored his first playoff goal to tie the game in the second period. Eddie Johnstone and Mike Allison got the assists.

"The Flyers had trotted out some tough guys on the line. I think [Behn] Wilson was on the deep pair. I think there were a couple of tough guys up front, whether it was [Paul] Holmgren or one of those guys, I can't remember. We won the draw, we'd dumped it in and, pretty sure it was Eddie that had the puck in the corners, him or Allison. I got open in front and yelled for the puck and threw it out and it was just a little too far behind me to get it on my stick and fire it on net because I was off to the side of the net and kinda tight. I did something that I'd never done before and I don't know why, but it's that moment. Instead of trying to shoot it on my forehand, I knew it wasn't gonna happen. I just grabbed it and I spun and threw it on a backhand. Sort of a spin-o-rama move and I don't think the goaltender was ready for it. I think he thought I was going to shoot on my forehand and he had committed a little bit. Then I spun and just wielded at the net on the backhand and it went in. What startled me was how loud it was in the rink when I scored because I never played in an arena that big with that many people.

There must've been a lot of people from the Rangers in the rink that day because that startled me."

FIRST RANGERS PLAYOFF GAME AT MADISON SQUARE GARDEN: April 9, 1983 vs. Philadelphia Flyers, Game 3 of the Patrick Division semifinals, 9–3 win.

"I remember Nick Fotiu telling me that it'll be so loud in there [the Garden], the hair on your arms is going to stand up. It's exactly what he said and when we got there, a couple of hours before the game, he said, 'Come with me,' and wearing our hockey underwear, we walk out the locker room. We walked down to some elevators and we took the elevator to the top floor, up to the blue seats and they're right where the elevator opened up. You just had this amazing sort of panoramic view of the whole rink and the logo in the ice and everything else. It was really something special. Nick was the kind of guy that would take the time to show a young guy something like that and you never forget it. I'm grateful to him for him doing that. I'll never forget that image because it was something to see. It was quiet. Nobody was there at that time, but it was something to see. Then, a couple of hours later, it was the loudest thing that I'd ever heard, and we won. I think we won the game 9–3 or something crazy."

FIRST EXPERIENCE OF THE RANGERS-ISLANDERS RIVALRY: April 14, 1983 @ Nassau Coliseum vs. New York Islanders, Game 1 of the Patrick Division finals, 4–1 loss. Rangers lost the series in six games.

"I really thought we could beat them. We started the series on the Island, and I remember, I think it was the first period that we really had them on their heels and were coming up and coming at them, just weren't getting the goals to beat them. I thought we were a lot closer in that series. It's my recollection anyway to beating them. They seemed to get stronger as the series progressed, shouldn't surprise anybody, they were a heckuva team. That's what I remember, playing on a line with [Ron] Duguay and [Mike] Backman at that time. I think we actually got to start Game Two, which was amazing.

"The Flyers-Rangers rivalry is as bitter as it could get as well. To me, like every one of those games was just this monumental playoff game against the division rival. It was just every game seemed to be incredibly loud. I always thought the Islander and Flyer games were different than any of my games."

FIRST REGULAR-SEASON GOAL : October 10, 1983 @ Madison Square Garden vs. Los Angeles Kings, 2–1 win.

McPhee's first NHL goal gave the Rangers a 1–0 lead in the first period.

"I didn't realize that it was the first one in the regular season. I didn't realize that. Nope, for me my first NHL goal was against the Flyers in the playoffs. That's the way I would regard that. I remember that goal against the Kings. My best friend was playing for the Kings. We had played together at Bowling Green and Brian MacClellan, he's playing for the Kings and I'm playing for the Rangers. Mike Rogers had the puck and threw it over to me in front of the net and wasn't quite in the wheelhouse, so I had to kick it up with one foot as I was falling backwards and just hit it with my stick and I was falling down and it went in, so like every NHL goal, it's special. I remember the goal; I didn't realize that was the first one that I had scored."

FIRST RANGERS FIGHT: October 7, 1983 @ New Jersey Devils, 3–1 win.

McPhee fought New Jersey's Joe Cirella and was a goal shy of a "Gordie Howe hat trick," as he had an assist in the game.

"The puck was coming around the boards to him and I was coming in so I laid him out and he wasn't very happy with it and I don't blame him. So he got up and had a fight. I don't know that it was much of a fight. He was a really strong guy and he had a hold of my arms and I couldn't really throw them the way I wanted to, we sorta rustled. Then, he threw me in the ground and it was over."

FIRST REACTION TO BEING TRADED FROM THE RANGERS:

McPhee was traded from the Rangers to Winnipeg for a draft choice in September 1987.

"Really disappointed. I think we're in Denver and we're going to play an exhibition game against Winnipeg, and I've hurt my neck in a fight in a preseason game and I was really struggling and I couldn't play for a couple of games. I was doing the back skate after practice and I remember looking down and I forget which coach was skating me but John Ferguson and Dan Maloney, the coach of Winnipeg, Fergy was the GM, were standing behind the glass, watching me. It was a different kind of watching 'cause I was the only guy on the ice and the two of them seemed serious. I think something might be going on here. Later that night, I got a call from Phil Esposito [Rangers GM] at the hotel and told me I was traded and that's it.

"It [being traded] can rattle you. I was rattled, I was disappointed. Certainly can empathize with players now when they get traded when I have to make a trade. You can't be flippant about it, it's a big deal. So it was a difficult thing to do to go through because your first team was your first team and I really enjoyed being a Ranger. I tried to have breakfast, even the next morning with Johnny Vanbiesbrouck and James Patrick and I didn't have much of an appetite. I just looked at them, shook their hands and walked out the door and get on the Winnipeg bus.

"There was a silver lining for me. I remember flying, I guess we were flying to LA, now on the Winnipeg flight, going to LA to play in an exhibition game. It was an awful feeling, you know, sort of projected by one team, you're with another team, really don't know anybody and everything you own is in New York in your apartment. Began figuring out how you're going to do all that, but I remember just being on a plane and saying to myself, you just have no control over your life right now and I guess this what you have to do if you want to be in the NHL, but I didn't like that loss of control. That was I think, really my inspiration for going to law school a few years down the road. Wanted to make sure that I am sort of in control of what was going to transpire in my life, but when it comes to looking at the schedule, wondering when the play the Rangers and so on, I don't recall ever doing that and I'm glad I never had to play the Rangers as a player. In some ways, it's fine the way it is. I got to play for them, and it would not have felt right to play against them. You know you're disappointed in your organization that you're traded but going on the ice and playing against your friends would not have been easy."

FIRST MANAGEMENT POSITION AFTER HIS PLAYING CAREER WAS OVER:

McPhee was the VP and director of hockey operations for the Vancouver Canucks team that met the Rangers in the 1994 Stanley Cup Final that culminated in the Rangers winning Game 7 at Madison Square Garden.

"I could tell you I thought we were going to win the Stanley Cup that night. The police escort from the hotel to the Garden was amazing. There must have been 12 motorcycles taking us over there. I really felt that the way the series was going, we had all the momentum and that we were going to win. The Rangers and that home crowd were just better that night and I remember just being devastated that it wasn't going to happen. Going down to the coaches room after the game and missing out on the Stanley Cup for the first time you had a chance to get one was devastating. I remember talking to a reporter after the game and telling him then, and I really believed it, that if it couldn't be us, I thought it was great for hockey that it was the Rangers, an Original Six team. It was the New York Rangers, 54 years or whatever it was, knowing what it would mean to that city, to that organization and again, for the league. I thought it was a really neat thing to experience."

FIRST REACTION TO SEEING HIS SON DRAFTED BY THE NHL:

In the 2016 NHL Entry Draft, McPhee's son, Graham, a left wing, was drafted in the fifth round by the Edmonton Oilers.

"It was [an amazing feeling] and I guess it's different but it allows you to relate to players better. What I mean is when I was traded, I know what that feels like. So it's helped, I think as a manager and doing things right. When things have to be done like that with my son, you know I was always certainly aware of how important it was to kids when they're at the draft to be drafted, to feel they're included and they're wanted and everything else, but when you go through it with your own kid, it's certainly magnified. You just want them to be drafted because it makes them happy. Again, it's a big day in a kid's life, so it was a big day for him and as a parent, just to have a son that [is] drafted by an NHL team and gets to go off and play Division I college hockey now. You're really lucky, and if you're lucky to be drafted by an NHL team and lucky enough to play Division I college hockey and then after that, you take your shot as a pro.

George made his NHL debut in the playoffs. (Public domain)

39
RICK MIDDLETON

I Rick Middleton was a promising young right wing who played two seasons with the Rangers before being involved in an ill-fated trade with the Boston Bruins that brought Ken Hodge to New York. Middleton, who scored 46 goals during his two-year Rangers tenure, went on to play 12 seasons with Boston. The Toronto product scored 448 goals in his 14-year career.

FIRST HOCKEY IDOL: Hall of Famer Frank Mahovlich

"Frank was the guy I remember. He was big, rangy winger with a big slap shot, and he was pretty fast. I remember he was kind of like a north-south guy but he'd go down and wind up with that big slapper. I swear, I saw him take a slap shot in the penalty shot once. Who does that way out? I can't remember if he scored, but wow."

FIRST CONTACT WITH NHL:

Rick Middleton was the 14th overall selection by the Rangers in the 1973 NHL Amateur Draft.

"I believe it was the Mount Royal hotel in Montreal. They were all in Montreal in those days and my parents were there and it was very exciting. There's always rumors going around, I remember being kinda in the hotel room beforehand. I don't remember the actual draft, it wasn't like the ones today, but even right up until the end, there was rumors that Buffalo was going to take me and the Rangers. I might've heard one. The look on my Mom and Dad's face when I got drafted in the first round, 14th taken by the New York Rangers. I remember that it was pure joy as you can imagine, pure joy. I had a great junior year that year but there was no guarantee that I was going in the first round. To be chosen by an Original Six team like the Rangers, it was, obviously, a dream come true, but the thing I remember is the look on Mom and Dad's face."

FIRST RANGERS COACH: Emile "The Cat" Francis

"Meeting "The Cat" was great. In those days, he smoked a Lucky Strike; he had a voice like gravel, and you know, just a little guy but he was an NHL icon and I was so thankful that he drafted me. I've always liked "The Cat," not only because of that, but I liked him as a coach too. That whole second year fell apart and when they got rid of him, that was the beginning of the falling apart.

FIRST RANGERS CAPTAIN: Brad Park

"I remember being treated so nicely. You're nervous, you're trying to make the team. You don't know how the veterans are gonna treat ya, you're a kid, you might even be taking one of their jobs. I just remember, that was the year after they went to the Finals and lost in the Stanley Cup to Boston. Everybody was totally first class. I'm pretty sure it was Brad Park. Brad and I spent a lot of years together, both in New York and Boston after that."

FIRST RANGERS TRAINING CAMP:

"I was a "dipsy-doodle" guy trying to go around the defensemen, which I got better at, but in my first training camp, I remember trying to beat Gilles Marotte. I thought I had him beat, I'm halfway around him and he just stuck his arm out and it was like running into a gate. It was like, okay, you're not going anywhere yet. He didn't grab me, he just put it out and it was like running into a steel gate. To me, that was an eye-opener 'cause I'm thinking, you know, these guys are men. I can do all the moves I want, but they're so strong that they're just going to, if they get a piece of me, they're going to slow me down or really hit me good. So I have to be a little smarter and pick my spots a little better, instead of just thinking I can go around everybody. It was a good lesson that Gilles gave me."

FIRST RANGERS GAME: October 9, 1974 @ MSG vs. Washington Capitals, 6–3 win

Middleton scored two third-period goals in his first Rangers game. It was also the first-ever game in Capitals franchise history.

"All these years, I had heard I had gotten two, but I didn't know it was Washington and I didn't know, historically, their first game."

FIRST RANGERS HAT TRICK: November 17, 1974 @ MSG vs. California Golden Seals, 10–0 win

Middleton scored four goals and added an assist in the Rangers' rout. The rookie winger scored twice in the first and third periods.

"We had a really good team, now the California Golden Seals weren't that good but to beat a team, 10–0. Our team was on a roll as I remember, early in that year. Once you start winning, you almost think it's gonna be too easy. I remember thinking, Jeez,this is gonna happen all the time. We've got a really good team, you know I'm playing with some great players. This is gonna be fun, and it was, but the four goals never happened again. I had I think I had 18 by Christmas, then I ended up getting a stick in the mouth in January, lost my first four teeth and I broke my ankle the following week and that was it for the Rookie of the Year."

FIRST RANGERS FIGHT: April 3, 1975 @ Philadelphia Flyers, 1–1 tie

"I've seen the grainy tape on YouTube, and I know Davey [Schultz] over the years from doing charity stuff and charity games and everything. So, I was somewhere in a bar having a few drinks with him and I might've been telling somebody else' story. I wanted to see what he would say, so I said, 'Davey, you know you're my first fight in the NHL,' and he turned and looked at me and went, 'I fought you?' He goes, 'How did I fight you?' I had not seen the tape before that and I said, 'I don't know, I must have elbowed you in the face or something.' I remember you turned around and dropped your gloves and you said you're going to 'take my friggin' head off.' I said 'I grabbed on and went for the ride, 'cause I didn't know if you're going throw a right, left or whatever. I think I grabbed both arms and went to push him up against the glass. As the tape shows, I really didn't have him up against the glass and he elbowed me in the face and my blonde hair goes flying back and he jumped me and he threw a right and then an uppercut and he missed with both of 'em."

FIRST TIME DRIVING TO NEW YORK:

"I believe I drove straight from Canada. It was an exhibition game before the season at Madison Square Garden. I don't think I went to Providence first. I think I just came right down to play a game. I remember going over the Triborough Bridge at like 2:30 in the afternoon and the big sign was Rodney Dangerfield (Dangerfield's comedy club in Manhattan). It was 'cause I was a big Rodney fan and you go over the bridge and this huge sign, Rodney Dangerfield, which I went to a couple times. I almost missed the game 'cause I had to go all the way across town and I'd never been in New York with a car in New York period. Honest to God, I thought I was going to miss the game. It must have taken me four hours."

FIRST RANGERS PLAYOFF EXPERIENCE: 1975 best-of-three preliminary round vs. New York Islanders (Rangers lost

third game, 4–3 in overtime on J. P. Parise's goal just 11 seconds into the extra session)

"It was before they [Islanders] had the big guys in there and the big '80s team but they were on their way to forming a good squad. They had some very good players. I think all the pressure was on us because they were the startup [team]. They had no pressure on them and the only had to win a two out of three, not a four out of seven. By that happening really helped spurn what happened the next year. It was just time to clean house and change the old guard. If we had won that series, we could've gone places. It was only two years [actually, three] after the Stanley Cup Finals. Losing two out of three to another New York team for the first time ever, I think it embarrassed some of the people upstairs. It was a tough series but most two out of three series are, especially when you go to the third game, the deciding game. We had it at home, we should've won it."

FIRST GAME AGAINST THE RANGERS AT MSG AS AN OPPOSING PLAYER: October 13, 1976 vs. Boston Bruins, 5–1 Rangers loss

In one of the worst trades in Rangers' history, Middleton was dealt to the Boston Bruins in May 1976 in exchange for winger Ken Hodge. The 14-year veteran never panned out during his season and a half in New York. Middleton assisted on Boston's first goal of the game.

"Even to this day, I get goosebumps going into Madison Square Garden. I was not mad a at the New York Rangers for trading me. Nobody ever wants to get traded. I was pretty sad about it when it did happen, but then, I'm thinking, Jeez, I'm going from a team that didn't make the playoffs in '75 to a perennial Stanley Cup contender with Boston. Bobby [Orr] was still on the team and Brad [Park] and the more I thought about it, the more excited I [got].

"That had to be, what, two weeks into the season. I was probably a little surprised that I was even playing as a regular. I'm not sure how many goals I got but what I do remember is that I usually had good games in New York and I liked that. I didn't do it out of any reason about being hostile, any hostility or anything. I just loved playing at Madison Square Garden; it kind of worked out well for me that I had some good games down there."

40
EDDIE MIO

Goaltender Eddie Mio spent two of his nine NHL seasons with the Rangers. Mio's best season in New York was 1982–83 when he played in 41 games and had two shutouts.

FIRST CONTACT WITH NHL:

Eddie Mio was chosen by the Chicago Black Hawks in the seventh round of the 1974 NHL Amateur Draft. Mio began his pro career in the World Hockey Association with the Indianapolis Racers before joining the Edmonton Oilers for the 1978–79 season. Mio and the Oilers joined the NHL the following season.

In December 1981, Mio was traded from the Oilers to the Rangers in exchange for center Lance Nethery. Mio played the rest of the 1981 season and the 1982 season with the Rangers before being traded to Detroit in June 1983 as part of a six-player deal.

"Well, our draft day was a little different back then. There wasn't the hoopla where you went to a building and everybody was there. It was a 20-year-old draft, you were contacted by phone. At least that's the way I was contacted, but it was still an exciting, nerve-wracking day, to say the least. I had Hall of Famer Bobby Orr call me because he was assistant GM at the time. He had just retired because of a knee injury and he was with Chicago. Wow! So that was a big thing for me, getting a phone call from him and saying I was drafted in the sixth [actually, seventh] round with the Chicago Black Hawks. I don't think you really care who the one is calling but in this situation, if it's Wayne Gretzky, Mario Lemieux, Bobby Orr, or you name it, you know, it's the fact that you are getting drafted and it's just an excellent bonus who's making this phone call."

Getting drafted by the Black Hawks was "not a position where I thought I was going to make it because they had Hall of Famer Tony Esposito, Michel Dumas, and Mike Veisor, so they were pretty set there."

FIRST REACTION TO BEING TRADED TO RANGERS: December 11, 1981

"Well, I was sent down [by Edmonton] to Wichita to get some playing time and Glen Sather [Oilers GM at the time] said, 'Hey, sit down there, we'll try and trade ya.' I had asked for a trade before I went down. So we're spending the time now, it's actually living with the owner, Larry Gordon, and he was also the GM at the time because we knew each other from Edmonton. He was the GM of Edmonton two years before that. In any case, I was just sitting there and it was Larry that happened to get the phone call from Glen Sather. It was the fact that I was going to New York was a great thing. When I got to New York, a fellow by the name of John Davidson picked me up at the airport."

FIRST RANGERS GAME: December 19, 1981 @ Pittsburgh Penguins, 3–3 tie

"The next day they were coming back from Colorado, I think it was. So they had a practice and the equipment manager had come over and said what number do you want to wear, and I said, well what numbers do you have available, you've got a few goaltenders here. Says, we got number 1 and I say, well, no I'm not wearing that, it should be retired. It's Eddie Giacomin's, and I said, 'Can I make up a number?' And he said, sure, so I made up 41 because my number was 31 throughout my high school and junior and college days. The first day I put the jersey on, I was a little nervous 'cause I was playing that night.

"Pittsburgh, I had played against them in Edmonton for two years. Going in, the one thing that, I just wanted to make a good example and have a good game. When you're coming in from a trade, it's your first game, you want the guys, especially for a goaltender, you want the guys to respect you and say, 'Wow, he gave us an effort, we're gonna give him an effort.' So I was pretty nervous, my first game going into Pittsburgh, but as the game got going, I got comfortable with the team. All I wanted to do was stop the puck and get that first victory and get outta there, just so that, at least, the players knew I came into play hockey for them."

FIRST RANGERS WIN: December 27, 1981 @ MSG vs. Pittsburgh Penguins, 5–3 win

"Sure, I got the [game] puck, somebody gave me the puck but I wasn't worried about the puck. We had the two points. We had a good game and I came out of it feeling really, really good, so that was more important that the puck, because if I did get the puck, I don't know where it is now."

FIRST RANGERS COACH: Herb Brooks

"I had known Herb from college. I played [at] Colorado College and he was coaching [the] Minnesota Gophers. Although, we had met at All-American banquet, I had met him there but nothing with any discussion. I think he knew me coming in after four years of playing college, so it was an easy transition to saying hello and welcome. I was a little in awe because obviously they had just won a "Miracle on Ice," the [1980] Olympics, but even during my college days, I had heard he was a pretty tough coach, pretty no nonsense type guy.

"This guy was one of the best coaches, the way he could adjust in a game. I was in awe because I just loved the way he got ready for games, especially in the playoffs. You know, when he talked to you, you felt, 'Wow, we got something to prove, we got to do this,' and then he gives you that excitement that I'm wanting to go out and play."

FIRST RANGERS CAPTAIN: Barry Beck

"Barry is awesome, I ended up rooming with him my second year there. He was a humorous guy, so he kept you on your toes with the one liners and all that between him and Nick Fotiu and then even Herb [Brooks] would get involved. He wasn't the big, kinda in your face, but he led by example. He went out, played hard every night. He loved wearing that jersey, he loved wearing the 'C' and he played like a captain should, so he led more by example.

"He [Beck] was more of an awesome presence. I mean, six-four, the guy was in great shape. You know you just wanted to play well with him on the ice. You didn't want him yelling at ya, but there was also times where you needed that little push, he was there to give you the push."

FIRST START IN A RANGERS PLAYOFF GAME: April 7, 1982, Game 1, Patrick Division semifinals vs. Philadelphia, 4–1 loss

"Going into the Garden, again, nervous, you know from getting the start, so we went out and I didn't have a good game. I did not have a good game. I'll give the Flyers and "Clarky" [Flyers Hall of Fame center Bobby Clarke] and all them, they were coming off strong. I think we had the circus was in town, so it was a late start. You know how they used to get the circus out of there and we would go on the ice.

"Coming into the dressing room after the game, everybody was disappointed. We had a good year. Philadelphia ended up in third, we were second, so losing that game kind of put a damper on me the whole year, or so we thought until Herb came in. It was a pretty good talking to and then as you know, we took the next game and then the next two in Philly [to win the series]."

Eddie loved playing for Herb Brooks. Photo courtesy of New York Rangers

41
DOMINIC MOORE

Center Dominic Moore played with ten teams over a 13-year NHL career. Moore, who was known as a defensive stalwart, had two stints with the Rangers. During his second time around in New York, Moore was named the winner of the Bill Masterton Memorial Trophy in 2014. In Game 6 of that season's Eastern Conference finals against Montreal at Madison Square Garden, Moore scored the only goal as the Rangers won 1–0 to advance to the Stanley Cup Final.

FIRST PLAYER WHO HE IDOLIZED AS A KID:

"Doug Gilmour. Toronto had some pretty lean years when I was like under twelve. Then, when I was 12, 13, 14, they had these epic seasons with Gilmour and Wendel Clark and Cliff Fletcher was the GM at that time. I was pretty undersized as a kid; I was always really, really small. I was a late bloomer and Doug was this small and pretty slight guy, but he always seemed to have two black eyes, you know, growing up with two older brothers, I kinda knew what it was like to have that gritty mentality. I just loved the way he played and admired him a lot.

"When I was in high school, I went to St. Mike's, which is [in] downtown Toronto. The Leafs used to sometimes practice at our arena. I had heard through the kids whispering around the halls that there were some NHLers in the rink practicing and this is the middle of the school day. I heard Gilmour was there so between classes you had like six minutes and I ran over to the arena. I was pretty small, so I was able to like sneak in around people and the crowd in there. I went into the locker room and the players were off the ice and there was all this media in the locker room interviewing Doug. I kinda just shimmied in there and there happened to be a media guy, Jim McKenny, who used to play in the NHL and ended up working for CityTV in Toronto. The only reason I knew him was because the week before he had done these features on CityTV where he picked an athlete of the week and the community. He had happened to pick me the week before and did a report on CTV news, highlighting me and he knew that I loved Gilmour. So I went up and said hi to him and as the media was done asking Doug the questions, he kinda came over and introduced me to Doug and Gilmour gave me a stick and he couldn't have been nicer. I can't even describe the thrill; I was like shaking and I went back to class with this Gilmour stick in my hands and I was late for class. I obviously could care less but I walked into class with the stick in my hand signed by Gilmour. The teacher could pretty quickly see what was going on and he was an astute guy and he gave me a little bit of a hard time for being late. He was nice enough to hold onto to the stick for me the rest of the day. I went home and immediately picked up the six-inch nails from the basement. My parents weren't home from work yet and I put these huge nails into the wall in my bedroom and put the stick on the wall. It's been there ever since. That was my hero, Dougie Gilmour."

FIRST CONTACT WITH NHL:

Dominic Moore was chosen by the Rangers in the third round of the 2000 NHL Entry Draft.

"Bob Crocker. I don't know if you've heard his name but he's a longtime scout, I would suspect. He's in his eighties now. I remember meeting him; he came to interview me and he was a scout in the New England area. He'd watched me play my freshman year in college and interviewed me at one point, just an incredibly kind man. I remember being at the draft in Calgary and sitting in the stands. I had a pretty good view of the Rangers' table. I was probably 20 rows up, but I could see the Rangers' table right down in front of me on the floor. When the third round came around, I could see during the Rangers' pick, the table deliberating. I saw Mr. Crocker kind of pointing at his head. Kind of my guess was that he was making a case for me, saying I was a smart player. Sure enough, they picked me, and I couldn't have been more thrilled. I had only been to New York once ever and that was like when I was 18, before I went to college. My Mom and Dad and I drove, rented a motor home, and drove down and parked it in New Jersey. That was my first trip to Manhattan. It was an awe-inspiring trip at that point so to be picked by the big city, the Big Apple, is a huge thrill. The first thing I did after I got picked was meet the brass, take some pictures and everything, but I felt like I wanted to go to the gym before I went out to celebrate. As special as the draft was and everything, to me it was like a stepping-stone. I hadn't proven anything. If I wanted to be an NHL player, it was a stepping-stone, not an arrival. I remember going with my brother [Steve, who played for the Colorado Avalanche], who had already been drafted, we went to the gym and got a workout before we went out toe celebrate. It wasn't like we didn't celebrate; we still went out as a family to celebrate after that."

FIRST RANGERS TRAINING CAMP:

"The scrimmage, I picked up the puck in the neutral zone and I was skating towards the offensive zone and I cut across the blue line to my right, out of the corner of my eye, I could see someone lining me up, you know, the whole "trolley tracks" thing, like you cut across the middle, you gotta be ready. So I saw this person coming but I thought I would make it seem like I didn't and at the last minute, I'd kind of reverse shoulder then. So, that's what I did, unfortunately it was Mark Messier. Honestly, it might've been the best hit of my career. I don't know if I had a better hit in 15 years in the league 'cause he literally went flying and within about three milliseconds they had like Chris Simon and [Matthew] Barnaby, must've been like Dale Purinton, like all three of them. One of them might've been been on my team in the scrimmage, they rushed me. Glen Sather was actually officiating the scrimmage and he just couldn't stop laughing. I apologized to Mark afterwards. I definitely didn't know it was him. I was just trying to protect myself. In truth, he probably was letting up right as I leaned into him, but he couldn't have been nicer. He was very understanding and good about it, which was pretty impressive of him. If it were me, I don't know if I would have been as understanding as he was."

FIRST TIME PUTTING ON THE RANGERS JERSEY:

"Pretty special. My first game was in Montreal so even more special in terms of the history of that building, [the Forum in Montreal] especially as a Canadian kid. Even though I'm from Toronto, I was very steeped in all of the history of the game and collected hockey cards, knew everything about it. To be able to be in the locker room, in Montreal, playing my first game for the New York Rangers, looking around the room and seeing these players that I'd watched on TV so many times, then putting that jersey on. Pretty, pretty, amazing, special feeling."

FIRST RANGERS COACH: Glen Sather

"I remember what he said to me before that first game. It was basically just, 'Hey kid, go out and have fun.' Glen had a way of knowing the right thing to say and he was a lot wiser. Sometimes a simple message like that was more than anything else went a longer way than anything else that a coach could've said. Played a good game, went out there and tried to follow his advice."

FIRST RANGERS CAPTAIN: Mark Messier

"He just had such a presence. When you grow up, having watched someone and you know their history, they have even more of a presence. Even without all that, he had a dynamic presence in the locker room. Just the way he carried himself, the respect he commanded. He was very warm. When I first got called up, it looked like I might stay around for a while and he was already talking about trying to help me find a place and things like that, things that you didn't need to think about. He had enough to worry about on his own, being the best player on the team, but that was the kind of guy he was.

FIRST RANGERS GAME: November 1st, 2003 @ Montreal Canadiens, 5–1 win

Moore had three primary assists in his first game with the Rangers.

"I don't know if I ever had a moment where I felt I belonged. I remember playing with, I think it was Dan LaCouture and Jamie Lundmark. We only played about seven minutes. I remember all the points, but I don't know which one was first. One was kinda off a pass off the pads where I don't know if Chris Simon buried the rebound. Second assist, it was just kind of a breakout and I ended up making an outlet pass to Jamie Lundmark and I think he went down all the way and kind of spotted up and scored. Then the third point, I think it was a power play where I got the puck along the goal line to the left of the goalie and kind of put it through the crease and it ended up going in on the backside. Sometimes you get fortunate as well. I think I played a good game. I had good energy but it was also a fortunate night where things happened, things happened for me so it was pretty special for sure."

FIRST RANGERS GAME AT MADISON SQUARE GARDEN: November 2, 2003 vs. Colorado Avalanche, 3–2 overtime loss

"There's a huge amount of lore and respect for Madison Square Garden and I had been there for some of the exhibition games and things like that. Some of the coolest part of being in Madison Square Garden is kind of seeing the things that you would never see as a fan. So, as a player, when you first see kind of the locker room and the space underneath the stand like that, that's when you feel like, Man, I'm really here, I'm really somewhere, and then going out onto the ice. In some ways, it's just more familiar. MSG has always been one of the most special places for me. Obviously, it's my favorite place to play in the league. It's just the environment, the atmosphere, you know the "true blue" fans in the upper deck. Those things are very unique. My brother was playing that game too, so that was pretty special. My parents were able to watch us play against each other. My first home game and my brother's first full season in the league. There's some pretty cool pictures of that game with both of us in the picture. There's a hilarious hockey card where I'm actually hitting my brother from behind into the boards, which is great, but that was a great experience for me."

FIRST RANGERS GOAL: October 6, 2005 @ MSG vs. Montreal Canadiens, 4–3 OT loss

Moore's first NHL goal tied the game late in the third period.

"I felt like it was a point shot and either a tip or a rebound. I was coming from the goalie's right, across in front of him. I don't remember too much about that goal, other than the kind of exhilaration part of it and celebrating. Kind of being aware of the whole atmosphere and the crowd cheering for the goal and that special feeling that you get from that."

FIRST RANGERS PLAYOFF SERIES: 2006 Eastern Conference quarterfinals vs. New Jersey Devils (Rangers were swept in four games)

"I don't know if I want to talk about that. I mean the regular season was really special because the Rangers hadn't been in the playoffs for eight [seasons] and we made the playoffs. So it was a huge, huge accomplishment and to be a part of that was very special. Then, to be swept by New Jersey, after that, was pretty tough to take. New Jersey was obviously a seasoned playoff team and you could argue that we weren't. I recall [Jaromir] Jagr separating his shoulder, trying to hit [Scott] Gomez. That was a tough moment for us where it looked like things were turning for the worst. That was a tough one to swallow after a really successful season."

FIRST TIME PLAYING AT MSG AS AN OPPOSING PLAYER: October 12, 2006, 6–5 Rangers loss

Moore returned to the Garden for the first time since he was traded to the Pittsburgh Penguins in July 2006. Moore had one assist against his former team.

"I had that feeling many a time in my career. There's obviously a little extra motivation but I think for the most part, you're just focused on doing your job well and making a difference for your team. There's definitely an element of 'Yeah, I want to show that team, you know, what I'm capable of and what I can do.'"

FIRST RANGERS STADIUM SERIES GAME: January 26, 2014 @ Yankee Stadium vs. New Jersey Devils, 7–3 win

Moore had a goal and an assist in the game.

"That probably was one of the standout memories from that year is the Yankee Stadium games and playing catch. It's just one of those things that as a sports fan, someone who appreciates history of things. Being able to play a hockey game at Yankee Stadium, with a storied franchise like that, you just want to kind of enjoy it. Doing the typical warm-up routine underneath like you would for a normal game and it was all fine. Embracing the moment and time to relish it was something that I wanted to try and do. I think the game got delayed because of the glare, so had the idea of going out and having a catch with Billy Southard, the equipment manager. That was amazing. I'll never forget that."

FIRST RANGERS STANLEY CUP FINAL: 2014 vs. Los Angeles Kings

Moore scored the only goal as the Rangers beat the Montreal Canadiens, 1–0, in Game 6 of the Eastern Conference finals to advance to the Stanley Cup Final.

"That goal is obviously the most important and memorable moment of my career. Never forget that. I mean it was an awesome, incredible play by Brian Boyle there to find me in the slot and it was a very tight game. Obviously, they [Montreal] were without [goalie] Carey Price [who was injured in the series opener] and things could still have gone either way very easily. To be able to wrap that game up in six was huge for us. It was just an incredible moment. Again, the history of the Rangers for me is important. Having it been 20 years exactly to when the Rangers were last playing for the Cup was surreal too. To kind of have been a part of getting back there and the kind of jubilation and stuff after that game on the ice sharing that with our teammates and coaches and staff, was a pretty special feeling for me."

FIRST MASTERTON TROPHY: 2013–14 season

"It's a testament to some of those qualities that I hopefully displayed throughout my career. It's also a testament to the people that are part of that and whether it's family or teammates, friends or whoever, no one perseveres on their own really. To me, it's kind of a testament to all of those things and to be recognized in that way was amazing. It was also a nice cap on an amazing season."

Dom rates his series-winning goal against Montreal in Game 6 of the 2014 Eastern Conference finals as the most memorable moment of his career. (Photo by Mark Rosenman)

42
JOHN MUCKLER

John Muckler was a five-time Stanley Cup winner with the Edmonton Oilers. Muckler won four of those Cups as an assistant coach and was the head coach in 1990 when the Oilers captured their fifth Cup in seven seasons. Muckler was hired to replace the fired Colin Campbell during the Olympic break in February 1998. During his 2½ years behind the Rangers bench, Muckler compiled a 70–88–24 (with 3 overtime losses) record.

FIRST GAME ATTENDED AS A KID:

"Toronto Maple Leafs. I was maybe about 15, 16. Montreal played Toronto that night, Rocket Richard scored a goal. I think Montreal beat Toronto.

"Syl Apps lives in Paris, Ontario. That's where I lived. I guess I looked up to him. He wasn't playing at that time, but he was the only person from Paris, Ontario, to ever be associated with the National Hockey League."

FIRST EXPERIENCE AS A PLAYER-COACH FOR THE NEW YORK ROVERS:

John Muckler was a player-coach for the New York Rovers of the Eastern Hockey League in the 1960-61 season. Muckler took over for the fired Lloyd Ailsby in midseason. The goalie on that team was future Ranger Eddie Giacomin.

"Well, Eddie was a great goalkeeper. [Gilles] Villemure came after Eddie. Eddie turned pro, I guess for a couple of years and then Villemure came in to replace him who also ended up in New York. So my two goalkeepers in Long Island (Rangers played their home games in Commack) were eventually New York Rangers."

The Rovers became the Long Island Ducks for the 1961–62 season. Former Rangers color analyst Sal "Red Light" Messina was a goaltender on that team.

"Sal was a great guy. I loved Sal and he was really into hockey and tried his best. He'd go out, put on the pads, practiced with us. He did a good job, really. Players liked to shoot at him. He is all about hockey and he was a great, great person."

Muckler coached the Ducks for two seasons beginning in 1961.

"We were the only professional hockey team on the Island at that time. The Commack Arena was an incomplete building, actually. Every Sunday, I don't know what it sat, maybe 4,000 people but it was jammed full and they enjoyed themselves. They drank beer. I can remember one instance, a lady who attended her first game. They were booing the referees as they came off the ice and she had a broom in her hand. I don't know where it came from, but it hit the referee over the head. They brought him into the dressing room to give him aid. We didn't have a Zamboni. We used to flood the ice with a hose in between periods, but the fans were great. We loved playing in front of the fans.
"Eventually, we became a good hockey club and go on to win a championship."

FIRST GAME BEHIND THE RANGERS BENCH:
February 26, 1998 @ Toronto Maple Leafs, 5–2 win

"We won that day and [Wayne] Gretzky was phenomenal. He really played well in that game. General manager hired me, Neil Smith, and it wasn't much of a hockey club really. It was a lot of veterans who were making a lot of money and they couldn't compete with the younger people in the National Hockey League. I think I was there for two and half years and we never did get any better, never made the playoffs."

FIRST RANGERS TRAINING CAMP:

"We couldn't make many, many changes. We had a draft choice [Manny Malhotra] I forget the kid's name, wasn't really ready to play [and] when he did play, he played on the third and fourth line. He became a good third-line center ice man in the National Hockey League and had success in that area, but he wasn't good enough at that particular time to make any difference in our hockey club. So we basically went with the same players that we had the year before."

Muckler was the Rangers' coach for Wayne Gretzky's final career game.

"Sad, very sad. He was a great person, a great hockey player who knew he couldn't go any further and retired. That was the best decision he made. Everybody was sorry to see him go. I tried to talk him into staying for another year, but he said, 'No, John, it's time for me to hang up the skates.' So it was very sad.

"For the final game, my daughter was pregnant. I told the PR guy [John Rosasco] as soon as it's born, come down and tell me. So it was the third period of the last game he [Gretzky] played. He had told me, 'John, your daughter's going to have a boy.' So I called timeout and I brought him over to the bench. I said, 'Gretz, you're right. I have a baby boy grandson and now I want you to go out there and score him a goal. He backs up a couple of steps and says, 'Muck, I could've done that maybe five or six years ago. Don't ask me to do that.' Everybody thought I was calling timeout to give him recognition, but that's what we were talking about."

FIRST RANGERS CAPTAIN: Brian Leetch

"Brian was at the tail end of his career and gave everything he had left. I loved Brian. He's a true professional and he gave you what he had every night. A great personality, everybody loves him. You couldn't have a better teammate or a better player for a coach. Those two [Gretzky and Leetch] were just super people and super Hall of Fame hockey players."

FIRST STANLEY CUP WIN AS A HEAD COACH:

"We were down three games to one to Winnipeg [in the 1990 Smythe Division semifinals] and then we came back and we won that series. Then I think we'd beat LA, Chicago, and into Boston. Boston was the number one team that year but 'Slats' (Glen Sather) made a trade for [Joe] Murphy and [Adam] Graves. I tried to make them feel at ease so I said I'll put 'em with first line veterans. Well, that didn't work out because they were scared to do anything with the puck. They were always throwing it to the veteran. So I took 'em off of that and made a line of Graves, [Martin] Gelinas, and Murphy. It was probably one of the best lines that we had going into the playoffs. They were just super, the kid line and they scored important goals for us, they were physical, they did more than what we could ask for, and that kind of turned our team around because we'd lost a lot of players through age or whatever. 'Fuhrsie' [Oilers goalie Grant Fuhr] didn't play, I think he was hurt and Billy Ranford took over. [Paul] Coffey wasn't there, Gretz wasn't there. During the year, we kind of bounced around a little bit. Not even finished much over .500 to get in the playoffs. From there on, we hit Winnipeg and it took seven games, but from there on, they couldn't stop us. We were really good. Played Chicago before we went to Boston. I remember the first game which was four (actually three) overtimes, which is a league record for a Stanley Cup Final. I remember one instance, it was late in the third period and one of their defensemen got the puck and as he received the puck at the blue line, somebody hits Billy and knocked him out of the net. You could hit the goalkeeper at that time, it was never called. Left-hand shot, he went to his backhand, instead of firing it forehand, and he misses it and we came on and win. On top of that, you know the [Petr] Klima story."

Note: Klima scored the game-winning goal in the third overtime of Game 1 of the 1990 Stanley Cup Final.

FIRST REACTION WHEN THE GAME ENDED AND THE CUP WAS WON:

"Happy, happy for my assistant coaches, my players. It was a big family that we were. It really carried us. I don't any team in the National Hockey League can win a Stanley Cup without being a family to be able to support their teams, protect their backs, we had that and we had talent on top of that. During the playoffs, it came to the top. Everybody got along well, they supported each other. When they made mistakes, they get it out of the dressing room. Everybody was very positive, and it was nice to see 'em raise the Stanley Cup in Boston."

Coach Muckler had a special request of Wayne Gretzky in The Great One's final game. (Public Domain)

43

DON MURDOCH

Right wing Don Murdoch was a promising young player who never reached his full potential. The 20 year old collected 56 points in 59 games in his rookie season of 1976–77. Murdoch was plagued throughout his career by drug problems and legal issues. He played parts of four seasons with the Rangers during his six-year NHL career.

FIRST CONTACT WITH NHL:

Don Murdoch was the sixth overall pick by the Rangers in the 1976 NHL Amateur Draft.

"I was with a friend of mine; his name was Barry Dean and he was playing for the Phoenix Roadrunners of the WHA and I was down visiting him in Phoenix. I can remember it was the night before [the draft] and there were a couple of other hockey players there. They said, 'All right, it's your big job day so we better take you out.' We went out and had a few cocktails and of course, I was nervous. You don't know what's going to happen. I can remember getting up the next day. Unfortunately, I was in Phoenix and they were in New York, so like 6 o'clock, my time was like 9 o'clock here. I remember I got a phone call from my brother, Bob [who had just finished his first NHL season with the California Golden

Seals], and I'm thinking I might go in the first round, 'cause everybody interviews you; I was praying I was gonna go in the first round. I figured everybody said I was going to be in the top ten or fifteen. They tried to locate me, so finally I get a phone call and Barry Dean wakes me up, I was sleeping and a little hungover. He said, 'Your brother is on the phone.' So I get up and I answer the phone and my brother Bobby is there and he says, 'You awake?' and he says, "Congratulations, you got drafted by the New York Rangers in the second round. I was kinda like, 'Oh, okay,' I wasn't overjoyed, and he said, 'Yeah, you went six in the second round, aren't you happy?' I said, 'I'm excited.' Then he says, 'No, no I'm just kidding, you were the Rangers' first pick and you went sixth overall in the first round,' the son of a bitch. Then all of a sudden, I'm all excited.

"It's like 6:30, quarter to seven in the morning there and you're kinda trying to wake up. He said, 'They're trying to locate you.' I was over visiting my brother, Bobby in California and then I shot over for a couple of days to stay with my friend, Barry Dean. He said, 'Yeah, you better get ready because John Ferguson [Rangers GM] is going to give you a call. Then, I got up, brushed my teeth, and washed my face to get ready 'cause I better be wide awake here. About half an hour later, John Ferguson called to congratulate me."

SEEING THE RANGERS JERSEY FOR THE FIRST TIME AND PUTTING IT ON:

"It's unbelievable. I can remember even going to training camp, to get in the dressing room to see your number there. Opening night with your number on it and your jersey, it was phenomenal. Especially, the Original Six. As a kid growing up, we watched TV. The big day was Saturday. Mom and Dad used to let us eat with them and then we'd watch *Hockey Night in Canada* and have hamburgers and to watch the Original Six and to be part of it was just phenomenal, it was an unbelievable feeling."

FIRST RANGERS TRAINING CAMP:

"We had a rookie camp and we had it in Montreal. Team Canada was playing, and Phil Esposito was on Team Canada. I don't know if Rod [Gilbert] was playing that year, my agent got me down to see them before the game and I got to meet Phil Esposito before the game. Going into main camp was pretty phenomenal too. When you get into the dressing room and being a first rounder, I got to go into the major dressing room. I believe I sat beside Rod Gilbert my first training camp so that's when it really came surreal. Is when you get to training camp and you see all the guys there. Rod Gilbert, Phil Esposito, Steve Vickers, Ron Greschner, Dave Maloney, all the guys that have played before. That's when it really became a reality for me, when you're sitting in the same dressing room as all those guys."

FIRST RANGERS COACH: John Ferguson

"It was pretty amazing because in Canada you grew up watching a lot of the Montreal Canadiens and John Ferguson was the tough guy. He was a little intimidating. I remember when I signed my contract, it was a little intimidating. He's just an intimidating guy to look at. John was really good, he treated me a hundred percent. He had confidence in me from the start. Just said, 'Kid, keep working and you're here to do one thing and that's to score goals' and that's what I kinda did."

FIRST RANGERS CAPTAIN: Phil Esposito

"Phil, he was just a big guy. He was such a good guy to get along with. I remember going in there and Phil always had a smile and was always joking with the guys. Phil just made you feel comfortable and he was really good to all the rookies. We had a lot of rookies that year. We had Davey Farrish, Mike McEwen, myself. The other good thing was that it was a young team to start with because you still had [Ron] Greschner and [Dave] Maloney and a couple of other guys who weren't much older than us. One thing I loved about him [Esposito] was that he just always seemed to be in a good mood. He was a bit of a prankster and just really took care of the young guys. Phil was phenomenal."

FIRST RANGERS GAME: October 6, 1976 @ MSG vs. Minnesota North Stars, 6–5 win

"I mean, surreal. That's when it comes. I can remember Madison Square Garden, stepping on that ice to start the season. I just couldn't sleep but the stuff on the ice and obviously your first NHL game. For me to get two goals in that first game, I remember when I scored my first goal, I've got a picture of it and I think I jumped four or five feet in the air. I believe it was Rod Gilbert got the puck for me. I think it was on the power play, if I'm not mistaken. Then, to score another one, that's when you knew what it was, stepping on that ice in the first home opener."

FIRST RANGERS HAT TRICK: October 12, 1976 @ Minnesota North Stars, 10–4 win

Murdoch set a Rangers franchise record and tied an NHL rookie record by scoring five goals against Minnesota. The 19 year old scored three goals in the second period to complete a hat trick and added two more in the third.

"I think that was my third game in the NHL and I scored two in the first. If I'm not mistaken, I don't think I even scored a goal until the second period. I think I got three in the second period. To get the hat trick was unbelievable. It just seemed everything I touched was going in. I remembered the fourth goal. I was on the bench and there was like ten seconds left in the game. I wasn't even on Phil's line at that time, I was playing with Walter Tkaczuk and Steve Vickers. Phil skated over to the bench and said to Fergy [Rangers coach John Ferguson], 'Put the kid out, let's see if we can get him another one.' I jumped up and I was over the boards before Fergy even said I could go. I can remember I went to the faceoff, it was in Minnesota's end and Phil said, 'Look kid, you stand right here,' he says,

'Don't move. If I lose the draw, still don't move.' He said, 'I'll get it to ya.' Phil lost the draw but still got it back to me and I rifled it and the fifth one went in. Another one I could jump ten feet in the air on that one. I can remember after the game, everybody's coming up [reporters]. It didn't really comprehend in your head that you scored five goals in the game. I remember in the shower and just like 'Holy shit, that just really happened?' You wanna get on the phone and call your family and everything. I remember getting on the bus and Bill Chadwick [Rangers TV analyst] came up to me and he said, 'Donnie, you tied the record in the NHL,' and I said, 'Oh, is that right?' He says, 'Yeah, you and a guy named Howie Meeker. You tied his record scoring five goals in the game as a rookie.' So that was pretty phenomenal."

FIRST PENALTY SHOT: November 3, 1976 @ Vancouver Canucks, 6–1 win

"Harold Snepsts [Canucks defenseman] pulled me down and I got a penalty shot in the first game in front of my parents. When I took that penalty shot, I can remember going in on it. I went in there and I was focused and I scored. When I was coming back, the referee said to me, 'If you woulda missed, I would've given you another shot.' I said, 'What do you mean?' He says, 'You didn't see that puck land in front of you?' I said, 'No, I was so focused.' I guess when I went to shoot the penalty shot, some fans with a puck, were way up top in the stands. I guess it bounced right beside me and it went to the side, but I was so focused, I didn't even see it."

FIRST RANGERS FIGHT: January 23, 1977 @ Vancouver vs. Vancouver Canucks, 6–2 loss

"We were playing in Vancouver and I'm from British Columbia. I had people down from my hometown, relatives and stuff and my Mom and Dad were there. I remember just when the game started, Walter [Tkaczuk] got a draw back to me. I shot it, it hit the crossbar and went up in the stands. I remember Jack McIlhargey come up to me and he said, 'Kid, if you touch that puck again,' he says, 'I'll cut your fucking eyes out,' and I'm like, "Yeah, yeah, okay,' so sure as shit, the puck comes back to where we are. Walter gets it back, I rifle it and then all of a sudden, I see this guy come flying at me and he's got his gloves off and his stick off and all of a sudden, just before he gets to me, and I threw my gloves off, he stepped on his stick and he fell into my stomach. So I just kinda grabbed him and started punching like crazy. Then, everybody came in there. Jack McIlhargey would've killed me in a fight. He was a tough guy, but unfortunately, he tripped on is stick and kinda fell into me so I was able to grab him and start swinging. After that, Nickie Fotiu kind of tuned him up. He went after him and then things settled down."

FIRST ALL- STAR GAME AS A RANGER: January 25, 1977 @ Vancouver

"My Mom and Dad are there. Playing in the All Star game was unbelievable 'cause Rod Gilbert got picked for a first All-Star right wing and I got second All-Star wing. Him and I stayed behind and we roomed together. They had the Vancouver Canucks players sitting at a table with with each one of the players' parents. Guess who was at my table with Jack McIlhargey. I remember my Mom said to him, 'It's a good thing you didn't beat my son up.' She says, 'I'd really hit ya.' It's funny because Jack and I ended up being pretty good friends after."

FIRST STANLEY CUP FINAL GAME: May 13, 1979 @ Montreal Canadiens, Game 1, 4–1 win. Rangers went on to lose the series in five games

"Getting through the Islanders [in the semifinals] was almost like the Stanley Cup. In playing in Montreal, the Forum, I remember that first game. Obviously, you know the story. A lot of we got there was because of JD. He just stood on his head as the goaltender. I can remember us going in there and, obviously we're just happy to get by the Islanders. So that alone, being the Stanley Cup Final and playing against the great Montreal team. There must've been ten, twelve, there could be more Hall of Famers on that team. To get in there and to win that first game, I mean, you had to pinch me, is this for real! I mean, let's be honest. I think we ended up fourteenth or something in the standings, but everything, in playoffs, just fell into place. Montreal and being the Stanley Cup Final, I mean, that's where you've got everybody phoning and sending congratulations and stuff, but to win that first game and then unfortunately, we JD in the second game. I don't know if that blew the sails out on us or what but it definitely put a damper on things."

Murdoch set a Rangers franchise record and tied an NHL rookie record by scoring five goals against Minnesota. (Public Domain)

44
RICK NASH

Rick Nash, a 6'4" left wing, was the first overall pick of the Columbus Blue Jackets in the 2002 NHL Entry Draft. Nash played nine seasons in Columbus before being traded to the Rangers in July 2012. Nash scored 145 goals during his six seasons in New York before being traded to Boston in February 2018.

FIRST CONTACT WITH NHL:

Rick Nash was the first overall pick of the Columbus Blue Jackets in the 2002 NHL Entry Draft.

"I remember meeting with Columbus and [Blue Jackets general manager] Doug MacLean at the time, you know, they had the third overall pick and there was a bunch of speculation. He was telling me that Philly was trying to move up to that number one spot, [as] was Florida, to get me and he was telling me how much they wanted me, and I was like, well then I guess, you know, there's only one thing to do. And then he said, 'I love it. I'm going to try and move up and get that spot.' Funny enough, we were sitting there and Gino Reda, (TSN correspondent) came running up, probably 10 minutes before the draft started and he said, 'We just got work that Columbus traded for the number one pick and right then and there, it's kind of when it first hit me that I might be taken first overall."

FIRST NHL GOAL: October 10, 2002 @ Columbus vs. Chicago Blackhawks, 2–1 win

"It was a blur for sure, I still have the puck and game sheet. Just to play in your first NHL game, growing up in Toronto and you know, being a dream of a lifetime and then to score a goal, you know put the icing on the cake. It was incredible."

FIRST REACTION TO BEING TRADED TO RANGERS: July 23, 2012

"I was actually at a golf tournament. I remember Scott Howson [Blue Jackets GM] called me and he said, 'We finally got a deal done and it's the New York Rangers.' The first thing that kind of hit me was Original Six, you know, growing up in Toronto and a hockey environment and then come to Columbus. College football mainly is number one here and hockey is kind of second fiddle to that. So first thought to me was Original Six, you know, New York Rangers, the blue sweater and give them the chance to play at MSG and be part of an organization that kinda, I was used to growing up with the Maple Leafs."

FIRST RANGERS GAME: January 19, 2013 @ Boston Bruins, 3–1 loss (lockout delayed start of the season)

"It was just one of those things where you're so excited to go to MSG and play in front of the Ranger fans and that kind of gets put on hold, but for the right reasons. Everyone wants a fair deal, but I do remember putting on the white sweater. It was in Boston and there's so much history behind it and the only thing that I can relate it to, which, you know, American fans might not understand, but it's like putting on that red and white Maple Leaf when you play for Team Canada here, there's so much history, there's so many stories behind it. There's so much passion behind it and I have the same feeling with putting on the Ranger shirt."

FIRST RANGERS COACH: John Tortorella

"The one thing I appreciated about "Torts" was honesty. You always knew where he stood. I truly felt like he changed the culture in New York, with all those guys in their great years that they had. There were no games with him. He didn't play head games or mind games, what you get with some coaches. I think over the years he kind of wears on some players and then he's gone and then you realize how good it actually was when he was there once he's gone."

FIRST RANGERS CAPTAIN: Ryan Callahan

"He [Callahan] was a captain who led by example. The way he played, it was so impressive. Obviously, playing against him for a lot of years and then to get the chance to play with him. You just see all the work and dedication that he put into the game."

FIRST RANGERS GOAL: January 20, 2013 @ MSG vs. Pittsburgh Penguins, 6–3 loss

"I think they were beating us pretty bad funny enough and it was towards the end of the third period. I think it was a pretty nice goal. I forgot who passed it and then I sprung in and made a backhand, forehand move and beat (Marc-Andre) Fleury."

NOTE: Derek Stepan got the assist on Nash's first Ranger goal. The Penguins goaltender was Tomas Vokoun.

FIRST STADIUM SERIES GAMES AND WINTER CLASSIC: January 26 and January 29, 2014 @ Yankee Stadium, January 1, 2018 @ Citi Field

"The Stadium Series ones stick out just 'cause of Yankee Stadium and all the history with that organization. Getting to play twice was pretty cool, and then the Winter Classic with everything that comes behind that and doing it at Citi Field. You know it was crazy cold."

FIRST STANLEY CUP FINAL GAME: June 4, 2014 @ Los Angeles Kings, 3–2 loss in overtime

"Yeah, in LA, it was incredible. It all just kind of becomes a blur. Like once you get into the elimination rounds, you know you're out there and it's kind of like an out of body experience. You don't really remember every detail, like some things stick out. I remember warm up of game one, I remember warm up of game three, coming back to New York and everyone being so excited and having a chance. Just that season in general and that playoff run, you just think of everything that has to go right and has to fall into place to even get the opportunity to do it. You know one of the things that stick out is just all the Rangers fans along the glass in LA and not only in LA, no matter where you went. It's something that I wish every NHL player could experience."

Rick wishes every NHL player could experience what playing in a Stanley Cup Final as a Ranger is like. (Photo by Mark Rosenman)

45
BERNIE NICHOLS

Center Bernie Nichols put together a spectacular 18-year career in the NHL. Nichols played parts of three seasons with the Rangers and scored more than a point per game in his Blueshirts career. In 104 career games with the Rangers, Nichols scored 110 points. The Rangers acquired Nichols from the Los Angeles Kings in January 1990 for Tomas Sandstrom and Tony Granato. On October 4, 1991, Nichols was a part of one of the most important trades in Rangers franchise history when they acquired Mark Messier from Edmonton. Nichols went on to score 475 career goals while playing for six teams during his long career.

FIRST CONTACT WITH THE NHL:

Bernie Nichols was a fourth-round selection of the Los Angeles Kings in the 1980 NHL Entry Draft.

"That was actually really cool. I just came home, I drove home and my Mom comes out, 'cause we didn't go to the draft back then. My Mom came out and said, 'You're just drafted by the LA Kings.' Honestly, growing up in a real small town in Canada, I never even knew the LA Kings played in the NHL. I really didn't. It was like, you know it's Toronto, Montreal, Boston, New York, and I get drafted by the LA Kings. First thing I did is I went and told my

Dad. Then went back and started looking them up and finding out who they got and what I got to look forward to, and then LA. You know I come from the smallest town in Canada, there may be 75 people in my hometown. Now, I'm going to 10 million people in sunny California. So there's a culture shock, bit of a shock just in itself. Me going there."

FIRST REACTION TO BECOMING A RANGER:

"I just had my big year, 150 points. I go to the owner [Bruce McNall]. It was a million- dollar house [Nicholls was interested in buying]. I said, 'Look, I want to buy this house. It's a lot of money,' and his exact words were, you know, I'm not a businessman and I was friends with the owner, he's a smart guy. He says, 'Yeah, it's a good investment,' he said, 'I'll never trade you.' So sure enough, we're actually at the All-Star Game and there's been no rumor, nothing. I was having a good year again but [Calgary goaltender] Mike Vernon comes up to me after the skills competition and said, 'You just got traded to New York,' and my exact words, 'The fuck you talking about, I got traded?' He said, 'Yeah,' so I go look for Bruce McNall. He said, 'Yeah, we just traded you to New York.' I go, 'Are you kidding me right now?' Like, I was shocked. The next day I'm playing in the game, I'm on the West [All-Star squad], I'm actually playing against Brian Leetch. Now, I'm a member of his team but once you sit back and realize you're traded, to go to New York, like there couldn't be a better place like New York. That part, Original Six, New York Rangers. Like I'm playing with Wayne Gretzky [with the Kings]. I don't know what it would be like honestly to play with Wayne for five, ten years, but I get traded and it's New York, so it was pretty cool going to New York."

FIRST GAME AS A RANGER: January 21, 1990, NHL All Star Game @ Pittsburgh

Despite being traded to the Rangers, Nichols played for the Campbell Conference (West) in the All-Star Game. The Rangers were part of the Wales Conference, which won the game, 12–7.

"I'm numb the whole game and I even say something stupid, like I felt bad saying after, like you're just dumb and stupid. Anyway, they interviewed me and I go, 'Yeah, New York got the better end of this trade,' and it was just, just stupid 'cause I loved Tony Granato and [Tomas] Sandstrom, great players [who Nicholls was traded for] but I was numb the whole game. Like, I'm in shock as far as going to New York, getting traded, like I said, I just bought this big house. LA, I'm playing with Wayne Gretzky. The last thing in the world you're thinking about is you never want to leave, so that was tough. That whole day was really tough 'cause I'm still shocked from the night before. I think we had a press conference that night with [Rangers GM] Neil Smith and the media, but now I'm a member of the Rangers and then I go back and I'm playing with the West [Campbell Conference] in the All-Star game. So that was tough and that's why they made the rule. Now, you can't trade during that time because of that trade."

FIRST TIME SEEING THE RANGERS JERSEY:

"Ulf Dahlen gave me [uniform number] 9, which was really pretty cool. That's the only number I ever wore. He gave me that, which was special. There's something about, like I love the Ranger uniforms, the red pants, but just the whole thing going in the Garden. You talk about the Garden, walking in there and you what the people, like when you're a Ranger, they love you there. I'll never forget I was late, I felt kind of embarrassed, but I was late getting dressed 'cause I don't know what I was doing. I always go out last anyways, but the team [was] kind of already gone and I'm lagging now. So, now I come out like maybe 30 seconds after, but it's like I'm making a grand entrance, which wasn't my intent. I was just running late but now I come walking out late and you know the Ranger fans, they're excited and they showed me they were awesome."

FIRST RANGERS GOAL: January 25, 1990 @ Calgary Flames, 8–5 loss

Nichols scored twice in his second game with the Rangers.

"We went on the road for three games, Edmonton, Calgary, LA. The toughest part was getting back to LA, but I scored in Calgary. Then I went to LA and I score, we win 3–1 and I score a goal there. I couldn't feel my body that whole night, but I'm pretty sure I scored two goals in Calgary."

FIRST RANGERS PLAYOFF GAME: April 5, 1990, Game 1, Patrick Division semifinals @ MSG vs. New York Islanders, 2–1 win. Rangers won series in five games.

"I think they might have had [goalie] Mark Fitzpatrick. He got traded while I was in LA, and I like Mark, for Kelly Hrudey, so we're playing against them. They had a tough team too, but you know, it's still a rivalry. Like it's Edmonton, Calgary, New York, Islanders, Rangers. It is the best and to win that was pretty cool too."

FIRST RANGER HAT TRICK: April 19, 1990 @ MSG, Game 1, Patrick Division finals, 7–3 win. Rangers lost series in five games.

"Nothing better than doing it in New York. Both years, Washington put us out. I can't believe it but I remember scoring three in the Garden. What a place to score three goals and a playoff, obviously playoffs are even better, so that was pretty cool."

SIGNIFICANT FIRSTS AS A RANGER:

"The first game I thought was really cool. There's so many. What's your best memory of playing in the NHL. Well, your first game, I did this so that. Just honestly walking out my first game at the Garden was cool. The first playoffs are just such a different animal.

Scoring three goals in a playoff game, there's just so much. Getting a speeding ticket in New York and the guy wouldn't give me a ticket 'cause I played for the Rangers. Another cop stopped me outside the Garden one time and she comes over and she's going to write me up and I got the Chief of Police card and she said, "What's that?' and I showed it to her and she threw it back at me. Said, 'Get out of here.' Wouldn't give me a ticket."

Nothing better than scoring a hat trick in playoffs as a Ranger for Bernie. Photo courtesy of New York Rangers.

46
CHRIS NILAN

Right wing Chris Nilan made his mark in the NHL as a member of the Montreal Canadiens for parts of 10 seasons. Nilan, who played a total of 13 years in the NHL and was a Stanley Cup winner in 1986, was a tough competitor to play against. Nilan led the league in penalty minutes in 1983–84 and 1984–85. He played parts of three seasons with the Rangers.

FIRST HOCKEY GAME ATTENDED AS A KID:

"Boston Garden, Chicago against the Bruins. I remember about 16,000 people throwing bottles on the ice. Bobby Orr got in a fight with Keith Magnuson and he got the extra penalty and the place went nuts. It was like a minute and a half left in the game. There were broken glass bottles on the ice, and they ended up not finishing the game."

FIRST HOCKEY IDOL: Bobby Orr

"He could skate, he was the best guy on the ice. Every kid in Boston wanted to be Bobby Orr. Any kid who aspired to play hockey or want to be hockey players looked up to him and he was the one that was just the best player on the ice."

FIRST CONTACT WITH NHL:

Chris Nilan was chosen by the Montreal Canadiens in the 19th round of the 1978 NHL Amateur Draft.

"I walked into the Cask 'n Flagon (a tavern near Northeastern University) with a teammate of mine at Northeastern, Mike Sanford. He and I walked in and someone said, 'Hey, you just got drafted by the Montreal Canadiens.' I said, 'No way.' 'No, it was on the sports.' So we ran to the back bar and we had them change the station because the sports was already on one and we're trying to catch it on the other one. They had two bars, one out front and one in the back. We ran off to the back and we had the bartender, who we knew would change the station and the sports was just comin' on, and we saw it, and I was shocked. It was just incredible. I went home and told my parents. I just remember they were happy for me. We really didn't have a party or anything. Just happened I got drafted."

FIRST REACTION TO BEING TRADED TO RANGERS:

Nilan was acquired by the Rangers from Montreal in January 1988.

"I got traded, I was in Buffalo. The coach had told me, Jean Perron. The assistant coach, Jacques Laperriere, said, 'Hey Chris,' and I knew something was up 'cause I had had a problem with the coach the game before [that] we lost. The next day was practicing before we head to Buffalo and coach was going around the room, calling everybody out. He came to me and said to me, 'Chris Nilan, when's the last time you had a fight?' and I told him basically where he could go and what he could do. He certainly didn't like that, so I guess he got on the phone and talked to Serge [Savard, Canadiens GM]. I got to Buffalo, we had a morning skate and I was off the line I had been on [with] [Guy] Carbonneau and Gaines [Bob Gainey]. I went back to the hotel; I didn't have a roommate and I got a phone call from Jacques Laperriere. 'Hey, the coach, he wants to talk to you, so he wants you to go down to his room.' I said, 'Jacques, I like you, I respect you, but tell the coach if he wants to fuckin' talk to me to call me himself.' Two minutes later, Perron called me, 'I want to talk with you. Can you come down to my room. I want to talk about your ice time.' Couldn't even fucking tell me the truth. Anyway, I went down to the room, the door was open and soon as I get there, I said, 'What's up?' He goes, 'Serge, he's on the phone, he wants to talk with you.' Anyway, he traded me to St. Louis and I told him, 'I don't want to go to St. Louis, I ain't goin'." So where you want to go?' I just don't want to go to St. Louis, I just want to stay in the East.' So I said, 'Boston' and he said, 'I can't do that, I'm not going to do it.' I said, 'How about New York?' 'cause I knew Phil [Esposito, Rangers GM] was interested in me and I ended up in New York."

FIRST RANGERS COACH: Michel Bergeron

"Bergy, I loved him. I'd go through a wall for him. He was great for me. I really liked him. A lot of guys were upset that he got let go on April Fools Day. We thought it was a joke, probably the worst time to do it if there was a time to do it. I really liked playing for him."

FIRST RANGERS CAPTAIN: Kelly Kisio

"Kelly was a quiet captain. Bob Gainey [Nilan's captain in Montreal] never said much. He just kind of led by the way he played. When times were tough, Bob would speak up. He certainly was a great leader in the sense that, a lot of the player realized that Perron really wasn't the brightest coach. There wasn't a whole lot of respect for him from the group, but we ended up winning the Stanley Cup. Larry Robinson and Bob Gainey kept the whole thing together. So yeah, Kelly's a good captain. It was a whole different thing, all of a sudden with the Rangers, I had a tough time.

"It almost broke me getting traded, to be honest with ya. I didn't let it, it's still my job, I still stuck up for my teammates and I played hard. Every time I put that sweater on, I ran into a bunch of injuries in New York. I started to break down. It was a difficult time 'cause I loved the fans, I loved the city, playing for the Rangers, but the injury took its tool on me. I broke my arm twice, I hurt my knee and I had a hockey hernia. It seemed like I was jinxed and got hit with the whammy. Other than that, I really liked being in New York and playing there but the injuries, they took their toll on me mentally."

FIRST TIME PUTTING ON THE RANGERS JERSEY:

"It was just cool [that] the three teams I played for [were] Original Six [Nilan also played parts of two seasons with the Bruins]. I grew up in an Original Six city, I was drafted by an Original Six team. It was just cool to be able to play for those three teams. I only wanted to play for one. I never wanted to leave Montreal and I never wanted to be anywhere else, but when I was asked where I wanted to go, it was Boston first, and then New York, second, so I ended up going to New York. The Original Six teams have so much history, the fan base, and I'm aware of all that history, most of them and it's kinda cool to be part of that."

FIRST RANGERS FIGHT: January 28, 1988 vs. Craig Berube @ Philadelphia Flyers, 5–2 win

"I remember that fight. It was in front of the bench and I hit him with a left that he was like, shocked. I hit him with a stun gun 'cause he knew I was a righty, but I could throw my left. He was kind of throwing away his right and I was trying to tie him up and keep him from throwing and throwing my right. Then he threw about five and I had my head buried. After the fifth one, I let go and dinged him with a left and kind of stood him up."

FIRST RANGERS GOAL: January 30, 1988 @ Boston Bruins, 4–2 win

"It was nice. I know my first goal with the Habs. Being in Boston, it's funny, I don't remember my first goal with Boston."

FIRST TIME PLAYING THE CANADIENS AS A

RANGER: November 21, 1988 @ MSG vs. Montreal Canadiens, 4-2 loss.

"It was really strange because I was so invested in the city. I was so invested in that organization. The intensity and passion I had playing for them. It was at a very high level and I was fortunate. I'd gotten my opportunity there and I never wanted to be anywhere else. Honestly, I couldn't care less if I hadn't played another game for another team. I did my best when I was there. It was not the same for me with the Rangers; it just wasn't the same. I didn't have the same investment as far as my feelings for playing for that team."

FIRST TIME TOUCHING THE STANLEY CUP AFTER WINNING IT: 1986

"It's just awesome. I tore ligaments in my ankle in a fight in the previous game. I tried to play in the game they clinched it. I had an injection, they let me go in warmup. I told them I could play and they said, 'Watching you, you can't keep up with your left and blah, blah, blah.' So they said, 'We're gonna play someone else.' You know, that hurt, but we won, which I was so happy about but being on the ice afterwards with the uniform on, sweat, it's certainly a different feeling than being on the ice with a suit and tie and a couple of beers in ya already."

FIRST TIME HOSTING A RADIO SHOW:

"Scared to death and not a whole lot gets me but the night before, I was like nervous as anything. I was nervous going in and I didn't know anything about it. I was looking at the clock all the time, make sure I get out of the segment on time, come in on time, I just had no clue. Honestly, my partner who's on with me, Sean Campbell, if it wasn't for him carrying me through it. He really helped me and Mitch Melnick's the guy who really got my foot in the door there. He wasn't sitting with me when I went in there and certainly, Sean Campbell really helped guide me. The first few months was like horrendous. I was horrendous. I was brutal and it was real nerve-wracking. As much as I tried to prepare myself, it was still difficult. I had to learn how to prepare. I had to learn how to not be so worried about time and the clock and that all comes with doing that. My girlfriend, Jamie, said she never seen me nervous before. I told her I wasn't that nervous playing my first NHL game. It was difficult, but I guess my own critique is I've come a long way in radio."

FIRST TATTOO: Nilan sports a tattoo of the Canadiens' famous "CH" logo

"Most people get tattoos when they're drunk or shit faced or messed up. And I got it when I got sober. You know, I got sober back in 2011 and yeah, I was sober and living out West living in Oregon, and, I just felt like getting a tattoo and I said that I'll start with the CH, you know, so I did, went and got it done."

47
MARK OSBORNE

Mark Osborne, a 6'2" left wing, played parts of five seasons with the Rangers in two separate stints. Osborne was acquired from Detroit in June 1983 in a controversial trade that saw popular winger Ron Duguay traded to the Red Wings. Osborne's best run with the Rangers was in the 1986 Stanley Cup playoffs. Osborne was a key player in the Rangers' run to the Prince of Wales Conference finals where they lost to Montreal in five games. In March 1987, Osborne was traded to the Toronto Maple Leafs.

FIRST GAME HE ATTENDED AS A KID:

"I grew up in Toronto, so born and raised in 'Maple Leaf Land.' Obviously, going down to the old Maple Leaf Gardens with my Dad, I mean, it was a thrill because *Hockey Night in Canada*, you watched it as a kid. You were enamored with the bright lights, these guys that you idolized, no helmets and then you got a chance to see how bright that rink was. As kids, you're used to being in cold rinks, growing up in Canada. It was like, 'Man, it's warm in here,' and underneath the lights, it felt hot. It was so exciting to be part of that first game as a kid."

FIRST HOCKEY IDOL:

"Without a doubt, it was Bobby Orr. Growing up and watching the Maple Leafs but, ever since I could remember, watching TV with my Dad, that was when Bobby Orr was just really starting out as a young player in the mid '60s. I don't remember the Leafs' Stanley Cup in '67, I was only six, but Bobby Orr came on the scene and I started following and cheering for the Bruins and [Phil] Esposito, around '69 and '70, eight, nine years old. Yeah, I jumped on that Bruin bandwagon pretty quickly and Bobby Orr, he was, no doubt an idol as a kid growing up."

FIRST CONTACT WITH NHL:

Mark Osborne was chosen by the Detroit Red Wings in the third round of the 1980 NHL Entry Draft.

"It was 1980 that I was drafted. It was only, I think about maybe the second year, I could be mistaken, of the underage draft. So, I had a feeling that I was gonna get drafted. That year, you heard through the grapevine that you were gonna get drafted 'cause we had a pretty good, young junior team. A lot of the guys that were represented by a guy by the name of Gus Badali, who was Wayne Gretzky's agent at the time. Wayne was our same age, but there was a bunch of guys that we played junior together with Steve Ludzik, Daryl Evans, and Steve Larmer, Paul Coffey, they all were represented by Gus Badali and all those guys end up going to the draft. It was in Montreal and I never went to the draft. It was likely you sit by the phone and you wait to see who ends up drafting you. It wasn't long after that the phone rang and I got drafted in the third round by the Detroit Red Wings. Initially, I gotta be truthful, I was disappointed. You hear different teams, maybe are interested in you. You know, growing up in Toronto, Detroit wasn't a very good team. The city didn't have a very good reputation and I thought, Oh my gosh, I'm going to a place that is not doing very well and doesn't have a good reputation as far as the city goes in the United States.

"After the fact, you started to learn about the history of the Red Wings and Ted Lindsay and Gordie Howe and all those [great players]. Ted Lindsay was part of the management team when I got drafted. So, going to Detroit and then getting a start there was great for me as a young kid out of junior 'cause I got to play as a 20 year old, right away."

FIRST REACTION TO BEING TRADED TO THE RANGERS:

"My first year as a Red Wing in 1981 as a 20 year old, right out of junior, I mean, much to my surprise, I shocked myself and everybody else. I led the Red Wings in scoring, I went to the World Championships. I started having some dizzy spells in Finland, I didn't really feel very good. That next summer, after my rookie season, I had tests, I had CAT scans. I went into my second year. This was when Mike Ilitch bought the team. I played every game, but I did not feel 100 percent. Lo and behold, the draft in 1983 came and the Red Wings drafted fourth overall, a guy by the name of Steve Yzerman. Jimmy Devellano was our general manager at the time. I thought Jimmy was calling me right after the draft to tell me about, 'You know, we got this kid out of Ottawa, Stevie Yzerman, he's going to be a good player,' Right after he explained that to me, he goes, 'Mark, we made a deal and you're involved,' and that's when I found out. He said, 'We've traded [you to] New York Rangers, part of a, I think it was a six-player trade. There was [Willie] Huber, [Mike] Blaisdell, myself and [Ron] Duguay, [Eddie] Mio, and [Eddie] Johnstone coming over to Detroit. So that was pretty shocking, really as a young player, under a new ownership with Mike Ilitch and all that kind of stuff, but I didn't feel very good my second year. I didn't have a very good year. Jimmy D. felt they needed a little bit of a change or whatever. Hence, the trade coming here [to New York].

"I didn't really know what I was getting myself into. I mean, I loved coming to play in an Original Six arena as an opposition player for the first couple of years. Then, you come here to this organization and again, an Original Six franchise and this city that never sleeps, it was an awesome place to come to."

FIRST RANGERS COACH: Herb Brooks

"I loved playing for Herb, I really did. My first couple of years in the NHL, I got to tell you, and all due respect to the guys who I played for, I didn't really learn very much. Now, when I came and played for Herb here, it was refreshing. The older guys didn't necessarily like Herb, but for me, as a young player, I mean his practices were upbeat, intense, they were moving and all that kind of stuff. I really, really enjoyed it. Obviously, him being fresh off the 1980 Olympic gold medal team and some of those college guys, I really did enjoy it. I thought we had some good teams, obviously, the Islanders were in their heyday, coming off four Stanley Cups in a row, but we felt competitive. I thought that Kenny Morrow overtime goal (Game 5, 1984 Patrick Division semifinals) was a heartbreak of a series. It was a few years later that we got a chance to go to the Stanley Cup semifinals."

FIRST RANGERS CAPTAIN: Barry Beck

"Barry had quite the reputation. Not only you heard his reputation as a junior at New Westminster, you know, that they had a real tough team and Barry was like six-four. Both him, and Willie Huber immediately were paired together. They were the twin towers. He [Beck] was big, he was strong, he could shoot the puck, I mean, coming into the NHL at that time, it was a different brand of hockey, right? You're coming off the '70s with the Broad Street Bullies [Philadelphia Flyers] and just a whole pile of things. He was a good captain."

FIRST TASTE OF RANGERS-ISLANDERS RIVALRY:

"Islanders-Rangers rivalry, and again, I'm comparing that to Leafs-Canadiens 'cause I also played six years in Toronto, so Habs-Leafs was awesome. Rangers-Islanders, I mean, the amount of Ranger fans going to Long Island. That was so much fun 'cause they were still such a good team. We were so competitive with them. The following of the Rangers on Long Island was awesome. Then, you think about that group of players that they had assembled. I mean, look at those Hall of Famers right from [Mike] Bossy and [Bryan] Trottier and [Clark] Gillies and Billy Smith, it was like iconic."

FIRST RANGERS PLAYOFF SERIES: 1984 Patrick Division semifinals vs. New York Islanders. Rangers lost best-of-five series in five games.

"My first two years in Detroit, there were no playoffs. To be able to experience what that means. There's nothing better for a player is to be playing for the Stanley Cup and into the playoffs. What a tremendous introduction for me, wearing the Ranger jersey. Again, you hate to admit it, but that's your first experience is playing these guys [Islanders]. You think about the Stanley Cup playoffs and just getting in, but the level is elevated even higher because of the rivalry. That even made it so much more enjoyable."

FIRST RANGERS PLAYOFF GOAL: April 15, 1986 @ Philadelphia Flyers, Game 5, Patrick Division semifinals, 5–2 win.

Osborne's first playoff goal in the second period gave the Rangers a 3–1 lead.

"It was 1986. It was three of five back then. I think we probably would have played four games in five nights. So, who's tired. Four games in five nights, hard-hitting hockey and all that kind of stuff. We went up two-one games in the series and we had Game 4 here at Madison Square and we got beat pretty good. I mean, I don't remember a score [7–1] but it was a bit of a whitewash. I remember looking down to the Flyers, Mark Howe was a member of that team. Those guys were going off to the tunnel here and you could see them really smiling and rightly so, they were enjoying themselves, but I think they were all smiling a little bit more 'cause they thought that Game Five, going into the Spectrum, that game was gonna be in the bag. 'Beezer' [Rangers goalie John Vanbiesbrouck] stood on his head and I was able to score that goal, a move that I don't think I've ever made again. Nor did I ever make it before then. You know, [Flyers goalie] Bob Froese came out of his net quite a distance and I didn't have really anything to shoot for. I decided to hold onto the puck a little bit. Ended up being the game-winner in a clinching, deciding game [of a] series."

FIRST FORAY INTO FREE AGENCY:

After parts of eight seasons with Toronto, Osborne returned to the Rangers as a free agent signing for the 1994–95 season.

"The Rangers won in '94. I was part of a Maple Leaf team under [coach] Pat Burns that went to two years in a row of the semifinals. Like, how'd we beat Vancouver? We would have played the Rangers so coming off back-to-back season of Stanley Cup semifinals in Toronto, like we had a pretty good team too. We were competitive with [Doug] Gilmour, [Wendel] Clark and Pat Burns behind the bench but [Leafs GM] Cliff Fletcher elected to go with some of the younger employees. My contract expired and I was really disappointed in not getting resigned but being familiar here. Neil [Smith] had called my agent and tendered me a contract offer. It was kind of almost, what goes around, comes around because I had two stints in Toronto as well. Eddie Olczyk and I got traded to Winnipeg and I came back to Toronto. With the Ranger opportunity, I said I'm familiar, this it'd be an easy transition to come to New York. When teams are interested and they show interest in you, I mean, that's an honor after the Stanley Cup year, so it was a pretty easy decision to come back. Albeit, it only lasted one year, we got locked out [delaying the start of the 1994–95 season]."

FIRST TIME BEING ON THE ICE WHEN STANLEY CUP BANNER WAS RAISED:

"You had goosebumps because the dim of the lights, the Cup coming out of the score clock, the smoke, standing in center ice around the Cup coming down out of the ceiling. Petr Nedved and I were the only two guys that were not on that team. So here we are with the Stanley Cup banner going up and everything, but we had nothing to do with it and weren't part of it. Being a Ranger for four years in the mid-'80s, knowing the Islander fans cheering 'Nineteen-forty,' all that kind of stuff. So it was a little bit of a mixed bag 'cause you're like, 'Oh, this is great for the Rangers, I wasn't part of this team.' So it was just an odd moment I guess in some ways."

FIRST TIME HE SAW HIS ACTRESS WIFE ON THE BIG SCREEN:

In 1988, Osborne married actress Madolyn Smith.

"I was playing here with the Rangers and it was a girl who was working with CBS, who wrote for the Ranger magazine, who actually introduced us. She [his wife] was on [the cover of] TV Guide because there was a mini-series *If Tomorrow Comes* on CBS with Tom Berenger, that was the first introduction for me. Seeing her on TV and everything like that. I mean, as a 24, 25 year old, I was little bit intimidated by the fact that she was a Hollywood movie star, I'm a Ranger hockey player. I'm an athlete but she was on another plane altogether. But 32 years later, we're still married but it all started here when I was in New York, so lots of fond memories for sure."

Having the Islanders as the opponent in first NHL playoff series made the experience more enjoyable for Mark. (Public Domain)

48
BRAD PARK

Hall of Fame defenseman Brad Park put together a stellar 17-year NHL career. Park played his first seven seasons and part of an eighth with the Rangers before he was traded to the Boston Bruins in a controversial five-player trade in November 1975. With the Rangers, Park was a five-time All Star and a four-time runner-up for the Norris Trophy.

FIRST CONTACT WITH NHL:

Brad Park was the second overall selection by the Rangers in the 1966 NHL Amateur Draft.

"I had no idea when they had drafted me. I read about it in the Toronto Telegram. It was in the transactions section. There was no article or anything, it just said who drafted who."

FIRST RANGERS TRAINING CAMP: Before 1968–69 season

"It was in Kitchener [Ontario] and I kinda knew about Walter Tkachuk and a lot of these different guys who I played against. I remember driving to training camp and checking in. My first roommate was Reggie Fleming. Going in and meeting him and saying hello and everything like that and finding out when the first practice was, etc."

FIRST RANGERS COACH: Hall of Famer Bernie "Boom Boom" Geoffrion

"The first thing was how much of an authoritarian he was. It was his way or the highway and 'Boom Boom,' we're gonna do it my or the highway and whatever he said goes. I mean that's as far as I was concerned, I was just a 20-year-old kid."

FIRST TIME PUTTING ON THE RANGERS JERSEY:

I remember when I went to training camp the first year and they gave me number 2 because I'd worn 2 with the 'Marlies' [Park's OHA-Jr. team, Toronto Marlboros]. The last guy that wore number 2 was Wayne Hillman [a 6'1" defenseman who played four seasons with the Rangers] and this thing was so, it hung down past my pants. You couldn't see my pants. I was afraid to face the trainers; you know this thing is a little big for me. The next day I came back and they had another sweater with number 2 on it and it fit me better."

FIRST RANGERS GOAL: February 23, 1969 @ MSG vs. Boston Bruins, 9–0 win

"I'd gone for a while without getting a goal. We were playing Boston, we were leading
8–0. Late in the third period, I shot one from the point, it went off both posts and beat [Bruins goaltender] Eddie Johnston. I was so excited, I jumped up and forgot to put my feet down and came down in a hump."

FIRST RANGERS HAT TRICK: December 12, 1971 @ MSG vs. Pittsburgh Penguins, 6–1 win.

"I remember the third goal, it was a pass from behind the net from one side of the net to the other, behind the net. I kicked it out to my stick and put it in and got a hat trick."

FIRST ALL-STAR GAME AS A RANGER: January 20, 1970 @ St. Louis

"I was excited, I remember it was in St. Louis and [Rangers defenseman] Jimmy Neilson was injured and he wasn't gonna play. I remember sitting on the bench and I'm sitting between Bobby Hull and Gordie Howe and I'm like, 'Wow.' Claude Ruel is the coach and I'm sitting to next Gordie who gives me an elbow and says, 'What does don't stop to skate mean?' and that's Claude Ruel behind the bench going, 'Don't stop to skate, don't stop to skate.' Gordie asked me, 'What does that mean?' as a joke."

FIRST RANGERS PLAYOFF GAME: April 2, 1969 @ Montreal Canadiens, Game 1 Stanley Cup quarterfinals, 3–1 loss

"We played Montreal, I think it was in Montreal. We ended up that series, we lost four straight. I was so disappointed we never even won a game."

49
JAMES PATRICK

Defenseman James Patrick provided a steady, two-way presence during his 11-year tenure with the Rangers. Less than weeks after playing for Canada in the 1984 Winter Olympics, Patrick joined the Rangers for his NHL debut. Patrick scored a career-high 17 goals in 1987–88 and had a career-high 57 assists and 71 points in 1991–92. Patrick played 671 games and finished his Ranger career with a plus-66 in the plus/minus category. Patrick is a member of the Manitoba Hockey Hall of Fame.

FIRST HOCKEY GAME HE ATTENDED AS A KID:

"I do remember going to a Winnipeg Jets game when I was nine years old. It was the first year of the WHA (World Hockey Association) and my father had gotten season tickets. I don't remember where the seats were, and I remember seeing Bobby Hull. I don't remember too much about the game, but I do remember it was such a big deal that Bobby Hull came to Winnipeg and seeing him skate, seeing him on the bench. Our seats were pretty close to their bench or behind the bench and so, those are probably the images of my memory. That would've been '72, I guess the first year of the WHA."

FIRST HOCKEY IDOL:

"Bobby Orr, I can remember being six or seven years old, watching a game with my father and brother and maybe the earliest memory of watching the hockey game. My dad pointed out Bobby Orr and said, 'He's gonna to be the best player,' I remember him saying, 'He's gonna be the best player in the NHL.' In that moment he was my favorite player, whether just because my dad said that, because he was a young player in the NHL. Literally, I followed his career, game by game, when I was learning how to read. I would read the newspaper as far as to see how Bobby Orr did. He was even God to me as a hockey player."

FIRST CONTACT WITH THE NHL:

James Patrick was selected by the Rangers with the ninth overall pick in the 1981 NHL Entry Draft.

"I was going to school in Prince Albert. Back then, the draft was on a Wednesday. It wasn't like it is now, but then it was always in Montreal. I was in Saskatchewan time, which was maybe an hour difference on the East Coast, an hour or two hours difference. For me, it was so much different then. Until Christmas of that year, I didn't even know I was drafted. I was told that they had dropped the age a year from there. That's gone from a 19-year-old draft to an 18-year-old draft. I was playing tier-two hockey, not a major junior, so I think I was a bit under the radar. A couple of scouts had interviewed me so I knew I could be drafted. Then I saw the *Hockey News*, I was rated, maybe the last pick in the first round, so I obviously knew the draft was happening and there was a chance I could be drafted. It was an exciting thought for me. I remember that morning getting a call from [Rangers GM] Craig Patrick telling me that they had drafted me in the first round and just a nice conversation."

"Anyone who knows Craig, he's the nicest, softest spoken, polite guy. I remember that very first conversation then he put me on the phone with two reporters, a reporter maybe from the New York Post and one from the [*Daily*] *News*. I talked to them briefly, the conversation ended, and I was so excited. Then I went to school, told my teammates. There's about four or five of us who were on the hockey team, so I was telling them, and they were super excited. By the end of the day, I think there was about seven players from our team that got drafted which was really unique for a junior a-team and that was it. There was no celebration. I ended up talking to my parents after and just being excited about it. My brother was a first-round draft pick the year before [Steve Patrick was taken 20th overall by Buffalo] so this was a year later. I knew New York was a big city. I knew the Rangers were an Original Six team. I grew up watching Montreal and Toronto. Those are the games you got in Canada, I was a Canadiens fan and I remember watching the Canadiens play the Rangers two years before in the playoffs and then to get drafted by them was super exciting. I mean I was just so excited to be drafted and hoping that someday I would play for them. I look back at it, someone being really young and naïve, just pure joy to be drafted by an NHL team because it was my dream, since I started idolizing Bobby Orr, to be an NHL player."

FIRST NCAA CHAMPIONSHIP:

In 1982, Patrick was a member of the NCAA hockey champion North Dakota Fighting Hawks. North Dakota beat Wisconsin, 5–2, in the championship game.

"I went to North Dakota, now being a first-round draft pick and there were high expectations, I just remember how difficult the adjustment was at first. I mean it was definitely a step up in hockey against fast and stronger, bigger guys, but I remember, I mean we had a real good team. There's just a lot of good players in college hockey. More physical brand under John "Gino" Gasparini our coach, we had Darren Jensen and Jon Casey too, a goalie that played in the NHL. Craig Ludwig was probably our best defenseman who had a long NHL career. Rick Zombo was also on the team. Troy Murray who had that long NHL career and Phil Sykes. Phil Sykes was our leading scorer and a great college player who played in LA and kind of became my checker in LA. Dave

Tippett and I both played junior together and we both went there together. We were roommates together and we had a lot of really good hockey players.

"For me personally, I just remember how hard the adjustment was and how hard the expectations were. It felt like it took me half of the year to really start contributing but felt the second half [I was] playing better and better and becoming a bigger part of the team. Then, we had a fantastic second half. We were almost .500 for half a year and then we started winning most of our games, like sweeping a lot of teams every weekend, the second half, and carried it right through and eventually played Wisconsin, our WCHA rivals, in the finals and it was two-all after two periods, so it couldn't get any closer. Phil Sykes, I think scored two goals in the third period. I just remember he was outstanding and Wisconsin had a great team. They had [Chris] Chelios and [Bruce] Driver and Mark Behrend and Pat Flatley. They had a lot of real good players so it was a real big rivalry. We fought against them, just battled them all year. We had a brawl with them halfway through the year. There was a lot of dislike between the two teams. They were coached by Bob Johnson and we were coached by Gino Gasparini, who had a long history against each other but that was a fantastic year. It was a really good learning year for me. It was awesome. I mean, you become so close with your teammates, lifelong teammates, but it was just a fantastic year, fantastic finish to it, so a good year."

FIRST OLYMPIC EXPERIENCE:

Patrick played for Canada in the 1984 Winter Olympics in Sarajevo, Yugoslavia.

"When I look at my Olympic experience, we started training camp in August and the Olympics ended near the end of February. When you look at that seven-month span, I looked at it as a grind. We were a lot of young [players] most of our time was between 18 and 22 and we lived together. We practiced twice a day, most of the year. It was just our daily schedule. Get up, have breakfast, go to the rink, practice, do some off ice, come back, hotel, lunch, nap, go back to the rink, skate for an hour and a half, come back, have dinner, go to bed. I know we played the Americans thirteen times, we played the NHL exhibition season, we played teams in the Central Hockey League that counted in their standings. It was such a unique year that you've spent so much time with your teammates all for that single goal of the Olympics and the build up of that. I know we were evenly matched with the Americans, but I remember the last exhibition game. We probably played them, I want to say sometime in January before we went over to Europe. We went to Europe about a month before they left and they beat us like 8–1 and we were gonna play them in the first game of the Olympics. I just remember there was a lot of disappointments with the year, you know, built up expectations and then we were struggling with the teams in the Central Hockey League. They were a lot more physical, they tried to run us out of the building. I know we had a lot of changes to our lineup. We were bringing in players or trying out new players and I guess that's normal. That was normal back then compared to Olympic teams. There [were] guys getting cut at the last moment so those are some of my memories of the year.

"When we got to Sarajevo, probably the two things that stand out for me was the day before our first game. We had three guys who had played professionally, and we were trying to use them in the Olympics and the day before, they were ruled ineligible so that day before that, a couple of guys got cut. One, being Kevin Dineen, which was shocking because Kevin had been with us all year. He was a good player. He played defense in college, but he could play forward. He was one of the main 10, 12 guys who had been with us the whole way and he got cut the day before the Olympics. These guys who had played some pro games were ruled ineligible like Don Dietrich, Mark Morrison was one, so they couldn't play and then Kevin was allowed to play. When we came into the Olympics, Kevin was one of our best players and Kevin probably had the best pro career of any of us that were left from that team. I think probably about 15, 16 guys on that team played in the NHL. We beat the Americans in the first game and they had a lot of pressure on them. The US had won in '80 so now the expectations for them were a lot different, but we made it to the medal round. We played good throughout to get to the medal round but then we lost to Russia, 4–0, to Czechoslovakia, 2–0, now we were playing Sweden for the bronze medal game and we lost, pretty sure it was 2–0. I just remember how devastating it was to lose because our goal was to go to the Olympics and win a medal. We had a chance, I think it was zero-zero after two periods, kind of close game that anyone could have won. Probably, as big a heartbreak as I had my whole career with not winning a medal. Having an opportunity and losing that. Again, it was a great experience."

FIRST NHL CONTRACT:

"I remember coming home after the Olympics and my agent negotiating the contract that took about a week. Agreeing to the contract and then flying to New York and I'm watching the Rangers play. They lost to Vancouver and I'm pretty sure they lost, 5–0 [actually 5–4] and the next morning signing the contract and then having practice with the team. I hadn't skated, I maybe skated once or twice in 10 days since the Olympics had ended. Then, having practice and Herb Brooks telling me it was going to be a real hard practice. I just remember dying. I can remember at the end there, Herb loved doing '45.' Three laps in 45 seconds. We did about 10 of them and I was so far behind the other, I think all the defenseman went together. A couple of lines in groups of three, so I remember my first practice, just being dead."

FIRST TIME SEEING HIS NAME ON A RANGERS UNIFORM:

"It was a dream since I was six years old, wanting to play in the NHL and now this dream had come true. You move up, you're drafted and then you're on the Olympic team and I got to play in the world championships when I was 19 years old. So I got to play with NHL players and felt I belonged with them. So I was confident, but I was also like giddy with excitement that I'm finally here. This has been my dream, but wondering, will I be good enough there? There's questions in your mind but I think one thing that made it easier, Bob Brooke, who was on the US Olympic team, and myself, we both signed the same day. We were first in the hotel together so both of us came into the dressing room. I felt like I had someone who I could hang out with. The players were awesome. Like any NHL team, once you're on the team, they take care of you. Dave Maloney was fantastic. Tommy Laidlaw, Mike Rogers, Pierre [Larouche], Nicky [Fotiu], Gresch [Ron Greschner], they were all really good. I mean, they're all real nice guys but Dave Maloney, more than anyone, took me under his wing and helped me out. I didn't know it at the time, but I know it meant at the time that he was another defenseman on the team who was going to play a little less. He didn't dress for all the games, but he still was incredible. He's just a really good character person. That's in a minute after walking in the room, he showed that, and he's been like that as long as I've known him."

FIRST RANGERS GAME: March 7, 1984 @ Minnesota North Stars, 6–3 loss.

"I remember feeling pretty good in the game. I remember Nick Fotiu set me up, I'm wide open in front on the net at one point in the game and I double clutched, double clutched and waited too long. Then, their defenseman got a stick on my shot. I remember Nick coming to talk to me on the bench after, [saying] 'You don't have that much time here in the big leagues.' I remember it was in Minnesota, in Bloomington, where the North Stars used to play."

FIRST NHL POINT AND MULTI-POINT GAME: March 9, 1984 @ Winnipeg Jets, 6–5 OT win.

Patrick had three assists including one on the game-winner in overtime for his first mutli-point game.

"I mean, Bobby Orr is my idol, but the Winnipeg Jets were gods to me when I was nine or ten. I remember seeing Bobby Hull in the rink, watching his son play against my brother when I was younger. Like any 10-year-old kid to see Bobby Hull, it's all you talked about the next day. Then, when Anders Hedberg and Ulf Nilsson came to play in Winnipeg, I think the European invasion changed hockey forever. I still remember the FIRST time I saw the Jets play, they had nine Europeans on their team whom they had brought over. Hedberg, Nilsson, Veli-Pekka Ketola, and Willy Lindstrom. The first time I watched them, it was so different to me. It's almost like my brain could comprehend what was going on with them switching lanes and cutting into the middle of the top with the puck back. Hockey wasn't played like that and instantly, everyone in the city fell in love with Hedberg and Nilsson. I mean they were in their prime playing with Bobby Hull. They had the great ones. One of the greatest lines I've ever seen in my life. To this day, I think Hedberg and Nilsson were good when they went to the Rangers, but I think that later in their career, because when they came to the Jets, they were so unbelievable. Even like Ulf and Anders, you ask anyone, any kid who grew up in Winnipeg, I mean they were so special and so to end up going to the Rangers and for a short while to be a teammate of theirs was incredible."

"I remember my first assist was on the power play. I basically got the puck to the point. I walked to the middle, passed it to Anders, pass it to someone on the back door and put it in. I got an assist on that play, but I know Anders Hedberg either scored it, or he passed it to someone else or someone got the rebound." (Mark Pavelich scored the goal, Hedberg got the primary assist.) I remember getting an assist in overtime just throwing a blind puck. Getting on the rush and then throwing it in front and Mark Osborne put it in that time."

FIRST RANGERS GOAL: March 17, 1984 @ Philadelphia Flyers, 6–4 loss.

"Anders [Hedberg] passed it to Mark Osborne who went down the wing, kinda on his off wing on the right side. I joined the play coming from behind. He dropped it back to me and I took a slap shot, skated into it and off the post, in Philly. The goalie was Bob Froese. After that, we were up, 4–1, but lost, 6–4. I can picture the goal. I mean I can see it in my head, I will forever."

"I never thought about it at the time, but you don't really make it until you've scored a goal in the league, whether you belong or not. Playing defense, even playing junior or college, I always got a lot more assists and I wouldn't say I got a lot of goals. You wanna score a goal, everyone wants to. I can remember that goal clearer than any I've scored. I kind of vaguely remember a few others. Not that many, just little parts of them, but I remembered all of that goal. The team gave me a VCR, videotaped copy of it. I haven't watched it in 30 years, but I remember watching it a few times after. It stays with you for sure, I think it stays with everyone. Every guy remembers his first goal, I think."

FIRST RANGERS COACH: Herb Brooks

Patrick is the coach of the Winnipeg Ice in the Western Hockey League.

"My first impression was, I really liked him. The thing about Herb, probably from his experience from coaching so long, I think he knew what each player brought, and he respected the players for what their talent or skill level was. Even at that time, he didn't try to change one player to something he wasn't. I remember his passion. He talked to me a lot I think as a young player. My first full year, I really struggled the first half. I remember him talking to me a number of times about putting the weight of the world on my shoulder, being down all the time and beating myself up. Just go out and play, be a 20 year old and get in and play and enjoy the love of the game. I remember him telling those stories.

"I remember him wanting motion. He would always go up to the board, he had magnets on the board and he'd say, 'I don't want you to just stay in here. I want us winding up here, I want this forward, coming back and winding up there, see if we can move the puck up, hit the center and then our wingers lined up and take some ice,' so he really wanted motion. I remember him wanting the guys to be skating and music motion. I remember how passionate he was talking about the game. I liked his practices. He would add it on the schedule once a week we are going to do a conditioning skate. We would play a lot of Saturday, Sundays and then Monday night be off. I think Herbie recognized and respected what the strengths were, the different strengths of each player and then his belief and conditioning. That has stayed with me and I believe in that for our players that I'm coaching."

FIRST RANGERS CAPTAIN: Barry Beck

"I look back at Barry as having as much presence as any player I played with. I played with Mark Messier, who played with passion. When you look at players with presence, how they carry themselves, the confidence and the presence they had. Bubba had presence when he was in the room, he had presence on the ice, presence amongst the other guys on the other team. Everyone knew when he was on the ice. I know that Barry had a window of probably seven, eight years in New York where he had a very big status. I'll be talking about past Rangers and I'm talking to younger players or younger people and they don't know Barry Beck. For a time, I mean this was like this guy Scott Stevens before Scott Stevens was Scott Stevens. This was a guy in the league who could score 20 goals, had a great shot and could skate, who could destroy guys physically. This guy was a dominant player with presence. Guys on other teams knew not to take liberties because Barry was on the team. I do think that the leadership of Barry was probably his presence and his intensity that you can't really emulate, but he was himself. That was probably the thing I took from him. You have to be yourself. You can't try and be someone else. I look at him as one of the greatest Rangers ever, especially looking back when he was at his best. I think my second year there, Barry hurt his shoulder. He had shoulder issues that I think ultimately led to the end of his career. He was a funny guy. There were times when he was so funny entertaining the room and teasing guys or making jokes about guys or laughing with guys. So you saw that part of him but then there'd come game time and he was tense and focused as it was, where I was like, 'Oh my God, don't stay in his way. He's ready to play.'

That's what I took from Barry."

FIRST RANGERS PLAYOFF EXPERIENCE: 1984 Patrick Division semifinals vs. New York Islanders. Rangers lost best-of-five series in five games.

"That's when the first round was best-of-five. The Islanders were going to their fifth Cup. They were coming off the four [time] Stanley Cup champs. They were a great team. They finally lost [that] year in the Final against Edmonton, but you know all those names. The great defense with [Denis] Potvin, [Tomas] Jonsson and [Ken] Morrow, all those guys. [Mike] Bossy, [Bryan] Trottier, [Clark] Gillies, [Bobby] Nystrom [Bob] Bourne, Brent Sutter, Duane Sutter, Butch Goring. I knew who they were, I knew from watching them when I was 13, 14, most of that same team. Being naïve helped me more than anything. I think coming off the Olympics, the pace of that year and the pace of the Olympics had me prepared. I took a break, but once I got my skating legs after about a week, playing in the NHL, I really felt as good, I mean it took me a number of years to feel that good again. I just felt I could skate at that level and play at that level. I felt that strong, so coming into the series, I think I knew enough from junior playoffs. Playoffs in college is different. It's a different world in the playoffs. It is hatred and intensity of battle. I know you're going to be tested and I didn't have any fear.

"We were up two to one in the series. They won Game Four and then Game Fve goes to overtime. Kenny Morrow's winning goal. I remember we tied it late. Donnie Maloney got that goal and batted that one out of the air. I remember the overtime, just get onto your shift and then get off, get your rest, get on to your shift, get off, get your rest. It was intense and you know it can go either way. Then both teams had chances and then they score on that kind of, scrambled up broken play with that puck off the wall that Morrow just threw at the net. It was fantastic. It was an incredible taste of the rivalry. Again, I was naïve, and I was so excited to be in the playoffs, loving it and it was disappointing to lose but I didn't understand the disappointment. I don't know if I shared the discipline of Gresh and Don Maloney and the guys who've been around for 10, 12, 15 years. Pierre, Mike Rogers, 'cause in my mind I thought, Oh yeah, this happens every year. Well, it took me five, ten years of real life, man it is hard. You better make the most of every chance you ever get. You don't know if you get another one."

FIRST RANGERS PLAYOFF GAME AT MSG: April 7, 1984 @ Madison Square Garden. Game 3 of Patrick Division semifinals, 7–2 win.

"I just remember there was a different Garden back then. It was the blue seats and I just remember it was incredible. That was the first time I remember the fans outside the building, you know hundred, thousand people outside the building. Coming in and going out after games. The passion and hatred of the Islanders. It was my introduction to a harder-edged fan. Extremely vocal and extremely passionate, it was in their family, in their lifeline, in their blood, their feelings of love for the Rangers. That was my first experience of it. I just remember how incredible that building went. Being in the new Garden now, it looks the same from the outside, but when you go in, its just that ol' shaped rink with the different colored teeth. I don't know if the lights were different, it had a little darker hue to the light and then the fans. It may be like that now but it's just a different feeling for me. Maybe it was because it was my first experience but that was why that series was so incredible. We didn't win, but I feel like either team could've won and we could've won just as easily, but the fans were part of that. They were part of the ride."

FIRST RANGERS GAME WITH HIS BROTHER AS A TEAMMATE: December 7, 1984 @ Madison Square Garden vs. Pittsburgh Penguins, 4–3 OT loss.

On December 6, 1984, the Rangers acquired Steve Patrick and Jim Wiemer from Buffalo for Dave Maloney and Chris Renaud.

"I remember the game, it was against Pittsburgh, I know we

lost. I know I got a goal, but I also know that I gave up the puck on the winning goal. I lost the puck. I remember my brother getting a real big hit, he really hit someone in the game. I remember obviously getting real excited about him coming. I remember meeting him at the hotel. Craig Patrick picked him up from there, him and Jim Wiemer right after they checked in. The year that he played for the Rangers, it was a real interesting dynamic probably for me because I was the older brother that my younger brother looked up to. I would describe us as real close to now being on the same hockey team. The first year, three quarters, but the next year he really struggled and coach didn't like him, and it really bothered me. I loved my brother and wanted the best for him, but I probably didn't have the right emotional makeup to handle how it played out."

FIRST TIME GETTING AN ASSIST ON A GOAL BY HIS BROTHER: February 22, 1985 @ Pittsburgh Penguins, 8–3 win

James Patrick had the lone assist on Steve Patrick's power play goal as part of a four-goal first period. In the previous game a day before, James and Steve had the assists on Mike Rogers's goal in the first period. Steve also scored a power-play goal in that game vs. the Hartford Whalers, a 4-3 loss at Madison Square Garden.

"Well, it's a big thrill. I can remember three of four goals or plays that I'm involved in in my career and you know it's one of the plays. I could still remember it. I remember the play he hit me and I was coming down on the wing, the defenseman went to jump at me. Just getting inside the blue line and I put it under the stick back to him, took one stride and picked the corner. It was kind of a quick play that happened, but yeah, I do remember it. It sticks in my brain for some reason. I'm really happy for my brother, that he got the experience of playing in New York. He got to play with Bubba and Gresch. Some of those guys are special guys but I also remember the hard part when [things] just didn't go well. He kind of became a healthy scratch a lot and it was heartbreaking when things weren't going good for him."

FIRST REACTION TO BEING TRADED:

In November 1993, the Rangers traded Patrick along with Darren Turcotte to the Hartford Whalers for Steve Larmer, Nick Kypreos, Barry Richter, and a draft pick.

"I remember the day. We had a team lunch, I had lunch and then I got home. I pulled in the driveway; my wife was waiting in the doorway. I got out of my car, she told me I got traded. No one had cell phones then and Neil Smith called the house. I knew there's a number of things that happened, but I knew when Mike Keenan took over the team, I wouldn't say I knew that I wouldn't be there long, but I'd been the longest guy in service [on the] Rangers in my 10th year. Even my agent said there's lots of times when Mike Keenan comes in, he changes a lot. You never know what's going to happen. I remember playing two of the exhibition games. I think we had like nine of them, so I didn't get into any exhibition games. Then, the first league game, I got three shifts. That had never happened to me, so the writing was on the wall. I maybe played the first two games and then two or three games and I was a healthy scratch. Obviously, I have mixed emotions. I knew that my time was coming to an end there, ended up maybe four or five days later, having a talk with Neil Smith. Neil came to me and said, 'I don't know if it's gonna work out here, I'm going to look to trade you if it works out.' Neil was really nice about it and really respectful. Neil said, 'I know when Mike comes, it doesn't always work for every player and he's going to have this type of player.' Maybe about two weeks later it ended up happening. I think I was about 30 years old and I still felt I could play and I still wanted to play. I wasn't gonna play there and I wasn't playing. They had good players. Sergei Zubov was now in his second year; he was a good player. They had a lot of different types of players who played real well. Beuk [Jeff Beukeboom] and [Brian] Leetch, Zubov and Kevin Lowe, so the writing was on the wall. There wasn't room for me. I still wanted to play. I mean, it wasn't bittersweet at that point. I said, hey, I would like to go and play somewhere. The trade to Hartford, I was there for about four months and then got traded to Calgary. So it was obviously an up and down year, somewhat unsettled for the family. As far as my emotions of the year, it's always tough to be traded and the team you get traded from goes on and wins it all. Brian Leetch was a real close friend but you're super happy for him, but I felt like I wasn't part of that team. I wasn't devastated though I could tell the first week of training camp that I wasn't going to be part of that team. That's kind of how I looked at it."

FIRST MEMORIES OF BEING BACK AT MSG AS A VISITING PLAYER:

"I remember going into the visiting dressing room. I remember the ceiling in the Garden, I remember the smell of the Garden, I remember the rink. I loved that day, I loved the ice there. I liked the dimensions with the rink, I liked the benches and this is the old Garden, the Garden that wasn't reconfigured. I remember walking up the driveway to the fifth floor where the rink is, which is unique for many buildings. I remember the smell of the building. I remember the memories every time I'm in that building. Ten years flashes before me and all my memories I have seen."

FIRST RANGERS OUTDOOR GAME: September 27, 1991 @ Caesar's Palace, Las Vegas vs. the Los Angeles Kings (preseason) 5–2 loss

"I remember flying in, I think we flew in the day of the game, got in the morning, checked into our hotel and then waited for the game. We stayed overnight but I do remember it being so different than anything we had ever experienced. I remember the stands, how they were set up. I remember there being 10,000 people. I remember there was concerns about the ice, but the ice was fine. I also remember that game. I thought we were outplaying LA and then [Wayne] Gretzky had to go get third period and they came back and beat us. It was a game we could've won. It was just an exhibition game, but still, because it was Las Vegas and outdoor attached to it. I do remember the grasshoppers on the ice. I remember how hot it was. It was humid into the evening and then I remember we went to the casino after the game."

50
MARK PAVELICH

Center Mark Pavelich was an undrafted free agent who made his mark as a member of the famous 1980 United States Olympic hockey team. Pavelich signed with the Rangers to play for his Olympic coach Herb Brooks. Pavelich has a couple of notable highlights during his five years with the Ranger. In his rookie season of 1981–82, Pavelich set a franchise record with 76 points, the most by a Ranger in his fitst year and he tied a franchise mark by scoring five goals in a single game.

FIRST MEMORY OF AN NHL GAME:

"I do remember when Chicago was playing and Bobby Hull, I forget who they were playing against. I remember him taking a slap shot and it actually went up and stuck in the boards above the glass. I just remember the crowd going, 'Whoa,' like he put it through the wood up there."

FIRST HOCKEY IDOL:

"I always wore nine, so Gordie Howe, when you could get the number. Of course, everybody, the older guys, when you're coming to the team, had first dibs, but that was always my desire, number nine. There was a lot of guys, like [Guy] Lafleur and

Bobby Orr. Orr's was the hardest number to get. I could never get that because that was probably the most sought-after number too, but for some reason, nine always resonated with me somehow."

FIRST OLYMPIC EXPERIENCE WITH THE US HOCKEY TEAM:

"I wasn't entirely sold when I first had the opportunity 'cause my dream was to go into the NHL. I didn't ever think I would play Olympics. It wasn't really on the list, the kind of bucket list, whatever you want to call it. Herb didn't play me a lot during that year because for whatever reason [I] sat on the bench a lot. We didn't play power play, didn't play penalty killing and when you don't play those two, mostly playing against the minors and the AHL, I forgot what other leagues they had back then. Most of them were filled with penalties, because they always tried to intimidate you, so you sat on the bench a lot. He'd have you playing seven minutes a game or five minutes of game. There's some players would enjoy that but it's tough to get into a game for me when you're only playing a limited amount of ice time, so it wasn't a really good year. The way Herb coaches was different too from any coach. He was incredible in ways and one of them was the shape he got you into, the physical shape. He was way ahead of his time, the personality he had around him and how to get that player into shape.

"It wasn't until the Olympics where I happened to bump into some of the Canadian players going up in the elevator. One of them was Glenn Anderson. He said to me, 'Boy, Brooks doesn't give you any ice time at all.' That motivated me to, one time during the first game in the Olympics, I said, 'Herb, if you want me to perform, you've got to give me some ice time.' That was a term that was like a signal to him that I wanted to play more or though he should play me more. So, I started to, at least, play on penalty killing and it changed the amount of ice time and it helped."

FIRST REACTION WHEN THE CLOCK HIT ZERO IN THE EPIC UPSET OF THE RUSSIANS:

"Against those guys, the whole Olympics was pretty amazing. So, yeah, I was wrong about the beginning of the year. The whole experience was amazing there. It was just a nice town [Lake Placid] to be [playing in] and the whole experience was amazing."

FIRST REACTION TO WINNING THE GOLD MEDAL:

"It was something you didn't expect. No one expected anything, to accomplish anything there but it was pretty amazing. That's all I can say."

FIRST RANGERS CONTRACT:

"The Montreal Canadiens wanted to sign me, but they didn't really send anybody to talk to me, so I took a bus to Portland, Maine, from Duluth [Minnesota] and they were offering me a two-way contract. Anyway, I showed up for practice there. They had a game that day, they were in Nova Scotia, so I took the bus out and I practiced with them in the morning. I didn't sign anything; I was just there to possibly sign if I wanted to. So, anyway, I jumped in practice with them in the morning. Most of the guys on the club, they're like, 'Oh great, who's this guy?' One wondering who's going to get replaced or what's going to happen, so they weren't happy. So I watched a game that night and it was just marred with fights and penalties and I thought, lucky I didn't play because even your own guys don't even want you there. Without saying anything, I don't think this is my route. I thought if they would have maybe sent somebody from the organization and explained here's what we want from me, but it was just like, 'Am I going to get stuck down here?' If I go out on the ice, where your own team's not even going to protect you, you're going to get hurt. I didn't want to be in a situation like that, so I didn't sign with them.

"I did go to Switzerland where Herb asked me if I wanted to try out the next, '81–'82 season. I said, 'Yeah,' so I actually started in the minor club at that time. They went over to Finland to train and New Haven was the farm club at that time. I played the games in there and Herb's attitude on me had changed too. It ended up really good because, after the first year, the vice president, Jack Krumpe, ripped up that contract, my two-way, and signed me to a new one and gave me a bonus. Then, after the second year, they ripped up that one and signed me to another contract."

FIRST RANGERS GAME: October 6, 1981 @ Madison Square Garden vs. Detroit Red Wings, 5–2 loss.

"You get out there and you wonder if you should even be there. All of a sudden your dream's fulfilled, but it's pretty amazing. You started to feel the pressure after a while, performing then, but it's an amazing feeling that when you finally fulfill it."

FIRST RANGERS COACH: Herb Brooks

"Herb was one of those coaches, they never get a day off. Herb was a disciplinarian and he had a strange way of coaching, though I wouldn't necessarily agree with it. He was incredible on training his players. He knew how to get them into the ultimate shape that a player needed to be in, so that was his big asset really. He did know the game. He just felt like he owed us for going through the whole Olympic experience. He was just a little bit more friendly and more appreciative of all the players that he achieved his Olympic goal through."

FIRST RANGERS CAPTAIN: Barry Beck

"He was awesome. I remember it was kind of funny. It was the first year, we were in Pittsburgh. I remember I was skating by the center ice and here's the Pittsburgh player and it ended up to be [Marty] McSorley. He came up high with his stick and caught me. I don't remember if it was by accident or purpose, but I think I swung back at him and maybe caught him too. He stopped and we kinda squared off. We were about ten feet apart and he took a few steps towards me and all of a sudden, he stopped and put his head down and kinda turned away. I didn't understand why until I turned around and here's Bubba standing right behind me. I thought, Well, that could have ended bad if he wasn't there. You know, he put his head down like a little puppy and skated away. So I thought that was pretty amazing. He didn't want to tangle with Bubba. Bubba was a great captain and great leader."

FIRST REACTION TO BEING TRADED FROM THE RANGERS:

In October 1986, Mark Pavelich was traded from the Rangers to the Minnesota North Stars for a draft choice that ended up being Troy Mallette.

"I didn't want to play really for the North Stars. I ended up playing for a short time. I did join them in March, I forget how many games I played [Pavelich played 12 games for Minnesota in the 1986-'87 season]. They offered me a contract after the season was over, a three-year contract but I never did take 'em up on it. I just didn't feel it was the right move at that time."

FIRST TIME FACING THE RANGERS AS AN OPPONENT: March 30, 1987 @ Minnesota. Rangers won, 6–5.

Pavelich had an assist in the game against his former team.

"It was kind of a strange feeling because so many of the personnel had switched around anyway. That's one thing you have to get used to in pro. You can be there one day and be in California the next, you know? So, that was kind of a strange experience, not knowing how the crowd would react or whatever."

Mark's reaction to winning the 1980 gold medal: "It was pretty amazing. That's all I can say." (Public Domain)

51
DALE PURINTON

Defenseman Dale Purinton played his entire five-year NHL career with the Rangers. At 6'3" and 228 lbs., Purinton was known as an enforcer. In 181 NHL games, he scored four goals and amassed 578 penalty minutes

FIRST CONTACT WITH NHL:

Dale Purinton was a fifth-round pick of the Rangers in the 1995 NHL Entry Draft.

"It was a real, special experience for me, for my family and for peers and guys I got to play with and against. It's really special and you know, it's one step closer. I'd always go along and say, 'Hey, if I get drafted and that's it, then that's amazing.' Then, when you get drafted, I go to my first camp and you're on the ice with [Wayne] Gretzky and Mess [Mark Messier].

**FIRST TIME SEEING THE RANGERS JERSEY:
December 1999**

"I get called up and we're in New Jersey, which you know, it's not a team that you really want to play against. I mean, [Martin] Brodeur is like a third defenseman. At that point. I don't think the Rangers beat him, they were like on a ten-game losing streak against him, so I'm in the locker room and my jersey's there and you're ready to go. Then I get called out, 'I'm sorry but we just picked up Richie Pilon off waivers.' So Richie comes in and you would think it's disappointing, but honestly, the truth was that it was a relief. It's such an overwhelming feeling, you're first kinda game, so for me it was actually kind of a blessing in a way because I got to go through that part of it and then you actually didn't get to play. Your nerves are just, it was crazy. As soon as that happened, it was a huge relief. The next time I get called up was the very last game of the season against the Flyers. So I get the call and I drive in from Hartford. Sure enough, Richie Pilon's my partner."

FIRST RANGERS GAME: April 9, 2000 @ MSG vs. Philadelphia Flyers, 4–1 loss

"I was very fortunate to be in New York with so many amazing guys; they made my experience incredible. They treated me like I was there all year. We're at home and just guys giving me rundowns like, 'Hey, keep it light, keep it out of the middle, move that puck, quick shifts,' you know, the whole deal. I'm prepared and I'm pretty fired up. Craig Berube's in the lineup and they had [Keith] Primeau as a captain, Rick Tocchet was still playing so these are guys that I grew up watching and it's surreal. I can't believe this is happening.

"So we go out and warm up, it's unbelievable. So this is where it gets really good. Last year, I think I had like 38 fights or 36 fights, I think I ended up with like 415 or 16 minutes in the minors, I was third in the league. Okay, I'm gonna probably go after Craig Berube, something dumb like that. Hopefully, you don't get your head taken off. Now we're back on the bench, they kinda do like the closing ceremonies of the year. The Christopher Reeve Foundation, the Rangers donated, I don't know the amount of money, you know, $100,000 dollars or whatever to his foundation.

Then, I'm sitting on the bench and it hit me, right? So now, there's a wave of emotion and I'm listening to him [Reeve] speak and everything's going down now. It's like your parents and your friends, and your family. Literally, I had tears running down my face but I have my glove over my face. I'm supposed to be like this "cop" coming up, throw your weight around and you know, scare some people or at least, leave your mark, and I'm literally having a friggin' meltdown on the bench. It's a major-league breakdown kinda thing. So when the anthem came on, I literally had my glove in my face. Like, I was having a breakdown and you don't want the cameras panning around and I pretended I was kinda like praying. It was too much because this is your moment, like reality, like it's here. Like, there's no more hiding. You gotta go out there and do your job and all that effort and all that work up to that point. You've accomplished what you set out to do as a kid, which is an incredible journey. I go out there and had a decent game. I think we lost maybe 3–2 to Philly that day, or 4–2 or something. I actually tried to fight Craig Berube and he sucked me in for two minutes and I think I did that later in the game and I ended up fighting Keith Primeau in that game."

FIRST RANGERS COACH: John "Torts" Tortorella

"Torts loved me at camp and would go out of his way to talk to me. He liked my work ethic and style because I'd run through the wall for any coach. I liked him and he treated me like a million bucks, he was firm, he wasn't easy about it. He was known for his training camps and how hard, his real tough style of coaching. He kinda just called me over and said, 'Hey, congrats and just stay simple, have a good experience out there,' it was real positive. I think he really liked how I played. I've always had a good experience with him. I think if you don't run through the all and block shots and play as hard as you can all the time, then you might have a different experience with him. If you do that, you're rewarded for it as well."

FIRST RANGERS GOAL: October 19, 2002 @ MSG vs. Nashville Predators, 2–2 tie

"The first one I missed, that was the one that really stuck with me. We're in Long Island and I jumped in the play, which rarely ever happened. I didn't even like to cross the far blue line. I liked the blue line back, especially on our end, I still just loved that style of game. So it was really rare that I jumped into the play and it ended up, I think it went from [Sandy] McCarthy to [Theo] Fleury, Fleury to McCarthy to me. I'm coming in all the way to the net, wide open and I shoot it wide and our whole bench stands up because there's no way you could miss that. It would've been so unbelievable to have those two guys, growing up, watching them, on that assist. It's haunted me to this day. Maybe they'll just get a plaque made up anyway.

"My first one, I pulled off the wall and just snapped it on net. Just kind of your head down and just threw it on net. It was unreal that I got it. It's always saying it's your first one but for me, it's like that's my second 'cause I already had one. I already had one that, you know, got away from me. Anytime you contribute that way is spectacular. It's something in your life that you can't ever replace."

Dale and his boys with two of his former coaches. Photo courtesy of Dale Puriton.

52
MIKE RICHTER

American-born Mike Richter is one of only four goaltenders in Rangers franchise history to win a Stanley Cup. Richter, who played his entire 14-year career with the Rangers, had 301 career wins and was a key to the Rangers ending their 54-year drought without a Stanley Cup in 1994. Richter made a memorable save of a penalty shot by Canucks star Pavel Bure in Game 4 of the Stanley Cup Final at Vancouver. Richter was a three-time NHL All Star and was named the MVP of the NHL All Star Game at Madison Square Garden in 1994. Richter's NHL debut came in Game 4 of the 1989 Patrick Division semifinals against the Pittsburgh Penguins. In 2004, Richter became the third player in franchise history to have his number (35) retired. In 2008, Richter was inducted into the United States Hockey Hall of Fame. In 2014, Richter was inducted into the Philadelphia Sports Hall of Fame.

FIRST GAME ATTENDED AS A KID:

"I grew up in Philadelphia so anything in the NHL was exciting to me. Back then, there were no hockey cards, we'd have stamps and there [were] only away games on television, on the radio. I sound like I'm 130 years old, but that was the case and we really tried to get everything we could, but the first pro game that I would have seen would have been a Philadelphia Flyers game for sure. I didn't get a chance to see an awful lot [of] games until I was a little older. We played games between periods of Pittsburgh Penguins games later on in life when we started to travel more. Next time I saw one in a different arena was after I was drafted by the Rangers, came up and saw some other games live. For the most part, it was all Philadelphia when I was young. University of Penn had a team, so every once in a while, would go down and watch a college game there too."

FIRST HOCKEY IDOL: Bernie Parent

"First of all, he was just a great goalie. It was obvious, the untrained eye to the trained eye, he understood how to play the game. The results were there pretty much every game, he just won a lot. They [Philadelphia Flyers] were a great team and he was a big part of their success. I mean he had a shutout [to clinch the Stanley Cup in 1974]. The Stanley Cup wins he had was just so impressive. On top of that, he was cool. He was French-Canadian, he had a great accent, he was always smiling. In the seventies, the Flyers had a really big personality and a bunch of interesting guys across their lineup. I really enjoyed following them and really loved supporting them. As tough as they were, like most great teams, they can beat you in a lot of ways. They had great skill upfront. They're tough as nails in an era where toughness really, really mattered. I guess it always does, but, back then, particularly the fighting, great defensively and unsurpassed in the net. So there were times you had to rely on him [Parent] and he'd steal a game or else other times, they'd find ways of winning offensively or just by being more physical than the other team, but he was a huge component of the ability to win."

FIRST CONTACT WITH NHL:

Mike Richter was chosen by the Rangers in the second round of the 1985 NHL Entry Draft.

"I went up to Toronto that year and my father was sick, so my mother was staying home with him. I went with my brother and my girlfriend at the time. We weren't sure where we would go and on draft day, anything can happen. It wasn't a lot of American goalies being taken back then. We had heard as high as second, we heard Philadelphia might take us in the third. I went up there with no expectations really. It was just incredibly exciting to meet some of the people that ran the world of professional ice hockey and some of the agents like Donnie Meehan. It was just like a dream come true to be up there and it's Toronto, right? You get to go and see the Stanley Cup and it's all things hockey and that weekend, so it was just such a treat. In the end, I did get drafted and on top of it, I got drafted by the Rangers which couldn't have been a better mix."

FIRST TIME PUTTING ON A RANGERS JERSEY: April 4, 1989, Game 4 of the Patrick Division semifinals @ Madison Square Garden vs. the Pittsburgh Penguins, 4–3 loss. Richter made his NHL debut in this postseason game. Rangers lost the series in a four-game sweep.

"It was amazing. There was a lot going on back then. We just had a very good team but they're playing against Pittsburgh Penguins in the first round, who had a fantastic team at the time. It was just where they were, coming into their own as one of those top echelon teams. I played in the minors after signing a contract. I had played on the '88 Olympic team. Tony Granato, Pete Laviolette, and myself played for the Denver Rangers at the time, who had a very, very good team. A couple of guys got picked up for the playoffs and you need a third goalie. So there it was and it was fantastic.

"Everything's a bonus. You get to practice with the team, you might be able to get into a game, free food, all kinds of great stuff but you're in the minors. To be able to be part of the big squad is a really big deal. Phil [Esposito] came up and looked and said, 'You know there's rumors,' that they might just try to shake things up. At the time, I felt so excited just to even be practicing with them and they said, 'Hey, you're going to play Game Four,' and I was like, 'Okay, let's go guy. We're going to come back from oh and three against the Pittsburgh Penguins,' not probably recognizing how big of a hole we were in against such a good team, but let's take it a game at a time. I promptly went out there and I think I had three goals scored on me very, very early and they stuck with me. We ended up in a 4–3 game. I played decent but not well enough to win it but not necessarily embarrassed myself and would've loved to have been able to turn the ship around, but it didn't happen, but it was an amazing experience. One of the coaches said, 'You haven't played your first game in the NHL and you never have to worry about your first playoff game.'"

FIRST GOAL HE GAVE UP:

Pittsburgh's Mario Lemieux scored the first goal against Richter in the first period of the playoff game.

"I do remember a two-on-oh they had coming down on me. I think it was he [Lemieux] and [Paul] Coffey were coming down on a two-on-oh and both of them were confused about which one was going to score [then] they overpass and went behind the net without getting a shot off. Is that much net being shown that you guys are fighting over the puck. It was kind of hilarious when I looked back on it 'cause those guys were just so bloody talented."

FIRST RANGERS COACH: Phil Esposito

Rangers GM Phil Esposito took over the team after he fired coach Michel Bergeron with two games left in the 1988–89 regular season.

"I loved him because he gave me an opportunity, so you could never say a bad word about him. I mean he was great to me in the sense that he believed and said, 'Look, maybe desperate times call for desperate measures,' but we weren't winning at the time. So, he put me in there. They had a great goaltending combination in John Vanbiesbrouck and Bobby Froese. I didn't take the opportunity to play lightly 'cause these guys are great and they don't need me. They've got other people that can play great hockey, and this was a real honor to be asked and a great opportunity.

"In my eyes, I will always owe him for that. He was great, really supportive. He was an old-time, obviously a great player, so you had a lot of respect for him as a player but that's a big moment. That first game was a huge moment for any player and for a goalie to get in and be entrusted in the playoffs, did wonders for me. It was just good to get in there and not be languishing in the minors forever. I went back to the minors and continued my development. It just gives you a sense of the speed and how the game is played. Going back to the minors then, you felt a sense of confidence that you could compete at a higher level, but you still need to work. It was a funny thing. A friend named David McNab, who was a scout for a long time for Hartford back then, he called me up afterwards. I went back to the minors and played a couple rounds and then we lost down there, I think the finals. The summer was there and you're done. He calls me up and says, 'Congratulations, you're the first goalie in Ranger history to lose, to end two playoff rounds.' It gave me a lot of confidence heading into the following year and a lot of motivation to get better. I mean they still have Bob Froese and John Vanbiesbrouck, two excellent goalies, great guys, very helpful to me and my career, but nothing motivates you like a little bit of a taste of where you can go with your talent and what you have to do to get better. That's what this thing was. I mean, I was playing the game to win and I was disappointed. We and particularly disappointed 'cause you know the year was over with that loss. It meant an awful lot to me."

FIRST RANGERS TRAINING CAMP:

"I already had a game under my belt. It was a higher level, obviously the playoffs are a higher level than you get when you're playing regular season. The intensity, the demand, the stakes are higher. So coming to training camp, I had a lot of confidence. I also knew that, you know, playing a single game doesn't make you an NHL goalie, it means you have the potential to be there. Perhaps if I had won and gone on to win the next couple of rounds, then you can start talking about it. I had a lot of hunger to get better. I worked hard that summer and came into camp in very, very good shape, mentally, physically and really had a strong training camp.

"After getting in a few games and having a couple of good opportunities to prove myself in training camp and the regular season, unless I was going to displace Bob [Froese] or John [Vanbiesbrouck] immediately, the right thing was to put me in the minors. When the coach finally brought me in there, he said, 'You're gonna stay up. We like you, you're playing well, get an apartment.' I was thrilled to get an apartment at that point. Then, at some point, after about a month it was like, 'Hey, you need to get some work, go down to the minors.' Roger [Neilson, the Rangers' new coach] was a good guy but he put me in the office and said, 'Hey Mike, we're going to send you down. That's the bad news, the good news is you get to work on your game and maybe another team who needs a goalie will be interested in, can trade for you and you'll get back up, you're good enough to play,' and I almost freakin' tapped out. Like I was, 'No, I'm a Ranger, like I was drafted, remember all I've been through, the three games that I've played. I'm thinking, how could you break this bond? The reality is he was saying the exact right thing I need to do to improve. I needed to get games in or else I'm not going to improve to the degree that I should. I need to kind of shut up and play and the minor leagues was a great opportunity for me to do that at that point. You just have to play through those things. You're going to get goals scored on you. A guy like Grant Fuhr, when he did get to the Rangers, Mess [Mark Messier] would talk about him. He could let in six goals, but if they needed to win, you need to save that seventh shot in overtime, he would be there and that's a real skill and that's the type of thing that you learn as you mature.

"I was so upset I can almost not bring myself to pack up the bag and go. I think part of it is maturity. I had lip on, you're upset and you're angry and all those things. Then I promptly went down there and played like crap for awhile. It was hugely important for me to pull it together and start playing. No one's going to give you this opportunity unless you weren't it. We didn't have a great team down there and we took our lumps and ended up being a good year to develop. The minors really, really helped me. I learned so much there so that by the time I did come up, I just felt like I got so much more. I was so much more battle tested and ready to play and it was the right thing to do and thankfully, the Rangers kept me."

FIRST RANGERS CAPTAIN: Kelly Kisio

"Kelly, number one, was an unbelievable person and a great, great player. I mean, he really was. He's an undersized buy back when the league did not take kindly to undersized guys. Skilled, professional, hardworking guy, played through injuries, all the things you want in a captain. Lead by example, was not an incredibly vocal guy. Like Mess he was inclusive. He was so good about that. I remember the first time he invited us over to have beef jerky in his basement. He made the beef jerky and he's down there, you know, 'Come over and have a beer and have some jerky. I make this stuff in the summertime.' This guy's been in the league for like a hundred years and he asked me to come over, as a rookie, and hang out, like treating you as a peer. There [were] some old veterans, great characters on that team when I came up to New York. Ron Greschner, James Patrick, Kelly Kisio was one of them, of course, [Chris] Nilan, [John] Ogrodnick. They were amazing to the young guys, like it was pretty intimate. We're walking out of the locker room and it was a little bit of a different era where rookies were to be seen and not heard and what not, but these guys were good. They include you in it and Kelly was spectacular about that. It really means something when someone comes up to you, 'Hey, sit next to me in the bus or whatever,' ask you about whatever, whatever's going on in your life, which clearly wasn't much when you're 20 years old. All you think about in the world is making that next game and sticking with the team was pretty straightforward, but they treat you with purism and that makes them an enormous difference. When you're talking about Kelly, that, to me, is one of the things I'll forever be grateful for how well he treated the young guys. Me, in particular, he was great to."

FIRST RANGERS REGULAR-SEASON GAME: October 19, 1989 @ Madison Square Garden vs. Hartford Whalers, 7–3 win

Richter made 24 saves in his NHL regular-season debut, including facing his first penalty shot. Richter didn't initially remember that Pat Verbeek scored the first goal against him.

"Patty Verbeek, that dirty dog. The only thing I remember was he had an illegal stick and the play was offside. I gotta give him shit the next time I see him. Honestly, I didn't think of that when he came to the Rangers. You know, I would have gotten maybe a free meal out of that or something.

"I do recall the penalty shot. [Kevin] Dineen, who was a great player. He had scored on me, I think, in training camp, high glove, you know he's a great player through his career, and went high glove, missed high [on the shot], I probably only gave him a yard or two. I don't know how much it was there. I was good at playing the angles and the game was a little bit different back then, so you're trying to take that away. I'm not a big guy but I could skate well so I would come out and give back. Not like I did years later on the Pavel Bure [penalty] shot. He [Dineen] was a great player and he scored on me before.

"A great goaltending coach I used to have when I was younger was Joe Bertagna who was a goalie for Harvard forever. He's written some books and he's just a funny guy. I mean, he would talk, kind of go into philosophy one night. 'You know, you can win that battle [one-on-one with a skater coming in on him] without doing anything. There's more pressure on the forward sometimes. He has to place a shot and you're in his way and you can come out and fall down, but he can miss the net.' You get the victory there. Sometimes you're fortunate too. You watch how good Henrik Lundqvist is, or even Georgie [Rangers goaltender Alexandar Georgiev] and they play their angles well and they're great. They move right, so they can force guys to shoot wide. [Dominik] Hasek was great at doing that but sometimes it's the luck of the draw and he missed the net on that one. I don't know honestly what I have to look at film of that one. What percentage falls in favor of him just missing or me forcing him."

FIRST RANGERS SHUTOUT: April 7, 1991 @ Washington Capitals, Game 3 of Patrick Division semifinals vs. Washington Capitals, 6–0 win. Rangers would go on to lose the series in six games.

"I would love to have a shutout every game. That's what you're aiming for. It gives your team the best chance of winning, but in the playoffs, it's all about buckling down and getting wins, wins on the road in particular. That was a good team the Washington Capitals had and we had a good team too. Roger Neilson played a good defensive style and that was a great game. I felt really good. We played well, we got the win and it was just a solid game. We were able to defend well; we were able to score goals. There was just so many good things about that game. It's just one of the solid wins where everybody felt good about themselves. The scoring, I think was pretty spread out from our point of view. I played well, but it wasn't overwhelming. It wasn't like we got lucky. It set you up for the series very well. They've kinda gotta look and go out, 'These guys can put the puck in the net and they can defend too,' so they're valuable games obviously for the win that you get, but also for the statement that they can make. That was a good team and they took it to us plenty of times over the next few years in the playoffs.

"In the playoffs, I thought it was easier to play in some ways because the intensity was so high and the players were so committed. You could read the plays where you know what your defense is going to do. Guys are so dialed into the responsibilities. I really like playing under those circumstances. We had a good defensive team, good communication, veteran defense. Doesn't mean you didn't lose games, didn't miss pucks, but sort of everybody was bought in at one when the playoffs started, in a way that almost never happens to the same degree during the regular season."

FIRST STANLEY CUP FINAL, 1994 vs. Vancouver Canucks. Rangers won in seven games.

"We used to really get books on other teams, you're playing them, essentially, for seven games, so you've got to learn this opponent quickly and understand them. You always have to play the same, kind of get yourself prepared in the same manner but each team has their own strategy and quirks that you have to deal with. You try to have consistency in your approach, you know that's gonna yield consistency and results. You don't, one game be up, one game be down. You go about the same way and once the playoff time comes, you know how that is.

"I mean it's not hard to get up for that [Cup Final] but that being said, it's different. I mean you're playing in the damn Stanley Cup Finals. Every time you step out on the ice or at practice or a game, it is a dream come true with the dream you had as a kid, but the Stanley Cup's the Stanley Cup. There've been so many great players across the history of this game that have never had the opportunity, so you don't know when you're getting back there again. All you know is the opportunity is a hard one and you don't want to squander it. It was an exciting [Eastern Conference finals] series against Jersey. You'll take every win, every battle. You're a better player for it, but you have work to do until that first shift of the first game, there's nothing else to think about, then go on to the second shift.

"You can't even think about winning that game. You have to think on a shift-by-shift basis. You can't even think, 'Oh, we just have four more wins.' That could be two weeks away, and in this case it was. Seven games and multiple overtimes and lots of air miles and adjustments and victories and defeats and mistakes. The minute you start talking about, 'We're four games away from the Stanley Cup,' you're miles away. Having people like Mark Messier, Kevin Lowe, and Jeff Beukeboom and these guys that have been through it multiple times is so valuable. Even that first series we played leading up to this seven games with Vancouver in the finals, we had won three games in a row against the Islanders. They were eighth seed, we were first. We were first in the league, they may have been the last team, the whole thing. Mark said that the fourth game is always hardest game for closing out. The other team can be embarrassed, their job's on the line, their pride, you know they're not going to go down without swinging. No one's going to give you anything for free. So, even in a first-round series, we're up three-nothing, you're going to have to scratch and claw to get that fourth one. The last game was like three to two when it was a dogfight, you don't want to lose that game. Now you go back home or else you go to their place and the momentum starts changing. Having that stability of the veterans that we had on the team was incredibly important. Heading into that final realm, it doesn't change, it shouldn't change but the expectations are higher. The media attention is greater, your expectations are higher. Your desire is through the roof. You have to stay on an even keel and keep yourself focused on the things that make you successful or you're going to be on the wrong end of this thing in a hurry. The irony is all that great intensity and effort and excitement, if not channeled properly, ends up getting in your way. You see it all the time. Suddenly, the press conferences are longer, before and after practices. What you say has to be a little bit buckled down.

"You're gonna see this opponent many, many times and all that stands between you and that's all that stands between you and hoisting the Cup, so I don't care who's on the other end, they're going to be a tough opponent. They don't give a crap that we were ranked high coming in, that we just beat New Jersey. They [Vancouver] defied the odds the entire way, they scratched and clawed. They won their own Game Sevens. That's a great team and they were playing very intense hockey and really relished the underdog status. So you know our fight was to focus on what made us successful, not have understandable expectations. They're going to score goals, they're gonna win games perhaps, momentum's gonna shift, but we can control how we play and that's what our focus needs to be, or else we'll be on the outside looking in. So heading into that first finals, I guess the Ranger team that had done that was with JD [John Davidson] years before and they had a great team. You hear their stories, they played so well to get to that spot, but then lost to Montreal. It's all over and your job's not finished. So we kind of felt like it's exciting, so happy about the New Jersey victory, but now let's refocus. Being that we went seven games, you don't have a lot of time to refocus, physically or emotionally. There's not a lot of resetting that you have to do and not a lot of time to do it, so you have to be very disciplined."

FIRST REACTION TO WINNING THE STANLEY CUP:

A controversial icing call was made with 1.6 seconds left in Game 7, so there had to be one more faceoff before the Rangers would win the Cup.

"We were an old enough team to have that discipline to have that kind of mental toughness to know that you can get scored on, the game's not over until the final buzzer, all that kind of stuff. If you remember, we got scored on with, whatever it was, seven seconds left from New Jersey series and Game Seven. By the way, they [Vancouver] scored in that same realm in the first game, put it into overtime, which they ultimately won with whatever tiny bit of time left [Canucks tied Game One with a minute left in the third period and won it in overtime]. So it wasn't like it wasn't fresh on our mind. Maybe as bad as those moments were, it helped us in this moment to be like, 'All right.' I think the real interesting part of that is you just reset. By then, you're so dialed in, you reset. Hard to do but I don't think it was an icing, it was a poor call, but whatever, he [the referee] said, 'Look, I'm gonna err for the side of being conservative and give these guys, so they're not bitching about it, an opportunity.' Sure, they had it and that is enough time, a shot and maybe a rebound. If you look at the final picture where Mess is jumping up in the air, but you watch that last faceoff, they put, what'd they put, two seconds on the clock or something like that.

"The puck's dropped. Mac-T [Craig MacTavish, Rangers center who took the final draw] throws it behind him into the corner. There's a great picture of Mark [Messier] after the buzzer sounds, jumping up and down. Mac spills his guy, he's turned him, he's put the puck in the corner, precisely as he should. Larms [Steve Larmer] is in the corner, tying up his guy. Like everybody's in the exact right position. If you think, wow, why would you go and get this old guy, MacTavish. They're giving up something. Yep, you're giving up something because in the seventh game of the Stanley Cup Finals, when you need to win the defensive zone faceoff and you have been scored on late and you need someone to win it clean and get it back and tie up his guy and never have to worry about it. That's the goddamn guy you want. I just think it's so cool, and Larmer the same way. These guys weren't going to play for another two decades. They were older guys, but their experience mattered, and that's why we won. We were able to weather those storms. These guys were doing their jobs perfectly. That famous picture, if you just watched a film of it, everybody does what they're supposed to do. Puck goes harmlessly in the corner, and you're winning. That's execution and it's not always easy to when you've had this false start. You know, they're already having fireworks go and stuff like that. Wait, we can't celebrate. So yeah, I thought it was a really interesting thing and kind of instructive to how important and great these veterans were for us."

FIRST TIME TOUCHING THE CUP AFTER WINNING IT:

"Honestly, at that point, you were so elated and so excited. You didn't care about anything. There was no, 'I need to get this before someone else,' or 'I'm going to do this with it.' You were just humbled by the strength of the moment. It's something you've dreamed about forever and there it is on home ice and with the team that drafted you. After all those firsts, this is the first that you've been pointing to forever. It's hard to process, you're just about blank. There's that great promotional video of guys with almost nothing to say. How's it feel? What'd you think? Give me some words to describe and people would just blank.

"You almost think about all the people that helped you along the way. You think about all the people you want to call on, share this with me. Think about, how thankful you are for your teammates, for your staff. I mean, endless everything in your life, everything my adult life has pointed to that moment. So where do you even begin to thank the people that got you there, to be appreciative of the opportunity. So many great players that I played with never got that chance. So much has to go right for you to be even in that position to fight for the Cup. You look at some of the names that never got to be there. The guys like JD [John Davidson] and that great team. Roddy Gilbert and the Rangers that didn't get a chance to hoist it. On a personal, on a team level, you know someone's going to win in each year but it's pretty amazing when it's you. You see guys who have won multiple, the first one is the first one, so you'll never forget that. Without that, there are no others of course, so it's maybe the most important, but each one is going to be a different story in order for you to get there and it's going to be a hell of a story because it's not a free ride to get to the finals."

FIRST STANLEY CUP VICTORY PARADE:

"It was just a really great moment in time. The city was so ripe for it. The hockey world was just at a great place. It had been a really exciting year with a lot of incredible instinctive talented players, not just on our team but the Devils were great in that rivalry. There's so many good teams and so much good competition. The NHL and New York has always been a great sports town generally, but always been a great hockey town it seems or at least has been for so long. To see them finally get rewarded after 54 years, you know how lucky are we to be in a position to compete for a Stanley Cup, to win it and doing it in a great city like New York. A great city like New York has a 54-year drought. I mean, it was just an amazing moment while the Knicks were going into the finals too and seventh game. It was like a perfect dream. It would have just been great if the Knicks could just finish it off, but so much was happening at that moment. So yeah, we were still processing it. You're still excited. You're doing circuit and late-night television and all the great things that you do and never want it to end. There's a crazy sense of freedom and almost oddness to the rhythm of your life.

"I was just unprepared for it [the massive crowd that attended the parade] and I knew it was a really meaningful moment, where we got a little bit of an inkling on how important it was for the city. There is this huge picture out there and very big city with an enormous stake in this thing. It's not just the guys in your locker room and you have to be playing for them but, wearing the colors and representing the team on your chest. That's New York and they have a ton of passion and they want to win as much as you. All the families and the players gathered at MSG. I think we may have had our picture taken and may even done Howard Stern [radio show] that morning, but it was a series of things like that. You're still trying to just process this and still say goodbye to some guys are getting ready to leave, go back to Europe. Adam Graves getting ready to get married. You're just holding it together.

"The parade always sounded like a great thing, I don't know how to describe it, just such an honor. It wasn't like I didn't understand the aspect of it, but how big it was and when the bus pulled out from under MSG, it was probably four buses with everybody. Trainers, family members and all that kind of stuff. Guys would come in late and we're all having a great time. Then, we got in front of the Moynihan building. The postal workers were lined up on the top stair, saluting us, clapping as we were pulling out of MSG. It was just inspiring. We were like, 'Oh my god,' like these people, they knew we were coming out, they knew what we just accomplished, and they were just saying, 'Thank you.' On the bus, we were all laughing and it just went quiet. I was really kind of taken aback by it. Then you go downtown and the staging area and all that kind of stuff. Again, you don't know how gigantic this parade is gonna be. Once you get on the float, you couldn't quite hear it, but as you approached the first turn where the actual parade starts and it's the 'Canyon of Heroes,' sounding like a jet engine. It was just this roar, this rumble. It was the film we saw the first day of training camp, only more intense of course or the astronauts coming home from the lunar landing or something. There were streamers coming down, people just emptying buckets of paper out their window, confetti, signs, people losing it. It was amazing.

They're 30 deep on each side, endless and just unbelievable. I just couldn't believe it. My brother and I had been out late, and he was up hanging out in New York for a few days and he's like, 'I don't think I can make it to the float, Mike.' I think my sister was coming up and I said, 'Grab him and get his ass down here.' I had no idea what a big deal it was. It was really amazing and just such a cool thing to share with the city. It was one of those great moments. Of course, you went to City Hall and those moments are so great when you feel like you can have that, you're not just playing and then getting off the ice. There's that kind shared experience that we're all acknowledging. I thought Mess was so good about that. When he picked up the Cup and kind of just glided over to the boards and let a pile of fans just touch it, I mean that was a thing after those weeks. It was a first for us, I'd never touched the Cup, I never carried it around, they'd never been to Manhattan with it. When you get the opportunity to do that, the reverence that people have for it and the respect is pretty inspiring."

FIRST OLYMPIC EXPERIENCE:

Richter played with the United States Olympic hockey team in 1998 and 2002, when Team USA won the silver medal. Richter also played for the United States in the 1986 World Junior Championships and was the MVP of the 1996 World Cup of Hockey when the United States beat Canada in the best-of-three finals including 5–2 win in Montreal in the championship game.

"It's an incredible honor on many levels. Easy enough because it's an accomplishment making the Olympic team. You think of all the good players within your country that can be taking your place. You've got to be one of the 20 best to be on that team and wear that jersey, so it's obviously a huge honor. Then your focus turns to who you're playing against. Whether, it's junior nationals, small international tournament as a Pee Wee, the Olympics or World Cup, you want to represent your country, your family, your locker room, all that as well as you can. It is the pride in the uniform they have and everyone's deep and hockey, such an international game that the same guys that were in your Ranger locker room, Adam

Graves and Wayne Gretzky and Mark, they're putting a Canadian jersey on and they've got an enormous amount of respect for that jersey, that flag. They're not gonna give up an inch. Look across, the Russians, the Swedes, the Finns, everybody. I think those international tournaments are so enjoyable to play in and now that I've retired, so enjoyable to watch because you are getting the best in the world. On just skill level, you're getting hundreds of players that can possibly be in one spot, but it's fueled by that passion and that pride in their countries, in their uniforms. The Finns, the Swedes, the Latvians, everybody has it. It's an enormous honor and responsibility to put it on and when you win, it's an amazing feeling. I grew up watching the Philadelphia Flyers, but the real international competition that rings true for me and stuff, probably all Americans, but as a young hockey player, we used to play in the driveway and be Bernie Parent, Rick MacLeish, and Bobby Clarke. In 1980, we came back. [USA goalie] Jim Craig and [Team USA captain] Mike Eruzione, [Team USA defenseman] Kenny Morrow. I don't think there's anybody that were on the next five Olympic teams that didn't take some kind of inspiration from what happened in 1980."

FIRST REACTION TO HAVING HIS NUMBER RETIRED:

On February 4, 2004, Richter's No. 35 became the third to be retired and hoisted to the rafters of Madison Square Garden.

"Well, I can remember being a free agent years before and wanting to sign with the Rangers, but you have to do what's right for your career at the time. Having a conversation with one of the team doctors, he said, 'The other good thing is your number could be retired here.' As a player, you don't really think in those terms. Truly, when my career ended [in 2003] I, of course, retired through injury, I wasn't thinking about, I think they had announced that they were going to retire my jersey and it almost didn't register with me 'cause I was thinking more about what I lost and the career and felt like I had some years left in me that I could play at a high level. I knew it would mean a lot to me but at the moment when it was announced, I probably didn't process it. Every day that goes by, every year that goes by, it's an amazing honor. It's there, it's there forever. You're left with memories, you can't play anymore, your career is over. To have that kind of sign of respect that the organization gives you is just humbling. It means more to me, certainly more now than the day they announced it, but every year it, it may be more. That was home [MSG] for everybody who put on a Ranger uniform and for guys that played the whole career there and don't know any other home and to be permanently up on display there, that was your family, that was your home, that was your work, that was everything. It's an amazing honor. Just thankful they gave me that, huge!"

ON NCAA TOP GOALTENDER AWARD THAT WAS NAMED AFTER HIM:

The Mike Richter Award was created in 2014 to annually honor the most outstanding goaltender in NCAA Division I men's hockey.

"It's amazing. You think of the great college goalies that have been out there. Kenny Dryden is the first one that spring to mind. Being an NCAA thing, an American thing, they want an American player to name it but I was amazed when someone asked me, 'Would I be accepting of this award,' to have it named after me, I was absolutely amazed. Yeah, I love it. It's not an easy job that the selection committee has because there are so many good goalies. I've watched a couple of these kids have multiple years of being in the running for the award. Some have won one and some haven't and they're just all great. NCAA has a great history of producing top notch player, but the top-notch goalies in particular. Right now, there's so many good players that are playing college hockey, Division I, and Division III, really capable guys that may or may not go all four years 'cause they're that good and will go on to a great NHL career. That was certainly a first for me and I'm very grateful for it. I really love it because in a sense, it forces me to follow these guys. The selection committee comes out in the first few rounds, and these are the guys that are being nominated. You follow them, you get to know them, you get to know their story. I have to say Connor Hellebuyck [now with Winnipeg] was the first and what an impressive guy he is, what a great story he has and what a great player he is. I love getting to know these guys and meeting them and just sharing a little bit of their success.

"Humbled by the strength of the moment." Photo courtesy of USEPA Environmental-Protection-Agency/Public domain.

53
EDDIE SHACK

Left wing Eddie Shack began his 17-year NHL career with the Rangers, where he played parts of three seasons. Shack began his junior hockey career with the Guelph Biltmores as a 15 year old in 1952. He signed with the Rangers and scored 47 goals in his fifth and final season in juniors as a 20 year old. After a year at the Rangers' AHL affiliate in Providence, Shack made his NHL debut as a 21 year old in the 1958–59 season. In February 1960, Shack and Hall of Fame defenseman Bill Gadsby were traded to Detroit for another Hall of Fame defenseman, Red Kelly, and Billy McNeill, but the latter two refused to report and the trade was cancelled. Later that year, Shack was traded to Toronto where he went on to win four Stanley Cups.

FIRST CONTACT WITH THE RANGERS:

"What happens in 'Junior-A' and Canada, 'Junior-B' or 'Junior-A,' then you can go right up to the NHL. That was when Andy Bathgate found that out. Dean Prentice, they were playing for New York and they came from the Guelph Biltmores and that's how they became New York Rangers."

FIRST RANGERS TRAINING CAMP:

"I lost my teeth in New York. They had the rink upstairs and [Lou] Fontinato, he swung and hit me, hit my teeth and knocked them out. I had a space in the middle and I was happy that I had them knocked out because I got false teeth and I liked it a lot better. Stupid, right?"

FIRST RANGERS COACH: Phil Watson

"When I played junior, I scored like 48 goals. Guelph was close to Toronto and New York was playing in Toronto and I felt like I should've been brought up there, I was hot but he didn't bring me up. The next year, he sends me to Springfield and then I broke my leg. He calls me up after, I didn't have my confidence in my hockey then and he brings me up then.

"After playing with New York, what happened? We lost five games and we're in Montreal and there was a meeting. The meeting [called by Watson]) was 'Nothing will held against ya. You can say what you want.' Then it [he] goes [looking for a response] to Bathgate, 'We should work harder.' He goes to Fontinato, he goes to Dean Prentice. They said, "Well, we should do this or we should do this.' I said, 'Phil, everything you said to me has gone in one ear and out the other.' Well it was cancelled then, the meeting was cancelled. So I walked out in the hallway and who was there? Frank Paice, the trainer. I said, 'What do you want?' He says, 'You're going to Springfield,' and that's when I got sent down to Springfield for two weeks, I guess for misbehaving. From there on, I liked Springfield. I was ready, sure I was. Don Cherry played there, so I enjoyed it. The money wasn't much. It was $4500 for playing the minor leagues and 75 for playing the NHL. I said, 'No, I don't want to [return to NHL] I'm going to stay down here.' "Then, Andy called me. I was to come back up there and that's when I got back to New York and then I got traded. I got traded to Detroit, Bill Gadsby and I for Red Kelly and Billy McNeill. Red didn't want to go to New York, he didn't want to go to play for New York, so he quit and he went to the farm and that's when Toronto picked him up [from Detroit] and then I got traded to Toronto."

FIRST RANGERS GAME: October 8, 1958 @ Chicago Black Hawks, 1–1 tie

"Playing in Chicago, the dressing rooms are downstairs and you have to walk up the stairs and then the rink and that. I liked Bobby Hull. I got his stick one time and I used it. You had to share what sticks. We had the 'CCM' and I had the curve in that. I got a hat trick. I said to Bobby, 'Thanks a lot,' and he got hell for that."

FIRST GAME WITH THE RANGERS AFTER PROPOSED TRADE FELL THROUGH:

"It was hell because I was a pretty mouthy kid at that time. Then, I have to go back to New York. It was hell. The coach was absolutely, he didn't have the balls to work you properly. When you're going good that's when you should be with the New York Rangers. I got sent down to Providence and then I broke my leg."

FIRST RANGERS CAPTAIN: Red Sullivan

"Red was a great guy, he was from Peterborough, Ontario. I really liked him and he liked me. I played with him a little bit but didn't play that much. I liked the guys there. I liked Andy Bathgate, Jerry Sullivan was a really good friend of mine, I was his best man. It was good, but the coach was absolutely hell."

FIRST REACTION TO BEING TRADED FROM THE RANGERS:

Shack was dealt to Toronto in November 1960

"I got traded to Toronto. I'm from Sudbury and played my junior hockey in Guelph, so it was close. Guelph and Toronto were close by. [Leafs GM] Punch Imlach, he liked me. I played with the right guys, I was happy with Toronto."

FIRST TIME HE TOUCHED THE STANLEY CUP

AFTER WINNING IT WITH TORONTO:

"It was great. Like we couldn't bring it to Sudbury. After the game you won it, that's where it stayed and then it went back to the Hall of Fame."

FIRST NHL PLAYER TO HAVE A RACEHORSE NAMED AFTER HIM:

"I lived on the farm and they [owners] named the horse after me. I rented their house for one of the trainers and it was like a 150 a month there. They had the horse named after me and it was M. J. Boylan, that's who owned the horse.

FIRST NHL PLAYER TO HAVE A HIT SONG WRITTEN ABOUT HIM:

"It was fantastic. When you turn the radio on, all you could hear [starts mimicking the song] 'Here comes Shack, you knocked him down and he gives him a whack. He scores goals, he's got the knack, Eddie, Eddie Shack.' Nancy Sinatra beat me out [of the No. 1 spot on the chart] so that was not too bad."

Shack went on to win four Cups with the Maple Leafs. Photo courtesy of Ralston-Purina Company, maker of Chex cereals /Public domain.

54
DAVID SHAW

David Shaw was a solid defenseman who played for six teams during a 16-year NHL career. Shaw was acquired by the Rangers in a trade with the Quebec Nordiques before the 1987–88 season. Shaw was a member of the 1982 Memorial Cup champion Kitchener Rangers, where he played alongside Hall of Famers Scott Stevens and Al MacInnis. Shaw played parts of five seasons for the Rangers but missed most of the 1989–90 season because of a shoulder injury. He was dealt to the Edmonton Oilers in November 1991 for defenseman Jeff Beukeboom to complete the trade for Mark Messier.

FIRST HOCKEY GAME ATTENDED AS A KID:

"Toronto Maple Leaf game, I grew up two hours outside Toronto. I went with my dad and my brother when they played Montreal. Montreal was good, Toronto was horrible. I grew up being a Bruins fan because Toronto was so bad, they hadn't won since '67. It was a great atmosphere, Toronto-Montreal games. So it was a lot of excitement."

FIRST HOCKEY IDOL:

"It was Bobby Orr, 'cause I think he's so much better than

anyone else. I was born in '64, so early '70s, it was the Bruins was the team. It was them and Montreal, but I like the Bruins for some reason. It was mainly for Bobby Orr, everyone idolized him. He definitely changed hockey. He was my idol growing up playing street hockey. Everyone wanted to be Bobby Orr."

FIRST MEMORIAL CUP CHAMPIONSHIP:

"It was my first taste of pro hockey because, for instance, Al MacInnis came, he went to Calgary's camp, he ended up coming back. He had sign a pro contract. A couple of guys signed pro contracts and I didn't realize the NHL was my next step, kind of like growing up. You don't really think you're there until you start playing with the guys that are on contracts. It was exciting and that team, I can't imagine another junior team having that many guys that go on to play pro. Even John Tucker played a long time, Mike Hough, Jeff Larmer, and Grant Martin. All those guys played at least a few games if not a thousand, so it was pretty special. We were a very talented team too, so I was fortunate to play in that organization."

FIRST CONTACT WITH NHL:

David Shaw was selected by the Quebec Nordiques with the 13th overall pick of the 1982 NHL Entry Draft.

"I was at the draft; it was in Montreal in '82. I went with Mike Hough and Bells [Brian Bellows] was the big talk of the draft that year, he was a great junior. They're talking about him going to be the next Gretzky, a little different style, but that's how dominant he was. So he was there and Stevens was there. Buffalo had three picks in the first round. That year, they had like six, I think 10th and 16th and I was rated at 17. So there was talks about Stevens going six and me going 16 'cause we were partners in junior. A lot of defensemen were taken early that round to bump me up to 13th, when I went to Quebec. No, Quebec wasn't my first choice by any means. Back then it was English speaking, the taxes were so high, it wasn't the preference of a lot of people who wouldn't wanna go or want to be drafted, but I was just so excited to be drafted anyways. I remember driving home that night. We got home and I was with my parents, my girlfriend, it was exciting. I knew I was going to go first round, but 13th was high and it was just the whole build up is great."

FIRST REACTION TO BEING TRADED TO THE RANGERS:

"Michel Bergeron was my coach in Quebec and then he was a coach of the Rangers too, my first couple of years there. Michel, he didn't really like me. He motivated through yelling at guys and he was never an X's and O's guy, so he didn't really relate real well to the young guys. He was good with the older guys and he was actually difficult. My last year in Quebec, I played there, I ended up having mononucleosis that year and I went from 210 pounds to like 187. No one can tell me what's wrong with me. So I played through and I had a bad year. I was weak, I ended up missing the last few games, plus the playoffs because I was diagnosed with mono and the summer comes that year and Bergeron, he leaves and signs with the Rangers. I'm like, 'Thank God he's gone.' Maybe, I'll have a better year just with Andre Savard [who] was the next coach. I think just get away from him [Bergeron] helped my career and then halfway through training camp, I get traded to the Rangers and he's there. The thing is when I got there, he changed and he's the one that actually I think helped my career, gave me a lot of ice time. He made me assistant captain. About two months into me being there, they took the captaincy away from Gresh [Ron Grechner] and Don Maloney and gave it to Kelly Kisio, who was captain. James Patrick and I were assistants, but I went from not wanting to be traded, especially to the Rangers, but it all worked out."

FIRST TIME PUTTING ON THE RANGERS JERSEY:

"I put my jersey on and it's the smallest jersey possible. I go to the trainer and said, 'What is this?' He said, 'Oh, that was George McPhee's jersey. He wore [size] 46, he was like a 52 size shirt and he used to cut the arms and play with it skintight. So I played with it that game and it was just ridiculous. That was my first impression of putting the Ranger jersey on."

FIRST RANGERS GAME: October 8, 1987 @ Madison Square Garden vs. Pittsburgh Penguins, 4–4 OT tie

Shaw assisted on the first goal of the season.

"It was awesome. It's a totally different venue than the Colisee in Quebec City. The guys I played with too, [were] awesome. Like the older guys, like Pierre Larouche was there, Gresh, Marcel Dionne was there, older Ron Duguay was there, but it was exciting to play with those guys too."

FIRST IMPRESSIONS OF BRIAN LEETCH:

"I remember the anticipation of Brian coming because it was right after the Olympics in '88. He was my partner for pretty much at least three years."

FIRST RANGERS PLAYOFF EXPERIENCE: 1989 Patrick Division semifinals vs. Pittsburgh Penguins. Rangers lost in four games.

"We lost four straight to Pittsburgh. That was a real strange time because Bergeron was just fired. He was fired April 1st. We in Pittsburgh when he got fired. He came in and said, 'Guys, thank you for everything, but I've been let go,' and went around shaking everyone's hand. It was April 1st, was this April fools? We were in first place but we weren't playing well at the time. Espo comes in after and says, 'Yeah, I've made a change. We're going in the wrong direction. I think we have a good team here to do something, so I'm going to take over as coach.' So he coached the last couple of games. I don't know if he won a game. For some reason, Espo had this thing with John Vanbiesbrouck. Our first two games in Philly, he sat Bob Froese too, Bob was the backup. Espo's philosophy was like Frozee was something ridiculous like

21 and 2 against Pittsburgh at the time, but most of those win came when he was playing for he Flyers, not the Rangers. Beezer ended up playing Game Three and [Mike] Richter for Game Four. It was kind of weird Espo came in and kinda switched everything, this should work, but it was horrible. So my first taste of players was exciting but it was very strange."

FIRST RANGERS PLAYOFF GAME AT MADISON SQUARE GARDEN: April 8, 1989 @ Madison Square Garden, Game 3 Patrick Division semifinals vs. Pittsburgh Penguins, 5–3 loss.

"It was exciting, it really was. I'm sure it would've been a lot different if we were up two games. We weren't playing well. We had a really good team too. I missed '94 obviously but each round gets more and more exciting."

FIRST TIME BEING ON THE ICE WHEN A NUMBER WAS RETIRED:

Shaw was on the Rangers when Eddie Giacomin's No. 1 was retired in March 1989.

"Well, it was pretty cool because Eddie was around quite a bit. He was our goalie coach. He actually helped a lot, he talked to Richter and Froese quite a bit and he's such a nice guy, so it was awesome seeing that go up. I was very excited; it was a neat moment. Never that I'd ever thought my number was ever going up there. It was cool to see someone that was worthy of it and a nice person."

FIRST RANGERS OUTDOOR GAME: September 27, 1991, preseason game @ Las Vegas vs. Los Angeles Kings, 5–2 loss.

"That was pretty cool at Caesar's Palace, walking through the lobby with our robes on to get out to the arena. It was pretty neat.

It was a 7 or 7:30 game, at five o'clock the ice was melted, it wasn't solid yet. It was still like a lot of moisture on top of it. The one thing I remember on the ice, there was bugs during the game on the ice. I guess 'cause the moisture, but there's no bugs in the desert but there was some hung out on that ice. It was cool and you put in [Wayne] Gretzky, how much Gretzky would actually play, but he did play a little bit in the exhibition games."

FIRST GAME AT MSG AS AN OPPONENT AFTER BEING TRADED FROM THE RANGERS: February 21, 1992 @ Madison Square Garden vs. Minnesota North Stars. Rangers won, 5–4.

"It was probably the worst day of my career when I got traded out of New York. I just got back off an injury and Roger Neilson called me up, like at 3:30 in the afternoon after practice and saying, 'Hey, can you come down? I'm gonna talk to you.' Okay, I said this isn't good and it came down to, 'Hey listen, we made a deal. You're going to Edmonton.' He goes, 'It's part of the Messier trade.' He goes, 'It was Messier and [Jeff] Beukeboom for Bernie [Nichols], Steve Rice, and Louis DeBrusk and someone else. Player to be named later basically. What I was told, they submitted a list to [Glen] Sather [Oilers GM] 'cause a couple of guys had surgeries that year. Mark Janssens did, Randy Moeller, couple of guys were just getting healthy, that he had up to a certain date to select someone. He [Neilson] goes, 'He [Sather] took you off the list and so you're going for Beukeboom.' Which was horrible for me because we went through a lot of like having decent teams. We're getting mid-80s to low 90s in points per year as a team. All of a sudden, they trade for Mess, they signed Gravy [Adam Graves] Richter's a better player. They turned into a franchise that is gonna do something. You can see it coming, also I've gone to a rebuilding team. I was so frustrated with that whole situation and I asked, I didn't want to be in Edmonton, so I asked to be traded and they traded me. Thank God they traded me to Minnesota like almost right away after I asked. Usually he has guys sit there and stew a little bit.

"When I played against the Rangers, it was just weird playing against your friends because after I was traded, everyone on their team came over to my house, wished me good luck and goodbye except Mess didn't come. There's maybe two or three guys living in the area, but everyone else came over. So I was really tight with everybody and when you get to play against your friends and it's a totally different atmosphere. You want to do better or you just don't want to mess up. I enjoyed it too, so that was good. Coming back into the Garden, there wasn't a huge reception or anything like that. A little bit here and there, a lot before the game, after the game. It seemed like a normal game at that point, so it wasn't that memorable for me. I had a lot of animosity towards the Rangers actually at that point because I hated leaving. The frustrating part was, the year before I had a horrible year with my shoulder. I only played like 22 games in one year. I played like two games, three games and I dislocated my shoulder and then I rehab for two weeks, two or three games and it would pop out again. I did that 'til January, then ended up having surgery on [it]. You give a lot for a franchise, you give a lot for a team and it didn't seem like reciprocated at the time. So I had a lot of animosity just leaving and the way it happened."

You Never Forget Your First: A Collection of New York Rangers Firsts

David barely fit into George McPhee's jersey in his Rangers debut. (Public domain)

55
MARTIN ST. LOUIS

Hall of Fame right wing Martin St. Louis came to the Rangers in a significant trade with the Tampa Bay Lightning in March 2014. In order to acquire St. Louis, the Rangers traded captain Ryan Callahan and two draft picks to Tampa Bay. With eight goals, the 5'8" St. Louis was the Rangers' leading goalscorer in the 2014 Stanley Cup playoffs that culminated with a berth in the 2014 Stanley Cup Final.

FIRST HOCKEY GAME ATTENDED AS A KID:

"I think I was 10, 12 years old. My dad took me to a Canadiens game. It was Toronto vs. Montreal at the old Forum. I had to be 10, 12 years old. Being in the old Forum and you'd see all the Stanley Cup banners. I was just in awe of seeing it live, I've always watched it on TV, *Hockey Night in Canada*, and now I was actually there and it's pretty cool."

FIRST HOCKEY IDOL:

"Mats Naslund [who] played for the Canadiens, who wore [No.] 26. A small Swede, so I totally associated myself with him. He's just the smallest guy on the team and he was a great playmaker for a 'pass-first' mentality and that's kinda like the way I played."

FIRST COLLEGIATE CHAMPIONSHIP:

St. Louis was a member of the Vermont hockey team in 1996–97 when the Catamounts won the ECAC Championship.

"What I remember that year obviously is the success we had and how close we were as a team and the whole city rallying behind us. It was a great time to be playing college hockey at Vermont in the old school barn, Gutterson Fieldhouse, and being packed. People were camping out for playoff tickets and that kind of stuff. So it's amazing when you have some kind of success, how much a town can rally behind that."

FIRST CONTACT WITH THE NHL:

St. Louis was undrafted and eventually signed a contract with the Calgary Flames in 1988.

"My draft year, I wasn't ranked, I wasn't even on the radar. So, for me, there was no support. I wasn't drafted, I wasn't expecting to be drafted. There's just playing hockey, having fun and I didn't know if I could play in the NHL, but once I went to college and I wasn't drafted. I was like, well, I'm just gonna see if I can play at this level. Once you start dominating, I'm like, 'Whoa, maybe I can go play pro,' and ended up signing after my senior year. To be honest, it was never a real disappointment. Being drafted just wasn't in the cards that time. I was just having fun playing hockey and getting better. All of a sudden, it became like more than something that could happen, and I actually signed a contract. I signed with Cleveland in the IHL. No NHL team wanted to sign me. I went to the All-Star game and I had a pretty good season [50 points in 56 games]. I scored three in the All-Star Game and the next day I signed in Calgary. Now I was one phone call from reaching my dream, get called up and it was pretty cool to have your name on an NHL contract."

FIRST REACTION TO WINNING A STANLEY CUP:

St. Louis won the Stanley Cup with the Tampa Bay Lightning in 2004.

"It's just hard work. The people that helped you, the training, the ups and downs, the injuries. Everything kinda gets like bottled into the great celebration of reaching that goal. When you lift the Cup and you just kinda have flashbacks and all that. There's this feeling of fulfillment and it was awesome."

FIRST OLYMPIC GOLD MEDAL: 2014

St. Louis played on the gold-medal winning Canadian team in the 2014 Winter Olympics in Sochi, Russia.

"The Olympics is epic, the experience. It's a two-week tournament. The guys from all over get put on one team, check their ego at the door and just play a role they want them to play. We did that, but when you win a Cup, its two months. It's the season, it's the ups and downs of a season, the injuries and stuff. When we win a gold medal, it's a two-week tournament, it's not the same. You're not emotionally invested as in a Cup run, but they're both very gratifying."

FIRST REACTION TO BEING TRADED TO THE RANGERS:

"I always kinda wanted to finish my career in New York and I saw an opportunity. Unfortunately, we fell short in the Stanley Cup Final, but it was quite a run. The emotional time for me, losing my mom, To play at MSG, for the Rangers, it was something I'm glad I got to experience."

FIRST RANGERS GAME: March 5, 2014 @ Madison Square Garden vs. Toronto Maple Lears, 3–2 OT loss.

"Pretty much a blur. I got traded about 11 [a.m.] and I left Tampa. They [the Rangers] had a plane waiting for me and I ended up landing in Teterboro [Airport] and getting on a helicopter and get into Manhattan. I think I walked in the dressing room like an hour and a half. There's a lot of stuff that happened and you just got to go play a game. I had just been somewhere for 14 years and now, a different jersey. So, it was not easy."

FIRST RANGER COACH: Alain Vigneault

"He had a good proven track record, his success in Vancouver. I felt he coached stars before. He wasn't an 'overcoach,' just kind of let you do your things inside the perimeters that he had, but it was a good experience."

FIRST RANGERS GOAL: April 1, 2014 @ Vancouver Canucks, 3–1 win.

St. Louis's first goal with the Rangers came in his 15th game and was a short-handed tally in the third period.

"Short-handed, with [Rick] Nash. It was long overdue, so, for me, it was good that I finally got it, yeah."

FIRST RANGERS PLAYOFF EXPERIENCE AT MADISON SQUARE GARDEN: 2014 Stanley Cup Playoffs

"A lot of energy at MSG in the playoffs. It was pretty cool. Got to score some big goals in the playoffs in that run. That was fun to see a Ranger fan, like when I scored in overtime against Montreal [Game 4, Eastern Conference finals], it was so loud."

Three days after the death of his mother, St. Louis scored the first goal of Game 6 of the Eastern Conference semifinals vs. Pittsburgh on Mother's Day. The Rangers won,

3–1, and were in the process of rallying from a 3–1 series deficit to beat the Penguins in seven games. Many felt the team got an emotional lift from the untimely death of St. Louis's mother and that carried them past Pittsburgh and eventually into the Stanley Cup Final.

"A lot of emotion. I was angry, I was happy, there's so many things I went through. It was on Mother's Day. My dad's there, my sister's there. It was just very fitting at the moment, you know to get one early on Mother's Day and the whole crowd was, I think, going through it with me. It helped me, definitely helped me cope with what I was going through."

FIRST RANGERS PLAYOFF OVERTIME GOAL: May 25, 2014, Game 4 Eastern Conference finals vs. Montreal Canadiens, 3–2 OT win. Rangers beat Montreal in six games.

"You always want to score and help your team win, but when you do it in the playoff, in that building against the team I used to idolize growing up. You put it all together, it was pretty cool. It was fun."

FIRST RANGERS STANLEY CUP FINAL EXPERIENCE:

"It was such a great run. We got Philly in seven, against Pitt [Rangers came from 3–1 down in the series to win] so we would face a lot of adversity. What's funny is Montreal ended up coming back on Boston and winning in seven and that meant my whole team is going to be able to come to my mom's funeral 'cause we were playing the Canadiens. So that was a pretty special time. What I was going through and how we did things. We became really close; I only had been there for a couple months and I became really close to my teammates because of what was going. So yeah, it was a really cool experience to get as far as you did."

FIRST GAME AS A RANGER IN TAMPA: November 26, 2014 @ Tampa Bay Lightning, 4–3 loss.

"I was just uncomfortable. A little bit uncomfortable for sure. I can't really remember the game, to be honest, but I remember just being very uncomfortable coming in there."

ON BEING THE FIRST PLAYER TO HAVE HIS NUMBER RETIRED BY A COLLEGE AND NHL TEAM:

St. Louis had his number retired by his college team at Vermont (8) and by the Tampa Bay Lightning (26).

"It's pretty special. You know that doesn't happen a lot and I was the first for both. It's flattering, the fact that they think I had that much of an impact. It's pretty cool"

ON BEING A FIRST-BALLOT HALL OF FAMER:

"I didn't expect to be a first-time ballot. When I got the call, I was surprised. I wasn't really waiting for a call. To me, you figure there's nothing I could have done. I was very comfortable. How I came into the league, all I left and what I did in between. The fact that people value my impact on the game to give me that honor. It was awesome."

His Mothers Day goal is one of the most memorable Ranger playoff goals (Photo by Mark Rosenman)

56
MARC STAAL

Defenseman Marc Staal has been a steady presence for the Rangers in the defensive zone since 2007. Staal made his debut in the 2007-2008 season, after he won the Lars Erik-Sjoberg Award as the best rookie in the 2007 training camp. At one point of his Ranger career, Staal played in 247 consecutive games. Staal suffered a serious eye injury in March 2013 after he was struck by a puck and missed the final 27 games of the regular season. When he returned for the Stanley Cup playoffs, he started wearing a protective visor. Staal has played the fourth most games by a Ranger defenseman, trailing only Harry Howell, Brian Leetch and Ron Greschner.

FIRST GAME HE ATTENDED AS A KID:

"First game was in Calgary at the Saddledome, played the San Jose Sharks and we always have family there. So we're visiting, it was around Christmas time. I remember being down by the glass for warm ups and actually had a San Jose coat, for whatever reason, for no reason at all, but I had one and I had it up against the glass and I remember Bernie Nicholls skated by and winked at me and that was kinda my first NHL experience. It's a moment that I've always remembered." So, it was pretty cool."

FIRST HOCKEY IDOL:

"Doug Gilmour, I would say. As I was growing up through that time, the Leafs were on all the time. We had only two or three channels and Saturday night was a big Leafs night. He was their captain and leader and someone that you looked up to as a kid."

FIRST CONTACT WITH NHL:

Marc Staal was chosen by the Rangers with their first-round pick (12th overall) in the 2005 NHL Entry Draft.

"It was a little different for me 'cause it was the lockout. I was in Ottawa, it was in a hotel, so we were 30 guys in a conference room. It was just silence and anxiety. It was an interesting day. Remember, just sitting there, my parents, my agent and the New York Rangers traded up with Atlanta. I was kind [of] nervous, to be honest, that Atlanta was going to pick me. Not like you pick and choose, then New York traded up, they picked me and I couldn't have been more excited and it was a dream come true. Then, that night we went out with dinner with Glen [Sather], scouts and everyone that night. That was pretty much it, had some dinner and relaxed and went back home the next day."

FIRST RANGERS COACH: Tom Renney

"He was a really good coach for me. He's very passionate about the game and gave me my first chance and had a lot of confidence in me. I really enjoyed playing for him and he gave me my start and put a lot of confidence in me and that's huge as a young player. It's something, looking back on, you don't appreciate as much as when you're in it. I definitely appreciate that."

FIRST RANGERS CAPTAIN: Jaromir Jagr

"The biggest thing I took away was his work ethic. Passion he had for the game. He came to the rink every day, excited to be here and he put the work in. When you're a young player and you look at a guy like that, sometimes you think they're so talented that they just show up and get three points tonight and it's easy, but you don't realize how much work that goes into it. That's the thing I learned from him the most."

FIRST RANGERS GAME: October 4, 2007 @ Madison Square Garden vs. Florida Panthers, 5–2 win.

"It was probably the most nervous I've been for a hockey game, ever. I remember the anthem going and trying to get my thoughts in order and focus on the game. I think we won; I didn't play that good. I remember Nathan Horton toe-drag me and just turn me inside out. Maybe my third or fourth shift and I'm like, I'm in one ear, but definitely something you don't forget. A very cool feeling."

FIRST RANGERS GOAL: November 14, 2007 @ New Jersey vs. New Jersey Devils, 4–2 win.

Staal's first NHL goal closed out the Rangers scoring in the third period.

"I think [Brendan] Shanahan passed it to me or [Scott] Gomez. He came around the weak side, Aves [Sean Avery] was in front. I just shot as hard as I could and it went in. I honestly thought that 'Aves touched it at first but he came over to me like I scored, so, obviously an incredible moment. I'm not a goal scorer by any means, but it was good to get the first one.

Staal still has the puck from the first goal:

"The Rangers do a nice job. They put it into a little frame and a picture of the goal, so yeah, it's pretty cool. Then you get the starting lineup sheet (of his FIRST game) too, which is very cool."

FIRST STANLEY CUP FINAL: 2014 vs. Los Angeles Kings. Rangers lost in five games.

"When you're going through a run like that, it's like *Groundhog*

Day. You're here, you're numb to pain and feeling. You're just getting up and focusing on trying to get on the ice and do your job. When we got to the Final, the two teams, it's a pretty good sense of accomplishment. Obviously, a devastating ending, but when I look back, I still have really good memories of a lot of those guys on that team over there. Very close team, and its something that we'll have for the rest of our lives. You don't win but you remember the memories along the way to get to that point and there was a lot of good ones."

FIRST TIME PLAYING AGAINST HIS BROTHERS IN THE NHL:

Marc's brothers Jordan (14 years) and Eric (16 years) are veteran NHL players. Eric played with Jordan on Carolina and with Marc as a member of the Rangers for 20 games during the 2015–16 season.

"I played against Jordan in junior, so I was kind of used to playing against him. Seeing Eric was different. It's gotten a little bit more normal, obviously the more you do it, but sometimes you find yourself watching them more than you do your own team or what's going on when you're on the ice. It's a different connection that you have with them but we've always really enjoyed it and we're very lucky to have been playing for as long as we have and have been able to do that."

"When you're going through a run like that, it's like *Groundhog Day*. (Photo by Mark Rosenman)

57
PETE STEMKOWSKI

Center Pete Stemkowski joined the National Hockey League the 1963–64 season when he played one game for the Toronto Maple Leafs. "Stemmer" would go on to a 15-year career including parts of seven seasons with the Rangers. Stemkowski's Rangers moment came in the 1971 playoffs when he scored the game-winning goal in the third overtime of Game 6 of the Stanley Cup semifinals to force a Game 7 that the Rangers eventually lost.

FIRST REACTION TO BEING TRADED TO THE RANGERS:

Pete Stemkowski was acquired by the Rangers from the Detroit Red Wings on October 31, 1970.

"I was with the Detroit Red Wings. I was living with Garry Unger in Dearborn, Michigan, at the time. [Detroit general manager] Sid Abel's daughter Linda's boyfriend was playing in Toledo that night. So we were getting in the car and we're going to Toledo and watch the game. As we're heading for the car, the phone, you know there were no cell phones back then, picked it up. It was Sid Abel on the other end of the phone. 'Want to let you know we just made a trade, we just traded you to the New York Rangers.' I said, 'What?' He said, 'Come down to the office tomorrow, nine o'clock in the morning and will let you in on all the details.' So needless to say, I was pretty upset. I was living with

Garry, I was being productive, playing with Gordie Howe. I wasn't in a very good mood the rest of the day and the rest of the night. We did go to Toledo and I wasn't really there. I was really out, I was upset.

"The next day, I go into the Olympia [Stadium] and there's Sid Abel and Ned Harkness and there might've been two other guys in there. They said, 'We're just putting the final touches on this and it looks like you're going to be going to the New York Rangers, just hold off, no practice.' I remember I walked out of the office and who came behind me was Ned Harkness, who was, back then, our coach. As I learned later on, he wasn't telling me the truth but he said, 'You know, this wasn't me really pushing this deal.' Meanwhile, I think it was. I didn't find out until later on that day and I went home, back to Dearborn and I sat it out for a day, just thinking. I was very, very upset. I shouldn't have been because I got traded from Toronto to Detroit a couple of years earlier. So I should've taken it in stride, but the fact is there was no rhyme or reason. I mean, I was a younger guy, I was probably the only physical forward they had. As it turned out, I ended up coming to New York, landing at LaGuardia Airport and having a fellow named Steve Bernheim picked me up, he was waiting at the gate for me and he said, 'It's a Monday night, all the guys are in the city, it's a Monday night off.' They're in a place called El Vagabondo on 62nd Street between First and Second [Avenues] so he took me there. I had my suitcases with me and we went to El Vagabondo and Brad Park was there, Walter Tkaczuk was there, maybe another guy or two. When the night was over, they said, 'Okay, we're going home,' and I go, 'Where's home?' He says a place called Long Beach, New York, and I didn't know that from Timbuktu. So I came out to Long Beach and I moved in with Mike Robitaille and Jim Krulicki, a couple of single guys, back then, who had an extra bedroom. I came to Long Beach back there in the early '70s and some 30, 40 some odd years later, that's where I call home, Long Beach. So it's amazing how that thing worked out."

FIRST OVERTIME PLAYOFF GOAL AS A RANGER:
April 18, 1971 @ Chicago Black Hawks, Game 1 Stanley Cup

semifinals, 2–1 win in first overtime

Stemkowski scored at 1:37 of the first overtime to give the Rangers a road win in Game 1 but his triple-overtime goal in Game 6 overshadows his first overtime playoff goal.

"I remember Stan Mikita hitting both goalposts and putting his head on the net and saying, 'How could I miss that?' I remember Bill White coming in and hitting Eddie Giacomin just underneath the neck and he went down, so they had some great, great chances. I remember something about the fact, people say I mentioned the fact that we were able to get this over with because all the gin mills are closing early and nobody's going to be able to get a drink after this. I wasn't thinking of New York, I mean they're open 24 hours. I remember the goal and getting to see Teddy Irvine shoot it in. You were at such a high back then. I really didn't get to sleep until about five or six in the morning.

"We went to a restaurant in Long Beach, I think Teddy Irvine, myself, and I think Dale Rolfe came with us. We just sat around just having a cold one. I remember the guy telling us, 'When you're finished and done, just lock the door behind you.'"

FIRST RANGERS COACH: Emile "The Cat" Francis

"I broke into the league in the '60s, so that's a long time ago. I've seen a lot of guys, played with a lot of guys, played against a lot of guys and a lot of coaches. I would say if they asked me to pick the top five best human beings that I came across in my career, both as a player and a broadcaster, I'd say Emile Francis is in that top five. He not only wanted to win badly, but he cared for his players. When we were in Boston once and we got to the hotel, he wasn't on that trip, I think Ron Stewart was the coach at the time, and I think there was a fender bender. A couple of guys in a taxicab were involved. When Ron Stewart called "The Cat," and said, 'Hey, you know what's happened?' I remember Cat saying, 'Why are you here? You should be at the hospital, where are you?' so he really cared about his players. He's a tremendous human being, very fair. If you were a 50-goal scorer and you did something wrong, you heard about it, like I shouldn't. Sittin' at the end of the bench, you know the rules apply to you."

Stemmer's triple-overtime goal in the 1971 playoffs is one of most memorable in franchise history. (Public domain)

58
KEVIN STEVENS

Left wing Kevin Stevens was a 15-year NHL veteran who came to the Rangers in the latter part of his career. Stevens won back-to-back Stanley Cups in 1991 and 1992 as a member of the Pittsburgh Penguins. In the 1991–92 season, Stevens scored 54 goals and set a record for an American-born player when he collected 123 points.

FIRST GAME ATTENDED AS A KID:

"It's probably one of those ol' Bruins games. They used to play the Flyers on Saturday afternoons in the early '70s when Bobby Orr and all those guys were around. So I used to go to a lot of those Bruins [vs.] Flyers Saturday afternoon games, which are crazy."

FIRST HOCKEY IDOL: Bobby Orr

"In Boston, pretty much the guy. He kinda changed hockey around here. Bobby Orr translated the game, the way he played."

FIRST CONTACT WITH THE NHL:

Kevin Stevens was chosen by the LA Kings in the sixth round

of the 1983 NHL Entry Draft.

"I didn't even know I was going to get drafted. The next day I got a call. It wasn't like it is now, everything hyped up. I didn't know I was gonna get drafted, I had no idea. I knew the draft was going on, it wasn't a big concern of mine. I think I was playing baseball. I got a call from someone from LA. That's who I got drafted by and I was traded to Pittsburgh. I was drafted by them and then I got my rights traded in college, which is another thing. I didn't even find that out, I think my sister called me."

FIRST REACTION TO BEING TRADED TO THE RANGERS:

Rangers acquired Stevens from the Kings in August 1997 for Luc Robitaille.

"I kind of knew this thing was developing that Luc would come back to LA. Gretzky was in New York, so I knew him and he knew what kind of what's going on. I think Luc knew what was going on too. He was coming back to LA too. I think Neil [Smith] called me, I was in LA for maybe a year and a half or so and then I got traded to New York. It was good. It was a team where were trying to win in New York, but we couldn't."

FIRST TIME SEEING THE RANGERS JERSEY WITH HIS NAME ON IT:

"It was an honor. Everything they had there in New York, you know what I mean. They were building and just being in New York City and being in Madison Square Garden. Being in that whole atmosphere, I played in it, but I'd never been on the same side of it; it was exciting."

FIRST RANGERS COACHES: Colin Campbell and John Muckler

Campbell was the coach for 57 games but was fired and replaced by Muckler in Feburary 1998.

"Good coaches, top coaches. Like old-school guys, which was new. It was old school back then. Muck was a loud guy. Good hockey guys, real good hockey knowledge. I liked them both. Straightforward guys, no bullshit with either one of those."

FIRST RANGERS CAPTAIN: Brian Leetch

"Leetchie's great. He's always the same, kinda leads by [example] on the ice but when he talks, people listen because he doesn't talk a lot. He was awesome, he's just a good friend of mine so he made it a lot easier to come in there."

FIRST GAME AS A RANGER: October 3, 1997 @ Madison Square Garden vs. New York Islanders, 2–2 OT tie

"Crazy, obviously the rivalry is a rivalry and it's always going to be a rivalry, but it was crazy. It was like I imagined. I remember playing the Islanders, we [were] both 20 points out of the playoffs, one of the last games of the year. Crazy, and the fans even with the players. It was definitely a big rival, it was exciting."

FIRST OLYMPIC EXPERIENCE:

Stevens played for the United States Olympic hockey team in 1988

"Olympic experience was great. We're still amateurs, a lot of Boston guys like Leetchie and [Craig] Janney, Stevie Leach, Scotty Young, Clark [Donatelli], [Tony[Granato, [Mike] Richter. We traveled around, we ate lunch together and played. That was awesome, that was a great experience."

59
JASON STRUDWICK

Jason Strudwick, a 6'4" defenseman, played two-plus seasons with the Rangers. Strudwick was signed as a free agent in July 2004, but the season was wiped out by a lockout. He left the Rangers in September 2006 to play in Switzerland but returned near the end of the 2006–07 season and then played one more season with the Blueshirts.

FIRST CONTACT WITH NHL:

Jason Strudwick was a third-round pick of the New York Islanders in the 1994 NHL Entry Draft.

"I was actually sleeping when I got drafted. This was a time, there wasn't a lot of computers, so the phone rings and my Mom comes in and it's like, 'Hey, Islanders on the phone [for] you.' I'm like, 'Hello' and they're like, 'We just drafted you in the third round' and I think it was [GM Don] Maloney [and] I'm like, 'Okay, great,' and I was just laying in bed and then my Mom says, 'What happened?' 'I think I just got 'docked' by the Islanders.'"

FIRST REACTION TO SIGNING WITH THE RANGERS:

"Glen Sather, I'm not gonna lie, [growing] up, I liked his teams.

He was a huge part of that so getting a chance to be with Glen Sather was something I was very interested in. When I got the call about New York, I was really excited. You know, I'm like this. The team that I love playing[at] the Garden, I love New York City. I want to say I'm a natural New Yorker but you know, I really wanted a chance to live there, play for the Rangers at the Garden underneath Glen Sather. I was so happy to make that deal happen."

FIRST RANGERS COACH: Tom Renney

"Tom was really proud to be the Ranger coach and he was going to be very organized. He had a long vision, he wanted to build this properly. I'm a little biased but he was the perfect guy for that coaching spot at that time with the Rangers."

FIRST GAME AS A RANGER: October 5, 2005 @ Philadelphia Flyers, 5–3 win (scoring his first Ranger goal)

"I'll never forget taking warmup, I'm skating around and I go to stretch and I hear banging on the glass. I turn around, there was like a nine or ten year old kid giving me the finger and beside him, his Dad is like 'Yeah, yeah, F-you, F-you' and I'm like 'Oh my God.' This eight or nine year old is giving me the finger and his Dad is cheering him on and I played the "Phillies" so I knew what it was like already. So I was like let's just stick it in their ear. I don't even remember the goal but I remember thinking like, Thank God I scored already 'cause I won't have to wait like forever. It was a fun game."

FIRST RANGERS FIGHT:

"I remember preseason I fought Colton Orr and I think it was pretty quick."

FIRST SHOOTOUT GOAL: November 26, 2005 @ MSG. (3–2 win vs. Washington in a 15-round shootout, which was a

record at the time)

NOTE: After Caps defenseman Bryan Muir scored in the 14th round to give Washington the lead, Strudwick Strudwick fired a wrist shot past Caps goalie Olaf Kolzig and that sent the shootout to a 15th round where Marek Malik scored his memorable shootout goal. The Rangers defenseman went between the legs with his stick and lifted it past Kolzig.

"We go to overtime, okay, no problem, there's no way I'm going to get into the shootout here. Then you know, get into five, six, seven, eight, nine. I'm like, holy shit, the goalies are still awesome, the players are getting worse, 'cause that's the way it works right. If they were good, you wouldn't be shooting at nine or ten. So, I remember Jim Ramsay [Rangers trainer] leans over, he's like, you better do your skates out there. Like, you've gotta be shitting me. Like, I was getting nervous, I wasn't even being called yet. So then, they'd get on deeper, I think someone scored around ten on both sides or whatever. Then it kinda makes it way down, I think Bryan Muir scored.

"Then, there's myself, [Darius] Kasparaitis, [Fedor] Tyutin, who had a broken finger and Marek Malik and the backup goalie, and I'm like, oh my god, please don't call my name. Tom [Renney] [is] like 'Next, Strud you're up' and I'm like I'm not 100 percent. I didn't hear him. It's extremely rough and I look over and he kind of like gives me a look and I'm like, oh my God. So, I jumped over the boards, my heart is pounding through my chest, like exploding. I remember flipping my stick around, like I was cool. I looked like such a tool. I looked like such an idiot 'cause I have no idea what I'm doing and everything. I'm going to shoot over his shoulder and this is Olaf Kolzig, he's like twelve feet tall so obviously not a goal scorer so I skate down the ice and I tried to hit on the right side but it doesn't go over [his] shoulder. I wouldn't call fan on it but I changed my shot and it went under his arm. I wasn't even happy, but I was just so relieved because I didn't want to let anyone down. The fans or my teammates, my wife was there, her Mom and Dad. I was just so happy not to let the guys down and then for Malik to do what he did afterwards. It's one of my all-time favorites, like non kind of, although we won, like non-winning moments in a hockey game. Like it was crazy and the guys were just giving it to us after. It was just such a great memory. Just a group of guys that just really randomly put together, but we came together and we had a special moment against the Caps."

60
STEVE VALIQUETTE

Steve Valiquette, a 6'6" goaltender, was an eighth-round pick of the Los Angeles Kings in the 1996 NHL Entry Draft. Valiquette began his NHL career with the New York Islanders in the 1999–2000 season and played parts of five seasons with the Rangers. After his playing career was over, the Ontario native transitioned into the media and is currently a co-host of the Rangers pre- and postgame shows on MSG Network.

FIRST CONTACT WITH NHL:

"I was actually drafted by the Los Angeles Kings in 1996; that was the draft in St. Louis. My grandfather was there, my sister, my parents of course and we were told probably fourth round I was going to go. I was a tall goalie, so coming off a good year, I felt like I had a chance to get into the top five rounds. Starting in the first round, I wasn't paying any attention at all. Waiting for the fourth round to begin and then I was going to start listening, listening attentively for my name. Back in those days, the draft would have started something like eight o'clock in the morning and I think I got drafted at like 6:30 at night and my grandfather had fallen asleep. My sister, I remember her saying to me, 'Steve, when are you going to get drafted?'

"When I finally did get taken, I was the first pick in the eighth round, so I wouldn't even be drafted now based on the fact that there's only seven rounds. I remember my agent saying to me, you know, 'Congratulations but probably would've been better if you weren't taken, you would've had more leverage as a free agent,' so it was a really bad experience."

FIRST REACTION TO BEING TRADED TO THE RANGERS: March 3, 2004

"Well, it was really bizarre because I always dreamed of playing for the Rangers, even when I was with the Islanders and that sounds bad. I signed that summer with the Edmonton Oilers and it was a really tough time for my relationship with my wife because she was from Milford, Connecticut. I met her when I was playing in Bridgeport and she was taking a surprise trip to visit me. So what ended up happening was she was on her way to come and visit me the day I was traded. I called her Mom because I couldn't get ahold of her and I said, 'Where's Chrissy?' She said, "She's on her way to visit you.' I said, 'She better turn around because I'm on my way to New York.' I got myself right away to New York and I was just thrilled. I couldn't have been happier."

FIRST TIME PUTTING ON THE RANGERS SWEATER: March 27, 2004

"When you start to play for an Original Six, there's a different level of pride there for anybody that was a fan as a child. Every time we played against an Original Six, it felt different. I remember taking off my Ranger jersey and I never threw it in the laundry bin. I would take it off and I would fold it and crest up. I would put it into the laundry. I just could never, I could never put it down or throw it or I just felt much pride about wearing it and looking at your name on the stall next to the logo."

FIRST SAVE: March 27, 2004 @ Philadelphia Flyers, 3–1 win

"My first save was not a save. It was almost a goal and it's my most memorable moment because the game could've gone the other way had it gone in. There was a shot from the point and I always, as a habit, I would look to see where the stick blades were on the ice and who was planning on deflecting the shot. I had some time to approach it that way on this particular play, and I looked to my right and I saw this blade. I saw this really screwed up blade, a really like inside-outside blade and I remember thinking to myself, Who the fuck stick is that, and then I look up and it's John LeClair and you can't take your eye off the puck for that long. I was a deer in headlights and I had a moment there was I was too much of a fan. The puck came from the point, it goes off of LeClair's wedged stick and it just hits the outside of the post and goes to the corner. That was my wake-up moment and after that, I was fine but, wow, it that would've went in, that game could've gone a different way."

FIRST PLAYOFF GAME: April 24, 2009, Game 5, Eastern Conference quarterfinals @ Washington Capitals, 4–0 loss

"My first playoff game was against Washington and it was a series that we were up three to one and Henrik [Lundqvist] was just like playing out of his mind and we did not deserve to be winning the series. I remember going home after these games and my wife's saying, 'How did the game go?' I'm like, you wouldn't believe Henrik right now, it's unbelievable. It's the best goaltending I've ever seen and I remember being up three to one and we should've been down three-one, but then it turned like it was just too much for him to do it alone.

"In Game Five, he got pulled about halfway through the game. I got to play the second half of the game against Washington. In Game Six, he [Lundqvist] got pulled again and I played half the game against Washington there. Because it wasn't a "cleanup," it doesn't count to me as a playoff game. I mean, starting a playoff game and getting thrown into cleanup are two completely different planets. So I got to touch the ice in the playoffs, but nothing to really be proud of or celebrate.".

61
JOHN VANBIESBROUK

Goaltender John Vanbiesbrouck played 11 of his 20 NHL seasons with the Rangers. "VBK" or "Beezer," as he was known, became the fourth Rangers goaltender to be named the Vezina Trophy winner when he won the award in 1985–86 when he led the NHL with 31 wins. During his Rangers tenure, Vanbiesbrouck won 200 games.

FIRST CONTACT WITH NHL:

John Vanbiesbrouck was chosen by the Rangers in the fourth round of the 1981 NHL Entry Draft.

"I didn't attend the draft. I knew that I was in the mix to be selected but it wasn't like they had central scouting lists, and they made it public and we had the internet, it was a little different then. That day in '81, I got a call from [Rangers GM] Craig Patrick, who said that the New York Rangers had selected me, you know, gave me the round, fifth round and just some of the details. He welcomed me to the organization. I was in Sault Ste. Marie at the time playing junior hockey for the Greyhounds. It really got a little bit quiet there for a while until you find out about training camp. They didn't e-mail you back then, so just got a bunch of stuff in the mail with that Ranger logo on it, Original Six team, it was just so invigorating."

FIRST TIME PUTTING ON THE RANGERS JERSEY:

"It was special, everything about it was special. The fabric, the stitching, the class, just everything about it. I remember walking up the steps of Madison Square Garden, carrying my bag, jumping out of a cab and hearing murmurs of people as I walked past and say, 'Hey, that must be that young kid that got called up' and walking into Herb Brooks's office. Just being in front of that legend and at the most famous arena in the world, it was bright lights and it was happening fast. You try and just engage in the moment and keep all your faculties together."

FIRST RANGERS COACH: Herb Brooks

"You don't plan for those moments. You don't plan what to say, you don't plan what's it's gonna go like. You're in a rush to get there and just to be on time and then all of a sudden, you're in front of a legend in the business, that was part of the greatest historical piece that ever happened in the game of hockey for Americans, but you weren't thinking that way, you don't plan for that moment. In the moment, just try and not say something dumb, which usually comes out of a kid's mouth."

FIRST RANGERS GAME: December 5, 1981 @ Colorado Rockies, 2–1 win

"I was an emergency call-up. There were a lot of injuries, so Steve Weeks was playing a lot of games and I just got to the point where I wondered if I was ever gonna play a game or not. I remember hearing that I was going to play in Colorado at the old McNichols Arena. We were in LA and we had a real challenging schedule, so I was going to get the call. I just remembered starting the framework of my mentality was, who are we going to be playing against and trying to get a book on who you're playing against. At the other end of the ice, it's going to be Chico Resch in goal. Some of the players that they had on their team were gonna be hard to stop. Just trying to get a book on all that.

"You'd go into the game just trying to be prepared, having a good skate. When you actually get out on the ice, you gotta really stay focused and not get caught up in the hoopla of the game. You manage the game the best you can, you know, the first part, the first minutes of the game, trying not to get scored on early in the game. The one thing I remember about the game. We won the game, obviously played good and gave up a goal. The response that I got by the crowd at Madison Square Garden, 'cause Steve Weeks had flown home and we had back to back. So we played Colorado and then we played at home. Goalies on the other team must've watched the game and they were tapping me on the pad saying, 'Great job last night, kid.' I just got a nice reception from Garden crowd and I was surprised that people actually paid attention to that game that late. I was wondering why I was getting so much attention. When you're focusing on just playing, you don't focus on the attention of the fans and the news and those types of things. I really felt good about that."

FIRST RANGERS SHUTOUT: January 2, 1985 @ MSG vs. Vancouver Canucks, 21 saves in a 6–0 win

"I had some success against Vancouver in my career. It was situation where Glen Hanlon couldn't play or something like that, then I was sick, he was sick and then I ended up playing. Got a shutout, we played a really good game. I didn't have a lot of work; I was really happy about that."

FIRST RANGERS PLAYOFF GAME: April 10, 1984 @ Nassau Coliseum vs. New York Islanders, Game 5, Patrick Division semifinals, 3–2 OT loss

"Actually, I had been a part of the playoffs when we lost to the Islanders. When we had them down in the series and then Barry Beck got hurt. Glen Hanlon was playing and we were gonna upset the Islanders. Herb [Brooks] was the coach of that team. I had played literally two minutes of that "goalie delay" thing. I went in there and it was just meant to be like a 30-second thing and my skates were dull and I didn't have great edges. All of sudden, there's a two-on-one with [Bryan] Trottier and [Mike] Bossy and fortunately Bossy missed the net. We lost the series and that was really my first [playoff] game that I was involved in.

"Then the series against Philly [in 1985–86] was one where we weren't supposed to win. We just made the playoffs and Philly, I think had 120 points [actually 110]. Just went in confident, had nothing to lose and the team had made some moves to get some toughness and some scoring and Pierre Larouche. We just started hitting on all cylinders. I remember playing, I think it was the first or second game there and I made a save on Brad McCrimmon on a power play from the point. Philly had a real deadly power play and I made a good glove save. I just remember getting some bounces and making that save. Thought we had a chance if I could just continue to play well and our team played well, we could upset them, and we did."

FIRST RANGERS OUTDOOR GAME: September 27, 1991 @ Caesar's Palace, Las Vegas vs. the Los Angeles Kings (preseason), 5–2 loss

"It was crazy because when we walked in for the game, the ice wasn't ice, it was a puddle and we were like, 'There's no way we're playing.' I just remembered a wind kinda kicked up and all of a sudden, there was ice but something happened where there were a bunch of like, locusts. We call them grasshoppers in the Midwest but they're kinda locusts. The ice was a little wavy. LA just got [Wayne] Gretzky and it was a big show and we had a good team. The thing I remembered about the game was Tie Domi and the fact that he missed on a breakaway and said that he tripped on a grasshopper or a locust. It was just hilarious because he had no hands anyway, but he went in on a breakaway and tripped on a locust. I mean, it was a funny episode. It was a great thing to be part of. I never thought we'd pull it off but there were some really funny moments of that game."

FIRST VEZINA TROPHY WIN:

"It was a special year. It meant that I belonged in the league at a high level but I got a lot of credit but we had a team and a team concept that really, we played well together and I benefitted a lot from sound team play and good structure. We had some good, young players on the team—Mike Ridley, Kelly Miller, but we had a good run. At the end, I tried to be consistent and be into the game all the time. I remember there were a lot of good things but there were challenging things too because with success comes attention and sometimes you can be viewed as a selfish player. I didn't want to be viewed as a selfish player but when you get attention, that's how other players view you. It was the first time I really had [to] handle some good pressure and I liked it. I engaged in it and I wasn't fearful of it. So, good things happen and then the one thing I point to is Pelle Lindbergh [Flyers goalie who was killed in a car accident] passing that year was tragic. He probably was on his way to winning another Vezina Trophy and I benefitted from his loss, which I'll remember until I pass."

During his Rangers tenure, Vanbiesbrouck won 200 games.
Photo courtesy of New York Rangers.

62
AARON VOROS

Six-foot-four center Aaron Voros played four NHL seasons, two of those with the Rangers during 2008–09 and 2009–10. Voros was known for his grit and toughness. He scored 11 goals with 12 assists in 95 games as a Ranger.

FIRST CONTACT WITH NHL:

Aaron Voros was chosen by the New Jersey Devils in the eighth round of the 2001 NHL Entry Draft.

"It was my goal to be a New York Ranger since I was five years old. They were my favorite team. Initially being drafted by the New Jersey Devils, it was kind of crazy because, obviously, in the late '90's, mid '90's, that was the number one rivalry. Once you start progressing through higher levels of hockey, you kind of lose your fandom there in terms of 'I always wanted to be a Ranger,' but your goals are more focused on personal development and your talent."

In July 2008, Voros signed with the Rangers as a free agent.

"Although I had more lucrative offers to go elsewhere, I still remember saying to my dad, I said, 'Dad, what do we want?' I said, 'I wanna be a Ranger.' I left money on the table to go to New York and it was a dream come true. It's definitely sculpted and curated my life that being a New York Ranger, compared to I would say any other team in the National Hockey League, carries a substantial amount of weight and pride. I definitely relate and see myself as a New York Ranger for the rest of my life. I'm very proud of my time, lifelong memories, and lifelong friends. I still have a restaurant with Henrik Lundqvist in Manhattan."

FIRST TIME PUTTING ON THE RANGERS JERSEY:

"I would say walking in, seeing my jersey, it's in your stall for the first time, seeing your jersey, seeing just the level of professionalism, the amount of staff. It is a well-oiled machine. A lot of the people, a lot of the staff have been there for 10, 15, 20, 30 years. I mean from the guys in the Zamboni entrance to the guys opening the dressing room door at Madison Square Garden to our trainers, it's just such a family like atmosphere. Where [with] other teams where they turn over ownership or coaches or GM's and they clean house, they've done a really good job of keeping continuity."

FIRST RANGERS ROOMMATE ON THE ROAD:
Brandon Dubinsky

"My roommate was always Brandon Dubinsky. We were best friends. It was me, Dubinsky and [Nikolai] Zherdev on a line. We kind of coined ourselves for the *New York Post*, telling them the "Playstation Line" 'cause we were young and having fun. We'd always play NHL, whatever it was, 2009 or 2008 or 2007, whatever it was, together. We still have a very close friendship."

FIRST RANGERS COACH: Tom Renney, who was replaced by John Tortorella during Voros's first season with the team.

"Coming from Jacques to over to Tom, Jacques Lemaire [Voros' former coach in Minnesota] was a guy's guy. I mean, if he spoke to you, it almost meant that you were not doing a good job. If he spoke to you, it was because you needed to pick something up. If he didn't talk to you, you knew that you were doing a good job. He also knew when to reinforce you. I always say this, coaches who have never played in the NHL, this isn't a knock against Tom, they don't understand how hard certain plays are to make at times. You look at "Torts." He'll defend his players to the hilt. As Rocky as mine and Torts' relationship was at the time, I was a little bit of a punching bag for him. I'd give my left arm to play one more game for him."

FIRST HOME GAME AS A RANGER: October 5, 2008 vs. Tampa Bay Lightning, 2–1 win (Voros had an assist).

"Looking back, I think when you're working so hard, you don't get a chance to sit and enjoy it. I look back and I'm very proud of it, but when it happened, I just took it for granted and wish I would've sat and enjoyed it. You're moving a million miles an hour. You're playing in New York City, you're stepping out of the Garden, you're off in a cab, you're hitting dinner. It's not like, you know, Minnesota per se, where you leave and the streets are frozen and you're looking to go grab a sandwich and go home. The city's moving at the speed of light. Looking back and reminiscing, it was very special."

FIRST RANGERS PLAYOFF GAME: April 15, 2009 @ Washington Capitals, 4–3 win

"I remember the electricity, I remember the intensity. Playing against them, with so much on the line, and knowing that we're up 3–1 [in the series], we ended losing Game Seven. Still remember the goal. Sergei Federov coming down the right side, stop and then goes barn in on Henrik [Lundqvist]. We had our chance to close them out and we didn't."

FIRST GAME ATTENDED AS A FAN: In Vancouver

"We lived about 15 minutes from the Pacific Coliseum, which is the old arena, the arena actually where the Rangers and Canucks played their playoff series, the Stanley Cup Finals. I didn't go to too many games; it was pretty expensive. My dad's a bricklayer. All my gear from the start of hockey until [age] 12 was secondhand. During that '94 Stanley Cup run for the New York Rangers, my dad got tickets and surprised me and we went to Game Three at the Pacific Coliseum. We didn't have a camera but we stopped by my papa's place to grab his camera. I'm walking into Pacific Coliseum and I'm wearing my Messier jersey and I get interviewed by CBC and I just freeze up. They ask who's my favorite player? I just blurted out Mark Messier, Mike Richter, and all this stuff. Anyways, I go to the game and I take all these photos. The next day, after the game, we go to get it developed and we didn't even check that there was film in the camera and there was no film."

Aaron wore his Messier jersey as a fan at Game 3 of the '94 finals. Photo courtesy of Huntingj38 at English Wikipedia / CC BY-SA).

www.ingramcontent.com/pod-product-compliance
Lightning Source LLC
Chambersburg PA
CBHW071644090426
42738CB00009B/1423